International Justice in Rwanda and the Balkans
Virtual Trials and the Struggle for State Cooperation

In contrast to the Nuremberg and Tokyo tribunals, the International Criminal Tribunals for the Former Yugoslavia and Rwanda lack police powers and must prod and persuade defiant states to cooperate in the arrest and prosecution of their own political and military leaders. Victor Peskin's comparative study traces the evolving capacity of these tribunals to build the political authority necessary to exact such compliance from states implicated in war crimes and genocide.

Drawing on 300 in-depth interviews with tribunal officials, Balkan and Rwandan politicians, and Western diplomats, Peskin uncovers the politicized, protracted, and largely behind-the-scenes state–tribunal struggle over cooperation. Key to his analysis is an explanation of how domestic politics – including the shifting balance of power between moderate and nationalist politicians – shapes and is shaped by the state–tribunal struggle over compliance.

In the Conclusion, Peskin examines the Special Court for Sierra Leone and the International Criminal Court, the next steps on the trajectory of international war crimes tribunals. His analysis focuses on how the diminished legal authority of these new courts affects their struggle for cooperation.

Victor Peskin received his Ph.D. in political science from the University of California, Berkeley, and is currently an Assistant Professor in the School of Global Studies at Arizona State University. His scholarly and teaching interests lie at the intersection of international relations, comparative politics, and human rights. His research examines the politics of contemporary international criminal tribunals and their contentious relationship with states implicated in war crimes and genocide and has been funded by the United States Institute of Peace and the Institute on Global Conflict and Cooperation. His articles have been published in *Europe-Asia Studies*, *Legal Affairs*, *International Peacekeeping*, the *Journal of Human Rights*, and the *Journal of International Criminal Justice*.

"In every respect, this is an outstanding analysis, original and much needed. This book represents a very important step in the general effort to subject a topic that has been dominated by activists and lawyers to serious social scientific and theoretical analysis. This will make it useful both to researchers and to a more general readership of people who have an interest in the regions under consideration and in issues of humanitarian law more broadly."
– Eric Gordy, University College London

"Both the promise and limits of international criminal courts emerge vividly from these pages, for it is a tale that's alternately heartening and sobering. This author has done tough legwork in the trenches and interviews on the ground with key players in several countries, and he joins them all to insightful and rewarding reflection on the evolving direction of international tribunals. It's a rare book that's so tersely written and tightly edited that, opening it at any page and reading any sentence, one immediately sees the connection to the central arguments. This is one; there's not one wasted word."
– Mark Osiel, University of Iowa

"Victor Peskin has written an outstanding book that should command immediate attention from anyone interested in international justice and international human rights. Emerging from years of field research in the Balkans, Rwanda, Arusha, and the Hague, Peskin concludes that state cooperation is a central but often overlooked issue that shapes how international human rights courts operate. Peskin's insight is straightforward, but it has profound implications. Peskin writes exceptionally well to boot, and he benefits from telling some extraordinary tales on the history of the tribunals. This is a terrific and riveting piece of scholarship."
– Scott Straus, University of Wisconsin, Madison

International Justice in Rwanda and the Balkans

Virtual Trials and the Struggle for State Cooperation

VICTOR PESKIN
Arizona State University

CAMBRIDGE
UNIVERSITY PRESS

CAMBRIDGE UNIVERSITY PRESS
Cambridge, New York, Melbourne, Madrid, Cape Town, Singapore, São Paulo, Delhi

Cambridge University Press
32 Avenue of the Americas, New York, NY 10013-2473, USA

www.cambridge.org
Information on this title: www.cambridge.org/9780521129121

First published 2008
Reprinted 2009 (twice)
First paperback edition 2009

Printed in the United States of America

A catalog record for this publication is available from the British Library.

Library of Congress Cataloging in Publication Data

Peskin, Victor, 1967–
International Justice in Rwanda and the Balkans : virtual trials and the struggle for
state cooperation / Victor Peskin.
   p.   cm.
Includes bibliographical references and index.
ISBN 978-0-521-87230-0 (hardback)
1. Criminal justice, Administration of – International cooperation. 2. International
criminal courts. 3. Milošević, Slobodan, 1941–2006. 4. Serbia – Politics and
government. 5. Tuđman, Franjo. 6. Croatia – Politics and government.
7. International Tribunal for Rwanda. 8. Rwanda – History – Civil War,
1994 – Atrocities. I. Title.

K5001.P48 2008
341.6'9–dc22   2007026194

ISBN 978-0-521-87230-0 hardback
ISBN 978-0-521-12912-1 paperback

Cambridge University Press has no responsibility for the persistence or
accuracy of URLs for external or third-party Internet Web sites referred to in
this publication and does not guarantee that any content on such Web sites is,
or will remain, accurate or appropriate. Information regarding prices, travel
timetables, and other factual information given in this work are correct at
the time of first printing, but Cambridge University Press does not guarantee
the accuracy of such information thereafter.

For Neva,
Harvey and Tsipa

Half-listening to the drone of the ongoing trial, I suddenly realized how in a sense the judges and prosecutors and investigators there in The Hague had set themselves a remarkably similar sort of reclamatory challenge. The tribunal's founding judges and officers have all repeatedly cast their work in terms of an attempt to stem the historic cycle of floodtides of ethnic bloodletting that recurrently afflict places like the former Yugoslavia, or Rwanda, the other principal locus of the tribunal's mandate. And in this context, it occurred to me that each of these individual prosecutions was like a single mound, a terp [sic] cast out upon the moral swampland of the war's aftermath – and the entire tribunal enterprise a system of interconnected dikes and sluices and pumps and windmills and canals designed to reclaim for each of the regions the possibility of fertile regeneration.

Lawrence Weschler, *Vermeer in Bosnia: A Reader*
New York: Pantheon Books, 2004

"Hands off our Holy War"

Placard at a nationalist demonstration in Croatia in 2001 against the International Criminal Tribunal for the Former Yugoslavia

Contents

Maps and Timelines

Maps

Timelines

Acknowledgments

This book deals with the most vexing challenge confronting today's international war crimes tribunals: how in the absence of enforcement powers can the tribunals move states complicit in atrocities to cooperate in the prosecution of suspects from their own political, national, or ethnic group. Such a focus requires a research methodology that accounts for the perspectives of all three major groups of players engaged in the political battles over state cooperation – the international community, the targeted states, and the tribunals themselves. I have set out to do this by conducting interviews with hundreds of diplomats, government leaders, and tribunal officials at the forefront of the cooperation issue. Over a span of eight years, I interviewed these informants in the Former Yugoslavia, Rwanda, Washington, D.C., and Brussels, and at the international war crimes tribunals in The Netherlands, Tanzania, and Sierra Leone.

My gratitude goes out to the many people in all three circles who, through their cooperation, made this book not only possible but, I hope, authoritative. With such a wealth of informants (and the need to protect the anonymity of those informants who requested it), I cannot thank everyone by name. But it is especially important to acknowledge the participation of prominent actors in the tribunal drama. At the tribunals, I am particularly grateful to Justice Richard J. Goldstone and Carla Del Ponte, who both served as chief prosecutors of the International Criminal Tribunals for the Former Yugoslavia (ICTY) and Rwanda (ICTR); to Luis Moreno-Ocampo, the chief prosecutor of the International Criminal Court; and to David Crane, the former chief prosecutor of the Special Court of Sierra Leone. Beyond the tribunals, I would especially like to acknowledge Zoran Živković, the former prime minister of Serbia; Gerald Gahima, the former attorney general of Rwanda; Joseph Mutaboba, the former Rwandan foreign minister and Rwandan ambassador to the United Nations; Amir Ahmic, Bosnia's liaison officer to the International Criminal Tribunal for the Former Yugoslavia; and David J. Scheffer, the former United States Ambassador-at-Large for War Crimes Issues.

A project of this duration and geographical scope can be quite lonely and daunting. Fortunately, it was anything but. I am indebted to all of those who helped me gain a foothold in societies, hosted me, and offered their friendship while I was far from home. They helped facilitate my research in many ways. I am most grateful for the support, hospitality, and friendship that Saleem Vahidy extended to me in Arusha, Tanzania, and Freetown, Sierra Leone, and Will Romans extended to me in Arusha. I am similarly grateful to Paul Farrell and Ursula Fraser in Arusha, Maria and Chris Farrar-Hockley in Kigali and Brussels, Katherine Gallagher and Monika Kalra in Amsterdam and The Hague, Vlatka Blagus in Zagreb, Guta Milovan in Sarajevo, Uroš Čemalović and Maryanne Yerkes in Belgrade, Sara Kendall and Michelle Staggs in Freetown, and Gregory Townsend, Cecile Aptel, and Jamie Williamson in Arusha and The Hague.

The process of researching, writing, and making sense of the contemporary war crimes tribunals owes much to conversations and interviews with tribunal experts, scholars, and practitioners. Among them I am indebted to Alison Des Forges, Filip Reyntjens, Luc Reydams, J. Alexander Thier, Lars Waldorf, Aloys Habimana, Dan Saxon, Danielle Cailloux, John Hocking, Liam McDowell, Anton Nikiforov, Jean-Daniel Ruch, Alexandra Milenov, Refik Hodžić, Graham Blewitt, Cees Hendricks, Ken Fleming, Robin Vincent, Luc Côté, Eric Witte, Jeremy Lester, William Haglund, and Ben Ferencz. I owe a special debt of gratitude to Thierry Cruvellier, the editor of the Paris-based *International Justice Tribune*, for his collegiality, generosity, and vital support of my research.

I would like to thank Tom Kennedy, who made it possible for me to conduct research at the ICTR, and Roland Ammoussouga and Beverly Baker-Kelly, who gave me the opportunity to intern for the tribunal's Witness and Victims Support section in Arusha and Kigali in 1999. At the ICTR, Gary Meixner, Constant-Serge Bounda, and Tom Adami provided me with library and archival support. In Zagreb, Ana Đorđević provided research assistance.

My advisers at Berkeley were a constant source of wisdom and support. I am grateful to Robert A. Kagan for his mentorship throughout my time at Berkeley. I am similarly indebted to Beth A. Simmons for her excellent guidance and for all that she has done to cultivate my interest in international justice and international institutions. David Leonard was an essential advisor, helping to prepare me for fieldwork and advising me throughout the writing process. David Cohen has been a devoted mentor, teaching me a great deal about the tribunals' jurisprudence and being instrumental in steering my work to publication. I also am thankful to David Caron whose expertise on international law and institutions greatly enhanced my understanding of the contemporary war crimes tribunals.

Research for this book would not have been possible without the generous fellowship support from the United States Institute of Peace and the Institute of Global Conflict and Cooperation. I am also grateful for fellowships from the Human Rights Center, the Center for African Studies, and the Institute of Slavic, East European, and Eurasian Studies at the University of California, Berkeley. While at Berkeley, Eric Stover and Harvey Weinstein of the UC Berkeley Human

Rights Center were a constant source of support and taught me profound lessons about human rights and human rights research. The Center's Summer Human Rights Fellows program enabled me to intern at the ICTR which, in turn, made my subsequent research and this book possible. I cannot imagine having embarked upon and completed this project without Eric, Harvey, and the Human Rights Center.

I am grateful to many people who provided critical feedback on my work, especially Rita Parhad, Alexandra Huneeus, Brownyn Leebaw, Diana Kapiszewski, Yuma Totani, Alison Kaufman, Robert Adcock, Rachel Shigekane, Mark Antaki, Jackie Gehring, Robin DeLugan, William Hayes, David Szanton, Laurel Fletcher, Naomi Roht-Arriaza, and Mary Kaldor. Emily Bazelon deserves acknowledgment for her excellent editing of my article on the ICTR – some of which I draw upon in this book – for the Yale-based *Legal Affairs* magazine. I am particularly grateful to Joe Nevins, who advised me on the publishing process and whose editing of an article of mine in the *Journal of Human Rights* proved critical in clarifying the arguments in this book. I thank Mark Johnson for teaching me about Bosnia and the Balkans and helping to plant the seeds for my research there. In a similar vein, I am grateful to Stanley Meisler, whose reporting and stories from Africa for the *Los Angeles Times* have long inspired me to study African politics. Larry Diamond and Alison Renteln have my gratitude for cultivating my interest in the role of legal institutions in post-conflict societies when I was a Master's student at Stanford University. My appreciation also goes to Kenneth Abbott for cultivating my interest in international institutions during my first year as a doctoral student at Berkeley. At the School of Global Studies at Arizona State University, I am appreciative of the support I have received from my colleagues, particularly David Jacobson and Michael Hechter. I am also grateful for funding I received from the School and from Arizona State that enabled me to conduct research in Europe in 2006 and 2007.

Mieczysław P. Bodusyński has my deep appreciation for being an outstanding colleague, co-author, and devoted friend throughout the course of this project. His invitation to visit him in Croatia in 2001, our travels in the Balkans, and our collaborative work marked a turning point in my research, leading me to bring principles of domestic politics into my study of the politics of international justice. I am also greatly indebted to my colleague and friend, Scott Straus. Since I first met him almost a decade ago, Scott has generously shared his expertise on genocide and African and Rwandan politics and has offered support at every turn. His extensive and incisive comments on two separate drafts of my manuscript proved essential in helping me reconceptualize key parts of the book and make subsequent revisions.

I would like to acknowledge Lewis Bateman, senior editor for political science and history at Cambridge University Press, for recognizing the merit in and the importance of this project and for everything he has done to bring it to publication. I am grateful to Ronald Cohen for his careful editing and am truly fortunate to have had such a dedicated professional working to improve the manuscript. Collaborating with him has made the final stages of this book project very rewarding. My appreciation also goes to an anonymous reviewer for constructive comments on an earlier draft of this book.

I am grateful to my parents, Harvey and Tsipa Peskin; my wife, Neva Peskin, and Drew Lehman, for reading multiple drafts of the manuscript and providing invaluable comments at different stages in its development. I am also grateful to Drew for designing the maps and timelines that accompany the book and for so generously giving of his time and wisdom. I also thank my brother, Aaron, my sister-in-law, Nancy, and the Keret and Ami families for all their loving support.

Throughout this project, my parents have been a well-spring of support and inspiration, encouraging me to leave no stone unturned. Whether during conversations at home around the kitchen table or through exchanges of letters and emails while I was in Africa or Europe, my parents have been there for me at each stage of this project. They have helped me maintain perspective and regain it when I either felt too detached from the world of international tribunals while at home or too immersed in that world while abroad.

My father deserves a special acknowledgment. The cornerstone of this book is a years-long conversation with my father about the vicissitudes of international justice and the importance of witnessing and acknowledging the complexity of this new experiment in international law and politics.

Above all, I am grateful to my wife, Neva, for her understanding and unwavering support during the many months of writing and rewriting this book and for learning about the tribunal process with me firsthand in The Hague and Sierra Leone. Since the day I met her, she has inspired me to do my best while never losing sight of the big picture – a picture that has grown bigger and brighter with the arrival of our son, Jonah, in June 2006. I dedicate this study to Neva and to my parents, Harvey and Tsipa.

Permissions

I would like to thank the following publications for generously giving me permission to reprint previously published material:

Europe-Asia Studies, for permission to use, in adapted form in parts of Chapter 5, material originally published as Victor Peskin & Mieczysław P. Boduszyński, "International Justice and Domestic Politics: Post Tudjman Croatia and the International Criminal Tribunal for the Former Yugoslavia," *Europe-Asia Studies*, Vol. 55, No. 7, 2003, 1117–1142, http://www.informaworld.com. Copyright © 2003 *Europe-Asia Studies*. Reprinted with permission.

Legal Affairs, for permission to use, in adapted form in parts of Chapter 8, material originally published as Victor Peskin, "Rwandan Ghosts," *Legal Affairs*, September/October 2002, pp. 21–25. Copyright © 2002 Victor Peskin, as first published in *Legal Affairs*. Reprinted with permission.

Journal of Human Rights, for permission to use, in adapted form in parts of Chapters 8 and 9, material originally published as "Beyond Victor's Justice? The Challenge of Prosecuting the Winners at the International Criminal Tribunals for the Former Yugoslavia and Rwanda," by Victor Peskin, *Journal of Human Rights*, 2005, 4: 213–231. Copyright © 2005 Taylor & Francis Inc. Reproduced by permission of Taylor & Francis Group, LLC, http://www.taylorandfrancis.com.

Note on Pronunciation

Many Serbo-Croatian proper names are used in this book. The following will aid in the approximate pronunciation of the names.

c   Pronounced 'ts' (as in 'dance') – *Srebrenica*
j   Pronounced 'y' (as in 'you') – *Sarajevo*
u   Pronounced 'oo' (as in 'mood') – *Vukovar*

Diacritical marks are used to modify the pronunciation of the following:

Č č   Pronounced 'tch' (as in 'scratch') – *Račan*
Ć ć   Pronounced 'ch' (as the 't' in 'future'). Commonly seen in the combination 'ić' at the end of a surname – *Mladić*
Š š   Pronounced 'sh' (as in 'shed') – *Milošević*
Ž ž   Pronounced 'zh' (as in 'measure'). In the combination dž, this becomes more like the 'j' in 'jam' – *Karadžić*
Đ đ   Pronounced as a soft 'dy' (as in 'adieu') – *Tuđman or Đinđić*

MAP 1. Map of the Former Yugoslavia.

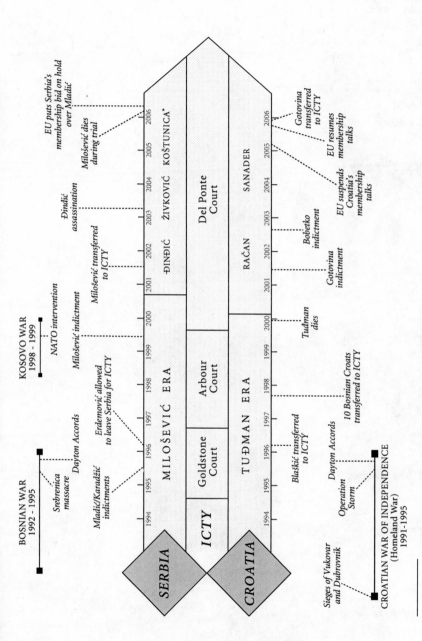

BOSNIAN WAR
1992 - 1995

KOSOVO WAR
1998 - 1999

Srebrenica
massacre

Dayton Accords

NATO intervention

Milošević indictment

Mladić/Karadžić
indictments

Erdemović allowed
to leave Serbia for ICTY

Milošević transferred
to ICTY

Đinđić
assassination

Milošević dies
during trial

EU puts Serbia's
membership bid on hold
over Mladić

SERBIA

| 1994 | 1995 | 1996 | 1997 | 1998 | 1999 | 2000 | 2001 | 2002 | 2003 | 2004 | 2005 | 2006 |

MILOŠEVIĆ ERA | ĐINĐIĆ | ŽIVKOVIĆ | KOŠTUNICA*

ICTY

Goldstone
Court | Arbour
Court | Del Ponte
Court

CROATIA

| 1994 | 1995 | 1996 | 1997 | 1998 | 1999 | 2000 | 2001 | 2002 | 2003 | 2004 | 2005 | 2006 |

TUĐMAN ERA | RAČAN | SANADER

Sieges of Vukovar
and Dubrovnik

Operation
Storm

Dayton Accords

Blaškić transferred
to ICTY

10 Bosnian Croats
transferred to ICTY

Tuđman
dies

Gotovina
indictment

Bobetko
indictment

EU suspends
Croatia's
membership
talks

EU resumes
membership
talks

Gotovina
transferred
to ICTY

CROATIAN WAR OF INDEPENDENCE
(Homeland War)
1991–1995

* Koštunica first took power as president of the rump Federal Republic of Yugoslavia (FRY)
in October 2000 and served in this position until the FRY dissolved and became the union of
Serbia and Montenegro in February 2003. In March 2004, he became prime minister of Serbia.

TIMELINE 1. Timeline of key events in the Former Yugoslavia and at the International Criminal Tribunal for the
Former Yugoslavia.

xix

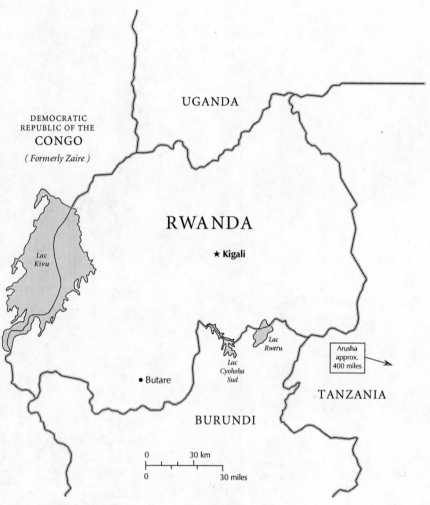

MAP 2. Map of Rwanda.

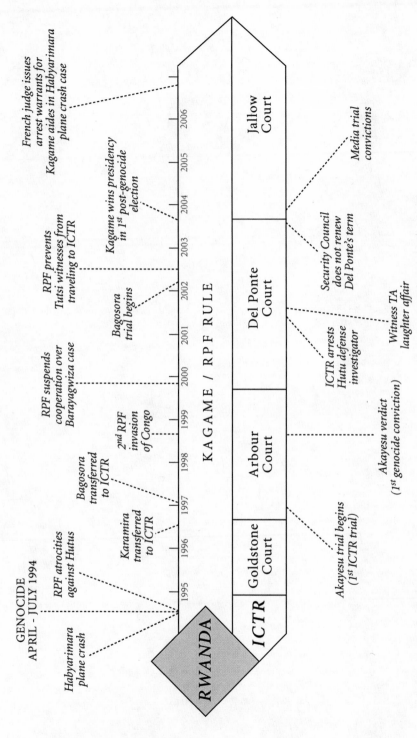

TIMELINE 2. Timeline of key events in Rwanda and at the International Criminal Tribunal for Rwanda.

PART I

INTRODUCTION

I

International War Crimes Tribunals and the Politics of State Cooperation

1.1 Prologue: Survivors and Suspects

On the morning of Friday, June 7, 2002, security officers working for the United Nations war crimes tribunal in Rwanda gathered several survivors of the 1994 genocide and brought them quietly to the airport on the outskirts of the capital, Kigali. The group of survivors – mostly poor Tutsi peasants – was set to board a UN plane for the two-hour flight that crosses the vast expanse of Lake Victoria en route to the tribunal's courtrooms in Arusha, Tanzania. The survivors had been chosen to testify for the prosecution in two trials of Hutu genocide suspects at the international court.

Moving witnesses from the green hills of Rwanda to the windowless courtrooms in Arusha some 400 miles to the east had become routine in the six and a half years since trials first began at the UN war crimes tribunal. But as the events of that day and the next few months would illustrate, the tribunal's existence depended on carrying out the seldom-noticed task of taking witnesses out of the country and, most importantly, on the willingness of the Rwandan government to permit it to do so.

When the tribunal's security officers escorted the survivors to the airport, the officers were stunned to learn that the Tutsi-led Rwandan government had just instituted travel restrictions that blocked the Tutsi prosecution witnesses from traveling to Arusha to testify against Hutu suspects on trial for genocide. Without witnesses to take the stand, tribunal judges were forced to adjourn two scheduled trials. The wheels of international justice ground to an abrupt halt until August, when the Rwandan government finally allowed witnesses to travel to the tribunal. The ease with which the government could jeopardize this new experiment in international law underscored the tribunal's lack of enforcement powers and the court's dependence on state cooperation for the functioning of its legal process.

While state cooperation with the ad hoc International Criminal Tribunal for Rwanda (ICTR) worsened during 2002, prospects for state cooperation steadily improved for its sister tribunal in The Hague, the International Criminal Tribunal for the Former Yugoslavia (ICTY). After years of showing no inclination to cooperate with an institution that targeted its political and military leaders as well as those of its Bosnian Serb allies, the Serbian government changed course and turned over some high-level suspects to the tribunal. The Croatian government, which had provided only limited assistance to the tribunal during the 1990s, also began to ease its resistance to the ICTY.

The start of the Slobodan Milošević trial in February 2002 was dramatic proof that the ICTY could induce cooperation from the once obstinate states of the Balkans. Milošević's refusal to recognize the tribunal's legitimacy notwithstanding, the former Serbian president was actually in the dock facing charges of war crimes, crimes against humanity, and genocide during the Balkan wars of the 1990s. Back home in Belgrade, top Milošević allies indicted by the court found it increasingly difficult to escape the widening reach of The Hague tribunal. Just a year before, indicted war crimes suspects went about their political or military business as usual, flaunting their visibility in Belgrade's finest restaurants. But by 2002, many of these suspects had gone underground, afraid that the once protective Serbian regime would arrest them. One top indicted war criminal, former minister of internal affairs Vlajko Stojilijković, made a defiant last stand against The Hague, preferring martyrdom to surrender. In April 2002, Stojilijković shot himself on the steps of the Federal parliament building in downtown Belgrade to protest the parliament's decision to pass a law designed to speed the arrest and transfer of Serbian war crimes suspects to the ICTY. Such suicidal protest was one more indication that the tribunal was gradually gaining the upper hand in its battle for state cooperation.

1.2 Key Questions and Central Issues

The rise of state cooperation in the Balkans and its decline in Rwanda indicate a surprising reversal of fortune for the two tribunals. What explains these shifts in state cooperation with the international courts? What accounts for the Rwandan government's initial support of the ICTR, and the Serbian and Croatian governments' previous opposition to the ICTY? The principal objective of this book is to address these questions by determining the conditions under which Rwanda and the states of the former Yugoslavia cooperate with the international war crimes tribunals. Specifically, this book examines the issue of state cooperation with the tribunals in its most difficult circumstance – when war crimes suspects belong to a government's own ethnic, national, or political group.

By many accounts, the turn of the twenty-first century ushered in a golden age for international human rights.[1] By the end of the twentieth century, the norm

---

[1] Geoffrey Robertson, *Crimes Against Humanity: The Struggle for Global Justice* (New York: The New Press, 1999); Aryeh Neier, *War Crimes: Brutality, Genocide, Terror, and the Struggle for Justice* (New York: Times Books, 1998).

of international justice had grown in remarkable ways, as seen in the establishment over the previous five decades of numerous international conventions and treaties outlawing human rights abuses.[2] In the 1990s, the creation of the UN International Criminal Tribunals for the Former Yugoslavia and Rwanda,[3] the passage of the Rome Statute that led to the creation of the International Criminal Court (ICC), and the use of universal jurisdiction to attempt to prosecute former Chilean dictator Augusto Pinochet and former Chadian dictator Hissène Habré signaled a sea change in the global expansion of the principle of accountability. More than codifying new elements of international humanitarian law, legal institutions have actually been created to hold suspects criminally accountable for their involvement in atrocities. To tribunal advocates, these new institutions represent the zenith of the international human rights movement. With such institutions in place, getting away with mass murder would no longer be the norm but the exception.

Whether these new judicial institutions will actually be effective depends ultimately on whether they can obtain and sustain the state cooperation needed to carry out investigations, locate witnesses, and bring suspects to trial. The striking scene on the airport tarmac in Kigali shows how much tribunals must look to the targeted states because it is these states that often control the most vital aspects of cooperation.

The framers of the ICTY and ICTR were well aware of the need for state cooperation and for safeguarding the courts against being manipulated to serve states' political agendas. Indeed, independence and insulation from external pressure lie at the core of the tribunals' mission to deliver justice fairly and impartially. It was believed that the tribunals' international makeup, their legal professionalism, and location far from the scene of conflict (The Hague for the ICTY and Arusha, Tanzania, for the ICTR) ensured their neutrality and protection from the lures of political expediency.[4] Nationals from the countries in which war crimes took place have so far been excluded from serving as judges, and usually also as prosecutors and administrators, at the ICTY and ICTR.[5]

---

[2] W. Michael Reisman and Chris T. Antoniou, *The Laws of War: A Comprehensive Collection of Primary Documents on International Laws Governing Armed Conflict* (New York: Vintage Books, 1994).

[3] The Security Council established both the ICTY and ICTR by invoking its Chapter VII powers, granted under the UN Charter, to respond to threats to international peace and security. The Security Council voted to create the ICTY in May 1993 and the ICTR in November 1994. See Security Council Resolution 827, adopted May 25, 1993, and Security Council Resolution 955, adopted November 8, 1994.

[4] Nevertheless, as will be discussed, the tribunals have come under heavy fire in Rwanda and in the Balkans for being too remote and unaccountable to local communities. Such criticism has been a major factor in the ICTR and ICTY's decision to launch "outreach programs" designed to close the geographical gap between the tribunals and Rwanda and the former Yugoslavia as well as the decision to locate the Sierra Leone tribunal in the capital of that West African country.

[5] This stands in contrast to the more recently created "hybrid" tribunals in Sierra Leone, East Timor, and Cambodia that provide for domestic judges and prosecutors to work alongside their international counterparts.

By acting outside the cauldron of domestic politics, the tribunals' international judges and prosecutors would uphold the law and not fall victim to the political forces that have characteristically undermined the legitimacy of domestic war crimes trials in deeply divided societies. Independence was also essential to realize other elements of the tribunals' mission, such as creating an accurate historical record of wartime atrocities and contributing to reconciliation and societal healing. Tribunals controlled by one or more states could not be counted on to deliver credible truth and lasting justice. To achieve these goals and protect the tribunals' autonomy, the UN Security Council granted the ICTY and ICTR legal primacy to trump state sovereignty and demand full and immediate cooperation from all UN member states, particularly targeted states.

The principle of neutrality stands in sharp contrast to the form of justice meted out by the victorious Allied powers in the Nuremberg and Tokyo military tribunals. Despite their jurisprudential precedents, the Nuremberg and Tokyo tribunals continue to be plagued by the criticism of "victor's justice" since only the vanquished Axis powers were punished for their atrocities. In contrast to these World War II-era tribunals, the ICTY and ICTR were given a mandate by the Security Council to prosecute serious violations of international humanitarian law regardless of whether the suspects came from the winning side or the losing side of an armed conflict. But withholding cooperation can give states power to turn the tribunals into vehicles for the political interests of the targeted state. These ad hoc tribunals can effectively become victor's courts insofar as the winners of a conflict may be able to control a tribunal's prosecutorial agenda. By the same token, the losers of a conflict may be able to control the courts by blocking investigations and prosecution of their nationals.

Rwanda and the states of the former Yugoslavia are not the only actors that seek to exert political control over these courts. In many circumstances, powerful international actors such as the United States, the European Union (EU), and NATO may effectively direct the tribunals. It is precisely this charge that was strategically leveled against the ICTY, most notably by Slobodan Milošević in his courtroom tirades. Under the broad cover of UN principles that created the tribunals – especially territorial and temporal jurisdiction and the type of human rights abuses to be prosecuted – international actors may take it as their prerogative to influence who is eligible for indictment and prosecution. Not unlike the targeted states, international actors may also hamper investigations and block indictments by withholding valuable evidence in their possession.

The courtroom has taken center stage in many scholarly analyses of international war crimes tribunals. But beyond the courtroom are political dramas largely hidden from both public view and scholarship that are crucial in determining the level of state cooperation and in shaping the dynamics and outcomes of the trials taking place in The Hague and in Arusha. This book focuses on two levels of such political activity beyond the courtroom: first, the political struggles and negotiations *between* tribunal, state, and powerful international community actors that occur prior to as well as during the courtroom trials; second, the political struggles and negotiations *within* states.

Embedded in these two levels of analysis is the crucial but understudied question of the power of international tribunals to influence targeted states to cooperate with war crimes prosecutions. Although the tribunals are often constrained, indeed even undermined, by the greater power of the international community and targeted states, at key junctures the tribunals have successfully developed and utilized a range of strategies in their struggle for cooperation with these actors. The tribunals have no enforcement power of their own. But they do have "soft power" – the capacity to affect change in the behavior of external actors by a multiplicity of strategies that do not depend on actual enforcement. Joseph S. Nye, Jr., who coined the term, defines "soft power" as the capacity for a state or institution to get what it wants "through attraction rather than coercion or payments."[6] Tribunals do not have the luxury of choosing coercion and payment over attraction. They have only the soft power of attraction. This type of power takes its force from legitimacy and moral authority. At least in theory, the UN tribunals possess a great deal of soft power because of their moral claim to being the ultimate judicial guardians of universal standards of human rights.

In reality, tribunals cannot afford to take their moral authority for granted because the actual practice of international justice often falls short of its idealistic goals. The real and perceived failings of the tribunals leave them vulnerable to attack from targeted states seeking to thwart prosecutions. Thus the soft power of the tribunals is not unalterable, but fluctuates with their standing among different international and domestic actors. To a significant degree, a tribunal shapes its reputation and in turn its soft power by the efficacy of its policies and practices as well as by the skill with which it markets itself.[7]

A core argument of this book is that the ICTY has been able to exercise its soft power more effectively than the ICTR because of the ICTY's greater success in completing trials, maintaining professionalism in court operations, and obtaining frequent and favorable international press coverage. By contrast, the ICTR has been beleaguered by a series of administrative scandals, the slow pace of trials, and negative media coverage that have undermined its reputation as well as its capacity to persuade international actors to intervene on its behalf when the Rwandan government withholds cooperation. However, just because the ICTY has wielded more soft power than the ICTR does not guarantee that the former's power will not deteriorate or that the latter's power will not grow. Failure to produce results in the crucial dimension of completed trials can deal a

---

[6] Joseph S. Nye, Jr., *Soft Power: The Means to Success in World Politics* (New York: Public Affairs, 2004), p. x. In his book, Nye focuses on the need for U.S. leaders in the post-September 11 era to develop soft power strategies as a complement to traditional hard power strategies such as the use of military force. Although Nye does not consider the potential of international war crimes tribunals to develop and wield soft power, he briefly discusses the ways in which the UN can cultivate this resource. According to Nye, the UN has a reservoir of soft power because of its "universality" and "legal framework" (p. 14).

[7] This point about the role of marketing is drawn from Clifford Bob, *The Marketing of Rebellion: Insurgents, Media, and International Activism* (Cambridge: Cambridge University Press, 2005).

blow to a tribunal's legitimacy and its diplomatic leverage. This may be particularly true when a tribunal fails to reach closure in the prosecution of its most
important suspects. A case in point is the death of Slobodan Milošević in March
2006, just weeks away from the end of his more-than-four-year-long trial and
amid revelations of lax tribunal procedures regarding his medical treatment
while in custody.

This book's attention to the strategic actions of tribunals poses a challenge to
realists who contend that international law and international legal institutions
have no independent power to influence events, being merely creatures of their
international creators. But by virtue of their capacity to craft strategies aimed
at prodding targeted states to cooperate and international actors to intervene
on the tribunals' behalf, tribunals matter more than realists have recognized.
Still, that the tribunals can act in this way does not necessarily mean they will
be free to do so or that each tribunal will do so in the same way or to the same
extent. The comparative nature of this book highlights the variation in each
tribunal's approach to the cooperation problem. The case-study chapters will
demonstrate how and why the ICTY has been much more successful than the
ICTR in developing effective strategies for state cooperation.

Just as it challenges realists, this book also challenges human rights cham-
pions of the tribunals. Their understanding of the tribunals as strategic actors
is often skewed by an idealistic outlook that views the tribunals as engaged in
a virtuous battle to save international justice and expand its global reach. This
perspective is particularly evident in the Western media's portraits of the tribunal chief prosecutor as a dogged and courageous crime fighter who brooks
no compromise in the pursuit of justice.[8] A major weakness of this analysis
lies in its narrow conception of what it means for tribunals to struggle with
targeted states and the international community for cooperation. To be sure,
human rights advocates do not inhabit a dream world where law alone gov-
erns international affairs and where international tribunals easily overcome the
resistance of defiant states. But they often contend that the tribunals' capacity
to alter the behavior of such states stems from the moral force of the tribunal's
mission and legal authority. Left unacknowledged, perhaps out of a reasonable
fear that such acknowledgment will undermine the tribunals' moral authority,
is the fact that the tribunals' fight for cooperation is frequently driven by a
legal and political calculus that involves bargaining with and concessions to
recalcitrant states. Largely absent in the human rights literature is a recognition that the tribunals' lack of enforcement powers often compels them to act
politically by negotiating with states to secure promises of cooperation or to
forestall threats to disrupt cooperation altogether.

Tribunal officials and advocates also argue that international war crimes tribunals can ameliorate the political climate in countries recovering from mass

---

[8] For example, see Ed Vulliamy, "Avenging Angel," *The Observer*, March 4, 2001; Helena Kennedy,
   "The Grand Inquisitor," *The Guardian*, March 6, 2002; Elizabeth Rubin, "If Not Peace, Then
   Justice," *New York Times Magazine*, April 2, 2006.

atrocity by reconciling former enemies, deterring new rounds of violence, and contributing to the development of a legal culture in which courts, not guns or machetes, resolve disputes. Faith in the transformative power of international law has cast the ICTY and ICTR (and ad hoc tribunals in Sierra Leone and East Timor and the International Criminal Court) not only as instruments of justice and morality but as indispensable tools for conflict resolution and prevention as well as nation-building. The long-term effects of the contemporary war crimes tribunals are, of course, not yet known. But the tribunals' short-term effects on targeted states – particularly in the Balkans – are not as benign as the human rights camp claims. This book challenges the inspiring Kantian vision of international law associated with human rights advocacy by highlighting the ways in which international tribunals may generate domestic crisis and threaten political stability. The domestic crises following tribunal indictments of top-level Serbian and Croatian military and political leaders have bitterly split governing coalitions, and during certain periods undermined the democratic transitions in Belgrade and Zagreb. While the ICTY has scored increasing success in compelling states to cooperate, these have at times been Pyrrhic victories that have undercut the tribunal's objective of contributing to domestic stability.

Finally, the book also disputes the claim that a state's decision to cooperate by handing over suspects to an international war crimes tribunal is proof of the growing legitimacy of tribunals and the universal acceptance of human rights norms. Behind such apparent state cooperation are layers of conflict and compromise. Even when state cooperation is forthcoming, stalwarts at home in the targeted states are unlikely to be swayed either by the value of international justice or by the state's responsibility for war crimes. In fact, state cooperation is all too frequently castigated at home as a violation of state sovereignty and a betrayal of the nation's honor.

1.3 Conceptual Framework

A. Between Tribunal, State, and International Community

The political interactions between tribunal, state, and international community are virtual trials of their own that determine a state's response to tribunal demands for cooperation. These interactions proceed over such matters as whether and how many nationals or members of a particular ethnic group will be indicted; how far up the political and military hierarchy will such indictments reach; and how many nationals of enemy nations or opposing ethnic or political groups will face indictment and prosecution. These virtual trials, which will also be called "trials of cooperation," are essential in establishing the level of cooperation the tribunals will ultimately receive from states and, consequently, the nature and outcome of the actual courtroom trials of individuals.

The idea of a trial of cooperation offers a conceptual framework that helps illuminate the features of the power struggles that occur between the ad hoc tribunals, the states of the former Yugoslavia and Rwanda, and influential international actors. Whereas the actual courtroom trials pit the prosecution

against the individual defendant over war crimes charges, the trials of cooperation pit the tribunals against the state and state leaders over charges of
obstruction of the tribunals' legal process. And whereas international jurists
sit in judgment of indicted war criminals in the actual courtroom trial, powerful international players – such as the European Union, the United States,
and the Security Council – sit in unofficial but influential judgment of states
in the virtual trial. Through these trials of cooperation, the tribunals' original
mandate to focus solely on determining individual guilt for the commission of
war crimes broadens, in effect, into determining state guilt for obstruction of
the legal process.

In their official statements and speeches, tribunal officials are often reluctant
to acknowledge that such virtual trials exist, primarily to discourage the perception that the tribunals have moved away from their original focus on the
guilt of individuals to casting blame on states. The raison d'être of the tribunals
is to determine individual guilt and thereby prevent the imposition of collective blame that often demonizes groups and nations and fuels new cycles of
violence. While insisting on the tribunals' legal right to obtain full state cooperation, tribunal officials often mute their adversarial rhetoric in the hope that
state assistance to the tribunals will become a matter of voluntary cooperation
rather than imposed compliance. The tribunals' strong preference for the word
"cooperation" over the word "compliance" speaks to their abiding hope of
winning universal acceptance and legitimacy. Still, states can become so openly
intransigent that the tribunals will make public – to international forums such
as the Security Council and the international media – these virtual trials in
which states stand accused of obstructing justice by sheltering war criminals,
hiding evidence, or blocking witness testimony.

These trials of cooperation, if "prosecuted" effectively by the tribunals, may
increase the prospects of state compliance by subjecting the state's violation of
international law to public exposure and condemnation. Without enforcement
powers of their own, tribunals will often resort to techniques of persuasion –
namely, shaming a recalcitrant state in the court of international public opinion. In lacking enforcement powers, tribunals are comparable to human rights
organizations[9] that even more so must rely on adversarial strategies that bran-
dish shaming. The Yugoslavia and Rwanda tribunals are different from human
rights organizations because, at least formally, these tribunals are arms of the
Security Council and have the legal right – granted under Chapter VII of the
UN Charter – to call on the Council for enforcement of a state's obligation to
cooperate with the tribunals.[10]

[9] For a discussion of the role of shaming by non-governmental organizations and transnational
advocacy networks, see Thomas Risse, Stephen C. Ropp, and Kathryn Sikkink, *The Power of
Human Rights: International Norms and Domestic Change* (Cambridge: Cambridge University
Press, 1999).
[10] Key tribunal actors such as the chief prosecutor have employed strategies used by non-
governmental organizations. This borrowing has been facilitated in part by the close collaboration between the tribunals and prominent NGOs such as Human Rights Watch. These

A non-cooperative state does not usually remain passive in the face of the tribunal's attempt to "prosecute" it by shaming. If the tribunal's aim is to put the non-compliant state on virtual trial, the state's aim is to wage a strong defense directed at instilling reasonable doubt as to whether it has actually failed to cooperate or whether its non-cooperation is justified by extenuating circumstances. Bold defiance of the tribunal is not necessarily in a state's best interest. Governments frequently seek to obstruct the tribunals by cloaking their actions in the language of compliance. States attempt this strategic obstruction in a number of ways. First, states can seek to justify their non-compliance on the basis of "good-faith" reasons, such as the specter of domestic backlash and instability if top-level suspects hailed as national heroes are turned over to the tribunal. Second, states can claim that they will take responsibility for prosecuting war crimes suspects in domestic courts rather than sending them to an international tribunal. This becomes a way to present a cooperative posture, despite the fact that refusal to hand over suspects indicted by the ICTY and ICTR is a clear violation of international law because these UN tribunals enjoy legal primacy over domestic jurisdictions.[11] Third, states can claim that they are willing to arrest fugitives but they lack the capacity (for example, adequate intelligence and police) to locate fugitives on their territories. In these situations, states react defensively against tribunal accusations of non-compliance. But states can also go on the offensive and change the terms of the debate. States will often attempt to fight back by employing "counter-shaming," a process in which states try to delegitimize the tribunal by magnifying its shortcomings and mistakes.

All non-cooperative states try such counter-shaming campaigns and, as will be shown, some succeed more than others. The extent to which a non-cooperative state can effectively put the tribunal on the defensive by counter-shaming depends on the substance and presentation of the state's criticism of the tribunal's shortcomings and on the state's international standing. Belgrade's counter-shaming campaign against the ICTY, while resonating loudly in Serbia, often falls on deaf ears internationally. Since Serbia was the major culprit in the Balkan wars, the international community has usually dismissed or simply ignored Serbia's complaints about being the victim of tribunal prosecution and persecution. Furthermore, the ICTY's international reputation as a credible institution making significant progress toward its goals has grown considerably in the West since its establishment.

The Rwanda case offers a very different story about what occurs when a state tries to counter-shame a war crimes tribunal. The Tutsi-led Rwandan

---

organizations also play a vital role in supporting the tribunals' efforts to expose state non-compliance and to pressure states to provide cooperation. While I document the role of such organizations at certain points in the case-study chapters, it is not the focus of this book.

[11] Under the principle of concurrent jurisdiction, the ICTY and ICTR permit domestic courts in the former Yugoslavia and Rwanda to conduct war crimes trials. However, these states must defer to the ICTY and ICTR if the tribunals request the handover of suspects.

government consistently has had the upper hand in the shame game, winning international sympathy for its self-portrayals as a victim state abandoned by the world during the genocide, and exposing the institutional shortcomings of the ICTR. The Rwandan government has proved especially adept at shifting international focus away from its non-cooperation by leveling trenchant criticisms of the slow pace of the genocide trials at the ICTR and by drawing attention to the tribunal's alleged malfeasance.

Much of the state–tribunal relationship is indeed adversarial and trial-like. But by no means is this the whole story. The state and the tribunal often resolve their differences through negotiations conducted out of the international and domestic media spotlight. The tribunals have crafted a repertoire of conciliatory strategies aimed at persuading these states to cooperate through offering concessions and compromises, including publicly crediting a state for its improved cooperation record, allowing states to prosecute some war crimes cases in domestic courts, and postponing or even quashing controversial indictments.

Still, negotiation runs the risk of placing the tribunals on a slippery slope where the boundaries of law and politics become blurred. The enduring quandary for the tribunals is how to influence states to cooperate without losing the moral and legal compass that is the source of their legitimacy. The uphill struggle for state cooperation has at times led tribunal officials – particularly the chief prosecutor who is in the forefront of the state cooperation battles, to cross the line into questionable dealmaking – into compromises that indeed compromise the tribunal's probity.

The state–tribunal struggle over cooperation cannot be understood without reference to the actions of powerful international community players. As "judges" or arbiters, these international actors play a decisive role in influencing the outcome of the trials of cooperation either by siding with the tribunal's claim of state obstruction of justice or by favoring the state's claim of not having violated its legal obligation to cooperate.

In the absence of police powers, the tribunals count on influential members of the international community to act as surrogate enforcers of a state's obligation to cooperate. In the UN, the Security Council can formally act once it receives an official tribunal grievance concerning state non-compliance. But the Security Council has usually been reluctant to take a decisive stand when the tribunals lodge such complaints. In the absence of Security Council action, other powerful international actors have at times filled the vacuum by using political and economic leverage to pressure states to cooperate. But by the same token, these international actors have also enabled states to violate their obligation to cooperate with impunity by remaining silent or otherwise passive when the question of a state's non-compliance arises. This point leads to a central argument of the book: influential international actors play a critical role in the trials of cooperation by significantly limiting or expanding the political space in which a targeted state acts to undermine a tribunal. Ultimately, the final "verdict" in these trials of cooperation lies not with the separate actions of the tribunals, the targeted states, or the international community, but is determined by their interaction, particularly the changing balance of power between these three different sets of actors.

B. *Within States and Governments*

Political battles over cooperation are waged not only on the stage of international politics, but also within the arena of domestic politics in targeted states. A state is not always of one mind on the question of cooperation with the tribunal. Regardless of regime type – be it authoritarian, established democracy, or transitional democracy – governments may be divided within themselves over their cooperation policies with war crimes tribunals. But such divisions are usually much less visible under an authoritarian regime, given the extent of state control over society. Internal Rwandan government discord over state policy toward the ICTR has occurred. But because of the particularly closed nature of the government, such splits are less evident. Discord within an authoritarian government may surface, especially in regimes such as that of Croatia's Franjo Tuđman, that allow a relative degree of press freedom. This book's treatment of domestic politics will focus mainly on the Balkans, where such divisions have been more transparent. In the cases under study, the most salient domestic divisions over state cooperation policy have surfaced in the transitional democracies of Serbia and Croatia, even while their transitions have coincided with increased cooperation with the ICTY. In contrast to the leaders of the authoritarian era, the leaders of the democratic coalition governments appeared to have greater incentive to cooperate with the ICTY. These leaders, unlike Milošević and Tuđman, had no reason to personally fear tribunal prosecution because they played no role in wartime atrocities. Yet this did not suddenly mean that these leaders or their constituencies were eager to embrace a court widely despised as an affront to national dignity.

Domestic crises over the state's cooperation policy have repeatedly threatened governing coalitions, and at times have imperiled stability. The decisions of the Serbian and Croatian governments to increase cooperation with the ICTY during the democratic era have been met with intense resistance from nationalists, military officers, and others opposed to seeing their prominent citizens and war heroes stand trial in The Hague. State cooperation has become "the issue of all issues"[12] for the democratic coalitions that took power in 2000 in Belgrade and Zagreb. The March 2003 assassination of Serbian Prime Minister Zoran Đinđić underscores the dangers to governments from domestic forces opposed to arresting and sending indicted war crimes suspects to The Hague. Đinđić's murder was motivated in large part by Serbian war crime suspects determined to stop the Belgrade government from sending them to the ICTY.

Serbian and Croatian leaders have been ever mindful of not alienating supporters or provoking a backlash among the still powerful right-wing groups. Although the nationalist parties lost power in the 2000 elections, they retained

---

[12] ICTY Press Conference by Chief Prosecutor Carla Del Ponte, July 19, 2004.

a strong hold over matters relating to the recently concluded wars and over issues of justice and the construction of national memory. For the nationalists, opposing state cooperation has become an effective way to mobilize supporters and increase the chances of winning power in the next elections. Nationalist groups have raised the political costs of cooperation by designing a rhetorical strategy that equates the tribunal's indictments against national war heroes with attacks on the country itself. In response to this threat, the fragile governing coalitions in Serbia and Croatia have stepped carefully when it comes to how fast and how much to cooperate with the ICTY.

In this book, I am also mindful that internal conflict exists within the international community concerning state cooperation in the former Yugoslavia and Rwanda. What is perhaps less obvious is that conflict even exists within tribunals themselves. In particular, the tribunals' three main divisions – the judicial chambers, the Office of the Prosecutor, and the Registry (the court's administrative division) – often differ over how to address the issue of state non-compliance. Discussion of the splits within the international community and the tribunals themselves will be included in the case study chapters when they help to clarify key events in the politics of state cooperation.

1.4 State Interests and the Battle for Victim Status

The armed conflicts between adversaries do not simply disappear overnight with cease-fires and peace treaties. The struggle between enemies often shifts from the use of the sword on the battlefield to the use of words in the post-war forums of war crimes tribunals. After internal or interstate conflict, indictments and prosecutions become new markers of victory and defeat between enemies. While the armed conflicts may have produced winners and losers on the battlefield, the subsequent rhetorical combat between tribunal and state is fought over which state or ethnic group will earn the mantle of victim and which side will be castigated as a perpetrator or aggressor.

As the struggle over obtaining international acknowledgment of victim status was a central feature of both the Balkan and Rwandan armed conflicts, the struggle for victimhood continues in the aftermath of war. In the Balkans, the Bosnian Muslims and the Kosovar Albanians stand out as the most aggrieved victims and Serb forces as the most obvious perpetrators of atrocities and ethnic cleansing campaigns. Yet all the major parties to the conflict – the Serbs no less than the Croats and the Muslims – have ardently claimed that they are the victims of genocide and that their involvement in the war was motivated by a need to defend themselves from destruction. In the Balkans, the belief in one's victimization has become, according to David Bruce MacDonald, "a central pillar of national identity"[13] and a source of continuing legitimacy in states' post-conflict, nation-building projects. The same may be said of the Rwandan

---

[13] David Bruce MacDonald, *Balkan Holocausts? Serbian and Croatian Victim-Centered Propaganda and the War in Yugoslavia* (Manchester: Manchester University Press, 2002), p. 5.

conflict. Members of the Tutsi minority obviously stand out as the main victims since their elimination was the aim of Hutu extremists, who planned and carried out the genocide. Nevertheless, Hutu extremists spin a revisionist history of the 1994 conflict by claiming that they have been the victims of genocide at the hands of the then Tutsi-led rebel army.

In the aftermath of armed conflicts, being designated as a victim is a source of political strength for governments. Victim status can confer global recognition of a nation's suffering and legitimacy to the government in power. This in turn may lead to increased international aid and support for the new regime. As MacDonald writes in his study of victim-centered propaganda in Serbia and Croatia in the 1990s, "We live in a world where victims are now the subject of pity and financial assistance, not scorn."[14]

In adversarial legal systems, prosecutors and defense lawyers contest each other's versions of a crime to persuade the jury of the defendant's guilt or innocence. Judgments cast one party as a winner and the other as a loser, while the scale of guilt determines the magnitude of punishment. The same zero-sum logic holds for international and domestic war crimes trials. But the stakes are often much greater in international and domestic war crimes trials than in domestic criminal trials since the former often have far-reaching political consequences. The moral opprobrium of being charged with and then possibly convicted of such offenses as crimes against humanity and genocide is unparalleled in domestic court systems. When it comes to international war crimes trials, the stakes are great not only for individual defendants in the literal dock, but for states and societies in the virtual or figurative dock.

From the perspective of governments involved in an ongoing or recently concluded conflict, the tribunal process can endanger state interests by undermining the government's official history of the armed conflict and the state's role in this conflict. For governments, the writing of this narrative plays a key role in maintaining their domestic and international legitimacy and in turn solidifying their grip on power. In Rwanda, the Tutsi-led Rwandan Patriotic Front (RPF) government has earned much of its international credibility by portraying itself as the force that ended the genocide and now pursues reconciliation between Hutu and Tutsi. This benevolent narrative invites favorable treatment from the international community for the government's authoritarian conduct at home and its military intervention in Congo. For the Rwandan government, the ICTR has been an invaluable tool in constructing this official narrative and in developing an international image of Rwanda as a victim country. But just as the tribunal helps validate the government's official history of the 1994 conflict by focusing on Hutu crimes, it also has the power to raise doubts about the government's actual role in the conflict by exposing Tutsi atrocities committed against Hutu civilians. The tribunal's attempts to investigate these atrocities sparked strong resistance from the government that led to its decision during the Summer of 2002 to suspend cooperation, as seen in its keeping the Rwandan witnesses at

[14] Ibid., p. 5.

the Kigali airport from reaching the courtroom in Arusha. The prospect of even a few indictments of RPF suspects was perceived as undermining the Tutsi-led government's claim to sole possession of victim status by uncovering its own complicity in crimes against humanity.

A government's official narrative may be further challenged by tribunal evidence that contradicts self-serving myths leaders use to justify going to battle and the human and economic toll of war. A government's claim that the country had to go to war or quicken the march to war may be contradicted by evidence showing that the government manufactured an internal or foreign threat. Such revelations may particularly stir the anger of veterans and families of loved ones that wars were heedlessly fought and lives needlessly lost. Moreover, tribunal prosecutions of individual defendants can render an aggressor state vulnerable to a civil suit at the International Court of Justice (ICJ).[15] Incriminating evidence uncovered during tribunal trials, if obtained by the ICJ, may implicate an aggressor state in genocide, perhaps leading to an order to pay reparations to the victim state. Tribunals can also threaten state interests by indicting top political and military leaders and directly threatening their hold on power. An indictment of a head of state does not necessarily or immediately lead to his fall from power and incarceration. Yet, even short of causing him to lose power, such an indictment can irreparably damage a leader and diminish his international stature. As this book will show, the power of the tribunal's "soft power" can therefore be formidable indeed.

1.5 Overlooked Issues in the Tribunal Literature

There has not yet been a study of state cooperation that focuses at once on the battles among the tribunals, key international actors, and the states of the former Yugoslavia and Rwanda.[16] The neglect of the cooperation issue is especially

---

[15] The Bosnian government established the precedent for such an action with its 1993 ICJ lawsuit accusing Serbia of violating the Genocide Convention of 1948. In February 2007, the ICJ ruled that the Srebrenica massacre was an act of genocide carried out by Bosnian Serb forces. However, the ICJ also ruled that Serbia could not be held liable for genocide in Srebrenica and thus was not required to pay reparations. The ICJ judges might have reached a different conclusion had they sought incriminating evidence of Serbia's involvement in the Srebrenica massacre, which had been in the possession of the ICTY during the Milošević trial. The ICJ did not request access to the documents held by the ICTY even though the Bosnian government had asked the ICJ to make such a request. In an apparent concession to persuade the Serbian government to hand over this important evidence for the ICTY's prosecution of Milošević, Chief Prosecutor Carla Del Ponte reportedly agreed to seal some portions of the evidence, thus making it unavailable to the ICJ. See Marlise Simons, "Genocide Court Ruled for Serbia Without Seeing Full War Archive," *New York Times*, April 6, 2007, A6.

[16] On the cooperation issue, several practitioners and legal scholars have provided useful legal analyses and policy reports with recommendations on ways to improve the ICTY's efforts to obtain custody of war crimes suspects. See Daryl A. Mundis, "Reporting Non-Compliance: Rule 7bis," in R. May et al., *Essays on ICTY Procedure and Evidence in Honour of Gabrielle Kirk McDonald*, (Kluwer Law International, 2001); Ivo Josipović, *The Hague Implementing Criminal Law: The Comparative and Croatian Implementing Legislation and the Constitutional Act on*

evident when it comes to the story of the Rwandan government's relationship with the ICTR.[17] Most examinations of the cooperation issue have focused on the ICTY's relationship with the West, and more specifically on NATO's early resistance to arrest fugitive war crimes suspects in Bosnia as well as the tribunal's subsequent success in prodding NATO to make arrests.[18] But there has been much less attention paid to what is arguably a more difficult challenge for the tribunals – obtaining cooperation from targeted states when there are no international peacekeepers on that state's territory to arrest fugitives. In these situations, a tribunal has much less leverage to apprehend indicted war crimes suspects. This critical but overlooked aspect of the cooperation problem poses an enduring problem for war crimes tribunals.

The reluctance to rigorously examine the cooperation issue is reflected in the literature's court-centered perspective, which has focused on analyzing and critiquing the tribunals' jurisprudential developments and rules of procedure and evidence.[19,20,21] The tribunal literature has also been strongly shaped by an activist mindset that emphasizes the political and normative virtues of international justice. Books, articles, and policy reports have often extolled the revolutionary promise of the tribunals to provide justice to victims, reconcile former

---

the Cooperation of the Republic of Croatia with the International Criminal Tribunal and the Commentary (Zagreb: Informator, Hrvatski Pravni Center, 2000); *Making Justice Work: The Report of The Century Foundation/Twentieth Century Fund Task Force on Apprehending Indicted War Criminals* (New York: The Century Foundation Press, 1998).

[17] Recently, however, there has been more scholarly interest in the political dimensions of the ICTR as seen in the following publications: Kingsley Moghalu, *Rwanda's Genocide: The Politics of Global Justice* (New York: Palgrave, 2005); Nigel Eltringham, *Accounting for Horror: Post-Genocide Debates in Rwanda* (London: Pluto Press, 2004).

[18] For example, see Rachel Kerr, *The International Criminal Tribunal for the Former Yugoslavia: An Exercise in Law, Politics, and Diplomacy* (Oxford: Oxford University Press, 2004); Gary Jonathan Bass, *Stay the Hand of Vengeance: The Politics of War Crimes Tribunals* (Princeton: Princeton University Press, 2000).

[19] Alex C. Lakatos, "Evaluating the Rules of Evidence for the International Tribunal in the Former Yugoslavia: Balancing Witnesses' Needs Against Defendants' Rights," *Hastings Law Journal*, March 1995; Richard May and Marieke Wierda, "Trends in International Criminal Evidence: Nuremberg, Tokyo, The Hague, and Arusha," *Columbia Journal of Transnational Law*, 1999.

[20] Some authors have sought to bring attention to the importance of expanding the types of atrocities a tribunal should prosecute, such as rape against women. For example, see Kelly Dawn Askin, *War Crimes Against Women: Prosecution in International War Crimes Tribunals* (The Hague: Martinus Nijhoff Publishers, 1997). Other works have focused on building the evidentiary basis of high-profile tribunal prosecutions. For example, see Norman Cigar and Paul Williams, *Indictment at The Hague: The Milošević Regime and Crimes of The Balkan Wars* (New York: New York University Press, 2002).

[21] A small, but growing branch of the tribunal literature has examined the relationship between international justice, reconciliation, and social reconstruction. See Eric Stover and Harvey Weinstein (editors), *My Neighbor, My Enemy: Justice and Community in the Aftermath of Mass Atrocity* (Cambridge: Cambridge University Press, 2004). A related study is Eric Stover's *The Witnesses: War Crimes and the Promise of Justice in The Hague* (Philadelphia: University of Pennsylvania Press, 2005), which inquires into the experience of survivors who have testified at the ICTY.

enemies, and deter new rounds of violence.[22] The writings of prominent human rights activists such as Aryeh Neier[23] and Kenneth Roth[24] and leading tribunal practitioners such as Richard J. Goldstone[25] provide notable examples of this trend. These authors have nourished a faith in the tribunals' capacity to withstand external pressure to capture the legal process for political ends. Moreover, human rights activists have envisioned that international war crimes tribunals, by virtue of the global rise of human rights, would take on a life of their own and inevitably realize their mission. In so doing, tribunals would surely become a force to be reckoned with in international affairs. Geoffrey Robertson in *Crimes Against Humanity: The Struggle for Global Justice* states, "The optimistic fact [is] that enterprises of this sort have a tendency to develop a momentum of their own, independent of the concerns of those who create them."[26] In this sense, the ad hoc tribunals have been lauded as precursors to the International Criminal Court (ICC) and part of a continuing campaign to broaden human rights protections worldwide.[27]

Not surprisingly, then, tribunal scholarship has shown more interest in the potential of these institutions to transcend politics than in analyzing the ways in which the political actions of the international community or states complicit in atrocities have actually undermined the autonomy and mission of these courts by withholding cooperation. In her study of the ICTY, for example, Rachel Kerr acknowledges that while the tribunal operates in a political context, and the chief prosecutor must engage in diplomacy, the prosecutor and the legal process itself are immune from politicization.[28] As much as her political sensibility is an improvement over other observers, Kerr brings little evidence to show that the ICTY can both be shielded from politicization yet be engaged in politics and diplomacy.

There has been limited scholarly analysis of the strategies that tribunal officials employ to prod recalcitrant states and international actors to provide cooperation. On this question, the most enlightening work is John Hagan's book, *Justice in the Balkans: Prosecuting War Crimes in The Hague Tribunal*. Hagan focuses on the organizational dynamics of the ICTY and the role that key tribunal officials play in turning the tribunal into an increasingly effective institution. Hagan argues that Louise Arbour, the ICTY's second chief prosecutor, became a charismatic leader within the tribunal and significantly developed the institution's diplomatic leverage. Hagan cogently describes how Arbour

---

[22] For example, see "Preventing Deadly Conflict Final Report," Carnegie Commission on Preventing Deadly Conflict, Carnegie Corporation of New York, December 1997, pp. 94–98.

[23] Neier, *War Crimes*.

[24] Kenneth Roth, "Introduction," in Geoffrey Robertson, *Crimes Against Humanity*, pp. xxiii–xxxiv.

[25] Richard J. Goldstone, *For Humanity: Reflections of a War Crimes Investigator* (New Haven: Yale University Press, 2000).

[26] Robertson, *Crimes Against Humanity*, pp. 288–289.

[27] See Neier, *War Crimes*, p. 254.

[28] Kerr, *The International Criminal Tribunal for the Former Yugoslavia*, p. 11.

devised strategies to successfully press NATO to arrest war crimes fugitives in Bosnia.[29] Crucial to Arbour's success was her resorting to secret indictments to prod NATO peacekeepers to arrest fugitives in Bosnia who might otherwise have been able to evade arrest if the indictments had been made public. Hagan also credits Arbour for her adroit use of the Western media to bolster the tribunal's prominence and political influence.

The strength of Hagan's analysis lies in his in-depth knowledge of the dynamics at play in rendering the chief prosecutor an effective actor. But his analysis is weakened by not examining the instances in which the chief prosecutor failed to act effectively in regard to obtaining cooperation from the Serbian and Croatian governments. Nor does Hagan consider the Rwanda tribunal in his study. An examination of that tribunal would have revealed a fuller and more realistic understanding of the chief prosecutor's efficacy as a strategic actor, both internally at the tribunal and externally in interactions with the Rwandan government and the international community.

The importance of a comprehensive picture of tribunal politics is further illuminated by considering the shortcomings of Gary Bass's prominent study of international tribunals, *Stay The Hand of Vengeance: The Politics of War Crimes Tribunals*. Bass explores the reasons why Western liberal states have historically established and supported international tribunals and skillfully examines several failed and successful efforts to create war crimes tribunals. Bass's case studies include the West's attempts to establish tribunals in the aftermath of the Napoleonic Wars, the Armenian genocide, World War I, and World War II, as well as during the recent Bosnian war.

Bass's book is a scholarly tribute to the West's ardent belief in international justice and the rejection of show trials and retribution. He argues that the West's faith in "legalism" – the idea that there should be trials governed by the principles of fairness and due process – has inspired its leaders to create a number of tribunals. At the same time, Bass qualifies this idealistic argument with a healthy dose of realism. He does so by acknowledging that even when Western liberal states create international tribunals, their logistical and political support is often grudging. This ambivalence is borne of fears that the pursuit of justice will interfere with more important foreign policy goals, such as the pursuit of cease-fires and peace treaties. In this regard, Bass's work is a cautionary tale about the West's reluctance to sustain the very tribunals it brings to life.

The Liberal paradigm in international relations theory,[30] which posits that a country's domestic political and legal orientation shapes its approach to international affairs, lies at the core of Bass's argument about what motivates Western

---

[29] John Hagan, *Justice in the Balkans: Prosecuting War Crimes in The Hague Tribunal* (Chicago: The University of Chicago Press, 2003), pp. 93–131.

[30] The term, "Liberal paradigm," is drawn from Anne-Marie Slaughter, "Law and the Liberal Paradigm in International Relations Theory," International Law and International Relations Theory: Building Bridges – Elements of a Joint Discipline, 86 American Society of International Law Proceedings, 1992, p. 180.

states to support international justice. To Bass, it is no coincidence that a democratic country, such as the United States, with a robust and independent court system and "principled legalist beliefs"[31] has historically supported the cause of international justice.[32] "After all," he writes, "a war crimes tribunal is an extension of the rule of law from the domestic sphere to the international sphere."[33] Accordingly, authoritarian states are not expected by Bass to support international justice. Thus, as a democratic country's support of the rule of law at home leads to its support of the rule of law abroad in the form of international war crimes tribunals, an authoritarian country's lack of support of the rule of law will lead it to oppose international tribunals. Bass concludes, "Liberal governments sometimes pursue war crimes trials; illiberal ones never have."[34] This implies that the Serbian, Croatian, and Rwandan governments have been opposed to the tribunals from the start largely because their governments are undemocratic and therefore lacked a principled belief in true justice.

Beyond acknowledging the Serbian and Croatian governments' defiance of the ICTY, Bass leaves largely unexamined the complex interests and actions of illiberal states toward the tribunals. The position and attitude of authoritarian states toward tribunals are not as absolute or static as Bass would have it. Whereas Bass bundles illiberal states together as hostile to international tribunals, the evidence indicates that illiberal states differ significantly in their posture toward tribunals. While Milošević's Serbia opposed the tribunal outright, the authoritarian governments of Franjo Tuđman's Croatia and Paul Kagame's Rwanda were actually in the forefront of calling for the establishment of a bona fide international tribunal – facts that go unmentioned by Bass.

The Tuđman government called for a tribunal in November 1991, at the height of the Serbian-Croatian conflict and a year and a half before the Security Council decided to create one. In the case of Rwanda, the Tutsi-led Rwandan Patriotic Front first called on the UN to establish a tribunal during the 1994 genocide. The RPF reiterated this call after it brought an end to the 100-day genocide and took control of Rwanda. In the face of international passivity during the genocide and the staggering death toll, the RPF's call for a tribunal had a strong influence on the Security Council's decision to create one in November 1994.

In the end, Rwanda voted against the UN resolution establishing the ICTR – a fact that Bass notes parenthetically and attributes to the UN's decision to bar

---

[31] Bass, *Stay the Hand of Vengeance*, p. 8.

[32] In a review of *Stay the Hand of Vengeance*, Joseph Nevins provides compelling evidence to counter Bass's assertion that the United States has historically shown strong support for international war crimes trials. "If we examine cases where liberal states are not victors with legitimate post-war grievances, but are perpetrators of atrocities or complicit in them, Bass's general argument is significantly weakened," Nevins writes. Joseph Nevins, "Truth and Justice in the Aftermath of War Crimes and Crimes Against Humanity," *Punishment & Society*, Vol. 5, No. 2, 2003: p. 210. My analysis of *Stay the Hand of Vengeance* is informed by Nevins's review.

[33] Bass, *Stay the Hand of Vengeance*, pp. 7–8.

[34] Ibid., pp. 8 and 35.

capital punishment for convicted Hutu defendants, a reason one might think befits an authoritarian ethos. Bass omits the several other reasons, not necessarily of an authoritarian mindset, that the Tutsi-led Rwandan government also cited for voting against the UN resolution. These reasons included wanting the UN to locate the ICTR in Rwanda and wanting more resources to be given to the tribunal to guarantee its viability. Most importantly, none of the government's initial objections contested principles of legalism, such as the level of due process afforded to Hutu defendants. In light of the ICTR's administrative problems and the slow pace of trials in its early years, the Rwandan government grew sharply critical of the tribunal. But this criticism, also sometimes echoed by Western liberal states such as the United States, should not be taken as proof of the Rwandan government's rejection of due process at the tribunal or its push for politicized show trials in Arusha. In fact, the government's vision of what it hoped the ICTR would become may not differ significantly from what a Western liberal government might also want if it had just emerged from a genocide.

The Rwandan government sought international trials because this was the only way to ensure that high-level Hutu suspects who fled the country after the genocide would stand trial. International trials also appealed to the new Tutsi-led government because it wanted prompt and numerous tribunal genocide convictions that could showcase Tutsi suffering. Indeed, the ICTR provided a credible legal forum where the finding of Tutsi victimization and Hutu culpability would be accepted and affirmed globally, and not dismissed as the poisonous fruit of an authoritarian domestic legal process. Although the Tutsi-led RPF had not suddenly embraced the principles of legalism, it quickly came to realize that bona fide international prosecutions could reap significant political benefits by solidifying the government's victim status on the world stage. As I demonstrate, then, where a country falls on the spectrum of liberal to illiberal states does not necessarily determine whether it will support an international tribunal.

Contrary to Bass's contention, the pursuit of international justice does not belong to Western liberal states only. A state's role in an armed conflict – whether it was, is, or may become a victim or perpetrator – may be a better predictor of its level of support for a tribunal than whether the state is liberal or illiberal. Even a democratic state imbued with a robust legal tradition may fear an international court, as demonstrated by the Bush administration's virulent opposition to the International Criminal Court. Indeed, United States leadership in creating the Nuremberg and Tokyo military tribunals and the contemporary ad hoc tribunals have not led to support for an international court that could indict American military and political leaders for alleged human rights abuses in Iraq and on other fronts in the "global war on terror."

The political landscape of the cooperation battles between targeted states and tribunals is not a still life, but can shift, at times dramatically, with changes in the domestic landscape of targeted states. Regime change in the Balkans offers a vivid illustration of this point. The demise of authoritarian rule in Serbia and Croatia in 2000 presented an opportunity not previously available to the ICTY to apprehend Serbian and Croatian fugitives who had been shielded by the Milošević and Tuđman regimes. In part of the afterword to the 2002 edition of *Stay the Hand of Vengeance*,[35] Bass turns his attention to Serbia after the fall of Milošević and his handover to the ICTY. But Bass does not modify his theoretical framework to account for Serbian (or Croatian) regime change from an illiberal state to a transitional democracy. His categorization of states as either liberal or illiberal therefore sheds little light on the behavior of states that are neither liberal nor illiberal. Inquiring into the actions and interests of states that fall between these two poles – particularly transitional democracies – is critical to developing an understanding of the conditions in which tribunals will receive cooperation.

A Liberal theorist may argue that transitional democracies such as Serbia and Croatia show a greater inclination than their authoritarian predecessors to cooperate with an international war crimes tribunal. The extent of this increased cooperation would reflect these states' increased embrace of principles of legalism and the domestic rule of law. As these states' political and legal systems grow stronger and the democratic transitions become consolidated, it might stand to reason that their support of international justice would grow yet stronger. But domestic antagonism to the ICTY in Serbia and Croatia has had a long half-life even during the democratic era. Even when the post-authoritarian governments have behaved cooperatively, such external factors as the timing and magnitude of international pressure are more consequential than the purported élan of a new democracy.

To better understand the dynamics of state policy toward international tribunals during democratic transitions, it is useful to draw on the transitional justice literature.[36] This literature – initially developed in the 1980s and 1990s by political scientists and legal scholars – examines the choices that newly democratic states make when deciding whether to prosecute or pardon the crimes of their authoritarian predecessors. Although the literature has tended to examine questions of domestic prosecutions and truth commissions, its insights can be used to shed light on the politics of state cooperation with international war crimes prosecutions.

Contemporary democratic transitions often give rise to calls for domestic trials and truth commissions from human rights groups and survivors who lived in silent anguish during the previous authoritarian period. The mobilization of domestic human rights activism, often in conjunction with the support of international non-governmental organizations, puts increased pressure on the state

---

[35] Bass, *Stay the Hand of Vengeance*, pp. 311–330.

[36] Prominent works include in this literature include Neil Kritz (editor), *Transitional Justice: How Emerging Democracies Reckon with Former Regimes*, Vol. I General Considerations; Vol. II Country Studies; Vol. III Laws, Ruling, and Reports (Washington, D.C.: United States Institute of Peace Press, 1995); Ruti G. Teitel, *Transitional Justice* (Oxford: Oxford University Press, 2000); Jon Elster, *Closing the Books: Transitional Justice in Historical Perspective* (Cambridge: Cambridge University Press, 2004).

to prosecute war crimes suspects. The case of Argentina in the 1980s[37] demonstrates that a democratic transition can increase state support for prosecutions because of the greater space given to civil society and human rights groups to air their grievances. For domestic proponents of prosecutions, accountability for past crimes is a moral imperative as well as a way to bolster a country's nascent democracy by removing individuals who may threaten the prospects of political reform. However, the transitional justice literature has also demonstrated the weak position in which human rights advocates find themselves during a democratic transition. Campaigns for domestic prosecutions thus rarely enjoy a consensus in society or government. This is particularly true when, in the immediate aftermath of authoritarian rule, many fear that prosecutions will provoke a rebellion from the barracks that may undermine the nascent liberalization project. With members of the authoritarian regime still in the country and in positions of leadership in the military, many fear that prosecutions will divide society just when unity is most needed.

By the same token, it is not inevitable that a new democratic government will provide an international tribunal with the cooperation it requires to investigate and prosecute state-sponsored atrocities. Indeed, the dilemma over whether to cooperate is particularly acute in transitional democracies. In the eyes of human rights proponents, cooperation with the tribunal is seen as congruent with state interest. In the eyes of nationalists, such cooperation is nothing short of collaborating with the enemy.

International pressure and incentives notwithstanding, the Balkan governments face a particularly difficult challenge when it comes to garnering domestic support for cooperation with the ICTY. First, unlike transitional democracies such as Argentina and Chile, where human rights advocates comprised significant numbers of citizens living within the state's borders, Serbia and Croatia have not had a significant civil society-base to campaign for prosecutions of the state's own political and military leaders. Indeed, beside the lone voices of several small human rights organizations and a few bold politicians, no vocal domestic constituency exists in Serbia and Croatia in support of tribunal prosecutions of their ethnic brethren. Second, in Serbia and Croatia, the state's participation and conduct in the Balkan wars are widely seen as legitimate and therefore above scrutiny from an international court. If Argentina fought a dirty war against internal "subversives," Croatians have widely come to see their breakaway from Serbia as a cleanly fought war of independence waged against an external occupier. The Serbian government too has seen its involvement in the Balkan wars as fully justified, particularly in protecting ethnic Serbs living in the territory of the former Yugoslavia. Moreover for both states, the domestic backlash against state cooperation with an international tribunal

---

[37] For a discussion of transitional justice efforts in Argentina, see Kathryn Sikkink and Carrie Booth Walling, "Argentina's Contribution to Global Trends in Transitional Justice," in Naomi Roht-Arriaza and Javier Mariezcurrena (editors), *Transitional Justice in the Twenty-First Century: Beyond Truth versus Justice* (Cambridge: Cambridge University Press, 2006), pp. 301–324.

has been more intense than the prospect of prosecuting its own nationals. The greater violation against these states, it seems, has been the violation of national sovereignty.

1.6 Case Selection and Field Research

Transcripts of the legal proceedings in The Hague and Arusha are readily available to researchers interested in understanding these courtroom trials. "Trials of cooperation," of course, have no literal transcript. It is the aim of this book to develop a virtual transcript and to draw on it to generate theory about the potential and limits of these experiments in international justice. I have attempted to make such a contribution by conducting extensive field research both at the tribunals and in the countries for which these tribunals have been created. It is from such primary source material that the trials of cooperation unfold.

This book focuses on case studies that examine the political interaction between the tribunals, Serbia, Croatia, and Rwanda, and the international community. In the Conclusion, I examine the politics of state cooperation in the context of the next generation of tribunals, specifically the International Criminal Court and the hybrid Sierra Leone tribunal. The changing dynamics of the state–tribunal relationship and the domestic politics of targeted states underscore the importance of conducting over-time and cross-regional field research. This has led me to conduct a total of fourteen months of field research over a span of eight years, from June 1999 through June 2007, and at numerous sites: The ICTY in The Hague, and Serbia, Croatia, and Bosnia; the ICTR in Arusha, Tanzania, and Rwanda; the ICC in The Hague; the Special Court for Sierra Leone in Freetown, Sierra Leone; the European Union in Brussels; Washington, D.C.; and New York.[38]

The case studies of Serbia, Croatia, and Rwanda provide a cross-regional comparison of the state–tribunal dynamic. A within-region comparison is provided by the two cases from the former Yugoslavia. The Serbian and Croatian cases allow us to see how the same tribunal pursues state cooperation differently and, in turn, how different states approach the same tribunal differently. Finally, the over-time study of these different states allows a within-state comparison. In the cases of Serbia and Croatia, this over-time study permits an examination of changing patterns of state cooperation with changing regimes – from authoritarian to transitional democracy.

In the former Yugoslavia, there are as many as five states and one province that could be selected for study. Serbia, Croatia, Bosnia, Montenegro, Macedonia, and the province of Kosovo all played a role in the Balkan wars and therefore have a subsequent relationship with the ICTY. The aim of this study, however, is to understand the challenges tribunals face in obtaining cooperation

---

[38] I also conducted interviews in Antwerp, Belgium; Harlaam, The Netherlands; Berkeley and Pasadena, California; and Sun City West, Arizona.

from fully sovereign states, since these states have a greater capacity to defy the tribunals. Thus, I have selected the Serbia and Croatia cases. Kosovo was not chosen because as a territory controlled by the UN it does not enjoy the status of an independent state.[39] I have not selected Bosnia because its sovereignty has been significantly constrained by the presence of an international peace-keeping force and by the High Representative, who acts as the de facto ruler of that divided country.[40] The Macedonia case has not been selected since its armed conflict in 2001 was relatively brief, and the tribunal has conducted only a limited number of investigations there. The Montenegro case is implicitly included in the Serbian case because of its former membership in the rump Yugoslavia and its subsequent membership in the political union of Serbia and Montenegro.

I conducted field research in Africa and Europe in 1999, 2000, 2001, 2002, 2003, 2005, 2006, and 2007. I also carried out extensive analyses of international, Balkan, and Rwandan media reports as well as tribunal and United Nations documents. My study is based in large part on in-depth, open-ended interviews with approximately 300 informants. I interviewed a wide range of officials and staff members at the Yugoslavia, Rwanda, and Sierra Leone tribunals. In addition, I interviewed government officials in Serbia, Croatia, Bosnia, Rwanda, and Sierra Leone as well as domestic legal professionals, Western diplomats, journalists, and human rights activists. My informants have included ICTY and ICTR Chief Prosecutors Richard J. Goldstone and Carla Del Ponte; International Criminal Court Chief Prosecutor Luis Moreno-Ocampo; Special Court for Sierra Leone Chief Prosecutor David Crane; Serbian Prime Minister Zoran Živković; Rwandan Attorney General Gerald Gahima; and David J. Scheffer, the former United States Ambassador-at-Large for War Crimes Issues. Wherever possible in the book, I identify and name my informants whom I quote or paraphrase. However, many people I interviewed requested anonymity as a condition for using their comments for publication because of the sensitive nature of the topics under discussion in my interviews or because certain informants were not authorized to speak publicly.

These interviews ranged in duration from one to three hours. I re-interviewed a select sample of the 300 informants over the course of my eight fieldwork

---

[39] It should be noted that the ICTY has faced some resistance to cooperation from the United Nations administration in Kosovo, which at times has been at odds with the tribunal over its prosecution of Kosovar Albanian suspects. This has been particularly the case with Ramush Haradinaj, the former prime minister of Kosovo with whom UN officials were politically allied. The ICTY indicted Haradinaj in March 2005 for atrocities against Kosovo Serbs and Kosovar Albanians. He resigned shortly afterward as prime minister. The trial of Haradinaj and two co-indictees began in the Hague in March 2007.

[40] There is significant variation in the levels of compliance in Bosnia. Although the Bosnian Muslim-dominated government in Sarajevo has provided much cooperation, the Bosnian Serb Republic has tended to provided little. However, beginning in 2004, Bosnian Serb cooperation began to increase notably because of pressure exerted by Bosnia's High Representative, Paddy Ashdown.

visits. Particularly in the Rwandan context, my interviews elicited material not in the public domain from tribunal and state insiders. The book has also been informed and enhanced by my observation of court proceedings at the Yugoslavia, Rwanda, and Sierra Leone tribunals, and by countless conversations with sources at the tribunals and in the former Yugoslavia, Rwanda, and Sierra Leone.[41]

* * *

This study of state cooperation in the international prosecution of war crimes seeks to illuminate a political process whose actors are often poised to avoid or downplay its public acknowledgment. The posture by both tribunal and state of non-negotiable rectitude has obscured the important issue of how international law actually operates in the context of political negotiations between tribunals and states. In the following chapters, understanding of this complex process is embodied in case studies that seek to reveal the dynamics of the state–tribunal relationship, especially by drawing on the testimony of some of the major actors who, when engaged by in-depth interviews, become witnesses to the politics of cooperation underlying this great experiment in international justice.

[41] In 1999, I conducted two months of participant observation as a tribunal intern at the ICTR headquarters in Arusha, Tanzania, and at its branch office in Kigali, Rwanda. During this internship, I participated in investigative and witness protection missions and other aspects of tribunal operations.

PART II

THE BALKANS: STRATEGIES OF NON-COMPLIANCE AND INSTRUMENTS OF PRESSURE

2

Slobodan Milošević and the Politics of State Cooperation

2.1 Introduction

Beyond the tribunal courtroom lies a virtual trial that determines who will stand actual trial for war crimes, crimes against humanity, and genocide. Whereas the courtroom trial is fought over the guilt and innocence of the individual defendant, a virtual trial – what I also call a "trial of cooperation" – is waged between the tribunal and the targeted state over whether that state will facilitate investigations, indictments, and prosecutions of members of its own national, ethnic, or political group. The aim of this case study is to reveal the dynamics of such virtual trials between the International Criminal Tribunal for the Former Yugoslavia (ICTY) and the Serbian government. These virtual trials are most consequential for the ICTY because Serbian war crimes lie at the epicenter of the Balkan wars and comprise the primary focus of the tribunal's prosecutions. With Slobodan Milošević's fall from power in 2000 and the demise of authoritarianism, Belgrade's defiance slowly gave way to increased cooperation. Still, Serbia has been the most difficult state for the ICTY, as underscored by Chief Prosecutor Carla Del Ponte's lament in my 2003 interview with her: "It is an incredible, incredible situation. We always have a problem with Serbia. Always."[1]

The Serbian case study will be divided into two chapters. In this first chapter, I will examine the struggle between the ICTY and the Serbian government during Serbia's authoritarian period that lasted until Milošević's fall from power in October 2000. In the next chapter, I will examine the conflicts over cooperation during Serbia's democratic period (from October 2000 through July 2007).

During the authoritarian and democratic eras, the international community – and particularly the United States and the European Union – played a critical role in defining the political costs and benefits for Serbia's defiance of the tribunal. The West's lukewarm support for the ICTY in its conflicts with Serbia helps explain why Milošević paid a small price for failing to cooperate and

---

[1] Fieldwork interview with Carla Del Ponte, The Hague, December 2003.

demonstrates the central role that international actors can play in enabling a targeted state to undermine international justice. Serbia's non-cooperation during the Milošević period was a foreseen and, curiously, often a desired outcome for the Western powers. In the interest of keeping Milošević as a deal maker for peace in the Bosnian war, the West refrained from exerting significant pressure on Serbia to give up war crimes suspects and evidence for their prosecution. While the West had an interest in establishing the tribunal and bringing low-level war crimes suspects to trial, it often had a greater interest in limiting the tribunal's prosecutorial reach, especially in regard to Milošević and other high-level government officials whose indictments would undermine Milošević's viability as a peacemaker.

The issue of peace must be taken into account to understand the West's own changing level of cooperation with the tribunal. The conditions under which a targeted state such as Serbia cooperates with the tribunal cannot be understood without recognizing the international community's frequent interest in prioritizing peace over justice. During the Milošević era the ICTY's struggle for cooperation occurred mostly in a time of war – for the Goldstone court in the Bosnian war and for the Arbour court during the Kosovo war. The pursuit of justice in wartime was complicated and frequently undermined by the West's efforts to avoid military intervention and seek a negotiated peace. Both the Goldstone and Arbour courts were severely tested whenever the West pressed the tribunal to subordinate justice in the interest of ending armed conflict. However, the international community's pursuit of peace did not always mean that the tribunal was regarded as an impediment to ending the Balkan wars. At times, Western diplomats supported the tribunal's quest for state cooperation because they believed that tribunal indictments and prosecutions could actually advance the prospects of peace. Accounting for the peace factor, then, will help bring order to the complex and often seemingly inconsistent stance of the international community toward Serbia's obligation to cooperate fully with the tribunal.

It is not only the actions of adversaries such as Serbia that tested the tribunal's soft power, nor even the actions of the international sponsors of the court. The tribunal tested itself too. The trials of cooperation became a training ground for top tribunal officials to develop and hone strategies aimed at pressing Serbia and other Balkan states as well as the international community to cooperate. By engaging Serbia in the trials of cooperation, the tribunal kept the government's defiance and the tribunal's resolve in the international spotlight. Doing so intensified pressure on Serbia to cooperate, once domestic conditions changed after Milošević's removal from power. Thus, in no small measure, the tribunal's losing battles with Milošević arguably would come to bolster its authority and leverage vis-à-vis Serbia in the post-Milošević period.

2.2 International Justice: A Looming Threat to Milošević's Serbia

Well before the Security Council authorized the establishment of the ICTY in May 1993, Serbia was warned that a war crimes tribunal would follow its investigations from the killing fields of Bosnia up the chain of command to Belgrade. Eight months into the Bosnian war, the acting United States Secretary of State, Lawrence Eagleburger, bolstered the emerging idea of a tribunal to prosecute those most responsible for the massacres of Bosnian civilians. In a December 1992 speech at a peace conference in Geneva, Eagleburger named ten suspects who might face trial in an international court for crimes against humanity. At the top of the list were Milošević, Bosnian Serb President Radovan Karadžić, and Bosnian Serb General Ratko Mladić. "We know . . . which forces committed those crimes, and under whose command they operated. And we know, finally, who the political leaders are and to whom those military commanders were – and still are – responsible," Eagleburger said. The Serbian people need "to understand that a second Nuremberg awaits the practitioners of ethnic cleansing, and that the judgment and opprobrium of history awaits the people in whose name their crimes were committed."[2]

Eagleburger's words were directed as much to the Serbian people as to Milošević and the other named war crimes suspects. With a presidential election only days away in Serbia, Eagleburger sought to emphasize that regime change provided the least painful option for Serbs to escape growing international isolation. For Eagleburger, the threat of a tribunal at this juncture was a useful tool to remove Milošević from power and to advance regional stability. Yet in the months and years to come, the United States and Europe would back away from Eagleburger's call, seeing prosecutions of high-level Serb suspects as jeopardizing efforts to negotiate an end to the war in the Balkans. In any case, Eagleburger's threat did little to scare voters into abandoning Milošević.[3] At the polls, Milošević won handily.

The judgment of history that Eagleburger spoke about would have to wait. Karadžić, who was actually in Geneva attending the peace talks, did not face imminent arrest. Nor did Mladić back in Bosnia or Milošević back in Serbia. It would take another six months for the Security Council to authorize the establishment of the ICTY and several more years for it to become fully operational. In the court's early years, its survival remained in question on two fundamental counts: first, the United Nations' ambivalence about whether it actually wanted an effective court; second, the non-compliance of the states of the former Yugoslavia with investigations and prosecutions. Although this book deals primarily with the second challenge, it must be understood against the backdrop of the first challenge, because international ambivalence weakened the tribunal by encouraging non-compliance from the Balkan states.

[2] Elaine Sciolino, "US Names Figures It Wants Charged with War Crimes," *New York Times*, December 17, 1992, A1.
[3] There is debate as to whether Eagleburger's speech actually backfired and helped Milošević win the election. Aryeh Neier argues that although naming Milošević as a war crimes suspect was a positive step, Eagleburger's speech was ill-timed and may have aided Milošević's electoral bid. Neier, *War Crimes*, pp. 125–126. Lord David Owen argues that Eagleburger's remarks did not prove decisive in helping Milošević win the election. David Owen, *Balkan Odyssey* (New York: Harcourt Brace & Company, 1995), p. 85.

The initial failure of the UN to support the tribunal undermined its institutional viability by depriving it of necessary resources, such as adequate funding and staffing. In light of the tribunal's many handicaps, policymakers and human rights activists remained apprehensive about its future. "There seemed a real possibility that the tribunal would flop," former U.S. Secretary of State Madeleine Albright writes in her memoir.[4] It would take a year and a half for the tribunal to issue its first indictment and almost three years for the first trial to get under way in The Hague. Most of the early defendants brought before the court were not the high-level suspects the tribunal was meant to target, but rather the foot soldiers at the bottom of the Bosnian Serb and Bosnian Croat military and paramilitary hierarchies. From the looks of it, the tribunal did not resemble Eagleburger's hope of "a second Nuremberg."

Nevertheless, the potential threat that the tribunal posed to Serbia was not lost on Milošević. A functioning tribunal threatened to further isolate and tatter Serbia's international reputation by revealing the extent of Belgrade's complicity in the ongoing Bosnian war and the dormant Croatian conflict. The tribunal could also one day indict Milošević himself. Although Serbia's conduct in Bosnia earned it pariah status[5] early in the Bosnian war, Milošević adeptly avoided this designation himself, at least in the eyes of many Western diplomats whom he frequently engaged. Preventing a thorough accounting of the Balkan wars and Serbia's direct role in it were central to Milošević's bid to maintain his image as a statesman with whom the West could work. From the start of the Bosnian war in April 1992, Milošević masterfully played "a two-tier game"[6] in which he aided the Bosnian Serb ethnic cleansing campaigns, but then presented a benign picture of Belgrade's non-involvement to international diplomats. There was a collusive element to the West's buying into this image of a statesman.

The tribunal also threatened to refute the myth of Serb victimhood, honed anew by Serbian leaders, intellectuals, and journalists beginning with Milošević's rise to power in the late 1980s. It was Milošević's galvanizing speech at Kosovo Polje[7] in June 1989, marking the 600th anniversary of the Serbs' defeat by the Ottoman Turks at that same spot, that reignited Serb nationalism and the depiction of Serbia as "a long-suffering, but heroic nation, struggling for centuries against annihilation."[8] In the speech, Milošević decried and trumpeted

---

[4] Madeleine Albright, *Madame Secretary* (New York: Miramax Books, 2003), p. 183.

[5] Lenard J. Cohen, *Serpent In The Bosom: The Rise and Fall of Slobodan Milošević*, 2nd. ed. (Boulder: Westview Press), 2002, p. 248.

[6] Louis Sell, *Slobodan Milošević and the Destruction of Yugoslavia* (Durham: Duke University Press, 2002), pp. 167–168.

[7] Two years earlier, Milošević highlighted the suffering of Kosovo Serbs in a highly publicized visit to Kosovo Polje (Fushë Kosovë in Albanian). Milošević's strong defense of Serb allegations of mistreatment by Kosovar Albanians, "elevate[d] him to the status of instant hero of the Serbian national cause" and gave momentum to his bid for the Serbian presidency. Kemal Kurspahić, *Prime Time Crime: Balkan Media in War and Peace* (Washington, D.C.: United States Institute of Peace Press, 2003), pp. 34–36.

[8] MacDonald, *Balkan Holocausts?* p. 63.

Serb victimization at the hands of Kosovar Albanians in response to some recent attacks against Serbs. The victim myth, employed in regard to the Serb minority in Kosovo, would soon be used by Milošević to stoke Serb fear of atrocities elsewhere in the dissolving Federal Republic of Yugoslavia.[9] With the media firmly under his control, Milošević played on the fate of the Serb minority in Croatia and Bosnia under the terror of the fascist Croatian Ustaša movement during World War II.[10]

The outbreak of war, in Croatia and then in Bosnia, did little to dampen Milošević's characterization of Serbs as victims. If anything, their sense of victimization increased when the Serbs found themselves on the receiving end of international condemnation and UN sanctions for wartime atrocities in Bosnia. Beginning in May 1992, the Security Council imposed a series of sanctions that crippled Serbia's economy and contributed to spiraling inflation rates not seen in Europe since Weimer Germany.

When the UN created the tribunal, Milošević would again portray Serbia as the victim of an international political vendetta. To Milošević and to many Serbs, the establishment of the tribunal underscored once again that Serbia was the target of persecution.[11] Serb resentment was magnified by the ICTY's decision to indict initially only ethnic Serb suspects. "That most of those indicted were Serbs," Tim Judah writes, "did not lead the Serbs to the conclusion that their side had committed more crimes but rather reinforced their prejudice that the whole world was against them."[12]

Importantly, the first chief prosecutor of the ICTY (and ICTR), Richard J. Goldstone of South Africa, moved quickly to broaden his investigations to target war crimes committed by ethnic Croats and Muslims against Bosnian Serb civilians.[13] In a 2003 interview, Goldstone told me that the decision to move beyond Serb suspects stemmed from the ICTY's "open mandate to investigate any war crimes committed since 1991 in the former Yugoslavia."[14] Upholding its neutrality by achieving proportionality in indictments could arguably boost the court's legitimacy in the region and, in turn, increase its chances of receiving state cooperation from Serbia. The ICTY's efforts to remain even-handed were especially important to counter Serbian nationalists' claim of the tribunal's anti-Serb bias. Nevertheless, the Serbian government's basic stance of victimization by the ICTY did not diminish with this effort at proportionality. Belgrade argued strategically that the tribunal's primary focus on Serb suspects

---

[9] Ibid., p. 75.

[10] Kurspahić, *Prime Time Crime*, p. 51.

[11] See U.N. Doc. S/25801, May 21, 1993 as quoted in Michael Scharf, *Balkan Justice: The Story Behind the First International War Crimes Trial Since Nuremberg* (Durham: Carolina Academic Press, 1997), p. 72.

[12] Tim Judah, *The Serbs: History, Myth & the Destruction of Yugoslavia* (New Haven: Yale University Press, 2000), p. 239.

[13] During Chief Prosecutor Carla Del Ponte's tenure, the tribunal also indicted Croatian and Kosovar Albanian suspects in connection with atrocities against Serb civilians in Croatia and Kosovo.

[14] Fieldwork interview with Richard J. Goldstone, Pasadena, California, April 2003.

distorted the balance sheet of atrocities committed in the Balkans. In Serbia and the Bosnian Serb Republic (referred to hereafter as Republika Srpska), the familiar refrain from politicians and citizens alike was that Bosnians, Croats, and Serbs all shared equal responsibility for wartime transgressions.

Serbia's non-cooperation also proved instrumental in obstructing the tribunal's efforts to prosecute Bosnian Serbs. As with Serbia during the 1990s, the level of cooperation from Republika Srpska was dismal during the same period.[15] Had Serbia given full cooperation to the tribunal, investigators would have been able much earlier to obtain evidence held in state archives in Belgrade implicating Bosnian Serb suspects in atrocities. Belgrade could have also played an instrumental role in pressing Bosnian Serb suspects to surrender to the tribunal, given Milošević's influence over the Bosnian Serb leadership and military. To a large extent, therefore, the key to Bosnian Serb cooperation lay with the authorities in Belgrade just as the key to Bosnian Croat cooperation lay in the hands of authorities in Zagreb.

From the start, Goldstone and other top tribunal officials realized that the ICTY would have little prospect of overcoming Serbian intransigence without a determined and strategic approach. To establish their effectiveness, the chief prosecutor and chief justice (hereafter referred to as the president)[16] often acted as international diplomats shuttling throughout the Balkans and between Western capitals, prodding the targeted states and the international community to cooperate. The prosecutor's and the president's official charge was, of course, that of the legal professional who administers the court and attends to the complex task of bringing a suspect to trial. The rules guiding the legal tasks of the prosecutor and the president were created in a spirit of experimentation that mixed aspects of the common law and civil law systems. But there were no rules when it came to tribunal diplomacy. Guidelines for this diplomacy would be forged through experience, yet they were rarely recorded or fully understood outside the small circle of those officials engaged in the quest for state cooperation. At the tribunal, the chief prosecutor and the president's diplomatic forays often went unacknowledged out of concern that they would be perceived by outsiders as promoting an agenda more political than legal.

As discussed in Chapter 1, tribunal officials developed a diplomatic tool kit consisting of both conciliatory and adversarial strategies. But given the inherent antagonism between the ICTY and the Serbian government, there was little foundation for a conciliatory relationship, although tribunal officials did try to cultivate allies in Belgrade by developing personal contacts with Serbian government officials. As Goldstone told me, personal diplomacy "does help because it becomes more difficult to refuse reasonable requests if you are in

---

[15] Fieldwork interviews with ICTY officials, The Hague, October-November 2001.

[16] The tribunal's chief administrator (or Registrar) also plays an important role in efforts to obtain state cooperation. This will become particularly apparent in my examination of the Rwanda case study.

that sort of relationship."[17] Still, no amount of diplomacy, short of the ICTY's abandoning key elements of its prosecutorial agenda, could significantly alter Milošević's hostility to the tribunal. Not surprisingly, the ICTY often resorted to an adversarial approach aimed at shaming Serbia before the international community. But Milošević's capacity for feeling shame was in short supply. Nevertheless, the shaming campaign – which focused on garnering international media attention to expose Serbia's defiance – continued as a source of pressure on Serbia as well as on international actors in a position to act as surrogate enforcers of Serbia's obligation to cooperate.

2.3 International Diplomacy and the Peace v. Justice Conflict

The Security Council imposed sanctions on Serbia for fueling the war in Bosnia. Yet both during and after the war, it did not impose sanctions or otherwise punish Serbia specifically for its failure to cooperate with the tribunal despite irrefutable evidence of non-compliance. With some exceptions, the Council, the United States, and Europe did not vigorously press Milošević to cooperate with the ICTY beyond statements criticizing his poor record and reminders of his obligation to honor international law.

The West's lack of concerted pressure on Serbia during the Milošević era stemmed in large part from fear that a tribunal empowered to achieve its mandate of prosecuting top-level Serbian war crimes suspects could interfere with the prospect of a negotiated settlement and spur the West to intervene militarily. Throughout much of the Balkan conflict, the avoidance of military intervention was the abiding intent of the U.S. government and its European allies. Both the Bush (senior) and Clinton administrations were fearful that intervention could lead to a military quagmire, distract attention from their domestic agenda, and spark an electoral backlash. While Clinton took a somewhat more forceful role than Bush in condemning the atrocities, Clinton too harbored deep reservations about sending troops to Bosnia or even bombing Bosnian Serb targets.

As the Balkans descended into war in summer 1991 with Slovenia's and Croatia's declarations of independence, the United States had no qualms about letting the Europeans take the diplomatic lead. Consumed with the aftermath of the Persian Gulf War, the deteriorating situation in the Balkans was not a priority for the Bush White House. National Security Advisor Brent Scowcroft recalls that President Bush told him weekly, "Tell me again what this is all about."[18] Unlike Bush, European leaders appeared eager to show that they could handle the crisis. But European diplomatic initiatives continually failed to deliver results. As the Balkan crisis dragged on, the United States under

---

[17] Fieldwork interview with Richard J. Goldstone, Pasadena, California, April 2003.

[18] See James A. Baker III and Thomas M. DeFrank, *The Politics of Diplomacy* (New York: G. P. Putnam's Sons, 1995), p. 637, as quoted in Richard Holbrooke, *To End A War* (New York: Random House, 1998), p. 27.

Clinton's leadership took a larger role in wartime diplomacy. Like its European allies, the United States pursued a negotiated settlement to the conflict. Toward that end, Washington increasingly sought to portray Milošević as a statesman and a deserving interlocutor. Not surprisingly, administration officials distanced themselves from Eagleburger's call to prosecute Milošević and other Serbs in his "naming names" speech.[19] In February 1993, one senior administration official defended the policy of meeting with high-level Serbian officials by saying that the United States was not about to bring indictments. "I don't think we're ready to bring any accusations or indictments at the present time," the official said in a statement that betrayed the administration's hope that the United States and not the prospective international tribunal would control the timing of indictments.[20] A year later, the Clinton administration still declined to call Milošević a war crimes suspect.[21]

Inevitably, this U.S. posture obscured the full extent of Serb atrocities and Milošević's role in them, playing up the Bosnian conflict as a civil war in which all sides committed atrocities and shared culpability. This, of course, echoed Serbia's own claim not to be singled out for war crimes. The effort to spread the blame for the Bosnia conflict went hand in hand with portraying the conflict as warfare bred from ancient hatreds and therefore beyond a moral obligation to send troops or even to hold modern-day leaders accountable. Clinton officials tried their best, as Samantha Power writes, "to dampen moral outrage, steering senior officials to adopt the imagery and wording of 'tragedy' over that of 'terror.'"[22] Just days before the Security Council established the ICTY, Clinton's Secretary of State Warren Christopher told Congress that all sides were to blame for atrocities against civilians and said that that shared responsibility meant there was no moral reason for international intervention.[23] Christopher's characterization of the conflict sparked a sharp rebuke from some in Congress as well as from a senior human rights official at the State Department. In a memo to Christopher that highlighted administration divisions over Clinton's Bosnia policy, James K. Bishop, a Deputy Assistant Secretary of State for Human Rights and Humanitarian Affairs, wrote that evidence demonstrated that Serb forces had carried out an "overwhelming majority"[24] of the massacres. Moreover, he said that the United States had clear evidence that many of the atrocities in Bosnia were committed with the complicity of the Milošević government.

---

[19] Elaine Sciolino, "In Bosnia, Peace at Any Price Is Getting More Expensive," *New York Times*, January 10, 1993.

[20] Elaine Sciolino, "U.S. Faces a Delicate Task in Intervening in Negotiations on Bosnia, *New York Times*, February 12, 1993, A10.

[21] Elaine Sciolino, "U.S. Accepts Easing of Curbs on Serbia: Three Reasons Why," *New York Times*, October 6, 1994, A14.

[22] Samantha Power, *"A Problem From Hell": America and the Age of Genocide* (New York: Basic Books, 2002), pp. 304–305.

[23] Michael R. Gordon, "U.S. Memo Reveals Dispute on Bosnia," *New York Times*, June 25, 1993, A3.

[24] Ibid.

Washington's attempts to downplay Milošević's culpability in war crimes in order to make him a palatable partner matched Milošević's own efforts. The Serbian leader was often careful to keep diplomatic channels open and appear committed to reaching a negotiated solution. Milošević had an uncanny ability, Power notes, of "cultivating the impression from the very start of the conflict that peace was 'right around the corner.'"[25] Milošević's personal charm, fluent English, and ability to present a moderate image helped drive Western diplomats' wishful thinking about his true intentions. "Many is the U.S. senator or congressman who has reeled out of his office exclaiming, 'Why, he is not nearly as bad as I expected!'" former U.S. Ambassador to Yugoslavia Warren Zimmerman wrote.[26]

In the hopes of burnishing his image abroad, Milošević was also quite willing on a number of occasions to denounce some Serbs as war criminals. As early as Fall 1993, his Socialist party announced that some Serbs, supposedly not supported by him or the party, had committed war crimes. In a statement designed to portray Milošević as a moderate and to win Western support to lift sanctions, his party lambasted Vojislav Šešelj, the notorious Serb paramilitary leader, for war crimes. At times, Milošević also distanced himself from Bosnian Serb leaders. In July 1994, Milošević cut his links with the Bosnian Serbs and turned on Karadžić by accusing him of war profiteering. Not surprisingly, Milošević's criticism of renegade Serbs did not translate into handing these suspects over to the ICTY, where they could use the courtroom to incriminate him.

Milošević seemed willing to betray the ideal of a Greater Serbia if his position internationally as a respected statesman were strengthened. In an interview, a veteran diplomat who dealt with Milošević during the Balkan conflict said of the former Serbian leader: "He's not a nationalist like others . . . He's not crazy like Karadžić. He's not stupid like Mladić. He's a very smart, intelligent, cynical politician whose only driving force is power."[27] Improving his international stature was critical to Milošević's goal to have the international community lift the economic sanctions that were weakening his power base at home.

The conflict between peace and justice was acute before and in the aftermath of the Dayton peace talks that brought an end to the Bosnian war. But this conflict was not static or unchanging. At times, diplomats realized that a robust tribunal wielding the threat of war crimes indictments complemented the search for peace by bolstering attempts to bring the war to an end. Even as the West feared the ICTY's interference in the peace process, Western diplomats, at times, also viewed the tribunal as an asset insofar as it could undermine and even remove undesirable leaders from both the domestic and international scene. Thus the West maintained an interest in pressing Serbia to provide some cooperation to the fledgling court. That the West needed to negotiate with Balkan leaders did not mean that it wanted to negotiate with all Balkan leaders.

[25] Power, *"A Problem From Hell,"* p. 260.
[26] As quoted in Power, *"A Problem From Hell,"* p. 260.
[27] Fieldwork interview with diplomat, The Hague, November 2001.

Indeed, some notorious figures, such as Bosnian Serb leader Radovan Karadžić and Bosnian Serb General Ratko Mladić, increasingly came to be seen as impediments to peace, both because of their role in perpetuating the war and their obstinacy at the bargaining table. Therein lies the international community's ambivalent and at times seemingly contradictory approach toward the tribunal and the question of Serbia's cooperation.

Against the backdrop of a horrific war on the doorstep of Europe – replete with televised scenes of Sarajevo under siege and emaciated Bosnian Muslims deteriorating in Serb concentration camps – a tribunal was both a powerful measure that conveyed the West's moral repugnance at the violence and a public commitment to hold the perpetrators accountable. The prospect of an international war crimes tribunal captured the imagination of many, especially in the international human rights community, who viewed the legal body as a moral force and a stepping stone for the creation of a permanent international criminal court and a new international legal order.

From another vantage point, the ICTY provided Western leaders with political cover for their ongoing failure to end the Bosnian war. Establishing the court was also meant, therefore, to pacify the rising condemnation – particularly leveled by Bosnian victims and human rights activists – of Western inaction to stop ethnic cleansing in the Balkans. The failure to stop the carnage in the former Yugoslavia created a crisis of leadership in the West. The post-Cold War promise of a new world order appeared suddenly to founder in the face of Western indecision. The Balkan crisis, wrote Richard Holbrooke, was "the greatest collective security failure of the West since the 1930s."[28] The decisions of the Bush and Clinton administrations not to intervene in the conflict sparked a barrage of criticism in the media, Congress, and even among some disenchanted officials in the State Department. This dissent within the U.S. government made front-page headlines with the resignations of several State Department officials to protest the lukewarm policy that bordered on appeasement of Milošević and the Bosnian Serbs. In this context, the Security Council's motives for creating the ICTY were strongly criticized in some quarters as "a fig leaf for inaction"[29] and a disingenuous way to portray itself as a staunch defender of human rights when it actually had abetted the destruction of Yugoslavia. "When it was established," Holbrooke recalled, "the tribunal was widely viewed as little more than a public relations device."[30] The tribunal itself acknowledged this skepticism. In its first annual report, the ICTY admitted that "however landmark in [its] breadth, not only was the promulgation of the Yugoslav Tribunal Statute painfully slow, but [it] effectively served as little more than [a] topical antiseptic in the treatment of the malignancy of genocide."[31] While there was a strong

[28] Holbrooke, *To End a War*, p. 21.
[29] Carol Off, *The Lion, The Fox, & the Eagle: A Story of Genocide and Justice in Rwanda and Yugoslavia* (Toronto: Random House Canada, 2000), p. 269.
[30] Holbrooke, *To End a War*, pp. 189–190.
[31] ICTY First Annual Report, quoted in Paul R. Williams and Michael P. Scharf, *Peace with Justice? War Crimes and Accountability in the Former Yugoslavia* (Oxford: Rowman & Littlefield Publishers, Inc. 2002), pp. 100–101.

consensus among international human rights organizations for the moral and legal necessity to establish a tribunal, there was also acknowledgment that it was created for the wrong reason. "It was a substitute for effective action to halt Serb depredations in Bosnia-Herzegovina," wrote Aryeh Neier, the former executive director of Human Rights Watch and president of the Open Society Institute.[32]

At the same time that the establishment of the tribunal scored public relations points for the West, it also had the potential to serve Western interests in the future. For the United States and its European allies, the ICTY could be invaluable if they could exert significant control over the timing and target of indictments. In particular, the tribunal could be used to target Milošević if and when the West deemed that his actions went beyond the pale. As events would demonstrate, going beyond the pale did not occur in Serbia's war in Croatia or Bosnia, but in Kosovo. The court's establishment, according to one European diplomat,[33] was intended in part as a warning to Milošević to curtail Serbia's ethnic cleansing campaigns. In effect, the UN put Milošević on notice that while he was safe for the moment, one day the tribunal might target him.

Just as a tribunal could serve Western interests, it could also undermine them. A fully functional tribunal able to operate independently of political influence from the West raised concern in Washington and some European capitals. As early as the Spring of 1992, Western leaders recognized that Milošević held the keys to a future settlement to the Bosnian conflict. "Diplomats looked for the solution to the Bosnian conflict not in Sarajevo or . . . [in] Pale [with Karadžić] but in Belgrade with Milošević," Louis Sell writes in his biography of the Serbian leader.[34] Despite international sanctions and Serbia's growing isolation, the West was careful to limit its marginalization of Milošević. Given his central role in the resolution of any conflict, not having Milošević as a partner in peace talks could, it was feared, prolong the war. In particular, the West feared that pressing Belgrade too hard to provide cooperation to the ICTY would brake or even break a prospective peace deal. An indictment against Milošević could also limit diplomatic maneuvering room by scuttling any proposals for amnesty in exchange for peace.

The international community's ambivalence about creating a robust and fully independent war crimes tribunal was foreshadowed by the ICTY's institutional precursor – the United Nations Commission of Experts. This temporary investigative body came to be seen as a way for the Security Council to demonstrate that it was taking action in response to atrocities[35] short of either military intervention or the establishment of an international tribunal. But by limiting funding and technical support, the Security Council hampered the Commission's work and raised doubts about the UN's commitment to uncovering the truth about the Balkan atrocities. Nevertheless, the Commission managed to

[32] Neier, *War Crimes*, p. 112.
[33] Fieldwork interview with European diplomat, Kigali, Rwanda, May 2002.
[34] Sell, *Slobodan Milošević and the Destruction of Yugoslavia*, p. 168.
[35] John F. Burns, "Balkan War Trial In Serious Doubt," *New York Times*, April 26, 1993, A9.

play a key role in the creation of the ICTY, due in large part to the tenacity of Commission members – particularly its second chairman, Cherif Bassiouni, an Egyptian-born American law professor – and to vital support from volunteers and non-governmental funding sources, such as the Soros Foundation. The Commission's interim report of February 1993 established that serious violations of international humanitarian law had occurred and recommended that the Security Council create a tribunal.

The West's lukewarm treatment of the Commission of Experts indicates how long-standing its ambivalence to international justice had been. This ambivalence toward the tribunal translated into inadequate funding for the court as well as a fourteen-month delay in selecting a chief prosecutor that all Security Council members could agree on. Over time, the ICTY received the institutional support it needed, in large part because of the effective pressure brought by tribunal officials and their advocates in the international human rights community.

2.4 Balancing Peace and Justice at Dayton

The Clinton administration's efforts to bolster Milošević's image increased with hopes for a negotiated peace agreement in the late summer and early fall of 1995. The conditions for a settlement improved as Serb forces lost ground in Bosnia and Croatia and international resolve increased for military intervention. The tide began to shift against the Bosnian Serbs in 1995 after they captured seventy percent of Bosnia in the early part of the war. Bosnian Muslim and Bosnian Croat forces, now allied against the Serbs after having fought each other in 1993, began to regain some of the territory lost to the Serbs. In early August, the Croatian armed forces launched Operation Storm, a massive military assault that recaptured approximately one-third of the territory in Croatia lost to breakaway Serbs in 1991. Continuing revelations of atrocities – particularly the July 1995 Srebrenica massacre – also increased American will to bring the war to an end.

For the United States, remaining a spectator to the Balkan wars was no longer viable. "The administration's muddle-through strategy in Bosnia was becoming a cancer on Clinton's entire foreign policy – spreading and eating away at its credibility," National Security Advisor Anthony Lake wrote in a memo at the time.[36] NATO's belated use of force – bombing Bosnian Serb positions in late August – set the stage for a peace conference. As the possibility of a summit grew near, American and European officials tried to raise Milošević's stature.[37] Commenting on Milošević's agreement to participate in peace talks, State Department spokesman Nicholas Burns lauded the Serb leader. "President Milošević is a respected leader among the Serbs, and for him to come out and dedicate his Government to a peace process is a positive sign," Burns

---

[36] Bob Woodward, *The Choice* (New York: Simon & Schuster, 1996), p. 253.
[37] Elaine Sciolino, "Trading Villains' Horns for Halos," *New York Times*, October 8, 1995, E1.

said.[38] But even as U.S. officials presented Milošević as a statesman, there was increasing public evidence and high-profile news coverage of his culpability in war crimes.[39] While lacking sufficient evidence to bring an indictment against Milošević, ICTY prosecutors announced, just as peace talks got underway at the Wright-Patterson Air Force Base in Dayton, Ohio, that the Serbian leader was under investigation.[40]

As it turned out, prosecutors were not close to indicting Milošević. Nevertheless, their announcement of an ongoing investigation may have been aimed at increasing the tribunal's leverage with U.S. negotiators and insuring that the ICTY would emerge from Dayton with enhanced authority in its battle for state cooperation.[41] For the ICTY, Dayton held both promise and peril. If Dayton produced an agreement binding Serbia to recognize the tribunal and guarantee cooperation, then the talks might bolster the tribunal's standing. But Dayton could also set the clock back by producing a weak agreement on cooperation, or even worse, granting high-level Serb war crimes suspects amnesty as a bargaining chip. That, in turn, could set a dangerous precedent whereby powerful actors such as the United States bargained away the tribunal's mandate to prosecute atrocities when the perceived need to do so arose in the future. As the peace conference drew closer, U.S. officials declined to commit to make the arrest of war crimes suspects a condition of any peace agreement. Chief Prosecutor Goldstone and others at the tribunal grew more concerned that U.S. negotiators might grant amnesty to the two most notorious war crimes suspects under indictment, Radovan Karadžić and Ratko Mladić.

Goldstone's moves, both before and during the November Dayton talks, to prevent an amnesty deal for Karadžić and Mladić, underscored his political skills and the important role the tribunal played in safeguarding and strengthening its own authority. Goldstone took several measures to remove a possible amnesty from serious consideration. First, in early 1995, but long before Dayton and before the war came to a close, Goldstone pursued investigations of Karadžić and Mladić. The investigations were not necessarily meant to preempt an amnesty, but nevertheless would help serve this purpose when the prospects for a peace conference increased over the course of the year. By April 1995, Goldstone let it be known that indictments would soon be handed down implicating the two Bosnian Serb leaders for their role in ordering atrocities in Bosnia.[42] Then, in late July, Goldstone indicted Karadžić and Mladić for war

---

[38] Elaine Sciolino, "What Price Peace? Balkan Agreement Offers All Parties A Practical, but Not Ennobling, End," *New York Times*, September 9, 1995 A4.

[39] See, for example, Roger Cohen's April 1995 front-page article in *The New York Times* that reported the release of incriminating documents by a former senior member of the Serbian secret police. "Serb Says File Links Milošević To War Crimes," *New York Times*, April 13, 1995, A1.

[40] Stephen Engelberg, "Panel Seeks U.S. Pledge on Bosnia War Criminals," *New York Times*, November 3, 1995, A1.

[41] Tribunal officials did not attend or play any official role in the Dayton peace talks.

[42] Roger Cohen, "Tribunal to Cite Bosnia Serb Chief As War Criminal," *New York Times*, April 24, 1995, A1.

crimes, crimes against humanity, and genocide in connection with atrocities committed earlier in the war.

The indictments raised the tribunal's profile as well as the notoriety of the Bosnian Serb leaders, although in some quarters the ICTY faced criticism for not having acted sooner. An unanswered question is whether Goldstone could and should have quickened the pace of his investigations and indicted Karadžić and Mladić earlier. The journalist Pierre Hazan maintains that Goldstone deferred to the West's wishes to protect Karadžić and Mladić – at least during the first half of 1995 when they still were seen by some Western diplomats as valuable negotiating partners – and focus on low-level suspects.[43] Had Goldstone indicted the Bosnian Serb leaders prior to the mid-July Srebrenica massacre, the ICTY would arguably have had a greater opportunity to isolate them and possibly deter the massacre. A question also remains as to why Goldstone did not indict Milošević or dedicate more tribunal resources and political capital toward doing so. Goldstone insists that he would have indicted Milošević if the tribunal had had sufficient evidence, and that he neither faced nor caved into international pressure.[44] The complex legal task of linking Milošević to the atrocities of Bosnian Serbs was made difficult by Serbian non-cooperation and by the refusal of Western governments to hand over incriminating evidence. Yet, arguably, the pragmatic Goldstone was likely more concerned with ensuring the tribunal's survival by securing Western support and funding. At least in the pre-Dayton period, it is, as Michael Scharf argues, "hard to believe that Goldstone did not intentionally delay pursuing an indictment" of Milošević because it "would have wrecked any prospect for peace."[45]

In the months and weeks leading up to the Dayton peace talks in November 1995, Goldstone and ICTY President Antonio Cassese issued trenchant public criticisms of any amnesty deal and insisted that an amnesty would not be legally binding on the tribunal, given its wide-ranging authority granted by the Security Council.[46,47] Goldstone also worked toward preventing amnesties by attacking the amnesties employed to resolve other armed conflicts.[48,49] He went a step

---

[43] Pierre Hazan, *Justice in a Time of War: The True Story Behind the International Criminal Tribunal for the Former Yugoslavia* (College Station: Texas A & M University Press, 2004), p. 65.

[44] Goldstone, *For Humanity*, p. 107.

[45] Scharf, *Balkan Justice*, p. 90.

[46] Roger Cohen, "U.N. in Bosnia: Black Robes Clash With Blue Hats," *New York Times*, April 25, 1995, A3.

[47] Elizabeth Neuffer, *The Key to My Neighbor's House: Seeking Justice in Bosnia and Rwanda* (New York: Picador, USA, 2001), p. 169.

[48] Peter S. Canellos, "Amnesty Plan Worries UN War-Crimes Prosecutor," *Boston Globe*, October 1, 1994, p. 8, as quoted in Scharf, *Balkan Justice*, p. 88.

[49] While reprehensible to many, amnesty deals brokered by the international community were common in the 1990s as seen in Haiti, El Salvador, Cambodia, Somalia, and Sierra Leone. Moreover, in Goldstone's South Africa, the creation of the Truth and Reconciliation Commission was in effect a mechanism for granting amnesty, albeit an innovative one based on trading truth telling for reprieves from prosecution.

further, wielding the prosecutor's power of indictment to raise the pressure on Richard Holbrooke, the lead U.S. negotiator at Dayton. Goldstone had already indicted Karadžić and Mladić in late July. But now, with the Dayton talks underway and rumors emerging of a possible amnesty, Goldstone moved to prepare a second indictment against the Bosnian Serb leaders. This new indictment, issued more than two weeks into the marathon peace talks,[50] added the Srebrenica massacre to the Bosnian Serb leaders' record of mass atrocities. When he announced the indictment, Goldstone threatened to resign if negotiators offered an amnesty deal.[51] Goldstone insists that the timing of the amended indictment was "a coincidence"[52] and had nothing to do with trying to sway American negotiators at Dayton. Yet he is somewhat equivocal about this assertion since he does acknowledge that he tried to "hasten" the indictment.[53]

Regardless of intent, the timing of the second indictment bolstered the argument against granting Karadžić and Mladić a reprieve from prosecution. Although the Bosnian Serb leaders remained legally innocent, the indictment reinforced their guilt in the court of public opinion and further illustrated the suffering of the Bosnian Muslim victims at Srebrenica. The November 16 statement by Fouad Riad, the tribunal judge who confirmed the indictment, searingly summarized the prosecution's case for bringing Karadžić and Mladić to trial:

The evidence tendered by the Prosecutor describes scenes of unimaginable savagery: thousands of men executed and buried in mass graves, hundreds of men buried alive, men and women mutilated and slaughtered, children killed before their mothers' eyes, a grandfather forced to eat the liver of his own grandson. These are truly scenes from hell, written on the darkest pages of human history.[54]

Against this statement, amnesty would have been appeasement by another name. American officials, however, maintained that no amnesty was considered at Dayton,[55] just as they insisted that they would not have agreed to such a deal during the earlier Vance-Owens peace negotiations.[56] It remains uncertain how seriously the Clinton administration considered an amnesty in the weeks and months preceding Dayton. The retrospective accounts of some key U.S. participants in the peace talks do not acknowledge that it was an option or that the tribunal posed an impediment to a peace agreement. In fact, U.S. officials concede little conflict between peace and justice, at least at Dayton. Holbrooke

[50] The Dayton peace talks began on November 1 and concluded on November 21. The formal signing of the Accords took place in Paris on December 14.
[51] Neuffer, *The Key to My Neighbor's House*, pp. 169–170.
[52] Goldstone, *For Humanity*, p. 108.
[53] Ibid., p. 108.
[54] "Radovan Karadžić and Ratko Mladić Accused of Genocide Following the Take-Over of Srebrenica," ICTY press release, November 16, 1995.
[55] Stephen Engelberg, "Panel Seeks U.S. Pledge on Bosnia War Criminals," *New York Times*, November 3, 1995, A1.
[56] See Madeleine K. Albright, "War Crimes in Bosnia," *San Francisco Chronicle*," December 4, 1993, A22, as quoted in Scharf, *Balkan Justice*, pp. 87–88.

lauded the tribunal as "a huge valuable tool"[57] by excluding extremists such as Karadžić and Mladić from the peace talks and forcing the more moderate Milošević to be their de facto representative. Writes Holbrooke: "We used [the tribunal] to keep the two most wanted war criminals in Europe...out of the Dayton peace process and we used it to justify everything that followed."[58] Holbrooke skillfully paints himself as the peace broker that he indeed was. But, more dubiously, he also portrays himself as a defender of justice. Recounting his message to Milošević during a pre-Dayton meeting, Holbrooke writes that he told the Serbian leader: "I want to be sure, since this is the beginning [of] a serious negotiation with you as the head of a unified Yugoslav-Srpska delegation...that you understand that we will not, and cannot, compromise on the question of the war crimes tribunal."[59] Holbrooke remained firm when it came to Karadžić's and Mladić's exclusion from Dayton and ultimately on the question of a possible amnesty for them. Yet compromise would become Holbrooke's guiding principal when it came to other aspects of the tribunal's fate.

Despite the U.S. interest in excluding Karadžić and Mladić from Dayton, it was still possible, at least months before the peace conference convened, that an amnesty would have been an attractive solution to brokering a settlement. In this regard, Goldstone's preemptive action appears to have played a critical role in making an amnesty an increasingly distasteful option at Dayton. While an amnesty might have appealed to U.S. officials earlier in 1995 – as a way to buy Bosnian Serb support for peace – it became less palatable over the course of the summer and the fall.

Goldstone also took other measures to ensure that the tribunal's authority was not undermined at Dayton, as demonstrated by his call for the handover of all indicted war crimes suspects as a precondition of any peace deal[60] and by his timing of indictments against the three senior officers in the Serbian-dominated Yugoslav People's Army for the 1991 massacre of 261 soldiers near Vukovar in Croatia. Until the November 10 indictments were handed down, the tribunal had indicted approximately fifty Bosnian Serbs, but no suspects from Serbia proper. The Vukovar Three were not only Serbian citizens but officers in the Yugoslav People's Army and as such ultimately under the command of Milošević, their commander in chief. The November 10 indictments made it much more difficult for Milošević to sidestep the cooperation issue or insist, as he had been doing, that he bore little responsibility for arresting ethnic Serb suspects who resided in Bosnia. Tribunal officials clearly hoped that the indictments of General Mile Mrkšić, Major Veselin Šljivančanin, and Captain Miroslav Radić would force Milošević to send these suspects to The Hague.

---

[57] Interview with Richard Holbrooke, "United Nations or Not? The Final Judgment: Searching for International Justice," *BBC Radio*, September 9, 2003.

[58] Ibid.

[59] Holbrooke, *To End a War*, p. 107.

[60] Stephen Engelberg, "Panel Seeks U.S. Pledge on Bosnia War Criminals," *New York Times*, November 3, 1995.

"The indictments... put direct pressure on Mr. Milošević," said ICTY Deputy Prosecutor Graham Blewitt.[61] "In the past, Belgrade has been able to say that Bosnian Serbs were separate units and inquiries should be made in Pale. That's not possible now."

The Dayton Accords yielded important benefits for the fledgling tribunal. The Accords committed the Serbian, Croatian, and Bosnian governments to comply fully with the court, which raised the prominence of the cooperation issue both regionally and in the eyes of influential international actors. Ever since the tribunal's creation, cooperation had been an obligation imposed on all UN member states and thus a source of bitter complaint in the Balkans. Significantly, the Balkan states had now signaled their consent to aid the court in its investigations and prosecutions. Although cooperation was not the central component of the Accords, Western diplomats increasingly regarded that provision as critical to securing peace in the region. The provision on cooperation was intentionally crafted to help bolster the prospects of stability by stipulating that indicted war crimes suspects – *in Bosnia only* – could not hold political office. One might see the application of this provision only to Bosnia as an attempt by American negotiators to insulate Milošević and President Tuđman of Croatia from the loss of their office if indicted by the tribunal. An indictment, even without a trial and conviction, would sideline those extremists, principally Karadžić and Mladić, most likely to spark a resurgence of warfare or block implementation of other bitterly contested aspects of the Dayton Accords (such as the return of refugees to their homes). Now, peace and justice appeared to complement each other.

Yet Karadžić was not forced to step down from his leadership position until more than a half a year after Dayton. Furthermore, the strategic timing of the ICTY's indictments notwithstanding, Milošević left Dayton without being forced to arrest and send the Vukovar Three (and other ethnic Serb suspects) to The Hague. Compelling the handover of the Vukovar Three was not a priority for Holbrooke, who feared that it could complicate efforts to reach a peace settlement. For U.S. negotiators at Dayton there was still in fact a conflict between peace and justice. "We're going to do as much as is realistic," one U.S. official said shortly after the Dayton talks got underway. "We're not going to take on a mission that may be unachievable and make it hostage to the larger peace settlement."[62] Yet, for Bosnian President Alija Izetbegović, justice was an indispensable element of the peace agreement, at least initially. Izetbegović's determination[63] to hold out for a guarantee of the surrender of war crimes suspects and Milošević's refusal to accede to this demand threatened to block an overall peace agreement. Not surprisingly, American negotiators proved unable to get Milošević to agree to language that spelled out the specific

---

[61] Roger Cohen, "Tribunal Indicts 3 Serbia Officers," *New York Times*, November 10, 1995, A1.

[62] Stephen Engelberg, "Panel Seeks U.S. Pledge on Bosnia War Criminals," *New York Times*, November 3, 1995, A1.

[63] Scharf, *Balkan Justice*, p. 88.

steps that Serbia would take to provide full cooperation to the tribunal. Curiously, Milošević did approve a provision that required all participating states at Dayton to abide by any tribunal order to arrest, detain, or surrender indicted suspects.[64] Yet the language of this provision proved too imprecise to expect Milošević's compliance. General Wesley Clark, who was part of the U.S. delegation, recalls that Milošević remained steadfast in his refusal to agree to provisions that might later be used to force his hand. "Milošević would do no more than agree with a formula that bound all parties 'to cooperate with the International Criminal Tribunal,' implying that he would act upon orders of the Tribunal, but without sufficient specificity to compel his action," Clark writes in his account of the Balkan wars. "This was an aspect of the agreement that would cause many difficulties in the years ahead."[65] Indeed, the Achilles' heel of the Dayton provision on cooperation lay in its vagueness and the subsequent ease with which Milošević could exploit it. When it came to issues of war crimes, Milošević conceded little at Dayton, which served to embolden him further to avoid cooperation without serious consequences.

The United States hailed the Dayton Accords as a just end to a painful conflict. The Accords, however, rewarded the Bosnian Serbs's ethnic cleansing by granting them a semi-autonomous region within Bosnia. After more than four years of war and atrocity in the Balkans, there was peace at last, or, more accurately, an absence of conflict.[66] The end of the Bosnian war, however, marked only a brief respite to the ongoing story of instability and violence in the Balkans. As Bosnia began to deal with the aftermath of its devastating war, Kosovo slowly began to unravel. Moreover, the end of the war on the battlefield did not bring an end to the war between the tribunal and the states of the former Yugoslavia over who would face indictment and trial for the atrocities of the recent past. The triumph of diplomacy at Dayton only provided temporary relief in the turbulent battles between The Hague and Belgrade over cooperation.

2.5 Broken Promises: Serbian Non-compliance after Dayton

In the aftermath of Dayton, Milošević's star rose at home and abroad. The instrumental role that Milošević played at the U.S.-sponsored peace talks boosted his image as a "peace-maker,"[67] a "moderate leader,"[68] and

---

[64] See Dayton Accords, Annex 1, Agreement on Military Aspects.

[65] Wesley K. Clark, *Waging Modern War: Bosnia, Kosovo, and the Future of Combat* (New York: Public Affairs, 2002), p. 65.

[66] After the Bosnian war, the commonly accepted death toll for that conflict was approximately 200,000. See Power, *"A Problem from Hell,"* p. 251. However, in mid-2007, a Sarajevo-based research center reported that the death toll from the Bosnian war was 97,000. The center's findings were based on a three-year investigation. See "Research shows estimates of Bosnian war death toll were inflated," *Associated Press/International Herald Tribune*, June 21, 2007.

[67] Lenard J. Cohen, *Serpent in the Bosom* (1st ed., 2001), p. 204.

[68] Raymond Bonner, "In Reversal, Serbs of Bosnia Accept Peace Agreement," *New York Times*, November 24, 1995, A1.

"world statesmen."[69] American gratitude won Milošević a reprieve from facing strong pressure to cooperate with the ICTY. American officials did, however, call on Milošević to cooperate and publicly declared that his obligation to aid the ICTY was non-negotiable. Since the imposition of UN sanctions on Serbia in 1992, Milošević had made it clear that his support for a peace agreement would have to be rewarded with a lifting of sanctions.[70,71] The lifting of the UN sanctions dealt a blow to the tribunal by considerably weakening the international community's leverage over Serbia on the cooperation issue during the rest of the Milošević era. The UN's actions appear to have encouraged Milošević to continue to defy the ICTY with virtual impunity.

America and Europe's reliance on Milošević did not end with the signing of the Dayton Accords. The West repeatedly turned to Milošević to compel Bosnian Serb compliance with different aspects of the Accords, particularly in regard to security, return of refugees, the transfer of Serbian areas near Sarajevo to Bosnian government control, and the removal of Karadžić from office. By comparison with the pre-Dayton period, the arrest of Bosnian Serb war crimes suspects and Belgrade's cooperation with the ICTY rose in significance, but these issues still remained of secondary importance to the Western powers. While Western leaders continued to extol justice as a cornerstone of peace, they were also reluctant to bear the costs of achieving it. To the Clinton administration, the success of Dayton lay primarily in securing the peace and ensuring that NATO's 60,000 troops – 20,000 of whom were American – suffered as few casualties as possible. Thus, the United States and other NATO countries remained reluctant to use troops to arrest war crimes suspects, fearful of a repeat of the U.S. military's disastrous attempts to arrest Mohamed Farrah Aidid in Somalia in 1993. That concern was heightened by Clinton's pre-election concern that casualties would jeopardize his prospects for a second term in November 1996. The story of NATO's reluctance to use its peacekeepers to arrest war crimes suspects has been well-documented elsewhere.[72] However, scholars and journalists alike have paid much less attention to the West's policy in regard to the Serbian government's lack of cooperation with the tribunal in the pre- and post-Dayton periods.

In the aftermath of Dayton, Milošević made a few concessions to the tribunal that briefly raised hopes in The Hague that the Serbian leader had turned over a new leaf, and inspired tribunal officials to make some conciliatory public statements. ICTY President Antonio Cassese, after returning from talks with Serbian officials in Belgrade, described his meetings as "frank and in-depth."[73] At one point, in March 1996, a tribunal spokesman went so far as to say that Belgrade

---

[69] Lenard J. Cohen, *Serpent in the Bosom* (1st ed., 2001), p. 204.

[70] Sell, *Slobodan Milošević and the Destruction of Yugoslavia*, p. 168.

[71] The United States, however, maintained "an outer wall" of sanctions that barred Serbia from receiving loans from some international lending institutions.

[72] For instance, see Bass, *Stay the Hand of Vengeance*, pp. 206–275.

[73] "President Cassese Holds High-Level Talks in Belgrade," ICTY press release, June 7, 1996.

had demonstrated "a new and genuine willingness" to cooperate.[74] But as the months passed, it became clear that Milošević remained steadfast in his determination to block the ICTY's investigations of Serbian war crimes suspects. In the wake of U.S. pressure in January 1996, Milošević belatedly agreed to allow the tribunal to open a liaison office in Belgrade and suggested that he might make it easier for the ICTY to conduct investigations.[75] The establishment of the office, however, directly served Milošević's interests because it was intended primarily to facilitate ICTY investigations of atrocities in which Serbs had been victims. Milošević also indicated his possible willingness to arrest and transfer non-Serb suspects living in Serbia to The Hague, but only on a case-by-case basis. However, he showed no inclination to arrest and hand over the Vukovar Three. Nevertheless, his decision to allow an unindicted suspect in the 1995 Srebrenica massacre to leave Serbia for The Hague in March 1996 did spark hope for an improvement in cooperation.

Milošević's decision to allow the suspect, Dražen Erdemović, to speak with tribunal investigators in Belgrade and then travel to the ICTY was regarded a "watershed"[76] event. At the time, the tribunal only had three suspects in custody, all low-level ethnic Serb suspects. In the face of intense international pressure, Milošević allowed the tribunal to take Erdemović out of Serbia. Milošević may have concluded that handing over a low-level, non-Serb, non-indicted suspect such as Erdemović was not a high price to pay, and might even be in his interest by showing a willingness to cooperate and by staving off pressure to hand over the higher level Vukovar Three suspects.

Although a low-level suspect, Erdemović was still a catch because of his willingness to provide evidence against high-level Serb suspects who ordered the Srebrenica massacre. Milošević made it clear that future cooperation – if it happened at all – would be on his terms. Throughout the 1990s, Milošević refused to hand over war crimes suspects and refused to adopt a national law on cooperation that would set clear procedures and timetables for cooperation. He and other Serb officials cited the lack of domestic legislation to justify their lack of cooperation.[77] Serb officials also persistently maintained the fiction that the Dayton Accords did not require Belgrade to send suspects to The Hague.[78]

The tribunal did not remain passive in the face of continued Serbian recalcitrance and uneven international community support. Goldstone and Cassese, followed by their respective successors, Louise Arbour and Gabrielle

---

[74] Alan Cowell, "A Croat, a Muslim and a Serb Are Held in Balkan War-Crimes Cases," *New York Times*, March 20, 1996, A12.

[75] "President Cassese Takes Stock of Current Co-Operation Between Croatia, the F.R.Y. and the Tribunal," ICTY press release, February 6, 1996.

[76] Jane Perlez, "Serb Leader Expected to Turn Over Key War Crimes Suspects," *New York Times*, March 13, 1996, A6. Erdemović was indicted and convicted for his role in the massacre.

[77] "Serbian ruling party official: Yugoslavia not to hand over suspected war criminals," *BBC Monitoring Original Source: Bosnian Serb News Agency, SRNA,* May 29, 1997.

[78] Jane Perlez, "In Montenegro, an Indicted Soldier Is Still a Hero," *New York Times*, January 5, 1996, A3.

Kirk McDonald, increased pressure on Milošević by highlighting precisely how Belgrade was sabotaging the tribunal's mandate. They took their case to the Western media, garnering sympathetic reporting and commentary from major media outlets. The tribunal also took its case to the Security Council, where it lodged formal complaints of Serbian non-compliance and called on the UN to impose sanctions. The tribunal had been reticent to issue such complaints against Serbia despite its flagrant non-cooperation. In fact, President Cassese made only one such complaint prior to 1996,[79] but after Dayton, he took a more activist stance. In the first half of 1996, he lodged three official complaints against Belgrade. The first complaint, in late April, lambasted the government for failing to arrest the Vukovar Three. The second and third complaints, filed in late May and mid-July, respectively, alleged that the Serbian authorities were harboring Radovan Karadžić and Ratko Mladić in Serbia.

The Council's response to the tribunal's protests sent mixed signals to Milošević. The Council responded to the first complaint by deploring Serbia's failure to arrest the Vukovar Three,[80] but did not reply to Cassese's second complaint in May. It agreed with Cassese's third complaint in July. The sum of the ICTY's complaints and the Council's responses raised the pressure on Milošević. But the UN's criticisms of Serbia were relatively gentle, and the issue of Milošević's non-compliance did not rise to the status of a major international issue. The result was that when it came to non-compliance with the tribunal, the UN was not willing to impose, or even seriously threaten to impose, economic sanctions that might have swayed Milošević. The tribunal's activist stance signaled its resolve to confront Belgrade's non-compliance. But Milošević kept the upper hand because the UN failed to intervene decisively on the side of the tribunal.

The ICTY's decision to file a series of official complaints of Serbian non-compliance in 1996 represented the ultimate method of shaming at its disposal. On the one hand, the three complaints increased pressure on the Security Council as well as on Serbia. On the other hand, the lackluster UN response arguably weakened the tribunal's leverage by exposing its dependence on a wavering Council. Ultimately, as Chief Prosecutor Arbour said in a broad critique of the Council, "The buck stops with the Security Council. That's where we finally have to go to denounce non-compliance. They created us. Either they are going to back us up or they are spending a lot of good money for nothing."[81] Tribunal officials faced a quandary that would confound them in the years to

---

[79] The tribunal's 1995 complaint, lodged by President Cassese, concerned the Bosnian Serb authorities' failure to arrest the Bosnian Serb suspect, Dragan Nikolić. The Security Council responded to this complaint by adopting a resolution that demanded that the Bosnian Serb government (and other states of the former Yugoslavia) comply with tribunal requests. See Mundis, "Reporting Non-Compliance: Rule 7*bis*," in May et al., *Essays on ICTY Procedure and Evidence*, footnote 15, p. 425.

[80] Ibid., footnote, 16, p. 425.

[81] Erna Paris, *Long Shadows: Truth, Lies and History* (Toronto: Alfred A. Knopf Canada, 2000), p. 417.

come – lodging too many official complaints could easily backfire by revealing the Council's passivity and the tribunal's helplessness, while declining to do so could further justify international inaction and diminish the tribunal's authority.[82] Rather than continuing to file unavailing complaints to the Council, ICTY officials protested state non-compliance to the media and public. The Western media and individual commentators played a critical role in articulating what was at stake for the tribunal.

In the aftermath of Dayton, the threat of international sanctions was focused on pressing Milošević to use his influence to remove Karadžić from his leadership position in Republika Srpska, given Karadžić's ongoing efforts to sabotage implementation of the peace accords. This threat, delivered by Holbrooke in a July 1996 Belgrade meeting with Milošević, finally compelled Milošević to remove Karadžić. In effect, Milošević revealed his control over the Bosnian Serbs.

Milošević feared that Karadžić would end up in tribunal custody. If put on trial in The Hague, Karadžić could try to deflect blame by pointing to Milošević as the Serb official most culpable for Bosnian atrocities. "He would sing like a bird," a Western diplomat predicted.[83] Unfortunately for the tribunal, the United States only tied the threat of sanctions against Serbia to Karadžić's removal from power, and not to his arrest and transfer to The Hague. This was, as Holbrooke later admitted, unfortunate for the quest for stability in Bosnia. "Of all the things necessary to achieve our goals in Bosnia, the most important was still the arrest of Radovan Karadžić," Holbrooke said.[84] When it came to arresting Karadžić, Mladić, and the Vukovar Three, the United States preferred to give Serbia leeway. Some U.S. officials had no qualms about publicly letting Milošević know this. "I think our present inclination is to give Mr. Milošević some time to work through this problem," said State Department Spokesman Nicholas Burns. "It's too early to rush to that kind of decision right now because if you rush to that kind of decision you might not get the action that you're intending to get."[85]

Milošević's efforts to evade the ICTY after Dayton were bolstered by two other developments: first, the tribunal's primary focus on securing cooperation from NATO peacekeeping troops in Bosnia, second, the U.S. decision to place more emphasis on pressing Croatia rather than Serbia to cooperate. In the post-Dayton period, the tribunal's attention was often consumed by its high-profile campaign to press NATO to use its peacekeepers to arrest Bosnian Serb and Bosnian Croat war crimes suspects and to provide the tribunal with access to Western intelligence. The tribunal's focus on pressuring NATO was a critical front in its battle for cooperation and institutional survival. The NATO mission, although reluctant to arrest war crimes suspects, presented a golden

---

[82] Fieldwork interviews with tribunal officials, The Hague, December 2003.
[83] Jane Perlez, "U.S. Presses Effort to Remove Indicted Bosnian Serb Leader," *New York Times*, July 19, 1996, A2.
[84] Holbrooke, *To End a War*, p. 338.
[85] "Call for Curbs If Top Serbs Are Not Held," *New York Times*, June 6, 1996, A3.

opportunity for the tribunal since NATO soldiers could potentially act as its de facto law-enforcement arm. In Serbia and Croatia, the tribunal confronted a much more difficult challenge, since it had to rely on hostile governments for the arrest of war crimes suspects. Starting in the Summer of 1997, the tribunal's battle with Western capitals reaped benefits as NATO began arresting war crimes suspects in Bosnia and sending them to The Hague. The tribunal's nearly empty detention center began to fill up, albeit with many low-level suspects. Nevertheless, the tribunal's focus on pressing NATO to come to its aid had the unintended effect of shifting international attention away from the issue of the Serbian government's non-compliance. The story most closely followed by the Western media and later by scholars was the tribunal's battles with Washington, London, and Paris, and not its battles with Belgrade and Zagreb. Locked in battle with NATO, the tribunal had less political capital to persuade the West to pressure Milošević to cooperate. Moreover, the focus on NATO's responsibility for arresting war crimes suspects seemed to lift some responsibility off the shoulders of the Balkan states. Prior to taking up her post as the tribunal's second chief prosecutor in September 1996, Louise Arbour underscored her resolve to shift responsibility back to Serbia as well as to the other Balkan states who were, she stressed, the tribunal's "primary source of cooperation."[86] Said Arbour: "It is important to remember that there are parties to the agreement who have undertaken to do something and they ought not to be relieved of this expectation simply because the focus" is on NATO's involvement.[87] Yet, when she arrived in The Hague, Arbour realized the difficulty of keeping the tribunal's spotlight trained on Belgrade's and Zagreb's defiance.

Milošević's effort to forestall international calls to aid the tribunal were helped by the U.S. decision to prioritize the issue of Croatia's compliance. After Dayton, the Clinton administration hoped that by putting more pressure on Croatia and seeing results there first, it would be harder for Milošević to continue to stymie the tribunal. Even some human rights activists believed that success in Belgrade depended first on success in Zagreb. "Milošević will never cooperate unless Tudman does," opined Kenneth Roth, the executive director of Human Rights Watch. "If the West's golden boy doesn't cooperate, why should Milošević?"[88] Actually, Tudman's cooperation gave little incentive for Milošević to take similar action. Concerted international pressure on Tudman did not translate into concerted international pressure on Milošević, thus giving Milošević little reason to match Tudman's beneficence by handing over Serb suspects. Instead, the U.S. strategy stoked resentment in Zagreb for holding Croatia to a higher standard of cooperation despite Serbia's greater culpability in wartime massacres.

---

[86] Barbara Crossette, "War Criminals Not NATO Job, New Judge Says," *New York Times*, March 5, 1996, A6.
[87] Ibid.
[88] Jane Perlez, "War Crimes Tribunal on Bosnia Is Hampered by Basic Problems," *New York Times*, January 28, 1996, A1.

Milošević's canny ability to exploit the gap between the words and actions of his adversaries is amply demonstrated again in his and Madeleine Albright's verbal jousting over Serbia's obligation to cooperate with the tribunal. The appointment of Albright as U.S. Secretary of State at the start of Clinton's second term and the rise of Prime Minister Tony Blair and his Labour Party in Britain marked the beginning of a more supportive Western attitude toward the ICTY and its quest for Balkan cooperation.[89] From the start, Albright was a strong ally of the tribunal's and a more forceful advocate than her predecessor, Warren Christopher. As U.S. ambassador to the UN during Clinton's first term, Albright was a critical force behind the creation of the ICTY. Indeed, some referred to her as "the mother of the tribunal."[90] As Secretary of State, Albright played a key role in persuading a hesitant Clinton to use NATO troops to arrest Bosnian Serb war crimes suspects against the recommendations of Pentagon officials who feared that such operations would incur casualties. Blair and his foreign minister, Robin Cook, also favored NATO's taking a role in arresting war crimes suspects in Bosnia. In July 1997, NATO made its first arrest of a war crimes suspect when British troops arrested one Bosnian Serb suspect and killed another in a gun battle. A few months later, U.S. forces made their first arrests. Albright also took a special interest in war crimes prosecutions, as seen in the creation of an at-large ambassador post for war crimes, which was filled by her former legal advisor at the UN, David J. Scheffer.

Albright's tough stance on state cooperation was demonstrated by her confrontational visits with Milošević and Tuđman in June 1997. In Belgrade, Albright demanded that Milošević hand over the "Vukovar Three." Albright provided Milošević with documents substantiating her claim that the suspects were in Yugoslavia.[91] When Milošević told Albright that she was misinformed about the suspects' whereabouts, the Czech native shot back: "Don't give me that. I'm from this region; I'm not naïve."[92] Still, Milošević managed to parry Albright's attempt to force him to hand over the suspects accused of carrying out the first major atrocity of the Balkan wars. Instead of simply refusing to cooperate, Milošević insisted that he would initiate domestic legal proceedings against the suspects, if he determined that the evidence in the indictments warranted prosecution.[93] In comments to reporters after the meeting, Albright let her anger show, saying she was "very unhappy" with Milošević.[94] Moreover, she expressed doubt about Milošević's promises to implement the Dayton Accords: "I told him, 'Words are cheap. Deeds are the coin of the realm.'"[95]

---

[89] Roy Gutman, "Albright Taking Tougher Stance," *Newsday*, July 14, 1997.
[90] Aryeh Neier, *Taking Liberties: Four Decades in the Struggle for Rights* (New York: Public Affairs, 2003), p. 231.
[91] "Albright Faces Off with Croatia," *Associated Press*, May 31, 1997.
[92] Tyler Marshall, "Albright Blisters Balkan Leaders," *Los Angeles Times*, June 1, 1997, A1.
[93] Albright, *Madame Secretary*, p. 268.
[94] "Albright Faces Off with Croatia," *Associated Press*, May 31, 1997.
[95] Ibid.

Her public criticisms of Milošević represented some of the toughest made by a U.S. secretary of state in recent years.[96]

In her meeting with Milošević, Albright promised that Belgrade's lingering international isolation could make way for integration with the West if Serbia met its international obligations.[97] "I told him Serbia could either comply with the [Bosnian] accords, cooperate with [the] war crimes tribunal . . . or keep stonewalling and assure its isolation," she said. "I'm sure President Milošević had no doubt about my message."[98] But the message coming from the United States and Europe was a mixed one and not nearly as firm as Albright presented. Albright's tough talk increased U.S. pressure on Milošević but did not fundamentally alter Milošević's incentive to continue to withhold cooperation. Without strong pressure, such as threats of international economic sanctions, Milošević likely calculated that the cost of compliance outweighed the cost of non-compliance. While Albright talked tough, the United States, and especially its partners in Europe, seemed intent on continuing to reward Milošević for his role at Dayton. The West still relied heavily on Milošević to ensure the implementation of the Accords and the compliance of the Bosnian Serbs in supporting them. Despite its increasing criticism of Milošević as seen in Albright's visit, the United States still had an interest in shielding Milošević from indictment. Milošević seized on the international community's own gap between words and deeds, which he himself had so masterfully manipulated.

2.6 The Ongoing Peace v. Justice Conflict: Crisis in Kosovo

Just months after the signing of the Dayton Accords, the uneasy relationship between Kosovar Albanians and the Serb minority in Kosovo slowly unraveled. Unlike the conflicts in Croatia and Bosnia, the conflict in Kosovo did not erupt into full-scale war overnight. Instead, Kosovo saw a steady escalation of violence between the Serbian police and the nascent Kosovo Liberation Army (KLA). Throughout 1996 and 1997, both sides launched attacks, although Serbian police were blamed for committing the majority of them. Beginning in late February 1998, the conflict took a turn for the worse when Serbian forces launched an all-out campaign to crush the KLA and its bid for independence. Countless Kosovar Albanian civilians caught in the crossfire were killed. Over the next year, Kosovo became the latest scene in the ongoing terror in the Balkans: scores of Kosovar Albanian villages were destroyed and 200,000 to 300,000 people were forced from their homes.[99] International military intervention would finally follow in March 1999 when NATO launched a

---

[96] This assessment is drawn from Tyler Marshall, "Albright Blisters Balkan Leaders," *Los Angeles Times*, June 1, 1997, A1.

[97] Albright, *Madame Secretary*, p. 268.

[98] Tyler Marshall, "Albright Blisters Balkan Leaders," *Los Angeles Times*, June 1, 1997, A1.

[99] Neier, *Taking Liberties*, p. 344.

seventy-eight-day bombing campaign against Serbian positions in Kosovo as well as in Belgrade, Novi Sad, and other parts of Serbia. In June 1999, Milošević agreed to remove his forces from Kosovo, and the approximately one million refugees who had been forced into Albania and Macedonia returned to their homes. The war dealt Milošević a serious blow since Kosovo, now occupied by a NATO force and run by the UN, was for all intents and purposes no longer part of Serbia.

The conflict in Kosovo hardly came as a surprise. Back in the late 1980s, Kosovo had briefly been the first site of violence in the early days of the Federal Republic of Yugoslavia's demise. Kosovo threatened to be a tinderbox, given Serbia's deep historical and religious attachment to the region and the growing resentment of Kosovar Albanians over being victimized at the hands of Belgrade and the Serb minority in Kosovo. Resentment was sharpened when Milošević in 1990 revoked the province's autonomous status. During the mid-1990s, Kosovo's claims for autonomy remained unanswered and the conflict simmered. The province's status was not addressed at Dayton and thus the situation remained unresolved. Kosovo's drive for independence only increased as its people eyed the fruits of success enjoyed by Slovenia, Croatia, and neighboring Macedonia, as well as the autonomy won by Bosnian Serbs in the Dayton-sanctioned Republika Srpska.

Milošević's incentive to resist the tribunal grew as the dormant tension in Kosovo made way to full-scale violence, and Serbian forces carried out numerous atrocities against Kosovar civilians. For Milošević, the tribunal's growing international stature made it a more formidable adversary than it had been during the Bosnian war. Indictments, especially if handed down shortly after the commission of atrocities, could cast Serbia as a perpetrator state and thereby increase international pressure for an earlier military intervention than might otherwise take place. During the Bosnian conflict, the tribunal fell well short of its mandate to deter wartime atrocities. But now human rights activists and others had more reason to hope that the ICTY could restore faith in its deterrent capability by promptly investigating atrocities before the violence exploded into a full-scale conflict.

The ICTY, however, was not able to interject itself quickly enough in the Kosovo conflict. As in Bosnia, the inability of the tribunal to make more immediate progress in investigating Serbian war crimes in Kosovo rested primarily with Milošević's non-compliance and with international reluctance to press Milošević to alter his position. And as in Bosnia, the West's hesitancy to press Milošević on cooperation was an outgrowth of its desire for a negotiated settlement. The West, once again, feared that an empowered tribunal would undermine the prospects for a peaceful solution in Kosovo by tarnishing Milošević and rendering him unsuitable to be seated at the negotiating table.

However, as the Kosovo crisis worsened and Serb atrocities continued, the West became more vocal in its criticisms of Milošević and also eased its initial reluctance to press him to facilitate ICTY investigations in Kosovo. Western leaders came to realize that pressuring Milošević and even calling on the

ICTY to investigate Serb atrocities could become a powerful instrument to sway Belgrade to temper its behavior. Thus, in the Kosovo context, Western diplomats began to regard the tribunal as an actor that could foster stability. In fact, the international community sometimes became a strong source of pressure on the tribunal to initiate investigations in Kosovo at a time when the tribunal appeared initially reluctant to do so. As the conflict escalated in early 1998, both the Security Council and the Contact Group[100] called on the ICTY to investigate atrocities in Kosovo.[101] The United States also called on the tribunal to begin probing the crimes and allocated $1 million to aid tribunal investigations.[102] But Western leaders still failed to provide the ICTY with the critical diplomatic support it needed to carry out investigations in Kosovo. A case in point is the West's reluctance to take measures that might have cleared obstacles from the tribunal's path, such as declaring the tribunal's right to enter Kosovo without first requiring visas from Serbian authorities in Belgrade. In a March 1998 statement, Albright oddly required that the ICTY still had to obtain visas from Serbia, which in effect left Milošević with an easy way of blocking investigators' access to Serbian territory.[103] It was only after NATO placed ground troops in Kosovo, after the conclusion of its air war, that the tribunal obtained unhindered access to mass graves and other valuable evidence. For the United States and Europe, calling on the ICTY to conduct investigations paid political dividends, first by portraying themselves as standing up to brutality in Kosovo, and second by shifting some of the responsibility to the tribunal for confronting Milošević.

An accounting of the tribunal's difficulty in obtaining cooperation from Serbia has also to consider the tribunal's own inaction. Chief Prosecutor Arbour's initial delay in investigating Serbian war crimes in Kosovo arguably emboldened Milošević's subsequent defiance of the tribunal. Arbour's cautious approach unwittingly suited Milošević's insistence that the Kosovo conflict was a purely internal matter in which the tribunal had no jurisdiction. Arbour's initial reluctance to investigate the Kosovo conflict stemmed in part from her conservative legal interpretation of the ICTY's jurisdiction. In this regard, Kosovo constituted a more complex legal case for the tribunal than either Bosnia or Croatia. The tribunal's jurisdiction in Bosnia and Croatia was unquestioned given the tribunal's right to investigate crimes that take place in international conflicts. But for Arbour, the violence in Kosovo was initially ambiguous because Kosovo's status as a part of Serbia may have rendered it an internal conflict outside the definitions of the Geneva Convention. Moreover, at the beginning of the conflict in 1996 and 1997, the prosecutor's office had misgivings about pursuing investigations of relatively minor atrocities in Kosovo when prosecutors faced a staggering case load from Bosnia and Croatia. The tribunal's

---

[100] The Contact Group consisted of the United States, Britain, France, Germany, Russia, and Italy.
[101] Williams and Scharf, *Peace with Justice?* pp. 177 and 179.
[102] Ibid., p. 179.
[103] Ibid., pp. 179–180.

statute, however, gave prosecutors the right to investigate atrocities that took place within both international and internal conflicts. In addition, in early 1998, the Security Council passed a resolution that gave the tribunal explicit permission to investigate war crimes in Kosovo. Arbour's hesitancy to open investigations was a source of deep frustration for some human rights activists, such as Aryeh Neier, who was "deeply disappointed by her failure to bring timely indictments."[104] In time, Arbour would take a more aggressive approach, culminating in the precedent-setting indictment against Milošević and four top Serbian officials during the NATO air war in May 1999.

The criticisms of Arbour's approach to Serb atrocities in Kosovo do not acknowledge the important steps she did take. When Arbour decided to turn her attention to Kosovo, she did so with resolve. In an attempt to focus world attention on Serbia's non-compliance, Arbour, in late 1998, dramatized Serbian recalcitrance by trying to personally visit Kosovo to ensure access for her investigators. She was turned back at the border. Although the attempted visit did not force Milošević to back down, it brought renewed international media attention to the tribunal's struggle for cooperation by projecting an image of action that is seldom associated with the cloistered world of courts.[105] Such a high-profile confrontation bolstered Arbour's authority, shamed Serbia for its non-compliance, and pressured the international community to intervene on the tribunal's behalf.

The tribunal campaign included a second round of formal complaints to the Security Council regarding Serbia's non-compliance. More than two years since its last formal complaint, the tribunal turned to this device to protest Milošević's ongoing defiance. Over the course of three months, beginning in September 1998, ICTY President Gabrielle Kirk McDonald lodged five official complaints against Serbia with the Council. Although McDonald focused on Serbia's non-compliance, she also took issue with the Council's failure to take action against Belgrade. "I urge you not to allow the Federal Republic of Yugoslavia's obstructionism to go unchecked for it sets a dangerous precedent, one which even transcends its noncompliance," she said. "Please show the international community that you meant what you stated when you created the Tribunal."[106] A year later, McDonald bemoaned the Council's refusal to condemn Serbian noncompliance despite her repeated complaints. "Justice, it seems, was not a high priority," McDonald said in reference to the Council.[107] As with its response to Cassese's complaints against Serbia in 1996, the Council in response to McDonald's complaints in 1998 criticized Serbia's

---

[104] Neier, *Taking Liberties*, p. 349.

[105] Jane Perlez, "U.S. Official Visits a Site Of Executions In Kosovo," *New York Times*, November 10, 1998, A14; Raymond Bonner, "Crimes Court Not Ready to Punish Kosovo Violence," *New York Times*, March 31, 1999, A11.

[106] Address to the Security Council by Gabrielle Kirk McDonald, December 8, 1998.

[107] "The International Criminal Tribunal for the Former Yugoslavia: Making a Difference of Making Excuses?" Speech delivered by ICTY President Gabrielle Kirk MacDonald at the Council of Foreign Relations, New York City, May 12, 1999.

non-cooperation on a number of occasions, but refused to take concrete steps to punish Belgrade.[108]

The low priority given to the tribunal was seen in the outcome of the October 1998 peace agreement with Milošević that was once again brokered by Richard Holbrooke. The short-lived agreement included provisions for 2,000 human rights monitors (from the Organization for Security and Cooperation in Europe) to be stationed in Kosovo. But the agreement contained no mention of Belgrade's obligation to cooperate with the ICTY or any specific provision that provided tribunal investigators access to Kosovo. As with the Dayton negotiations, the tribunal's bid for a guarantee of Serbian cooperation was perceived by U.S. officials as an obstacle to halting the violence through negotiations. The marginalization of the tribunal and its loss of leverage prompted McDonald to send a strongly worded protest to the Security Council. "I am gravely concerned that the agreements concluded on the situation in Kosovo lack an explicit recognition of the [Federal Republic of Yugoslavia's] obligation towards the International Tribunal," she wrote.[109] Within months, however, the tribunal's fortunes would change for the better as Serbian violence in Kosovo triggered the wrath of the United States and NATO.

2.7 The NATO Air War and the Milošević Indictment

The beginning of NATO's air war in Kosovo in late March 1999 gave a boost to the tribunal's efforts to bring indictments against Milošević and top officials in the Serbian government. Milošević the statesman had now become Milošević the villain. In late May, Arbour handed down the ICTY's most important indictment. For the first time in history, an international war crimes tribunal had indicted a sitting head of state. The indictment charged Milošević and four top Serbian government officials with war crimes, crimes against humanity, and genocide in connection with atrocities committed in Kosovo during the first half of 1999.[110] Now that they were at war with Serbia, the United States and its NATO allies, after years of resisting the tribunal's attempts to investigate Milošević, had an interest in aiding its criminal probe of Milošević. Still, the West was deeply divided over the wisdom of a tribunal indictment of Milošević. For some policymakers, there was once again a conflict between peace and justice. Some Western officials cautioned against an indictment during the war out of concern that it might prolong the war by limiting NATO's ability to negotiate an end to the conflict with Milošević and provoke him to intensify the conflict. Other Western officials favored an earlier indictment, believing

---

[108] Mundis, "Reporting Non-Compliance: Rule 7bis," in May et al., *Essays on ICTY Procedure and Evidence*, p. 423.

[109] Ibid., footnote 33, p. 431.

[110] It would be another year and a half until the tribunal indicted Milošević for Serbian atrocities committed in Croatia and Bosnia. The Croatia indictment was issued on October 8, 2001, while the Bosnia indictment was issued on November 22, 2001.

it would further isolate and weaken Milošević and help strengthen NATO's resolve to accomplish its military goals.[111]

The split between and within Western governments led to mixed signals being sent to the tribunal regarding the merits of issuing an indictment against Milošević. After the indictments were handed down, some in the Western media questioned whether Arbour had succumbed to NATO pressure, while the Serbian media lambasted her for doing so. In Serbia, the charge against Arbour was that the tribunal was nothing more than the judicial arm of NATO, subserviently following directions from Washington and Brussels in order to demonize Milošević and justify a non-UN sanctioned military attack on a sovereign nation. According to this view, cooperation from the West appeared to come at the cost of the prosecutor's independence. That charge grew louder when first Arbour and then her successor, Carla Del Ponte, decided not to pursue in-depth investigations of NATO pilots in connection with Serbian civilian deaths.[112]

Arbour rejected the argument that by indicting Milošević the tribunal had done NATO's bidding. Moreover, she contended that during the war there was no clear NATO position on the indictment question. "I find it ironic," Arbour said, "that many journalists asked me: Are you being pressured? It became very clear the only message I was getting in all of these capitals was one of total ambivalence and ambiguity."[113] This ambivalence, tribunal officials argued, meant that the court faced countless obstacles in obtaining incriminating evidence in the possession of Western countries in 1998 and early 1999.

Western governments, and their intelligence services in particular, held the keys to a Milošević indictment. Specifically, U.S. intelligence possessed satellite imagery and radio communications that could reveal what crimes Serb forces had committed and the role played by Milošević and other top Serb officials in Belgrade. Had Washington relinquished intelligence information earlier, Arbour would presumably have been able to issue a Kosovo indictment earlier in 1999 or even in 1998. But the United States held crucial evidence close to its vest until shortly before the May 1999 indictment was issued. Arbour, in fact, persistently lobbied Washington and other Western capitals to hand over such evidence.[114]

Prosecution officials maintain that the indictment was issued as soon as sufficient evidence was obtained and that it was not timed to either bolster the tribunal's authority or to aid or undermine the prospects of a NATO victory. Nevertheless, the tribunal had an interest in issuing the indictment earlier rather than later, given the rumors that NATO might grant Milošević amnesty

---

[111] Fieldwork interview with David J. Scheffer, Washington, D.C., September 2004.

[112] In 2000, tribunal prosecutors completed a preliminary investigation that concluded there was a lack of sufficient evidence to pursue a more extensive investigation of NATO's role in civilian casualties. For a probing analysis of the chief prosecutor's approach to the NATO question, see Luc Côté, "Reflections on the Exercise of Prosecutorial Discretion in International Criminal Law," *Journal of International Criminal Justice*, Vol. 3, No. 1, March 2005, pp. 179–183.

[113] Michael Ignatieff, *Virtual War: Kosovo and Beyond* (New York: Metropolitan Books, 2000), p. 124.

[114] Charles Trueheart, "A New Kind of Justice," *Atlantic Monthly*, April 2000, p. 88.

in exchange for his removing Serb forces from Kosovo.[115] ICTY Deputy Prosecutor Graham Blewitt told me in a 2003 interview that the tribunal issued the Milošević indictment realizing that it may have the unintended effect of actually prolonging the war.[116] The fact that the ICTY went ahead with the indictment, Blewitt said, underscores its efforts not to have its prosecutorial agenda determined by political events. Blewitt also told me, however, that prosecutors consulted with NATO in order to get a better sense of whether an indictment might hamper NATO objectives in Kosovo. These consultations, said Blewitt, were "just fed into our considerations. They're not primary, they don't determine the timing of things."[117] As it turned out, Milošević agreed a few weeks after the indictment to withdraw his forces from Kosovo, bringing the war with NATO to a close.

The timing of the Milošević indictment still raises questions about the extent to which the tribunal is an independent actor in charge of its own prosecutorial agenda. Arbour's insistence on the minimal U.S. role in providing last-minute cooperation for the Milošević indictment notwithstanding, the United States and other Western states played a key role in facilitating the indictment. NATO's decision to go to war against Serbia created the conditions that made it possible for the tribunal to receive the cooperation it needed from Western governments to indict Milošević. That did not mean that the West left the evidence tap fully open as soon as the war began. On the contrary, Arbour often had to struggle to obtain evidence. Nevertheless, the ICTY was the beneficiary of the West's paradigm shift vis-à-vis Milošević and its belated decision to treat him as an international outcast. The Milošević indictment was a vivid illustration of the court's growing ability to exercise its own soft power to wrest cooperation from recalcitrant states, albeit Western states, and not Serbia. At long last, the tribunal had fulfilled a crucial part of its mandate by indicting the biggest suspect in the Balkans.

2.8 Conclusion: After Kosovo

Indicting Milošević did not, of course, bring an end to the tribunal's interest in the Serbian leader. Now the tribunal was faced with the problem of gaining custody of the defiant Serb leader. For the tribunal, regime change in Serbia was the best hope for having Milošević sent to The Hague and overcoming Belgrade's refusal to cooperate.

With the war over, forcing Milošević from power became the focus of the West's policy toward Serbia. President Clinton launched a campaign toward this end, part of which involved encouraging Serbian officials to remove Milošević by staging a coup. Another element of the strategy involved supporting the tribunal's efforts to bring Milošević and other Serbian war crimes suspects

[115] Ibid., p. 88.
[116] Fieldwork interview with Graham Blewitt, The Hague, December 2003.
[117] Ibid.

into custody. In late June, Clinton offered a \$5 million reward for information leading to Milošević's arrest. Washington went one step further by explicitly linking future international aid to a post-Milošević government with significant progress in cooperation with the tribunal. The strong U.S. position on Serbian cooperation in the post-Milošević era grew out of the policy established immediately after the Kosovo war. For the Serbs to be welcomed back into the community of nations, Clinton said that they had to "come out of denial"[118] and confront their role in the Kosovo atrocities. To obtain Western aid, said Clinton, Serbs will have to "decide whether they think it's O.K. that all those tens of thousands of people were run out of their homes, and all those little girls were raped and all those little boys were murdered."[119] This meant nothing less than handing over war crimes suspects. Although belated, the West's condemnation of Milošević and its new-found interest in exposing Serbian crimes bolstered the tribunal's quest for cooperation from Belgrade, particularly after Milošević's fall from power in October 2000.

As domestic opposition to Milošević grew in reaction to the Kosovo debacle and the country's deteriorating economic situation, tribunal officials became more optimistic about the prospects of regime change and a new era of cooperation with Belgrade. Now, more than ever, the future of the international law experiment in The Hague depended on the turbulent politics hundreds of miles away in Serbia. It is to this turbulence that we turn our attention in the next chapter.

[118] Blaine Harden, "Live, in Belgrade, the Milošević News," *New York Times,* June 27, 1999, A8.
[119] Ibid.

3

International Justice and Serbia's Troubled
Democratic Transition

3.1 Introduction

Slobodan Milošević's fall from power on October 5, 2000, raised hopes in Serbia and at the International Criminal Tribunal for the Former Yugoslavia (ICTY) that a new era had dawned. For many Serbs, Milošević's loss in the national elections in late September and his decision – in the face of massive street protests and the loss of support from his elite police units – to finally abide by the election results meant a quick end to Serbia's international isolation and pariah status. With the embrace of electoral democracy, Serbia could now claim a rightful place in the international community. At the ICTY, Milošević's fall increased the prospects of state cooperation for the arrest and hand over of those Serb war crimes suspects who had long evaded the tribunal's reach.

As long as Milošević remained in power as president of the rump Yugoslavia, the tribunal expected and received little, if any, cooperation. The prospects for cooperation only grew worse following the tribunal's May 1999 indictment of Milošević and four senior Serb officials in connection with massacres in Kosovo. Without his removal from power, the tribunal's bid to prosecute Milošević and many other indicted war criminals would continue to be imperiled because many of these suspects were either Serb or Bosnian Serb citizens who enjoyed the protection of the Belgrade government.

The beginning of the democratic era in Fall 2000 marked a new chapter in the "trials of cooperation" between the Serbian government and the ICTY. Regime change coincided with a marked increase in state cooperation, but the transition did not spark a normative embrace of international prosecutions. While the emergence of democratic rule ushered into power certain government leaders willing and able to cooperate with the court, the government was bitterly divided over the question of how much to aid an institution still widely derided in Serbia as a Western instrument of Serb humiliation and victimization. These divisions, both within the government and between the government and

Serbian society, have had a profound effect on Serbian politics and its turbulent democratic transition ever since.

This case-study chapter will analyze developments during the following phases of the democratic era: (1) the initial post-Milošević period, (early October 2000 through January 2001); (2) the events leading up to and immediately following Milošević's arrest and his transfer to the ICTY (February through June 2001); (3) the period from July 2001 through December 2002; (4) the events leading up to and following the assassination of Serbian Prime Minister Zoran Đindic (January 2003 through December 2003); and (5) the period from January 2004 through July 2007.

This chapter – as does the book as a whole – imparts several lessons. First, to understand the dynamics of these virtual trials one must pay close attention to the volatile domestic politics surrounding state cooperation in Serbia. To a large extent, the government's willingness and capacity to cooperate with the ICTY is a function of the negotiations both within the government and between government and domestic constituencies. A second lesson is that powerful international actors frequently play a decisive role in the stance of a targeted state toward a tribunal. International community pressure prodded recalcitrant government leaders in Belgrade to hand over many Serb war crimes suspects. This pressure took the form of U.S. aid conditionality and the European Union's decision after 2000 to make Serbia's progress toward EU membership contingent on increased cooperation with the ICTY. Although decried in Serbia as excessive, international pressure was also timed and calibrated to give Serbian leaders some respite from the domestic crises that often accompanied the transfer of suspects to the tribunal. In practical terms, international pressure on Serbia to abide by its legal obligation to provide full cooperation was not taken to mean that it actually had to do so all at once. Rather, powerful actors, such as the United States and the European Union, expected Serbian leaders to periodically arrest and transfer suspects to The Hague and to provide access to government-held evidence.

A third lesson of this chapter is that the tribunal is not powerless in its efforts to prod Serbia to cooperate. The actions taken by top tribunal officials – the chief prosecutor in particular – can effectively shape the outcome of the trials of cooperation. But the prosecutor's actions also entail risks. First, there are risks associated with pursuing a policy of negotiation with the targeted state. Notably, emphasizing conciliation may send a signal to recalcitrant government leaders that the strict legal obligation to cooperate is actually open to compromise and dealmaking.

But dangers are legion as well in pursuing an adversarial policy that aims to shame the state for its violation of international law. Excessive shaming of the state can backfire by hardening domestic opposition to the tribunal and igniting a lasting war of words between state and tribunal that seriously undermines the opportunity for future negotiation. The chief prosecutor's shaming campaign can be turned against him or her by domestic detractors as an egregious act of tribunal bias against the country. Indeed, Serbian officials have sought to portray Chief Prosecutor Carla Del Ponte's campaign for cooperation as a crusade that casts collective guilt on the nation and threatens to undermine the country's fragile democratic transition. By impugning the tribunal's alleged breach of its own mission to pursue only individual guilt, Serbian officials have attempted to "counter-shame" Del Ponte and the tribunal.

3.2 First Encounters: Carla Del Ponte, Vojislav Koštunica, and Zoran Đinđić (October 2000 through January 2001)

The trials of cooperation framework introduced in Chapter 1 highlights the ways in which the chief prosecutor seeks to subject a state's violation of its legal obligation to cooperate to international scrutiny and condemnation. Yet, the chief prosecutor's bid for state cooperation also often involves a conciliatory approach that emphasizes persuasion and negotiation. As the following discussion of the early post-Milošević period underscores, the prosecutor may first employ a conciliatory approach in the hopes that this will create allies in government that, in time, will foster a willingness to cooperate.

The collapse of the Milošević regime and the election of a democratically elected leader changed the political calculus of the tribunal's relationship with Belgrade. But the transition also created a strategic dilemma for the tribunal – namely, how quickly and vigorously should it press the new government to cooperate? Del Ponte decided to give Vojislav Koštunica, the new president of the rump Federal Republic of Yugoslavia (FRY), a honeymoon period before forcefully calling for the handover of fugitive suspects. It appears that she did so out of concern that pushing for arrests too soon might complicate the country's nascent democratic transition by fueling protest against the government by Serbian nationalists opposed to cooperation. A backlash against the FRY government could also damage the prospects of the center-left Democratic Party in the December 2000 Serbian parliamentary elections. The Democratic Party and its leader, Zoran Đinđić, were perceived as stronger supporters of the tribunal than the more conservative and nationalistic Democratic Party of Serbia, led by Koštunica. Del Ponte may have also been concerned that moving against Belgrade too soon might alienate potential international supporters who, in the aftermath of Milošević's demise, gave strong backing to the new Koštunica government.

Del Ponte read the international politics of the moment correctly. Initially, the United States and Europe appeared more interested in bolstering Serbia's nascent democratic transition than in pressing Belgrade to make arrests of war crimes suspects that might destabilize the country. The West seemed as eager to bring Serbia within the fold as Serbia was to join. Even before voters went to the polls on September 24, 2000, the West indicated that a Serbia without Milošević would be quickly welcomed back into the community of nations. On the eve of the election, European leaders promised that "a democratic change would lead to a radical modification of the European Union's policy towards Serbia" and the lifting of economic sanctions.[1] The EU quickly fulfilled its promises. In doing so, the long-standing demands on Serbia to hand over war crimes suspects was, for the time being, sidestepped.[2]

Western leaders and media embraced the new democratic government and hailed Koštunica as a hero. *Time* magazine named the new Yugoslav president its runner-up for its 2000 "Person of the Year" award.[3] French President Jacques Chirac praised Koštunica for his democratic virtues, saying, "In his person, he represents democracy rediscovered in Yugoslavia."[4] With words of praise came tangible economic and political rewards for ridding Serbia of Milošević. Within weeks of Milošević's removal, the international community had lifted an array of sanctions against Serbia and pledged millions of dollars to help rebuild the country's shattered economy.[5] These steps were accompanied by invitations to rejoin regional and international bodies such as the Organization for Security and Cooperation in Europe[6] and the UN.[7]

Taking stock of the international mood, Del Ponte issued a statement welcoming Serbia's "newfound democracy," but also let it be known that she was ready for cooperation, particularly in regard to her number one priority – the handover of Milošević.[8] After his fall from power, Milošević remained in Serbia but not under arrest. Amicable words aside, it soon became apparent that there would be open conflict between Del Ponte and Koštunica. Koštunica exploited the warm reception he received from the international community and the tribunal. The absence of pressure appears to have emboldened Koštunica's defiance of the tribunal and his belief that such defiance would not prompt his new international allies to curb the flow of political and economic benefits to Belgrade. Even before he took office, Koštunica had grown optimistic that he would not face strong international pressure to cooperate with the tribunal. "I will ignore them . . . I'm encouraged in this by the fact that Europe is increasingly less insistent on that," he said.[9] Shortly after the election, he said there would be no immediate cooperation with the ICTY. "The question of cooperation is a fact, but it cannot be one of our priorities," he said.[10]

---

[1] "EU Carrot to Yugoslav Voters," *BBC News*, September 18, 2000.

[2] "Koštunica: War Crimes Must Wait," *BBC News*, October 14, 2000.

[3] Norman Cigar, *Vojislav Koštunica and Serbia's Future* (London: Saqi Books in association with The Bosnian Institute, 2001), p. 13.

[4] "Koštunica, at EU Debut, Pledges a 'Guarantor' Serbia," *Agence France-Presse*, October 14, 2000.

[5] "EU Eases Yugoslav Sanctions," *BBC News*, October 9, 2000; "EU Millions for Serbia," *BBC News*, October 13, 2000; "Koštunica, at EU Debut, Pledges a 'Guarantor' Serbia," *Agence France-Presse*, October 14, 2000.

[6] "Yugoslavia to Join Security Body," *BBC News*, October 19, 2000.

[7] "UN Embraces Yugoslavia," *BBC News*, November 1, 2000.

[8] Statement by Carla Del Ponte, October 6, 2000.

[9] As quoted in Cigar, *Vojislav Koštunica and Serbia's Future*, p. 75.

[10] "Koštunica: War Crimes Must Wait," *BBC News*, October 14, 2000.

Koštunica could hardly conceal his unease about cooperation and his antipathy toward the tribunal. Although a committed legalist and a proponent of Serbia's integration into Europe, Koštunica was also a nationalist committed to the ideology of a Greater Serbia that fueled the Balkan wars. In this respect, many Serbs regard Koštunica as more of a pure nationalist than Milošević, who on a number of occasions during the war had abandoned his ethnic Serb brethren in Bosnia and Croatia for his own political gain. Koštunica himself equated Milošević's lack of wartime support for the Bosnian Serbs as a "national betrayal."[11] This criticism went hand in hand with his praise of Radovan Karadžić, the former Bosnian Serb leader indicted by the ICTY.[12] Tribunal prosecutions of Serb suspects have directly challenged Koštunica's view of the purity of Serbian conduct during the war, his downplaying of Serb massacres, and his denial of the existence of concentration camps in the Bosnian Serb republic.[13]

Del Ponte quickly sensed Koštunica's hostility to the tribunal. By late November 2000, she put Koštunica on notice that her patience was running thin. In her annual address to the UN Security Council that November, Del Ponte sized up Koštunica as a manipulative politician who would do his utmost to avoid cooperation. Del Ponte also took aim at the Council for treating Koštunica with kid gloves. "The world has embraced President Koštunica despite the fact that he has repeatedly said that co-operation with the ICTY 'is not a priority' for him. If he chose that phrase himself, I admire him – it is a clever line, one capable of different interpretations – a true politician's phrase," she told the Council.[14] Although Del Ponte did not yet press for Milošević's immediate transfer, she made clear her intention to prosecute the former Yugoslav leader in The Hague: "The Milošević question cannot so easily be brushed aside," she told the Council. "Milošević must be brought to trial before the International Tribunal."[15]

The December 2000 parliamentary elections brought Zoran Đinđić, the leader of the Democratic Party, to power as Serbia's prime minister. Đinđić, a center-left politician who had received his doctorate in philosophy in Germany, had a reputation as a reformer and a pragmatist. The new political reality and the peculiar structure of governance in Serbia brought promise and complication to the tribunal's quest for cooperation. Del Ponte and other top tribunal officials had to deal with two heads of states: Koštunica, the popular president of Yugoslavia, which since the start of the Balkan wars consisted only of Serbia and Montenegro; and Đinđić, the prime minister of Serbia, the dominant republic of the rump Yugoslavia. The support of both leaders would be important for the tribunal. However, Đinđić, as the leader of Serbia, controlled the police

---

[11] As quoted in Cigar, *Vojislav Koštunica and Serbia's Future*, p. 29.
[12] Ibid., p. 38.
[13] Ibid., pp. 72 and 32.
[14] Address to the Security Council by Carla Del Ponte, November 24, 2000.
[15] Ibid.

force and therefore often wielded more power than Koštunica when it came to arresting war crimes suspects and sending them to The Hague.

With the Belgrade leadership in place, Del Ponte, in January 2001, sought her first meetings with Koštunica and Đinđić to establish working relationships with them and press them on the Milošević case. Her initial separate meetings with the two leaders underscored that her relationships with each of them would be markedly different. With Koštunica, attempts at dialogue soon broke into mutual recrimination. With Đinđić, a diplomatic relationship was quickly established.

Del Ponte's difficult relationship with Koštunica was brought into sharp relief even before she made her first visit to Serbia in late January. Koštunica, bolstered by his new international standing as the founder of Serbian democracy, sought to marginalize Del Ponte by refusing to meet with her. Publicly, he claimed that he could not receive Del Ponte because she is not a state leader or ambassador and therefore lacked adequate "accreditations."[16] Under heavy pressure from Đinđić and others, Koštunica acquiesced and granted Del Ponte an audience.[17] In a face-saving move, Koštunica explained that his decision to see her was sparked by his need to discuss the issue of NATO's use of depleted uranium-capped shells in the bombing of Belgrade.[18] To Koštunica, Serbia's victimization at the hands of the international community, not Serbia's victimization of others, deserved to be at the top of Del Ponte's prosecutorial agenda.

Koštunica used the meeting to launch an attack against the tribunal's anti-Serb bias. In my December 2003 interview with Del Ponte, she recalled Koštunica's diatribe and her response:

He told me 'Serbs are only victims. Why are you prosecuting Serbs?' I was trying to explain, that of course, Serbs are victims, but not only, not all Serbs are victims! But we have Serbs that are perpetrators... But he was not willing to listen to me. For him, [the] ICTY is bad, is politically under the political influence of the international community. And there was no dialogue possible, absolutely not. And so after... near[ly] one hour I left.[19]

In her remarks to the media following the meeting, Del Ponte tried her best to portray Koštunica as unreasonable in his opposition to the tribunal. In subsequent remarks, Del Ponte went further, rebuking Koštunica for his "incredible nationalism" and calling him "a man of the past."[20]

Del Ponte's criticism of Koštunica was accompanied by praise for the more moderate Đinđić.[21] In the months and years to come, Del Ponte would pursue

[16] "Koštunica Will Not Meet UN Prosecutor," *Reuters*, January 16, 2001.
[17] Željko Cvijanović, "Hague Tribunal Prosecutor Carla Del Ponte Storms Out of Meeting with President Koštunica," *Institute for War & Peace Reporting*, January 24, 2001.
[18] Vesna Peric Zimonjic, "Yugoslavia Wants DU Use Tried as War Crime," *The Independent*, January 19, 2001.
[19] Fieldwork interview with Carla Del Ponte, The Hague, December 2003.
[20] "Del Ponte Lambastes Koštunica," *CNN*, March 3, 2001.
[21] Jonathan Steele, "Del Ponte Chides Koštunica," *The Guardian*, January 26, 2001.

a strategy in Serbia of undermining adversaries while cultivating allies. Del Ponte did so through public statements that commended Đinđić as a cooperative pragmatist and discredited Koštunica as a symbol of the country's nationalist past. Toward that end, Del Ponte called on the international community to apply strong pressure on Koštunica. "Conditions, very tough conditions, have to be set so that Yugoslavia cooperates with us," she said, referring to the governmental entity that Koštunica headed.[22] Clearly, the honeymoon period that Del Ponte granted Koštunica had come to an end. Nevertheless, Del Ponte and Đinđić soon established a strong working relationship. "He was our interlocutor," Del Ponte said of Đinđić in my December 2003 interview.[23]

Del Ponte's characterization of Đinđić as "our interlocutor" underscores the tribunal's reliance on domestic partners with whom to negotiate the terms and the timing of state cooperation. Đinđić was a crucial tribunal ally. Yet that did not mean he was willing or able to cooperate on the tribunal's terms. Particularly when it came to the handover of war crimes suspects, Đinđić often proceeded carefully, given the ingrained opposition he faced from Serbia's elite police units, the military, politicians, and society as a whole. Indeed, the outcome of the negotiations between Del Ponte and Đinđić was often a function of the negotiations between Đinđić and his domestic interlocutors as well as between Đinđić and powerful international actors such as the United States. Arresting war crimes suspects was particularly difficult for Đinđić because of his close ties to police and military officials who had played a key role in Milošević's downfall, but were likely to be targeted for indictment by Del Ponte.[24] Đinđić feared the domestic fallout of arresting his erstwhile allies in the police and the military. Initially he indicated that he would never do so. "I would rather withdraw from politics than extradite them to The Hague," he said in December 2000.[25] Still, for tribunal officials, a pragmatic leader such as Đinđić engendered optimism that he would comply with international pressure to cooperate. He had "different political agendas," ICTY Deputy Prosecutor Graham Blewitt told me in a December 2003 interview. "But having said that, he [Đinđić] realized there was a moral and right thing to do. And he was determined to follow through on it."[26]

3.3 In Pursuit of Slobodan Milošević (February through June 2001)

A. *Milošević's Belgrade Arrest and Handover to The Hague*
A tribunal's pursuit of cooperation is often multi-faceted: gaining access to state archives, forensic evidence, and witnesses, and obtaining custody of suspects.

---

[22] "Del Ponte Lambastes Koštunica," *CNN*, March 3, 2001.
[23] Fieldwork interview with Carla Del Ponte, The Hague, December 2003.
[24] Željko Cvijanović, "Hague Tribunal Prosecutor Carla Del Ponte Storms Out of Meeting with President Koštunica," *Institute for War & Peace Reporting*, January 24, 2001.
[25] Ibid.
[26] Fieldwork interview with Graham Blewitt, The Hague, December 2003.

Inevitably, the chief prosecutor and other top tribunal officials determine what forms of state cooperation and what suspects from each side of an armed conflict matter most to them. By so doing, tribunal officials can establish the content and the timing of the trials of cooperation. Dependent as they are on the international community to pressure recalcitrant states, tribunals can instigate international scrutiny and pressure by initiating a trial of cooperation against a state and keeping this virtual trial in the media limelight. Carla Del Ponte's campaign to press Serbian authorities to send Slobodan Milošević to The Hague underscores the critical role that the tribunal plays in the battle for cooperation.

Del Ponte's first visit to Serbia, in late January 2001, coincided with the intensification of her calls to obtain custody of Milošević. Perhaps in a concession to Đinđić and an acknowledgment of political reality, Del Ponte called for Milošević's arrest and transfer, but gave government leaders some leeway. "I didn't expect the immediate arrest of indicted war criminals, but I cannot wait years until fugitives are transferred to The Hague," she said during her visit to Belgrade.[27] Del Ponte also signaled her willingness to delay pressure for the immediate transfer of Milošević, if other ethnic Serb suspects, especially the former Bosnian Serb general Ratko Mladić, were delivered to the tribunal.[28] But even then, the prospect of transferring other suspects, Mladić in particular, entailed serious political risks for Đinđić.

Initially Đinđić, like Koštunica, favored prosecuting Milošević at home on domestic corruption charges stemming from the excesses of his regime.[29] But in time, and in the face of increasing international pressure, Đinđić had a change of heart. Đinđić's meetings with U.S. officials in Washington in early February 2001 underscored the need for Serbia to demonstrate its commitment to the ICTY.[30] Unless the Belgrade government showed significant progress by March 31, the United States would withhold certification of its cooperation with the tribunal. Denying certification would mean the loss of some $100 million in nonhumanitarian financial assistance to the Federal Republic of Yugoslavia as well as America's support for World Bank and IMF loans.[31] The U.S. Congress had established this certification process and the March 31 deadline in the previous fall.[32] Although the Congressional legislation did not precisely specify how

---

[27] Jonathan Steele, "Del Ponte Chides Koštunica," *The Guardian*, January 26, 2001.

[28] Douglas Hamilton, "Give us Mladić as Marker, Tribunal Tells Belgrade," *Reuters*, February 19, 2001.

[29] "Đinđić: Serbia Must Cooperate with The Hague to Get U.S. Support," *Associated Press* and *Agence France-Presse*, February 4, 2001; "Milošević Trial: Home or Away?" *BBC News*, January 10, 2001.

[30] "Đinđić: Serbia Must Cooperate with The Hague to Get U.S. Support," *Associated Press* and *Agence France-Presse*, February 4, 2001.

[31] Curt Tarnoff, "The Federal Republic of Yugoslavia: U.S. Economic Assistance," Congressional Research Service Report for Congress, updated August 16, 2001, p. 4; Transcript: State Department Noon Briefing, April 2, 2001.

[32] Steven Woehrel, "Serbia and Montenegro: Current Situation and U.S. Policy," Congressional Research Service, updated January 18, 2005, p. 16.

much Serbia actually had to cooperate to win certification,[33] it became increasingly apparent to Đinđić that he would eventually have to arrest Milošević and send him to the tribunal.

The March 31 deadline prompted the Serbian authorities to arrest Milošević. The dramatic standoff that preceded the Milošević arrest also foreshadowed the power struggle between Đinđić and Koštunica. On Friday night, March 30, a day before the U.S. deadline, state security forces under Serbian Prime Minister Đinđić's control surrounded Milošević's villa in Belgrade.[34] An attempt on early Saturday, March 31, to storm the villa and arrest Milošević was stopped by Yugoslav army soldiers, who were ostensibly under Yugoslav President Koštunica's control.[35] During the confrontation, a defiant Milošević threatened he would "not go to jail alive."[36] But after Koštunica's army force backed away, Milošević surrendered in the early morning hours of April 1.[37]

Although Đinđić outmaneuvered Koštunica, Đinđić balked at sending Milošević to The Hague, forestalling the tribunal's legal claim to prosecute the country's former leader. Milošević was put in a Belgrade jail to face only domestic corruption charges, not war crimes. Thus, Serbian politicians continued to keep him beyond the tribunal's reach and to keep the question of the country's war crimes in Kosovo unexamined.

Although the Milošević arrest fell short of the American-imposed requirement for cooperation, the Bush administration quickly granted certification to Serbia.[38] However, the administration qualified its certification by threatening that U.S. participation in an upcoming donors' conference would be contingent on Belgrade's cooperation with the ICTY.[39] Serbia's reprieve from international pressure would be short-lived. The government's delay in sending Milošević to The Hague and Del Ponte's ongoing criticism of Belgrade led to increased international scrutiny. In early May 2001, Del Ponte traveled to Washington to lobby State Department officials to set a deadline for Serbia's transfer of Milošević. Del Ponte left Washington without a firm commitment on an American-imposed deadline, but she appeared to win agreement from Secretary of State Colin Powell that Serbia had not made sufficient progress.[40]

---

[33] Section 594 of the Foreign Operations Export Financing and Related Programs Appropriation Act of 2001 states that the U.S. President must certify that Serbia is "(1) cooperating with the International Criminal Tribunal for [the Former] Yugoslavia including access for investigators, the provision of documents, and the surrender and transfer of indictees or assistance in their apprehension." See Steven Woehrel, "Serbia and Montenegro: Current Situation and U.S. Policy," Congressional Research Service, updated January 18, 2005, p. 16.

[34] "Timeline: Milošević Arrest," *CNN*, April 2, 2001.

[35] Ibid. Also see Anthony Borden, "Milošević Arrested," *Institute for War & Peace Reporting*, No. 233, April 1, 2001.

[36] "Milošević on Trial," *BBC News*, April 1, 2001.

[37] "Timeline: Milošević Arrest," *CNN*, April 2, 2001.

[38] Transcript: State Department Noon Briefing, April 2, 2001.

[39] Ibid.

[40] Andrea Koppel, "War Crimes Prosecutor Urges U.S. to Push Milošević Transfer," *CNN*, May 8, 2001.

Over the next month, it became increasingly clear that the United States would not participate in the June 29 donors' conference unless Belgrade's cooperation markedly increased. Again, there was some ambiguity concerning what constituted sufficient cooperation. Koštunica apparently hoped that the Yugoslav parliament's adoption of a national law on cooperation would satisfy U.S. demands. But strong parliamentary resistance derailed any hope for quick passage.[41] Days before the donors' conference, Đinđić sought a way through the impasse by winning federal government support for a decree that would allow the handover of Milošević. But the Serbian Constitutional Court, filled with Milošević appointees, ruled the decree unconstitutional. Still, Đinđić ordered Milošević's handover, bassed on Serbia's international legal obligation to cooperate with the ICTY.

In the days preceding the donors' conference, Đinđić worked behind the scenes to ensure that Koštunica and the courts would not block him. In a sign of his concern that Yugoslav army forces might stop Milošević from being taken out of the country, Đinđić devised an elaborate scheme to keep the handover secret.[42] In the aftermath of the transfer, Koštunica maintained that Serbian authorities acted without his knowledge – perhaps a half truth in the sense that Koštunica may not have been privy to the details of the scheme. Đinđić backers refuted that claim. "He pretended that he didn't know ... [but] he knew when we arrested him and he knew when we extradited him," Zoran Živković, the Yugoslav Interior Minister and a close Đinđić ally, told me in a 2002 interview in Belgrade.[43] (Živković became prime minister of Serbia in 2003.)

In the end, Đinđić's decision to send Milošević to The Hague constituted a significant gamble given the uncertain political fallout. Yet Đinđić clearly saw it as a necessary step to obtain the international financial backing he needed to rebuild an economy badly hurt by years of international sanctions. "It was like deciding to cut your finger off without anesthesia when you have gangrene," Đinđić said, in reference to the handover of his longtime rival. "The question was whether we would all become infected because of one man."[44]

The Milošević handover succeeded because of the political maneuvering of Prime Minister Đinđić. But the story of the Milošević transfer is also the story of U.S. aid conditionality. "It was pretty clear what affected change in the end," a former Western human rights activist involved in the campaign to apprehend Milošević told me in an interview. "I'm not sure how far the ICTY would go without aid conditionality."[45] This conditionality was, in turn, a result of Congressional pressure on the State Department and the White House. In this campaign, two senators on the Senate Appropriations Committee – Patrick

[41] "Milošević in The Hague: What it Means for Yugoslavia and the Region," International Crisis Group, Balkans Briefing, July 6, 2001, p. 2.

[42] Carlotta Gall, "Serbian Tells of Spiriting Milošević Away," New York Times, July 1, 2001, A8.

[43] Fieldwork interview with Zoran Živković, Belgrade, Serbia, August 2002.

[44] Henry Chu, "Serbia Lionizes Its Slain Leader," Los Angeles Times, March 16, 2003, A3.

[45] Fieldwork interview with former human rights activist, Freetown, Sierra Leone, March 2005.

Leahy (D-Vermont) and Mitch McConnell (R-Kentucky) – played the leading roles.

To tribunal backers, Milošević's arrival in The Hague in late June proved the efficacy of linking economic aid to improvements in state cooperation. But to many Serbs, this cash-for-suspect transaction only confirmed their belief that international justice is inherently political. That perception was fueled by Đinđić, who justified cooperation not as a moral imperative, but as a way to obtain much needed American dollars.

B. The Milošević Transfer and the Rejection of Compromise

Notwithstanding the key role of the United States, Del Ponte had an important part in the Milošević transfer by being the first, most ardent, and most consistent voice calling for his handover. Perhaps her least noticed but most important contribution was in rejecting compromises that sought to derail a Milošević trial in The Hague in favor of a domestic trial. While Serbian politicians faced intensifying pressure for Milošević's arrest through the first half of 2001, Del Ponte herself faced increasing pressure from Serbian officials and some international actors who worried that the controversy surrounding Milošević's fate would undermine stability and the democratic transition.

During early 2001, Del Ponte contended with two compromise proposals aimed at thwarting her goal of trying Milošević in The Hague. At different points, Serbian politicians suggested that the state's own legal grievances against the deposed leader should take precedence over the tribunal's quest to try Milošević in connection with wartime atrocities. For the Belgrade government, prosecuting Milošević for his crimes against the Serbian people – for corruption and assassination of political opponents – would have been a preferable resolution to the emerging crisis by both thwarting the tribunal and assuaging public anger at the former leader, who was widely blamed for widespread corruption and for losing four wars.[46] The idea of trying Milošević in Serbian courts gained favor domestically in the aftermath of his April 1 arrest. There was, however, little prospect that Del Ponte would allow the Serbian courts to usurp the tribunal's legal primacy.

When the idea of a domestic corruption trial seemed improbable, Serbian politicians turned their attention to a face-saving measure: holding an ICTY trial in Belgrade rather than The Hague. Such a trial was more palatable to Serbian leaders, who feared the domestic uproar sparked by putting Milošević on a plane to The Netherlands. The "Hague-on-the-Danube" plan received avid backing from some international actors who considered an international trial in Belgrade as an ideal way for the ICTY to come closer to the region in which the atrocities under examination occurred.[47] At one point, it appeared that Del

---

[46] "Milošević in The Hague: What it Means for Yugoslavia and the Region," International Crisis Group, Balkans Briefing, Brussels, July 6, 2001, p. 6.

[47] For instance, see the op-ed article by Gareth Evans, president of the International Crisis Group, "Yes to a Hague-on-the-Danube Trial for Milošević," *International Herald Tribune*, January 9, 2001.

Ponte's office gave its blessing to holding at least part of the Milošević trial in Belgrade.[48] In early March 2001, Deputy Prosecutor Blewitt, declaring that the ICTY is "too remote in The Hague," signaled the tribunal's willingness to hold some of the Milošević trial in Serbia.[49] But Del Ponte quickly distanced herself from Blewitt's remarks and insisted on the tribunal's right to bring Milošević to trial in The Hague.[50]

Although The "Hague-on-the-Danube" plan might have enabled the tribunal to score a quick victory and put Milošević on trial sooner than many expected, the compromise could have sparked a negative reaction by encouraging Croatia and Bosnia to delay handing over suspects to the tribunal in the hopes that Del Ponte would permit other trials on domestic soil. If Del Ponte allowed Milošević to stand trial in Belgrade, the Croatian government would be on strong footing several months later to insist on equal treatment for its newly indicted generals. Del Ponte explained that holding the trial in Serbia would be unfair to those defendants already convicted by the ICTY.[51] Moreover, she rejected an ICTY trial for Milošević in Belgrade because it was not neutral territory and it would be difficult to persuade Kosovar Albanian witnesses to travel there to testify.[52] On a more pragmatic level, there was no pressing need for Del Ponte to give up her right to prosecute Milošević in The Hague when the tide of international pressure was building against Belgrade.

Interestingly, Del Ponte, in her capacity as chief prosecutor of the ICTR, was at the same time calling on that tribunal to hold some of its trials, or portions thereof, in Kigali, Rwanda. Del Ponte's different approach at the ICTR appears to be a reflection of her weak political position vis-à-vis the Rwandan government and the ICTR's need to respond to continuing criticism of its remoteness from Rwanda. Critics of the "Arusha-in-Kigali" plan have long maintained, in an argument ironically similar to Del Ponte's argument against The "Hague-on-the-Danube" plan, that Rwanda is not a neutral venue for trials and that Hutu suspects (as well as Hutu witnesses living in exile) will be justifiably afraid to travel to Rwanda.

3.4 After Milošević: New Battles with and within Serbia (July 2001 through December 2002)

A. A New Round of Virtual Trials
Within hours of his departure from Serbia, the grainy television image of Slobodan Milošević being escorted to the ICTY's detention center in Scheveningen

---

[48] A final decision on such a plan requires the approval of ICTY judges.

[49] "Hague Offer Milošević Compromise," *CBSnews.com*, March 7, 2001.

[50] "All Indicted Persons Must be Surrendered to and Judged by the International Tribunal," ICTY press release, March 8, 2001; "Trying Milošević," *NewsHour with Jim Lehrer*, transcript, May 8, 2001.

[51] Jonathan Steele, "Koštunica Snubs UN Call to Seize Milošević," *The Guardian*, January 24, 2001.

[52] Gabriel Partos, "Milošević Trial: Home or Away?" *BBC News*, January 10, 2001.

near The Hague became a defining symbol of the power of an international court. Tribunal officials hailed the date of his handover, June 28, 2001, as a critical juncture in their battle for state cooperation. "The transfer of Slobodan Milošević marks the real beginning of co-operation by Yugoslavia," said Del Ponte, the day after Milošević's late-night arrival.[53]

But did June 28 mark a turning point in the "trials of cooperation" with Belgrade? There was some reason to think that it had, as a number of tribunal officials interviewed during my research believed.[54] After all, the immediate public reaction in Serbia was relatively muted, suggesting to optimists abroad that domestic resistance to the tribunal had been broken. At the time, sending Milošević to The Hague actually caused fewer problems for the government than a gay pride parade held in Belgrade several days later – an observation recounted by Zoran Živković, the Yugoslav interior minister and Serbia's future prime minister, during my 2002 interview.[55] Živković noted that certain factors, such as Milošević's already being in police custody, made his transfer to the ICTY easier than that of fugitive suspects. "The Milošević arrest was one very short episode that we knew needed to happen," Živković recalled in the same interview. "He knew that, we knew that. The only thing we knew we needed to do was to do the job."[56]

However, if the Milošević handover demonstrated the resolve of the Đinđić government – and those international actors that pressured the government to act – it also underscored the exceptional circumstances that led to his arrest. Moreover, it demonstrated the tribunal's continuing dependence on the Western powers and their strong-arm tactics. That Đinđić acted decisively did not mean he would do so again any time soon. International pressure would continue, but it would come in bursts, thus enabling Serbian authorities to delay additional transfers until pressure mounted and financial inducements were offered. In this contest, Del Ponte continued to play a vital role as a campaigner for continued cooperation. Del Ponte's abrasive style frequently angered Serbian politicians and not infrequently irritated Western diplomats, who wished to proceed at their own pace. At times, Del Ponte faced international pressure to soften her high-profile pursuit of other war crimes suspects, even as she faced simultaneous international pressure to complete all her investigations and prosecutions to meet a 2010 deadline for the closure of the tribunal. The chief prosecutor bristled at the mixed message she was receiving. "We cannot be asked to complete soon our indictments and trials of top leaders and, at the same time, be told to be patient and not to rock the boat. This is an obvious contradiction," she told the Security Council in 2002.[57]

---

[53] "Statement of the Prosecutor, Carla Del Ponte, on the Transfer of Slobodan Milošević to The Hague," ICTY press release, June 29, 2001.
[54] Fieldwork interviews with ICTY officials, The Hague, October–November 2001.
[55] Fieldwork interview with Zoran Živković, Belgrade, August 2002.
[56] Ibid.
[57] Address to the Security Council by Carla Del Ponte, October 29, 2002.

B. International Pressure and Domestic Resistance

The warm praise Đinđić received from the tribunal and the West for his "coura-geous step"[58] in sending Milošević to The Hague earned him a respite from external pressure. Đinđić made clear that the timing of future cooperation would be an outcome of negotiation. "I think we should discuss that with The Hague," he said, in reference to Del Ponte's calls to transfer the other fifteen suspects then believed to be in Serbia. "They have enough for the moment to be going on with."[59]

Even as the tribunal faced increasing international pressure to complete its caseload, it had to cool its heels in the face of Đinđić's new resistance to arrest and transfer Serbian and Bosnian Serb suspects. The tribunal was also rebuffed when it came to securing archival evidence and access to insider witnesses, both keys to the prosecution of Milošević and other Serb suspects. The ICTY's list of indicted Serb suspects believed to be under Belgrade's protection was growing longer with new indictments. At the top of the list were former Bosnian Serb leader Radovan Karadžić and former Bosnian Serb general Ratko Mladić, both indicted for the infamous 1995 Srebrenica massacre. Immediately below were four senior Serb officials indicted, along with Milošević, in connection with Kosovo atrocities. The list of fugitives also included the three Yugoslav People's Army officers indicted for their alleged role in the murder of 261 wounded Croatian soldiers in Vukovar in 1991.

The Milošević transfer did not establish a government consensus over the need to cooperate and to adopt a domestic law on cooperation. Stiff opposi-tion from nationalists stopped the passage of such a law. Koštunica, the legalist, claimed erroneously that cooperation could not proceed without this law. Yet critics abroad charged that he did little to push for the law's adoption. "They never claimed that they needed it under Milošević," a high-level ICTY pros-ecution official told me in a 2001 interview. "Now they think it is necessary, but they don't [pass] it... At the Federal level, they simply do not want to cooperate."[60]

In the months following the Milošević transfer, the rift between Koštunica and Đinđić grew deeper, as seen in the collapse of the broad-based coalition – called the Democratic Opposition of Serbia – they had formed to topple Milošević.[61] Dissension also increased within the state security forces over the prospect of seeing many of their top officers sent to The Hague. Even the arrest and transfer of low-level suspects threatened a degree of unrest in Serbia. In November 2001, Đinđić ordered the special police forces to arrest two Bosnian Serb brothers – Predrag and Nenad Banović – who had been living

---

[58] Address to the Security Council by Carla Del Ponte, November 27, 2001.

[59] Carlotta Gall, "Serbian Tells of Spiriting Milošević Away," New York Times, July 1, 2001, A8.

[60] Fieldwork interview with ICTY official, The Hague, October 2001. Also see address to the Security Council by Carla Del Ponte, November 27, 2001.

[61] "Serbia After Đinđić," International Crisis Group, Balkans Report No. 141, March 18, 2003, p. 5.

in Serbia. Prior to making the arrests, leaders of the Red Berets police unit had reportedly not been told that the brothers had been sought by the ICTY.[62] In protest, Red Beret leaders said they would refuse to arrest other ICTY indictees without passage of a domestic cooperation law. The commandos took their protest a step further, using their armored vehicles to block major highways. The rebellion, analysts believed, was directly related to fear among the special forces that many of their members might face indictment for wartime atrocities. Đinđić put down the rebellion by removing two senior police officials and exerting more control over the special forces. Still, the revolt foreshadowed the danger Đinđić would face if and when he went ahead with Del Ponte's requests to arrest and hand over indicted suspects from Serbia's special police forces.

If even the arrests of two minor Bosnian Serbs came at a high political price to Đinđić, the arrest of high-level suspects such as Karadžić's and Mladić would be even more costly. Del Ponte – reiterating her earlier calls and those of her predecessors, Louise Arbour and Richard Goldstone – pressed for Karadžić's and Mladić's capture. The tribunal's bid for Karadžić and Mladić was complicated not only by their high rank and hero status, but by Belgrade's insistence that the two Bosnian Serbs were not actually in the territory of the rump Yugoslavia. To bolster her virtual "prosecution" of such state recalcitrance, Del Ponte had to persuade skeptics in the international community that Belgrade in fact had the capacity to arrest Karadžić and Mladić. Toward this end, Del Ponte's office gathered evidence that Mladić was in fact in Serbia. Until a few months earlier, Mladić had frequently been sighted in Belgrade, enjoying meals in fine restaurants. But by 2002, the situation had begun to change. Mladić and other Serb suspects had gone underground, afraid that the once-protective Serbian regime would arrest them. It was less clear, however, whether Karadžić could be apprehended by the Serbian authorities because he was probably hiding either in Bosnia or in Montenegro. Thus, when dealing with Belgrade, Del Ponte emphasized its obligation to arrest Mladić.

Still, even officials allied with Prime Minister Đinđić continued to insist during 2001 and 2002 that they had no idea where Mladić was hiding. Zoran Živković, the future Serbian prime minister, told me in an August 2002 interview: Del Ponte "is repeating for the last year the Karadžić and Mladić story...without any evidence that they are here...Whenever she is saying Karadžić and Mladić are in Serbia, I'm telling her 'OK, tell us the address [and] they will be arrested within four hours.'"[63] Del Ponte, in my 2003 interview, dismissed Živković's claim of government cooperation on the Mladić case, saying that Serb authorities usually did nothing to follow up on the information she gave them regarding his whereabouts.[64] "They don't want to locate him,"

---

[62] Daniel Sunter, "War Crimes Arrests Spark Serbian Mutiny," *Institute for War & Peace Reporting*, No. 243, November 5–10, 2001.

[63] Fieldwork interview with Zoran Živković, Belgrade, August 2002.

[64] Fieldwork interview with Carla Del Ponte, The Hague, December 2003.

she told me.[65] It was considerably more difficult for the government to make the same argument when it came to arresting those indicted suspects who were living openly in Serbia. While some suspects were in hiding, others, such as Milan Milutinović, were in full public view. Indeed, Milutinović was the president of Serbia.[66]

Regardless of the reasons offered, there was little cooperation from Belgrade in the nine months following Milošević's transfer. The U.S.-imposed March 31, 2002, certification deadline came and went without significant progress on cooperation. Washington reacted quickly, suspending approximately $40 million in economic aid.[67] However, U.S. officials made it clear that Serbia could still pass its annual certification exam and receive economic assistance if it showed signs of aiding the tribunal. Washington's use of aid conditionality prompted the Đinđić government to declare its intent to provide full cooperation. But, once again, Koštunica insisted erroneously that passage of domestic legislation was required to allow the government to send suspects to the tribunal.

Despite previous legislative defeats, the Yugoslav parliament finally adopted a cooperation law under intense international pressure. The law should have led to a marked increase in cooperation in light of Koštunica's insistence on the importance of domestic consent. Yet the law contained a number of loopholes that Belgrade intended to exploit to thwart cooperation. A key provision stipulated that the government only had an obligation to hand over those suspects already indicted, thus sanctioning state defiance when it came to those suspects yet to be charged by the ICTY. Tribunal officials and their international supporters remained skeptical about whether the new legislation would significantly benefit the tribunal.

At least some indicted suspects, however, viewed the law as another sign of the loss of Serbian sovereignty and the growing likelihood of their prosecution in The Hague. In a show of defiance, one senior government official indicted by the ICTY – Vlajko Stojilijković – shot himself in the head on the steps of the federal parliament building just hours after parliament passed the law on April 11, 2002. He died two days later. Stojilijković, the former Serbian Minister of Internal Affairs, was, along with Milošević, one of five co-defendants charged with atrocities during the Kosovo war. For anti-tribunal nationalists, Stojilijković's suicide was a courageous act that focused attention on the nation's victimization at the hands of a politicized, anti-Serb court. Koštunica sought to use the suicide as evidence of the destabilizing effect of international pressure to cooperate with the tribunal. Stojilijković's actions, Koštunica said, are a "warning to

---

[65] Ibid.

[66] Milutinović, who served as president of Serbia from 1997 to 2002, was indicted, along with Milošević and three other top Serbian officials, by the ICTY in May 1999 in connection with atrocities in Kosovo.

[67] Andrew Gray, "Belgrade in War Crimes Crisis After U.S. Aid Freeze," *Reuters*, April 2, 2002.

the international community that constantly sets conditions, pressures us and dictates behavior."[68]

The suicide did little to stop the flow of Serbian suspects to The Hague in April and May of 2002. In a major development, former Yugoslav People's Army Chief of Staff Dragoljub Ojdanić, also charged in the Kosovo indictment with Milošević, surrendered to the tribunal in late April. In early May, two more suspects, former Yugoslav Deputy Prime Minister Nikola Sainović and Momčilo Gruban went to The Hague. That was followed two weeks later by the transfer of Milan Martić, the former leader of the breakaway Croatian Serbs, and Mile Mrkšić, one of the Vukovar Three suspects. Later in May, the Serbian government received what it was looking for – the Bush administration's belated decision to certify Yugoslavia for economic aid.

Clearly the tide was turning in the tribunal's favor. This spurred ICTY officials and their advocates in the international human rights community to lobby for more cooperation, noting that many suspects still remained at large. Especially daunting were the serious obstacles that greeted tribunal investigators trying to obtain documents for use in the prosecution of Milošević and other Serb suspects.

Although the tribunal found itself in a generally stronger position vis-à-vis the government compared with the Milošević era, it still faced long stretches in which its leverage was relatively diminished. In the aftermath of the April and May surrenders, the tribunal found itself in a weak position to pressure the Serbian government to continue the handover of additional suspects or to provide access to crucial documentary evidence. As is often the case, mounting an international campaign for documents, as opposed to suspects, is particularly challenging because it is a relatively technical matter that is difficult to dramatize. In their public statements and meetings with diplomats, Del Ponte and other tribunal officials sought to call attention to Serbia's obstruction. During her annual address to the Security Council in October 2002, Del Ponte protested a provision of Serbia's cooperation law that required the destruction of archives more than ten years old. "Having been told many times in the past that access to certain military documents would not be possible before the enactment of the Law on Co-operation, we have recently been informed that some requested documents have now been destroyed," Del Ponte said. "If the consequences were not so serious, this kind of blatant defiance of international obligations would be almost comical. It cannot be allowed to continue."[69]

During 2001 and 2002, the festering divisions over the cooperation issue in Serbia and the prospect of continuing domestic crisis raised serious questions about the tribunal's claim that justice is in fact a precondition for peace and stability. The debate as to whether the tribunal fosters or undermines stability and

---

[68] "Suicide Attempt is 'Warning to International Community': Koštunica," *Agence France-Presse*, April 12, 2002.

[69] Address to the Security Council by Carla Del Ponte, October 29, 2002.

democratization soon became a centerpiece of the rhetorical battles between tribunal officials and state leaders. For Serbian politicians, leveling the charge that
ICTY indictments and pressure sparked instability was a self-fulfilling prophecy,
a prescient warning of domestic turmoil and a way to garner international sympathy for its non-compliance while delegitimizing the tribunal's avowed goals.
Use of the instability argument became a way for politicians to counter-shame
the tribunal by arguing that it actually exacerbated rather than facilitated the
country's democratic transition.

Serbian leaders also personally faulted Del Ponte for her aggressive and insen-
sitive approach to Serbia's predicament. "She is definitely not a good diplomat,"
Zoran Živković charged in my 2002 interview. "She is more or less always
angry with us."[70] Serbian officials also criticized Del Ponte for failing to launch
an effective prosecution in the Milošević trial. "At the moment . . . we can see
that they are going to make a national hero of him, not a war criminal,"
Živković said in the same interview.[71] That sentiment was echoed during my
interviews in Belgrade with a number of Serbian human rights activists otherwise generally supportive of the ICTY's work.[72]

Del Ponte saw a need to publicly counter the instability argument, contending
that in the long run, the prosecution of high-level suspects would aid Serbia by
removing potential threats to democracy. At the same time, Del Ponte and top
prosecution officials sought to provide a different context for Serbia's domestic
travails by shifting responsibility to Serbian politicians who failed to articulate
a moral imperative for cooperation. Sending war crimes suspects to an international tribunal was obviously difficult and "to be expected in any country
in the aftermath of armed conflict and political upheaval," Del Ponte told the
Security Council in October 2002.[73] But, she added, delaying indictments and
soft-peddling calls for cooperation would undermine her mandate to prosecute serious violations of international humanitarian law within the time limit
established by the Council.

When it came to dealing with government leaders in Belgrade, Del Ponte
faced an ongoing predicament. Employing an adversarial strategy of shaming
helped put Serbia's non-compliance under the international media spotlight and
galvanize international pressure. But shaming alone could backfire by alienating
international backers and hardening Serbian attitudes against the court. That, in
turn, threatened to raise the domestic political costs of cooperation for relatively
pro-tribunal actors, such as Prime Minister Đinđić. Yet, resorting to a conciliatory approach that emphasized negotiations with Serbian officials could also
derail cooperation by signaling the tribunal's willingness to compromise when it
came to Serbia's binding obligation to provide full and immediate cooperation.
Del Ponte would use both adversarial and conciliatory strategies. Negotiations

---

[70] Fieldwork interview with Zoran Živković, Belgrade, August 2002.
[71] Ibid.
[72] Fieldwork interviews with Serbian human rights activists, Belgrade, August 2002.
[73] Address to the Security Council by Carla Del Ponte, October 29, 2002.

with Đinđić occurred, although Del Ponte took pains not to give away too much or to acknowledge publicly that negotiations were in fact taking place.

3.5 The Murder of Zoran Đinđić (January through December 2003)

A. *Đinđić Moves Against the Serbian Mafia and War Crimes Suspects*

As the March 2003 deadline for U.S. certification approached, international and tribunal pressure on Belgrade increased once again. And, yet again, Prime Minister Đinđić and his allies grew more willing to facilitate the handover of fugitives by pressuring some suspects to surrender and by arresting and transferring others to the tribunal. Đinđić's capacity to do so was strengthened by the erosion of Koštunica's power since his failure to win the Serbian presidency during two elections in late 2002.[74] The impending demise of the Federal Republic of Yugoslavia prompted Koštunica, the Yugoslav president, to seek a new leadership position in the Serbian presidency. In February 2003, the rump Yugoslavia was dissolved and officially became the union of Serbia and Montenegro. Then, in May 2006, Montenegrin voters approved a referendum to become fully independent from Serbia.

Cooperation with the tribunal began to increase in late January 2003 when Milan Milutinovic, who had recently stepped down as president of Serbia when his term expired, surrendered to the tribunal. Still, pressure on Serbia mounted to arrest and transfer Ratko Mladić and other fugitives.[75] In addition to pledging to send more suspects to The Hague, Đinđić promised to initiate a crackdown on several organized crime groups, some of whose members had close ties to the state security services and were also sought by the tribunal for their alleged role in wartime atrocities. This crackdown was seen by Đinđić as an important albeit risky way to remove domestic obstacles to political and economic reform. These two decisions put Đinđić on a collision course with his erstwhile backers in the state security services.

Del Ponte reported that she had faith in Đinđić throughout his tenure as prime minister.[76] Therein lay Del Ponte's rationale to give Đinđić breathing room from public criticism and other forms of pressure. Toward the end of February 2003, Đinđić told Del Ponte that he would soon arrest Mladić. Del Ponte recounted this conversation in my December 2003 interview with her:

Two weeks before he was killed he told me, 'Prosecutor, I will give you Mladić in [the] Spring. But give me some more time because it's difficult.' And he explained to me why ... And I said, 'Yes, of course' ... because he informed me what he was doing and how he would achieve it. It was the same [as he did] with Milošević.[77]

---

[74] Despite being the top vote getter in both elections, the results were invalidated because a majority of voters did not cast ballots as required by Yugoslav law.

[75] In early 2003, the United States announced that the certification deadline for 2003 had been moved from March 31 to June 15. See Željko Cvijanović, "New Indictments May Follow Šešelj Charges," *Institute for War & Peace Reporting*, February 20, 2003.

[76] Fieldwork interview with Carla Del Ponte, The Hague, December 2003.

[77] Ibid.

Đinđić seemed to realize the personal risks involved in his bid to arrest more war crimes suspects and move against the Serbian organized crime groups. In late February, he was the target of an apparent assassination attempt when a truck slammed his motorcade. "He told me, 'They will kill me.' But he didn't believe it. He thought he was protected," Del Ponte told me.[78] In the end, neither Del Ponte's willingness to give Đinđić breathing room nor the prospect of the renewal of U.S. economic aid was enough to save the Serbian leader from his domestic adversaries.

B. Đinđić's Death and its Aftermath

Shortly after midday on March 12, 2003, a sniper's bullet killed the fifty-year-old Đinđić outside the Serbian government building in Belgrade. The assassination plot was quickly traced to current and former members of the elite special police unit formed years earlier by Milošević. In the aftermath of Đinđić's murder, the entire country was in mourning, as Misha Glenny observed in the following passage: "Hundreds of thousands turned out to pay their last respects as the funeral cortege moved through Belgrade in complete silence ... Almost everyone in Serbia had regarded Đinđić as a divisive figure, but in death he seemed to unite the country."[79]

For a moment it appeared that Serbia's grief would unify the nation and resolve its internecine battles over the country's relationship with organized crime and the international war crimes tribunal. Đinđić's murder indeed galvanized his successor, Zoran Živković, and the rest of the Serbian government. Acting under state of emergency powers, police quickly arrested numerous suspects believed to be involved in the assassination plot and pursued a harsh crackdown against mafia groups and senior members of Milošević's security structures. By the end of March, more than 3,000 alleged members of the Serbian mafia, including the former head of state security during the Milošević era, were arrested. The judiciary and the media were also targeted, with the head of Serbia's constitutional court dismissed and three publications closed down. In the aftermath of the assassination, government zeal led to human rights violations that included torture of some detained suspects.[80]

The crackdown prompted criticism from international human rights organizations,[81] even as it sparked hope at these organizations and the ICTY that at last the government had the will to move against indicted war criminals and their influential backers. For the first time since Milošević's fall from power, the democratic government appeared to gain the upper hand in its battle with organized crime. In turn, the prospects for political and economic reform appeared to grow stronger, notwithstanding the government's abuse of human rights.

---

[78] Ibid.

[79] Misha Glenny, "The Death Of Đinđić," *The New York Review of Books*, July 17, 2003, p. 34.

[80] "Serbian Reform Stalls Again," International Crisis Group, Balkans Report No. 145, July 17, 2003, p. i.

[81] "Serbia: Emergency Should Not Trump Basic Rights," Human Rights Watch, March 25, 2003.

In the aftermath of Ðinđić's murder, some commentators in Serbia and elsewhere blamed the tragedy and the country's turmoil on relentless pressure – from Del Ponte and the international community. Still, Del Ponte showed no sign of relenting after Ðinđić's death. If anything, the assassination seemed to increase her resolve to press Belgrade to hand over more war crimes suspects. In Del Ponte's view, easing the pressure now would not only undermine the tribunal bid for cooperation, but also hurt the efforts of Serbian authorities to ostracize organized crime groups and war criminals.[82] "Those who claim that cooperation with the tribunal is adverse to [the] internal stability of Serbia, and that Serbia has been under too much pressure to meet its obligations, are taking a dangerously short-term view," Del Ponte said in a visit to Belgrade shortly after Ðinđić's death.[83] Her decision to keep the pressure on Živković, as with her decision to pressure Ðinđić, involved a gamble that the long-term benefits for Serbian democracy would outweigh short-term instability.

The government crackdown initially coincided with a notable increase in cooperation. During the Spring of 2003, Serbian authorities arrested four suspects and transferred them to The Hague. The list included Miroslav Radić and Veselin Šljivančanin – the two remaining Vukovar Three suspects sought by the tribunal since their November 1995 indictments – as well as Jovica Stanišić, the former head of State Security, and Franko Simatović, the founder of Red Beret special forces. Belgrade also increased the handover of documents and relented when it came to its long-held refusal to grant waivers for government and military officials to testify at the tribunal.[84] Further, the government took steps to amend aspects of the domestic cooperation law previously used to impede cooperation. Toward that end, the parliament of the new union of Serbia and Montenegro (the successor to the Federal Republic of Yugoslavia) repealed the provision that barred the government from transferring suspects indicted by the tribunal after the law's adoption.

Serbia's cooperation prompted Del Ponte to act in kind with Prime Minister Živković. In a conciliatory move, she offered Serbian authorities two important concessions and indicated her willingness to offer more. Acting on Belgrade's request, Del Ponte quickly indicted Stanišić and Simatović, two high-ranking members of the state security service that the Serbian government had an interest in removing from the political scene.[85] The government's request for these indictments provided an example of how state cooperation actually served the government's domestic political agenda. In mid-May, Del Ponte complimented the government on its improved cooperation and, for the first time, mentioned the possibility of allowing Serbian courts to prosecute some tribunal

---

[82] Victor Peskin, "After Zoran Ðinđić: The Future of International Criminal Justice," *Open Democracy*, available online at: http://www.opendemocracy.net/themes/article-6-1107.jsp.

[83] Beti Bilandzić, "Hague Prosecutor to Keep up Pressure on Belgrade," *Reuters*, March 21, 2003.

[84] "Serbian Reform Stalls Again," International Crisis Group, Balkans Report No. 145, July 17, 2003, p. 4.

[85] Ibid., p. 4.

cases.[86] As in Croatia, Bosnia, and Rwanda, such deferrals were highly desired by the Serbian government because they offered a way to reassert state authority and take control of some war crimes prosecutions.

By the Summer of 2003, the flow of suspects, documents, and waivers for witnesses to testify at the tribunal had slowed down. This followed the U.S. certification of Serbia's cooperation in mid-June, two days after the high-profile arrest of Veselin Šljivančanin and his transfer to The Hague.[87] The arrest took place after a ten-hour standoff outside the ex-army colonel's Belgrade apartment between his bottle-throwing supporters and police.[88] The Serbian government had passed the American certification exam, but now it once again reduced its cooperation. This pattern was to be expected, complained Vermont Senator Patrick Leahy. "As co-author of this law, I can say that this is not what we meant by cooperation," Leahy said in a statement criticizing the Bush administration's decision to reward Serbia's limited cooperation with renewed economic aid.[89]

The tribunal's cooperation wish list remained long. Sixteen suspects, including Ratko Mladić, remained at large in Serbia. Moreover, the government continued to withhold crucial evidence that prosecutors sought in the ongoing Milošević trial. In the fall, Živković appeared increasingly reluctant to make other arrests that might upset his party's standing in the upcoming Serbian parliamentary elections.[90] Del Ponte planned a fall visit to Belgrade, prior to her annual address to the Security Council, to pressure Živković to hand over more suspects. But her efforts did not produce results, leading her to launch a shaming offensive against the government in her remarks to the Council[91] and in her other statements. By the end of the year, she had grown more pessimistic about Živković's commitment to the tribunal. At the same time, she was concerned that the moderate Živković and his Democratic Party might lose in the upcoming elections amid a rightward turn in Serbian politics.[92]

Just as in the aftermath of Đinđić's assassination, Serbian politicians and commentators in the Fall of 2003 blamed Del Ponte for destabilizing domestic politics by issuing new indictments and exerting excessive pressure for the capture of suspects on the heels of the upcoming elections. Serbian critics took aim at the chief prosecutor's fall indictments of Sreten Lukić (who had played a

---

[86] Ibid., p. 5. Also see Nick Hawton, "Prosecutor Hails New Belgrade Era," *BBC News*, May 20, 2003.

[87] David Gollust, "US Approves Aid for Serbia, Montenegro," *VOA*, June 17, 2003.

[88] More than fifty police officers were injured during the standoff. "Serb Arrest 'Will Unlock U.S. Aid,'" *CNN*, June 13, 2003; "Serbs Clash over War Crimes Arrest," *BBC News*, June 13, 2003.

[89] "Reaction of Senator Patrick Leahy to Secretary Powell's Certification of Serbian Compliance with Legislative Conditions Linking U.S. Aid to Compliance with the War Crimes Tribunal," Leahy press release, June 16, 2003.

[90] "Serbian Reform Stalls Again," International Crisis Group, Balkans Report No. 145, July 17, 2003, p. 5.

[91] Address to the Security Council by Carla Del Ponte, October 9, 2003.

[92] Fieldwork interview with Carla Del Ponte, The Hague, December 2003.

key role in the spring crackdown on Serbian organized crime groups) and three other generals for their alleged involvement in Kosovo atrocities. These attacks against the tribunal came not only from those on the right, but also from more moderate voices such as Živković, who found his bid for election increasingly threatened by the new indictments and domestic backlash against the tribunal. But given Belgrade's recent defiance – for instance, Živković's threat to suspend all cooperation if Del Ponte issued the indictments of the four generals[93] – Del Ponte did not see the need to be as conciliatory to Serbia's new prime minister as she had been with Đinđić.

The end of 2003 marked a clear shift to the right in Serbian politics. The ultra-nationalist Serbian Radical Party – led by Vojislav Šešelj, an indicted war criminal who had surrendered to The Hague earlier in the year – came away with the highest vote totals in the late December elections, leading to Živković's defeat. Following two months of protracted negotiations, a minority governing coalition, led by Vojislav Koštunica and his Democratic Party of Serbia, was formed in early March 2004. The fragile coalition – which excluded the Serbian Radical Party and Živković's Democratic Party – consisted of three smaller parties and also relied on the support of Milošević's anti-tribunal Socialist Party of Serbia. For the ICTY, the window of opportunity that opened in the aftermath of Milošević's fall from power appeared to be closing.

3.6 Back to the Beginning: The Return of Vojislav Koštunica (January 2004 through July 2007)

As many at the tribunal predicted, Koštunica's return to office as Serbia's prime minister made the ICTY's bid for cooperation more difficult. Koštunica reasserted his long-standing complaints about the tribunal and his resistance to cooperation. The only way suspects would end up in The Hague, he said, was if they voluntarily surrendered. But for much of 2004, Belgrade's cooperation had "deteriorated to a standstill," according to John C. Danforth, the U.S. ambassador to the United Nations.[94] This marked the first year that Washington withheld certification of Serbian cooperation, which in turn led to the suspension of some economic assistance.

Initially, Koštunica's stance was a continuation of his earlier approach when he had served as president of the now dissolved Federal Republic of Yugoslavia. In Del Ponte's annual address to the Security Council in November 2004, she dismissed Belgrade's surrender policy for failing to produce results and for being a "blatant contradiction" of Serbia's legal obligation to cooperate.[95] But toward the end of 2004, Koštunica actually took steps to pressure Serb fugitives

---

[93] Chris Stephen, "Del Ponte Reveals Serbian Obstinacy," *Institute for War & Peace Reporting*, October 17, 2003; Chris Stephen, "Belgrade Faces Indictee Dilemma," *Institute for War & Peace Reporting*, October 24, 2003.

[94] Text of Ambassador John C. Danforth's remarks, USUN press release, November 23, 2004.

[95] Address to the Security Council by Carla Del Ponte, November 23, 2004.

to "voluntarily" surrender. In this regard, the tribunal appeared to benefit from the June 2004 election to the Serbian presidency of the reformist Democratic Party leader, Boris Tadić. Koštunica's actions in encouraging these surrenders mirror the steps taken by Croatian Prime Minister Ivo Sanader. As will be discussed in Chapter 5, Sanader facilitated the "voluntary" surrender of nine indicted Croatian suspects during the first half of 2004.

In early 2005, the flow of Serb suspects departing for the ICTY increased markedly. These included Vladimir Lazarević, who surrendered in early February, Sreten Lukić, who surrendered in early April, Vujadin Popović who surrendered in mid-April, and Nebojša Pavković, who surrendered in late April. From the start of the year through the end of April, a dozen Serbian and Bosnian Serb suspects had been transferred to the tribunal.[96] At no other time up to that point had so many ethnic Serb suspects been sent to The Hague for trial.

The tribunal played a crucial role by sweetening the bitter pill of surrender and incarceration. The Office of the Prosecutor offered some suspects the prospect of provisional release (pending judicial approval) after their surrender and arraignment and prior to trial.[97] Prosecutors also pursued plea-bargaining arrangements to speed the disposition of cases and encourage more surrenders throughout the former Yugoslavia. Beyond the prospect of any concession that Del Ponte might offer, some suspects doubtless came to realize the benefits of surrender, nationalist rhetoric notwithstanding. The act of surrender could become a mitigating factor in sentencing if and when judges found them guilty. Moreover, it became increasingly apparent that defendants found guilty in their trials had a chance to win full or partial acquittal in the appeals process. War crimes trials, of course, remained a serious threat to defendant and nation, imperiling both the individual's freedom and the nation's claim to victim status. Still, it had become evident that the sentences handed down by ICTY judges were hardly draconian. Despite tribunal judgments that convicted many defendants for unspeakable atrocities, judges demonstrated little inclination to hand down heavy sentences.[98]

As important as tribunal incentives were, American and European pressure proved to be the most critical factor in inducing the new wave of surrenders. In 2005, Washington once again conditioned aid to Belgrade on transfers of war crimes suspects.[99] Moreover, U.S. officials withdrew their previous support for a deal that would have allowed the Serbian courts to prosecute four generals (indicted by the ICTY in Fall 2003) in exchange for the arrest and

---

[96] Nicholas Wood, "Balkan Federation to Start Talks with EU," *International Herald Tribune*, April 13, 2005.

[97] See "Provisional Release Granted for Vladimir Lazarević, Milan Milutinović, Nikola Sainović and Dragoljub Ojdanić," ICTY press release, April 14, 2005.

[98] By April 2005, the ICTY had delivered only one life sentence. The tribunal's second longest sentence of forty-six years was given to Radislav Krstić in 2001. On appeal, Krstić's sentence was reduced to thirty-five years in 2004.

[99] Steven Woehrel, "Serbia and Montenegro: Current Situation and U.S. Policy," Congressional Research Service, updated January 18, 2005, p. 14.

transfer of Ratko Mladić to the tribunal.[100] The Serbian government had a strong incentive to delay the handover of some fugitives as long as there was a possibility of American backing for this domestic prosecution deal. The EU also played a pivotal role by indicating that talks on a stabilization and association agreement – a necessary step for eventual EU membership – would be contingent on increased cooperation. In mid-April 2005, the European Commission deemed Belgrade's cooperation sufficient and recommended that the EU start negotiations on a stabilization and association agreement.[101]

By April 2005, it was clear that the tribunal was steadily winning its trials of cooperation with the Serbian government. Since Milošević's removal from power in 2000, the tribunal had, in fits and starts, reaped the benefits of a democratic government that was less antagonistic to cooperation, albeit when faced with formidable international pressure and attractive incentives. Yet the ICTY's growing success in apprehending suspects did not carry over to its two most wanted fugitives – Radovan Karadžić and Ratko Mladić. More than eleven years after the Srebrenica massacre, these two prime Serb suspects were still at large.[102]

For the tribunal, obtaining custody of Karadžić and Mladić grew in importance after the death of Slobodan Milošević in March 2006. Milošević's fatal heart attack – shortly before the completion of his more than four-year-long trial and amid revelations of lax tribunal procedures regarding his medical treatment while in custody – was a major blow to the tribunal's reputation, and magnified the need to bring such major suspects as Karadžić and Mladić to trial. Milošević's death further undermined the ICTY's credibility in Serbia and handed nationalists another platform to attack the tribunal. While Serbia's counter-shaming did not often win over Western diplomats and media, the government's attacks against the ICTY in the wake of Milošević's death did resonate in the West. Even though Milošević contributed to his own death by failing to take his required medication, the tribunal bore responsibility for not having done more to monitor his heart condition. Moreover, despite Milošević's creative delaying tactics, it was in the tribunal's power to have conducted a shorter and less cumbersome trial. In the end, the ICTY – often lauded for its efficiency and professionalism – faltered. Richard Dicker of Human Rights Watch expressed the sentiment of many tribunal supporters when he called Milošević's death "a terrible setback first and foremost for the victims of horrific crimes in the former Yugoslavia and because it deprives the tribunal of a chance to render a verdict on his true role."[103]

---

[100] Bogdan Ivanišević and Geraldine Mattioli, "Real Progress in The Hague," Human Rights Watch Commentary, March 29, 2005; "Mladić a 'Priority' for Serbia," *BBC News*, October 23, 2003.

[101] Daniel Dombey and Eric Jansson, "Brussels Backs Closer Ties with Serbia Despite Concern over War Crimes Cases," *Financial Times*, April 13, 2005.

[102] By the end of 2006, four other Serb suspects indicted by the ICTY were still at large.

[103] Marlise Simons and Gregory Crouch, "Milošević is Found Dead in Cell, U.N. Officials Say," *New York Times*, March 12, 2006, A4.

Mindful of the leverage Serbian nationalists hoped to gain from Milošević's death, European officials warned Belgrade that it still had a responsibility to hand over Mladić. Arresting Mladić was, of course, never a risk-free proposition for the Serbian government. But Milošević's death and the resulting increase in anti-tribunal sentiment in Serbia raised the domestic political risk that Prime Minister Koštunica faced over the Mladić issue. Under intensifying international pressure, Koštunica pledged in early 2006 to arrest Mladić and send him to The Hague. The EU backed up its calls for the arrest by threatening to suspend the stabilization and association agreement talks with Serbia if Koštunica reneged. The prime minister's promise was highly significant because it was a tacit admission after years of denial that Mladić was indeed in Serbia and that the Belgrade government had the means to arrest him. However, by taking responsibility for Mladić's arrest, Koštunica committed himself to actually apprehending the former Bosnian Serb general, thereby backing Belgrade as well as Brussels into a corner. Since the EU had conditioned continuation of the stabilization and association agreement negotiations on Mladić's arrest, a failure to act would make it politically difficult for the EU not to suspend the talks because it would undermine the credibility of its conditionality policy.[104] When the EU's March 31, 2006, deadline passed with no Serbian action, Brussels extended the deadline for Mladić's transfer until the end of April. Then, when Koštunica failed to act again, the EU suspended the talks in early May, putting Serbia's nascent bid for EU membership on hold.

Even as it had a strong interest in reaffirming its conditionality policy and backing Del Ponte's bid for Mladić and the several other remaining Serb fugitives, the EU did not relish blocking Serbia's long path to membership. Indeed, in the second half of 2006 and the first half of 2007, the EU and the West grew increasingly concerned about the prospect of political instability and a nationalist resurgence in Serbia. In 2006, leaders in Belgrade were confronted with two blows – first, the May victory of an independence referendum in Montenegro, and, second, the rising prospects that the UN would soon grant some form of independence to Kosovo, which remained an anathema in Serbia. In this context, EU officials I interviewed in December 2006 expressed concern that the suspension of the stabilization and association agreement talks would further weaken Koštunica and increase the prospects that Šešelj's Serbian Radical Party would prevail in the January 2007 parliamentary elections. In November and December, Šešelj's hunger strike while in custody in The Hague further burnished his nationalist, anti-tribunal credentials and his electoral prospects. (In February 2007, ICTY President Fausto Pocar acquiesced to Šešelj's demand, made during his hunger strike, to dismiss the panel of judges selected to preside over his trial and appoint new judges. This provides a prominent example of how the tribunal's president can be involved in compromises that may undermine the institution's integrity.) Concern with instability in Serbia appears to have been the motivation behind NATO's decision in late November 2006 to

[104] Fieldwork interviews with EU officials, Brussels, December 2006.

invite Serbia to join the Partnership for Peace, a coveted stepping stone for membership in the military alliance.

In light of Serbia's fragile political situation and the looming confrontation over Kosovo, the EU sought to find a way out of the Mladić impasse and to restart the stabilization and association agreement negotiations. Toward that end, the EU indicated to Belgrade that short of arresting and transferring Mladić to The Hague, talks could resume if Koštunica presented a credible plan for arresting him. To exploit this new loophole and possibly win resumption of the talks, Koštunica worked on developing such a plan over the course of 2006. He also tried to provide persuasive evidence that the government was actively searching for Mladić, by publicly circulating the plan for Mladić's capture, staging a raid purportedly aimed at arresting Mladić, and arresting several people who helped protect him. Still, some European diplomats remained skeptical that this would quickly lead to Mladić's capture. "I will believe it when I see it," said Dutch Foreign Minister Bernard Bot.[105] In speeches to the Security Council in June and December 2006, Del Ponte faulted Belgrade for not seriously pursuing Mladić. Ever the prosecutor, Del Ponte told the Council in June that "on the basis of the facts in my possession, I cannot be convinced that Serbia is ready to arrest Mladić."[106] In December, Del Ponte dismissed Koštunica's arrest plan as "just another smokescreen."[107]

While Mladić drew increased Western scrutiny in 2006, interest in Karadžić seemed to fade, to Del Ponte's chagrin. As Del Ponte pointedly remarked in her June Security Council speech, the responsibility for Karadžić's arrest not only lay with Serbia and Republika Srpska, but with the West and its peacekeeping forces in Bosnia. "It is pathetic that today, nobody is searching actively for Karadžić,"[108] she said, adding that the planned reduction in the number of European peacekeepers in Bosnia would only make the search more difficult. In June 2007, Del Ponte told the Security Council that she had no current information on Karadžić's whereabouts and implicitly criticized Western intelligence agencies for not doing more to keep him in their sights.[109] This lack of certainty dealt a blow to Del Ponte's efforts to "prosecute" Serbian non-compliance and persuade the UN, the United States, and the EU to press Belgrade to take immediate action to track down and arrest Karadžić. But although the former Republika Srpska leader had disappeared from the world's radar screen, he remained a presence in Serbia, continuing to write and publish new books and poetry.

As the scheduled closing of the ICTY drew near, Del Ponte, at the end of 2006, intensified her efforts to bring Karadžić and Mladić to trial before the end of the decade, or barring that, to ensure that the UN would allow an international

---

[105] "Serbians Propose 'Mladić Plan' in Plea to EU," *Financial Times*, July 17, 2006.
[106] Address to the Security Council by Carla Del Ponte, June 7, 2006.
[107] Address to the Security Council by Carla Del Ponte, December 15, 2006.
[108] Address to the Security Council by Carla Del Ponte, June 7, 2006.
[109] Address to the Security Council by Carla Del Ponte, June 18, 2007.

trial in The Hague any time afterward. In her December 2006, speech to the Security Council, she invoked the memory of the Srebrenica victims and the West's abandonment of them a decade earlier in an attempt to safeguard the tribunal's prerogative to bring the two former Bosnian Serb leaders to account. Said Del Ponte: "There is no other place than The Hague to try them."[110]

In early 2007, another international court in The Hague added a new dimension to the trials of cooperation between the ICTY and Belgrade. In February, the International Court of Justice (ICJ) issued its long-awaited decision in Bosnia's genocide lawsuit against Serbia. In a major disappointment for survivors of the Srebrenica massacre and human rights activists, the ICJ ruled that Serbia was not guilty of the genocide that occurred in Srebrenica and did not owe reparations to Bosnia, even though the Court found that Belgrade had failed to take measures to prevent the massacre. The Court also held that Serbia was in violation of the Genocide Convention of 1948 for not handing over Mladić and Karadžić for trial to the ICTY. One might have expected that the ICJ ruling – the first one to ever find a state in violation of the Genocide Convention – would strengthen Del Ponte's hand and spur greater international pressure on Belgrade to arrest these top fugitives. But over the next several months, the chief prosecutor's leverage diminished as the West sought to placate Serbia and ensure that it did not move away from Europe and toward Russia.

The West's concern was heightened by the first-place showing in the January 2007 elections of Šešelj's Serbian Radical Party – which received 28 percent of the vote – and the uncertain composition of the new government. It would take almost four months of negotiations until a new government was formed, led again by Koštunica. However, in early May, the Serbian Parliament's election of Radical Party leader Tomislav Nikolić as its speaker raised fears in the West that that the pro-Moscow ultranationalists might join with Koštunica to form a new government.[111] Just before the deadline to form a new government expired in mid-May, Koštunica and Boris Tadić, Serbia's pro-Western president, agreed to a power-sharing deal that excluded the Radical Party. A relieved EU moved to reward Serbia.

In an effort to bolster the new pro-Western government and in a long-shot bid to ease Serbia's adamant opposition to Kosovo independence, European diplomats indicated that the suspended stabilization and association talks would soon resume.[112] But the exact date depended to a large extent on whether Del

[110] Address to the Security Council by Carla Del Ponte, December 15, 2007.
[111] Nicholas Wood, "Serbian Parliament picks ultranationalist as speaker," *International Herald Tribune*, May 8, 2007.
[112] In early May 2007, the Council of Europe – the institution charged with protecting human rights and rule of law in Europe – granted Serbia the rotating chair of its highest decision-making body, the Committee of Ministers. Elevating Serbia to the symbolic leadership of Europe's efforts to safeguard human rights foreshadowed the EU's decision the following month to resume negotiations with Serbia over a stabilization and association accord.

Ponte would render a positive assessment of Serbia's cooperation.[113] In a bid to win such an assessment from Del Ponte, the Serbian government suddenly became more cooperative. On May 31, the government facilitated the arrest and handover to the tribunal of Zdravko Tolimir, a top aide to Mladić, indicted for genocide and crimes against humanity at Srebrenica. Tolimir, who had been living in an apartment in Belgrade, was reportedly taken by Serbian police to Republika Srpska and arrested there in order to reduce the domestic fallout for Prime Minister Koštunica.[114] The next day, Olli Rehn, the EU enlargement commissioner, announced that Brussels would restart the talks later in June, but did not set a date.[115] By agreeing to restart the talks without first requiring that Belgrade send Mladić to the tribunal, the EU reneged on the condition it had established a year earlier when it suspended the negotiations.

Once it became clear that the EU would compromise its own conditionality policy, Del Ponte made a similar strategic compromise, dropping her insistence that Mladić be turned over before the stabilization and association talks resumed. Del Ponte now recognized that her best chance to maintain her authority and win the arrests of the remaining fugitives was by acquiescing to Brussels and holding talks of her own with Serbian officials to encourage more arrests.

Confident that it could court the weakened chief prosecutor, the government invited Del Ponte to a five-day visit to Belgrade in early June. Del Ponte – who described it as "the best visit I have had in eight years"[116] – gave Serbia the public praise it wanted, saying that the government had demonstrated a commitment to cooperate. She also predicted that Mladić would be handed over in three months, close to the September time when her tenure at the tribunal was initially scheduled to end.[117,118] She took conciliation to a new level when, on June 6 in Belgrade, she said, "I would be grateful if the [EU] negotiations can start as soon as possible."[119] On June 7, the EU announced that its talks with

---

[113] Sara Goodman, "Is Tolimir Arrest Evidence of New Cooperation?" *Institute for War & Peace Reporting*, June 1, 2007.

[114] "Crimes and misdemeanours," *The Economist*, June 7, 2007.

[115] The EU resumed the stabilization and association talks with Serbia on June 13, though it pledged not to sign an agreement with Serbia until all fugitives are handed over to the tribunal. Stephen Castle and Dan Bilefsky, "Serbia and EU resume formal talks," *International Herald Tribune*, June 13, 2007.

[116] Nicholas Wood, "EU confirms a new round of entry talks with Serbia," *International Herald Tribune*, June 7, 2007.

[117] Ibid.

[118] In summer 2007, Del Ponte agreed to stay on at the ICTY through the end of the year to allow more time for the Security Council to find a successor. Initially, it appeared that the Council would appoint Serge Brammertz, a former deputy prosecutor of the International Criminal Court who went on to head the UN's investigation into the assassination of the former Lebanese Prime Minister Rafiq Hariri. But by September, the Council had not yet selected a new chief prosecutor. Senior ICTY prosecutors lobbied strongly for the appointment of a tribunal veteran – ICTY Deputy Prosecutor David Tolbert.

[119] Nick Hawton, "*Del Ponte urges EU-Serbia talks,*" *BBC News*, June 6, 2007.

Serbia would resume the following week.[120] As Del Ponte's second four-year term and tenure at the tribunal approached its end, she hoped that this shift to a conciliatory approach would finally lead to the arrests of the last fugitives, particularly Mladić.[121] Shortly after her visit, and just a day before she was to give an assessment of Serbia's cooperation to the Security Council, Belgrade arranged the arrest and transfer of another indictee, Vlastimir Đorđević.[122]

As the longest serving prosecutor at the ICTY, Del Ponte has made considerable gains in the area of state cooperation, with 91 accused being sent to The Hague. Of the 161 suspects indicted by the tribunal since 1993, only 4 remained at large by the end of July 2007. Since its founding, the ICTY has registered 61 convictions and 9 acquittals. As impressive as these numbers are, they do not tell the whole story given the particular importance that victims, human rights activists, and the tribunal itself have placed on prosecuting Mladić and Karadžić. As Del Ponte told the Security Council in June 2007, not long before the twelfth anniversary of the tribunal's initial indictment of Mladić and Karadžić, the failure to apprehend the two former Bosnian Serb leaders "is a permanent stain on our work."[123]

3.7 Conclusion

This chapter demonstrates the key role that influential international actors, especially the United States and the EU, play in the trials of cooperation. Without international pressure and the promise of economic and political incentives, there would be little change in Belgrade's willingness or capacity to cooperate with the ICTY. Particularly when it came to the handover of war crimes suspects, state compliance predictably increased shortly before and after the imposition of conditionality deadlines and then decreased during other parts of the year. Even as Serbia's cooperation waxes and wanes opportunistically, this chapter also demonstrates that the confrontation and negotiation between state and tribunal matter greatly. Both state and tribunal each wage a battle to persuade the international community to intervene on its behalf. The tribunal seeks international intervention to condemn state non-compliance and to pressure the recalcitrant state to reverse course. The state seeks international support for its arguments of state exceptionalism to evade punishment for its non-cooperation. In this rhetorical combat with the tribunal, both the Milošević regime and its democratic successors argued for exemption from having to cooperate because of the tribunal's supposed anti-Serb bias. Milošević obviously had reason to fear the tribunal because of its power to indict him. Serbia's new political leaders do not fear such a fate because they did not play a role in the country's

---

[120] Nicholas Wood, "EU confirms a new round of entry talks with Serbia," *International Herald Tribune*, June 7, 2007.

[121] Fieldwork interview with ICTY prosecution official, The Hague, June 2007.

[122] On June 17, 2007, the indictee, Vlastimir Đorđevic, wanted in connection with atrocities in Kosovo, was arrested in Montenegro and sent to The Hague.

[123] Address to the Security Council by Carla Del Ponte, June 18, 2007.

ethnic cleansing campaigns in Croatia, Bosnia, or Kosovo. Yet indictments and the tribunal's calls on the government to send indictees to The Hague raise the fear of instability and crisis at home. Thus, in the recent democratic period, the tribunal simultaneously poses a threat to stability and provides Serbian politicians with a new device to use in their campaign for international forbearance for its non-compliance.

For politicians in Belgrade, playing the "instability card" has also become a means to counter-shame Chief Prosecutor Del Ponte for her efforts to shame Serbia for its non-compliance. By blaming Serbia's domestic turmoil – particularly the Đinđić assassination and the defeat of his Democratic Party in the December 2003 parliamentary elections – on the ICTY and Del Ponte personally, politicians have sought to damage the tribunal's foundational claim that international justice fosters stability and democratization. The instability that has accompanied tribunal indictments and handover of suspects in both Serbia and Croatia indeed raises serious questions about the compatibility of international justice and democratization and how vigorously and expeditiously a tribunal should pursue the prosecution of war crimes.

These questions deserve much more dispassionate and rigorous scrutiny by scholars and practitioners than they have so far received. When it comes to determining whether tribunals foster or undermine domestic stability, much is at stake, both for tribunals and their advocates in the international human rights movement and for recalcitrant states and their like-minded domestic constituencies. The same holds true when it comes to determining whether tribunals deter armed conflict or actually encourage its resumption. The contentious debate over whether international justice cultivates or imperils democratic transitions lays at the heart of the "trials of cooperation" between Serbia and the International Criminal Tribunal for the Former Yugoslavia.

4

Franjo Tuđman and the Politics of International Justice

4.1 Introduction

In this and the next chapter, I will examine the "trials of cooperation" that have taken place between the International Criminal Tribunal for the Former Yugoslavia (ICTY) and the Croatian government. In this chapter, I will examine these "trials" during the country's authoritarian period that lasted until the electoral victory of a democratic coalition in January 2000. In the next chapter, I will examine the ICTY-Croatian government "trials" since the beginning of Croatia's democratic period.

A major aim of the Croatia case study, as with the Serbia and Rwanda case studies, is to reveal the often hidden ways in which targeted states manipulate the course of international justice. The ability of the Croatian government to thwart the ICTY underscores the extent to which its prosecutorial agenda can be shaped by the political interference of targeted states. The Croatia case, as much as the Serbia case, also demonstrates the central role that key international actors such as the United States and the European Union play in both undermining and bolstering the tribunal's quest for cooperation from targeted states. The tribunal, however, is not predestined to be an arm of either the international community or targeted states. The Croatia and Serbia case studies point to a developmental process whereby the ICTY has evolved into a strategic actor with an increasing capacity to press states to cooperate while protecting itself from external manipulation. The tribunal, and particularly its chief prosecutors, have developed a tool kit of strategies that have proved increasingly successful in prodding Zagreb to cooperate. As discussed in Chapter 1, this tool kit contains adversarial strategies designed to shame and conciliatory strategies designed to persuade a recalcitrant state to cooperate. That Croatia has provided more cooperation than Serbia does not mean that it has done so willingly or provided nearly enough to suit an ad hoc court under intense international pressure to complete its work in a timely manner. Tribunal officials whom I interviewed often reserved their most scathing criticism for the Croatian government because of its frequent refusals to cooperate, its skillful delaying tactics, and its relentless "counter-shaming" attacks against the tribunal.

International concern over state cooperation in the Balkans has been largely focused on Serbia, making it relatively easy for the ICTY to garner worldwide media and diplomatic attention even as it struggled to press the international community to compel Serbia to cooperate. Both during and after the war, Serbia and its wartime leader, Slobodan Milošević, were the big story. In contrast, Croatia and its wartime leader, Franjo Tudman, were usually relegated to the inside pages of Western newspapers. Croatia, however, is a critical case to examine precisely because it has been in the shadows of both the Balkan conflict and the subsequent conflicts over cooperation between Serbia and the tribunal. While much is now known about Serbian war crimes and Serbia's subsequent defiance of the tribunal, far less is known about Croatian actions on both fronts.

The tribunal's prosecution of Croatian war crimes suspects has not been pursued merely for the sake of trying to appear evenhanded or to leverage cooperation from Serbia. Without sufficient cooperation from Croatia, the tribunal runs the risk of prosecuting suspects from the group most responsible for atrocities (i.e., the Serbs) while leaving suspects from the group next most culpable (i.e., the Croats) relatively untouched. This in turn runs the risk of turning the tribunal into a de facto victor's court, given Croatia's emergence in 1995 as the clear winner of the Balkan wars. (In fact, as we will discuss, this has been the fate of the International Criminal Tribunal for Rwanda (ICTR) where the priority given to Hutu genocide trials has meant that lesser Tutsi crimes evade prosecution.) A fundamental aim of the United Nations ad hoc tribunals has been to prosecute war crimes suspects from both the winning side and the losing side of armed conflicts and to overcome the legacy of victor's justice established at Nuremberg and Tokyo.

The dynamics of the ICTY's trials of cooperation with the Serbian and Croatian governments actually have a striking resemblance. During the authoritarian period in particular, Serbia and Croatia resisted the tribunal and frequently blocked its quest for state cooperation. In Serbia, President Milošević argued that the tribunal was an anti-Serb institution that cast collective guilt on the Serbian nation. In Croatia, President Tudman also used the collective guilt argument, maintaining that the tribunal was an anti-Croat institution. In both countries, the tribunal posed a similar threat to state interests by undermining each government's claim to be the main victim of the Balkan conflict and threatening each government's leader with arrest.

For all the parallels, there are sharp differences between the way Belgrade and Zagreb have approached the tribunal, underscoring the need for a separate examination of the ICTY–Croatian government relationship. Whereas Serbia provided virtually no cooperation to the tribunal during the authoritarian era, Croatia at times provided significant cooperation, as seen in its handover of a dozen Bosnian Croat war crimes suspects in 1996 and 1997. In contrast to Serbia, Croatia realized the benefits of compliance, given its initial experience as the main victim of the Balkan wars. But Croatia's changing wartime experience and its new-found identity as both victim and perpetrator soon rendered the government deeply ambivalent about international justice.

The Croatian and Serbian governments also employed different strategies of resistance in their dealings with the tribunal. In the Milošević era, the Serbian government's defiance was usually bold and straightforward, reflecting its unmitigated antipathy to the court. But Croatia's resistance, while often equally disruptive to the tribunal, took a more subtle form, seemingly more compliant and hence less assailable. Croatia tried its best to cloak its obstinacy in the rhetoric of cooperation, at least when it came to pledges to tribunal officials and statements meant for international consumption. At other times, the Tuđman government justified non-cooperation by resorting to a legalistic strategy that argued for exceptions to the Security Council's strict obligation on all UN member states to comply fully and immediately with all tribunal requests. In my interview with him, Richard J. Goldstone, the tribunal's first chief prosecutor, spoke of Croatia's determination to evade the ICTY's reach. The Croatian government, Goldstone said, was "much shrewder" than the Serbian government. "Belgrade said 'we don't recognize you.' Hence, zero cooperation. Croatia said 'we recognize you and we'll give you all the cooperation we can.' Only they didn't. It was much more shrewd and more . . . devious. . . . They were happy to cooperate when it suited them, but if it got close to home then they would shut up like clams."[1]

When it came to addressing audiences at home, Tuđman and top-level government officials stoked popular resentment against the tribunal for daring to prosecute Croatian suspects. In the aftermath of Croatia's victory in its so-called Homeland War, the government employed a rhetorical strategy that likened the tribunal to a new external enemy. The Homeland War (*domovinski rat*) is the term that many Croatians use to refer to the war of independence fought against Serbian forces on Croatian territory from June 1991 through August 1995. To Tuđman, the tribunal's transgressions not only cast unwarranted blame on all Croatians, but discredited the celebrated war of independence that had become a defining and mythologized moment for the new Croatian nation. Although the tribunal posed a serious threat to the regime, this newly declared enemy was also a blessing for Tuđman and his right-wing HDZ (Hrvatska Demokratska Zajednica, Croatian Democratic Union) party. Battling the tribunal provided an opportunity for the HDZ to burnish its image as defender of the nation's sovereignty and to reinvigorate its claim to authoritarian control over domestic politics, media, and civil society.

International pressure on Croatia to assist the tribunal was circumscribed. The United States and Europe pressured Zagreb to hand over low-level Bosnian Croat war crimes suspects, but did far less to press Tuđman to aid tribunal investigations of high-level Croatian generals suspected of ordering atrocities against Serb civilians on Croatian soil during the Homeland War. Washington's reticence to press Tuđman vigorously to cooperate with tribunal investigations

---

[1] Fieldwork interview with Richard J. Goldstone, Pasadena, April 2003.

of the Homeland War stems both from its interest in obscuring America's own role in aiding the Croatian military's 1995 attacks on the Serbian-held areas of Croatia and from its interest in ensuring Croatia's continued positive role in aiding the tens of thousands of refugees who had fled the Bosnian war. However, after Tuđman's death in late 1999, the United States grew more willing to press Croatia to facilitate tribunal investigations of Homeland War atrocities.

Although Croatia at times surrendered to strong international pressure, it was still able to draw a line in the sand and withhold crucial evidence that could have led to the indictment of President Tuđman and Defense Minister Gojko Šušak. In this regard, Tuđman was able to stymie the tribunal's mission and keep it focused on Zagreb's wartime proxies and post-war fall guys – the Bosnian Croats. The tribunal would eventually bring indictments for the crimes committed by high-level Croatian generals inside Croatia, but this would come well after Tuđman's death.

4.2 Croatia's Search for Independence through Victim Status

A. *Croatia as Victim in the 1991 War with Serbia*

In light of Croatia's bitter trials of cooperation with the ICTY, it is seldom remembered that Croatia (like Rwanda) initially welcomed the prospect of an international war crimes court. The Croatian government called on the international community to create a tribunal during the nadir of its war with Serb forces in November 1991.[2] Croatia's initial support for an international tribunal was driven by its image of itself as the main victim of the Balkan wars as well as by the political benefits it stood to gain from international prosecutions of Serbian war crimes. For the fledgling Croatian government, calling for a tribunal was a logical step in Croatia's quest for diplomatic recognition and for victory in its war with Serbia. "As one of the countries that were victims of the aggression during the first part of the 90's we were obviously interested in perpetrators of war crimes being brought to justice," a Croatian government official involved in issues of state cooperation with the ICTY told me in a 2001 interview in Zagreb.[3]

Beginning in the Summer of 1991, Croatian government forces fell victim to Serb attacks aimed at thwarting Croatia's bid for secession from the Federal Republic of Yugoslavia (FRY). Zagreb declared independence from the Serbian-dominated FRY in late June 1991 after the fabric of the once-cohesive republic was torn apart by the rise of nationalism in Belgrade, Zagreb, and other Balkan capitals over the previous year and a half. However, the battle for

---

[2] The Croatian government submitted a formal request for an international tribunal on November 22, 1991. See Government of Republic of Croatia, *The White Paper on Cooperation with the International Tribunal for the Prosecution of Persons Responsible for Serious Violations of International Humanitarian Law Committed in the Territory of the Former Yugoslavia Since 1991*, Zagreb, September 1999, p. 4.

[3] Fieldwork interview with Croatian government official, Zagreb, Croatia, December 2001.

independence would be formidable. During the six-month war that followed, the anemic Croatian army was outgunned[4] by the superior Serb-dominated Yugoslav People's Army (JNA), said to be the fourth largest army in Europe.[5] Serb forces were determined to take control of Eastern Slavonia and the Krajina – areas on the border with Serbia and Bosnia with sizeable ethnic Serb populations – and forced Croats from their communities in the tens of thousands, carrying out numerous atrocities against civilians. During this part of the Balkan conflict, Croatia was the main victim. However, Croatia was not purely a victim because its armed forces also carried out torture and atrocities against Serbs during 1991,[6] though these acts did not rise to the magnitude of the Serb crimes.

Croatia's victim status was at first insufficiently acknowledged internationally. International acknowledgment of victim status, as with diplomatic recognition of its independence, required a determined and strategic struggle. Particularly during the first half of the 1991 conflict, the United States and Europe, reflecting their desire to be neutral arbiters, declined to designate either Croatia as the victim or Serbia as the aggressor. During the Summer months of 1991 "there was still a strong feeling [in the West] that the Croats were as much to blame for the situation in Yugoslavia as the Serbs," writes Marcus Tanner in his history of Croatia.[7]

Milošević proved to be a formidable adversary when it came to Croatia's quest for victim status, since he too was trying his best to win this designation for the Serbs. At every turn, Milošević charged that Tuđman's forces were attempting to advance a genocidal policy and that Serbia was only trying to protect Croatian Serbs from annihilation.[8] Serbian government propaganda raised the specter of the return of Serbian victimization at the hands of genocidal Ustaša, an allusion to the Croatian fascist movement responsible for the murder of hundreds of thousands of Serbs and Jews during World War II. That four-year rule of the Nazi-installed Ustaša government marked Croatia's only experiment with independence. Milošević stirred fear that Croatia's new bid for independence would bring back the nightmare of the 1940s.

For his part, Tuđman accused Serbs of being "war criminals" involved in a "dirty, undeclared war."[9] In the rhetorical war that ran parallel to the actual one, the war crimes accusation proved the most frequent and potentially the

---

4 Stephen Engelberg, "Croatia Ousts Defense Chief As Serbs Outgun Its Forces," *New York Times*, A2.
5 Misha Glenny, *The Fall of Yugoslavia: The Third Balkan War* (New York: Penguin Books, 1992), p. 134.
6 Ivo Goldstein, *Croatia: A History* (London: Hurst & Company, 1999), pp. 229 and 236; Chris Hedges, "Croatian's Confession Describes Torture and Killing on Vast Scale," *New York Times*, September 5, 1997, A1.
7 Marcus Tanner, *Croatia: A Nation Forged in War* (New Haven: Yale University Press, 2001), p. 253.
8 Chuck Sudetic, "Serbs Refuse to Negotiate in Croatia," *New York Times*, August 5, 1991, A6.
9 Ibid.

most damaging to either side. Croatia's interest in a war crimes tribunal lay in the hope that a court of law could raise its accusations to the level of acknowledged fact while exposing Milošević's accusations as fabrications.

Tuđman did little to help his image among Serbs or the international community with his purge of many Serbs from their posts in the police force[10] and civil service, and the writing of a new constitution that relegated Serbs to minority status and declared that Croatia was the homeland for the Croatian nation alone.[11] This new constitution annulled the previous one in which Croatia was an expressly multicultural society.[12] Tuđman also sought to revive Croatia's brief interlude with independence in order to build the foundation of the new Croatian state. He did so by restoring controversial Ustaša symbols, such as the white and red checkerboard Ustaša coat of arms as the centerpiece of the new Croatian flag and the use of the Kuna as the nation's currency. Tuđman's anti-Serb policies – as well as his previous disparaging remarks about Serbs and Jews and his claims that the number of Jews killed in the Holocaust was greatly exaggerated[13] – diluted Western sympathy for Croatian suffering and complicated Croatia's bid for self-determination.

Croatia's declaration of independence was the spark that set off an already tense and escalating conflict. Milošević's JNA forces and their Croatian Serb allies quickly overwhelmed Croatia's ill-equipped army, capturing much of Eastern Slavonia and the Krajina and cutting off Zagreb from key parts of the country. By the end of 1991, Serbian gains amounted to approximately one-third of Croatian territory. With the backing of Milošević, the Croatian Serbs declared an independent Serb state in the Krajina.

The JNA attacks on Vukovar, Dubrovnik, and other frontline towns had a devastating toll on Croatia, but fortified its emerging self-identity and representation of itself as a victim nation. This sense of victimization was magnified by the international community's failure to resolve the crisis despite repeated cease-fire agreements or to punish Serbia with sanctions. The JNA's relentless bombardment of the walled city of Dubrovnik on Croatia's Dalmatian coast focused international attention on the damage inflicted on a world heritage site. This, in turn, helped build international support for Croatia's campaign for independence. If to many Croatians and even some Western commentators[14] the siege of Dubrovnik did not receive the international attention it deserved, the attention paid to Dubrovnik was significantly greater than to the more dire humanitarian tragedy unfolding in Vukovar. In contrast to Dubrovnik, Vukovar "had no priceless architectural treasures to capture the world's fickle attention," Tanner writes.[15] The three-month siege of Vukovar, which reduced this city of

---

[10] Tanner, *Croatia: A Nation Forged in War*, p. 231.
[11] Ibid., p. 230.
[12] Ibid., p. 230.
[13] Elaine Sciolino, "Trading Villains' Horns for Halos," *New York Times*, October 8, 1995, E1.
[14] Anthony Lewis, "Where is the Outrage?" *New York Times*, November 4, 1991, A19.
[15] Tanner, *Croatia: A Nation Forged in War*, p. 261.

45,000 people on the Danube to ruins, constituted the first major atrocity of
the Balkan wars and was "a crime without parallel in post-war Europe."[16] The
atrocity was magnified when, after Vukovar fell in mid-November, Serb forces
murdered 261 Croatian wounded soldiers who sought refuge in the town's hospital.[17] The fall of Vukovar was a low-point for the beleaguered country and a
grim indication of the barbarity yet to come elsewhere in the Balkans.

B. Croatian Victimization and the Role of International Justice

For the Croatian government, a war crimes tribunal promised to shine an international spotlight on the country's suffering at Vukovar and elsewhere. On
November 22, 1991, five days after JNA troops captured Vukovar, the Croatian government issued a formal request to the UN to establish an international
tribunal, pronouncing itself "the victim of Serbian aggression."[18] The Croatian
government's call for a tribunal received little international notice at the UN or
in the international human rights community.

Despite daily television images of bloodshed on Europe's doorstep, the Croatian conflict was still regarded dismissively in the West as "the little war."[19] The
United States and Europe had a strong interest in downplaying the human cost
of the war both to help keep Yugoslavia united and to fend off calls for international intervention. Moreover, for the West, the urgency of Croatia's request
for a tribunal seemed to fade quickly once a cease-fire was announced. When
Croatia issued its call for a tribunal in late-November, the war with Serbia was
nearing an end after Croatia's crushing military defeats. To Western diplomats,
there was little reason for a tribunal despite the possibility that a quickly established and effective tribunal might have helped deter or slow Bosnia's descent
into war several months later.

It is also important to emphasize that in 1991 there was not yet an international consensus concerning the utility of creating war crimes tribunals to prosecute atrocities in the Balkans or elsewhere. The Bush administration had briefly
considered an idea to create a tribunal to prosecute Saddam Hussein for atrocities committed the year before in Kuwait, but the plan never materialized.[20]
At the time, international war crimes tribunals belonged to the distant past
of Nuremberg and Tokyo. Nevertheless, Croatia's call for a tribunal reflected
an astute understanding of the power that tribunals can confer to states, especially to states victimized in war and searching for international support. The
Zagreb government realized what the Bosnian Muslim and Tutsi-led Rwandan

---

[16] Misha Glenny, *The Fall of Yugoslavia*, p. 115.
[17] The story of the forensic investigation of the Vukovar massacre is poignantly told by Eric Stover
   and photographed by Gilles Peres in *The Graves: Srebrenica and Vukovar* (Zurich: Scalo, 1998).
[18] Government of the Republic of Croatia, *The White Paper on Cooperation with the International
   Tribunal*, p. 4.
[19] John Tagliabue, "Croatia's Dying Dream," *New York Times*, September 15, 1991, E2.
[20] U.S. Department of State Dispatch, November 12, 1990, Vol. I (11), p. 260, reporting President
   Bush's remarks on October 28, 1990.

governments would later come to understand: international prosecution of one's enemies can bestow an official international imprimatur of victim status on one's nation and ethnic group. With this status in hand, Croatia hoped to extract international diplomatic recognition for its declaration of independence.

The Croatian government's bid for a tribunal was part of a larger strategy that emphasized its victimization. "The key to Croatia's victim strategy," writes James Gow, "was to force international recognition of its independence: the more Croatian towns were attacked, the more likely it became that international support for Croatia would grow."[21] A veteran diplomat who worked in the Balkans during the war echoed this perspective in a 2001 interview: "The Croatian government was saying 'we are victims, we are victims.' That was their strategy. 'We must be seen as oppressed people ... in order to get our independence.'"[22] In contrast to Slovenia, which made strategic preparations for war with Serbia, Croatia may have deliberately stayed unprepared for war in order to enhance its victim status. According to a number of analysts as well as Tuđman's right-wing rival, Dobroslav Paraga, Tuđman deliberately starved Croatian troops of more arms and reinforcements to focus global attention on the country's victimization.[23] But when it came to the defense of Vukovar, Croatian forces resisted beyond expectations.

It is important to view Croatia's call for an international tribunal in the context of its bid for international recognition of statehood. To be sure, the ICTY did not actually affect Croatia's bid for recognition. After all, Croatia received diplomatic recognition from the European Community in January 1992, almost a year and a half before the Security Council created the ICTY. Yet, from the vantage point of November 1991, the Croatian government viewed a tribunal as providing leverage in its dual goals of gaining recognition and isolating Serbia. At the height of the war in Fall 1991, the fate of Croatia's bid for international recognition remained uncertain. Although Germany's early calls for recognition gave Croatia reason for optimism,[24] other European powers, notably Britain and France, appeared reticent.[25] Moreover, the United States and the UN had deep reservations about recognizing Croatia, fearing that such a step would spark another bloody conflict in Bosnia.[26]

Croatia's prospects for diplomatic recognition seemed to increase as Serbian attacks on Croatian civilians intensified. The victim strategy began to pay dividends when in late August 1991, Germany warned that increased Serb violence

[21] James Gow, *The Serbian Project and its Adversaries: A Strategy of War Crimes* (Montreal: McGill-Queen's University Press, 2003), p. 239.

[22] Fieldwork interview with former diplomat, The Hague, October 2001.

[23] Fieldwork interview with Dobroslav Paraga, Zagreb, December 2001. Also see Tanner, *Croatia: A Nation Forged in War*, pp. 265–266.

[24] Chuck Sudetic, "New Croatia Strife After Bonn Warning," *New York Times*, August 26, 1991, A3.

[25] Tanner, *Croatia: A Nation Forged in War*, pp. 272–273.

[26] David Binder, "West Now Split On Yugoslavia," *New York Times*, July 3, 1991, A1.

might compel Bonn to recognize Croatia.[27] Arguably, an international tribunal, if it became quickly operational, might have provided a wider stage
to showcase Croatia's suffering and generate an international consensus for
diplomatic recognition.

It was the tragedy in Bosnia, not the dormant war in Croatia, that prompted
the Security Council to create the ICTY in May 1993. Although Croatia's long-
held desire for a tribunal had finally been realized, events in Bosnia would eclipse
Croatia's standing as the primary victim of the Balkan wars. Still, time had
not diminished Croatia's hope that an international court would seek at least
some prosecutions of Serb atrocities against Croatians. Securing second place
in the hierarchy of international acknowledgment could still bolster Croatia's
international standing and reap significant political rewards. Moreover, the
trials could increase global condemnation of Serbia's wartime conduct and, in
turn, help to further delegitimize the Serb occupation of one-third of Croatian
territory. On a more practical level, an international tribunal also provided the
only way to ensure that high-level Serb suspects, who were living comfortably
under Milošević's protection in Serbia, would face trial. In line with its desire
to expose Serb crimes, the Croatian government provided ample cooperation
to tribunal investigators when they turned their attention to Serb atrocities.

C. *Croatia's Military Intervention in Bosnia: From Victim to Victimizer*

While the Croatian government retained a strong desire for the new tribunal,
it soon would also have cause to fear it and to withhold cooperation. The war
in Bosnia fundamentally altered Croatia's role in the Balkan conflict. Whereas
Croatia in 1991 had mainly been a victim, it later became an assailant in neighboring Bosnia together with its Bosnian Croat proxies. Croatia's shift from
victim to victimizer raised the likelihood that the tribunal would investigate
Bosnian Croat war crimes suspects and complicit high-level Croatian officials
in Zagreb.[28] Much had changed in the two years since Croatia issued its initial call for a tribunal. After first siding with the Bosnian Muslim government
based in Sarajevo,[29] Croatia in late 1992 and early 1993 became a perpetrator, in light of Tuđman's decision to use military force to ethnically cleanse
parts of central and western Bosnia in an effort to guarantee Croat dominance.
Milošević's quest for a Greater Serbia found its parallel in Tuđman's quest
for a Greater Croatia. Intervention in Bosnia was an integral part of Tuđman's
nationalistic vision for the extended boundaries of the Croatian nation. As early
as 1990, Tuđman publicly expressed his desire to incorporate parts of western

---

[27] Chuck Sudetic, "New Croatia Strife After Bonn Warning," *New York Times*, August 26, 1991,
A3.

[28] In contrast to the ICTR's jurisdiction, which was limited to the time frame of January 1 through
December 31, 1994, the ICTY's jurisdiction was more open-ended. That meant that the ICTY
could investigate and bring indictments for serious violations of international humanitarian law
that took place in the territory of the former Yugoslavia from 1991 through the end of the
Balkan wars.

[29] Goldstein, *Croatia: A History*, p. 243.

Bosnia into Croatia. In 1991, Tuđman and Milošević reportedly agreed to divide Bosnia between themselves.[30] Squeezed by the Serbs and the Croats, Bosnian Muslim civilians stood to suffer the most as did the principle of a multi-ethnic state that the Sarajevo government represented. Choosing between Milošević and Tuđman, Bosnian President Alija Izetbegović once remarked, was akin to choosing between "leukemia and a brain tumor."[31]

Bosnian Croat forces, directed and armed by the Croatian government in Zagreb, launched attacks on Muslim civilians in central and western Bosnia in early 1993. In mid-April, approximately a month before the UN created the tribunal, Bosnian Croat forces committed their first massacre against Bosnian Muslim civilians, killing 117 civilians in the village of Ahmići.[32] The atrocities at Ahmići would become a major focus of the tribunal's Bosnian Croat case files. For the next year, a Croat–Muslim war ensued with both sides committing atrocities, although the Croat forces were accused of committing more of them.

Just as Milošević claimed that Belgrade had no hand in the Bosnian Serb violence, Tuđman maintained that Zagreb had clean hands in the Bosnian Croat violence. The declaration of a Bosnian Croat state in July 1992 was aimed at bolstering the argument that ethnic Croats were acting independently of the Croatian government.[33] But Zagreb came under fire from the international community for its part in ethnic cleansing. Still, international criticism was muted and did not lead to punishment. In contrast to the punitive measures it imposed against Serbia, the Security Council did not impose sanctions against Croatia. The Serbs, not the Croats, were perceived as the main culprits of the Balkans since their atrocities were committed on a larger scale. Furthermore, Western governments found themselves highly dependent on Tuđman since Croatia was caring for almost 300,000 Muslim refugees driven from Bosnia by the Serbs.[34]

Croatia's military intervention in Bosnia and its direct and indirect role in atrocities against Bosnian Muslim civilians undermined the government's assertion that it was the central victim of the Balkan wars. The war in Bosnia "damaged Croatia immeasurably," the Croatian historian Ivo Goldstein writes. "It lost Croats and Croatia the status of victim to which at earlier stages they could reasonably have laid claim."[35] Croatian war crimes in Bosnia planted the seeds for the government's subsequent defiance of the tribunal.

By 1994, the course of the Balkan war had changed again. Under intense American pressure, the erstwhile war between Croats and Muslims in Bosnia

---

[30] Hervé Clerc, "Last PM of the former Yugoslavia testifies against Milošević," *Agence France-Presse*, October 23, 2003.

[31] Roger Cohen, "Balkan Leaders Face an Hour for Painful Choices," *New York Times*, November 1, 1995, A1.

[32] Goldstein, *Croatia: A History*, p. 246.

[33] The Bosnian Croat state, which was called the Croat Union of Herceg-Bosna, was led by Mate Boban.

[34] Tanner, *Croatia: A Nation Forged in War*, p. 288.

[35] Goldstein, *Croatia: A History*, p. 247.

now made way for a military and political alliance aimed at defeating the superior Serb forces. In March 1994, the Croat–Muslim alliance was formalized in Washington. Tuđman's belated conciliation earned him appreciation among U.S. officials who hoped to use Croatia to counter Serb power in the Balkans. At the signing ceremony, President Clinton applauded Tuđman as a man of peace.[36] But Croatia's actions would continue to expose it to tribunal scrutiny. For Croatia, the image of the ICTY as a double-edged sword would become more pertinent with time.

4.3 Atrocities at Home: Croatian War Crimes During the Homeland War

Croatia's largest military campaigns – as well as its most egregious wartime atrocities – were yet to come. Since its stinging defeat at the hands of Serb forces in 1991, Croatia had steadily built up its armed forces in preparation to retake the one-third of the country lost to the JNA and breakaway Croatian Serbs.[37] As a prelude to a larger assault, Tuđman ordered an attack on Croatian Serb positions near the city of Zadar in the Krajina region of Croatia in January 1993. The attack succeeded. Then, in September 1993, Croatian armed forces launched another attack south of Gospić in the Medak Pocket area of the Krajina. During the operation, Croatian soldiers captured several villages and then killed more than 100 Serbs, including elderly civilians and several captured and wounded Serb soldiers. The atrocities would be the target of tribunal investigations and the subject of subsequent indictments against the Army's Chief of Staff, Janko Bobetko, and another top general, Rahim Ademi. For Tuđman, the Medak Pocket atrocities backfired by sparking international criticism that compelled Croatian forces to withdraw from the captured villages.[38,39] Nevertheless, international attention was still focused mainly on Serb excesses in Bosnia. Tuđman's agreement with Izetbegović to form a Croat–Muslim alliance greatly improved Tuđman's international standing, making it easier for the United States and some European countries to turn a blind eye to Croatia's next attempts to retake Serb-held territory in the Krajina.

In May and August of 1995, the Croatian military launched two military campaigns aimed at capturing the areas lost to Serb forces four years earlier. The May attack, dubbed Operation Flash, recovered Western Slavonia in less than two days and forced 18,000 Serbs to flee Croatia.[40] The August attack, named Operation Storm, was the bigger of the two military actions. In Operation

[36] Elaine Sciolino, "Trading Villains' Horns for Halos," *New York Times*, October 8, 1995, E1.

[37] During 1994 and 1995, retired U.S. army officials working under the auspices of a private company helped train Croatian forces. Roger Cohen, *Hearts Grown Brutal: Sagas of Sarajevo* (New York: Random House, 1998), pp. 303–318.

[38] Tanner, *Croatia: A Nation Forged in War*, p. 291; Goldstein, *Croatia: A History*, p. 250.

[39] Croatian soldiers destroyed Serb houses and barns before leaving the area. See Tanner, *Croatia: A Nation Forged in War*, p. 291.

[40] Laura Silber and Allan Little, *Yugoslavia: Death of a Nation* (New York: Penguin Books, 1997), p. 353.

Storm, a Croatian force of between 100,000 and 200,000 soldiers[41] recovered the entire Krajina region in just eighty-four hours. The rapid victory was facilitated by Milošević's broken promise to come to the aid of the Croatian Serbs in the event of an attack by Zagreb.[42] For Tuđman, the victories in Flash and Storm marked the fulfillment of Croatia's "thousand-year old dream" for independence[43] and established Croatia as the sole winner of the Balkan conflict. "The champagne corks can be opened in Zagreb – nowhere else," Misha Glenny wrote in a *New York Times* op-ed piece.[44]

Celebration in Zagreb was anguish for Croatian Serb civilians. Croatian forces involved in Storm were implicated in the murder of hundreds of elderly Serbian civilians and the destruction and looting of thousands of Serb houses. Some of the killings of elderly civilians occurred well after Storm had concluded and Croatian forces had won control of the Krajina. The military campaign, which included shelling of residential areas,[45] also led to the ethnic cleansing of 150,000 to 200,000 Serb civilians, who fled to neighboring Serbia.[46] As with its military actions in Bosnia, Croatia was criticized by some in the international community, most notably France, Britain, and Russia.[47,48] However, the United States and Germany refrained from condemning Operation Storm.[49,50]

For Washington, Croatia's resurgence came at a propitious time since it greatly weakened Milošević and increased his incentive to negotiate an end to the Balkan conflict, which he would do several months later in Dayton, Ohio.[51] On the eve of both of Croatia's 1995 assaults to regain the Krajina, U.S. diplomats grew silent, which to many observers was interpreted in Zagreb as a green light for military action.[52] At this point in the war, Croatia had become, as a top United States diplomat opined, America's "junkyard dogs."[53] Yet, the United States had an interest in not having its junkyard dog become too unruly since such behavior could embarrass Washington. The U.S. Ambassador to Croatia,

---

[41] Tanner, *Croatia: A Nation Forged in War*, p. 296; Goldstein, *Croatia: A History*, p. 253; Croatian Helsinki Committee for Human Rights, *Military Operation Storm and its Aftermath Report*, Zagreb, 2001, p. 11.

[42] Silber and Little, *Yugoslavia: Death of a Nation*, p. 353.

[43] Ibid., 298.

[44] As quoted in Holbrooke, *To End a War*, p. 170. Also, see Silber and Little, *Yugoslavia: Death of a Nation*, p. 345.

[45] In reference to the shelling in the Krajina, a Western diplomat told the *New York Times*: "With shelling like this, people don't stay. This is the goal . . ." Jane Perlez, "Serb Chief's Response to Events is Restrained," *New York Times*, August 5, 1995, A4.

[46] Silber and Little, *Yugoslavia: Death of a Nation*, p. 358.

[47] Goldstein, *Croatia: A History*, p. 254.

[48] Tanner, *Croatia: A Nation Forged in War*, p. 298.

[49] Ibid., p. 298.

[50] For a discussion of the split between Europe and the United States over Operation Storm, see Holbrooke, *To End a War*, pp. 72–73.

[51] Ibid., pp. 72–73.

[52] Roger Cohen, "Balkan Leaders Face an Hour for Painful Choices," *New York Times*, November 1, 1995, A1.

[53] Holbrooke, *To End a War*, p. 73.

Peter Galbraith, reportedly told Tudman that he would not protest Operation Storm provided that the war was kept "short and clean."[54] American officials hoped to have their cake and eat it too by supporting Tudman's offensive while discouraging human rights abuses against Serbs. However, there was a fundamental contradiction in U.S. policy, since a central aim of Tudman's Krajina offensive was to expel Serbs. Neither U.S. urging nor the prospect of tribunal investigations appeared to temper Tudman's bid to "rid [Croatia] of its historical cross."[55] Chief Prosecutor Goldstone, however, maintains that Croatian leaders paid close attention to the tribunal, which prompted them to call on their troops to abide by the rules of war and not to harm civilians during Operation Storm.[56] Yet that call appears to have been meant for international consumption, given the evidence that has surfaced indicating that Tudman ordered his troops to ethnically cleanse the Krajina. A confident Tudman, who was at the peak of his power after his battlefield victories, gambled that he could ward off attempts by the fledgling tribunal to search for incriminating evidence of Croatian atrocities in Storm just as he had long avoided international ostracism for his wartime conduct.

Tudman, however, was not blasé when it came to the potential threat posed by the ICTY. Before the tribunal began to investigate Storm, Croatian and other government officials crafted a vigorous defense of the army's conduct, insisting that it fought a perfectly clean war of national liberation. In foreshadowing the defense it would mount when the tribunal accused Zagreb of non-compliance, the government claimed that the ICTY had no legal right to scrutinize the army's conduct since it was not possible to commit war crimes during a defensive war, which in their view, referred to all actions taken by the army inside Croatia from the start of the war in 1991 through its end in 1995. Croatian officials also tried to forestall tribunal investigations by claiming, again erroneously, that Flash and Storm were domestic police actions and of such short duration that they were not subject to the tribunal's jurisdiction. The Croatian media usually echoed these arguments and rarely represented contrary views.[57] From an early date, Croatian officials also dismissed international criticism of the army's conduct as unjust attempts to discredit Croatia's newly won sovereignty. Croatia's new identity as an independent nation went hand in hand with its understanding of itself as both a victor and a victim, but not as a victimizer.

When it came to refuting international criticism of Flash and Storm, Tudman maintained that the Serbs had left the Krajina of their own accord. "The fact that 90 percent of them have left is their problem," he remarked a year after the war.[58] But Tudman's apparent delight at having a virtually pure Croatian state

---

[54] Silber and Little, *Yugoslavia: Death of a Nation*, p. 360.
[55] Roger Cohen, "Balkan Leaders Face an Hour for Painful Choices," *New York Times*, November 1, 1995, A1.
[56] Goldstone, *For Humanity*, p. 125.
[57] Josipović, *The Hague Implementing Criminal Law*, p. 229.
[58] Samantha Power, "Croatia's Threat to Peace," *New York Times*, July 18, 1996, A23.

raised doubt about his denials of Croatian culpability, as seen in the following pledge he gave to his generals a few months after the war: "We have resolved the Serbian question. There will never be 12 percent of Serbs" in Croatia again.[59] Even during Croatia's democratic era, government officials would insist that no ethnic cleansing occurred in Flash and Storm. But evidence provided by human rights organizations, including the Croatian Helsinki Watch[60] and later by tribunal investigators, revealed that it was government policy to cleanse the Krajina of Serbs through indiscriminate shelling of civilian centers[61] and the harassment and murder of Serbs who remained in their homes. This ethnic cleansing may have been permanently achieved because most Croatian Serbs had not returned to their homes almost a decade later.[62] Tudman publicly welcomed the Serbs to return, though both his warning to prosecute Serb war criminals[63] and the many subsequent domestic trials that took place – which were strongly criticized by international observers for lacking adequate due process guarantees for defendants – spread fear among Serbs of collective punishment.[64]

Although Tudman refused to cooperate with investigations of Operations Flash and Storm, he could never be certain how much evidence the prosecution had gathered from other sources and thus how close it was to handing down indictments. As early as November 1995 and early 1996, the European and the U.S. media reported that Defense Minister Gojko Šušak[65] and Tudman would soon be indicted. Interestingly, Goldstone seemed disturbed by the rumors. In an apparent sign of his desire to maintain good relations with Zagreb, Goldstone issued a press release denying that an indictment of Tudman was imminent.[66] But Tudman remained wary. By 1999, the Croatian president was reportedly convinced that he would face indictment.[67]

4.4 Croatian Cooperation and the Handover of Bosnian Croat Suspects

Croatia's defiance of the tribunal in regard to Homeland War investigations stood in contrast to its relative willingness to cooperate with investigations of Bosnian Croat suspects. The transfer of Bosnian Croats for war crimes committed in Bosnia was less politically sensitive than the transfer of Croatian army

[59] Raymond Bonner, "Harsh Verdict on Croatia," New York Times, March 3, 1999, A1.

[60] Fieldwork interviews with Croatian Helsinki Watch official, Zagreb, November and December 2001.

[61] Raymond Bonner, "Croat Army Takes Rebel Stronghold in Rapid Advance," New York Times, August 6, 1995, A1.

[62] Tanner, Croatia: A Nation Forged in War, p. 298.

[63] Ibid., p. 298.

[64] Fieldwork interviews with Organization for Security and Cooperation in Europe officials, Zagreb, December 2001.

[65] BOSNEWS Digest 471, November 19, 1995.

[66] Statement by the Prosecutor, ICTY press release, June 28, 1996.

[67] Raymond Bonner, "Croatia Branded as Another Balkans Pariah," New York Times, March 3, 1999, A1.

generals, since the Bosnian Croats were lower-level suspects and the military intervention in Bosnia was not as strongly supported in Croatia as was the Homeland War, which was an independence struggle fought inside Croatia. Nevertheless, handing over Bosnian Croat suspects also posed a danger to Tudman because his government played a direct role in the Bosnian conflict. As we will see, Tudman tried his best to withhold evidence that could lead to his own indictment.

Tudman yielded to the tribunal on the Bosnian Croat question in the face of concerted international pressure and the threat of economic and political retribution. To minimize the potential domestic fallout of bowing to such pressure, Tudman insisted that the suspects he sent to The Hague had surrendered voluntarily. The Western media often repeated Tudman's contention as fact even though Bosnian Croat suspects were usually forced to turn themselves in or face arrest. "I think it was as voluntary as going to the electric chair," Richard Goldstone told me in a 2003 interview.[68] "They were told probably what would happen to them and to their families if they didn't hand themselves over."

These transfers of Bosnian Croat suspects, coming in the face of continued defiance by Milošević and the Bosnian Serbs and the initial refusal of NATO peacekeepers to arrest fugitives in Bosnia, heightened the tribunal's dependence on Zagreb for arrests. Without assistance from Croatia, the tribunal's detention center would have remained virtually empty, rendering the tribunal's future increasingly uncertain. The court's reliance on Tudman, and the fact that he did actually hand over Bosnian Croat suspects, presented a quandary for Goldstone and his successor, Louise Arbour. Tribunal prosecutors likely feared that moving too vigorously to press Croatia to cooperate with Homeland War investigations would provoke Tudman's enmity and, in turn, spark resistance even on the question of the Bosnian Croats.

There is no evidence that the tribunal quashed or even slowed its investigations of the Croatian army's conduct role in the Homeland War. But for several years after the end of the war, the ICTY did not turn Tudman's refusal to cooperate on the Homeland War into a major issue. Despite Tudman's bold defiance – seen in his refusals to even acknowledge tribunal jurisdiction over the Homeland War – tribunal officials did not challenge Croatia in the Security Council on this crucial issue until late August 1999. When it came to cooperation with Homeland War investigations, ICTY officials preferred to emphasize quiet diplomacy in Zagreb and Western capitals. When asked in an interview why the ICTY did not make more of an issue of Tudman's defiance, Deputy Prosecutor Graham Blewitt told me that negotiations with Croatian authorities, while not achieving the tribunal's goals, did in fact yield some cooperation.[69] However, it is unclear whether the tribunal's reliance on a conciliatory strategy yielded enough cooperation to warrant such an approach. On the other hand,

[68] Fieldwork interview with Richard J. Goldstone, Pasadena, April 2003.
[69] Fieldwork interview with Graham Blewitt, The Hague, December 2003.

it is uncertain whether using an adversarial approach would have led to better results, at least while Tuđman remained in power.

4.5 The Blaškić Indictment: Cooperation on Tuđman's Terms

In mid-1995, Chief Prosecutor Goldstone signaled his intent to move beyond indictments of Serb suspects by also targeting Croat suspects. On August 29, Goldstone indicted Ivica Rajić, a Bosnian Croat. On November 10, the tribunal indicted six more Bosnian Croat suspects, including Tihomir Blaškić, a Bosnian Croat general, and Dario Kordić, an influential Bosnian Croat leader, for their role in the 1993 massacre of Bosnian Muslim civilians in Ahmići. In the Western press, these later indictments were overshadowed by the ongoing Dayton peace talks and by the tribunal's indictment, also on November 10, of three Serb suspects charged in connection with the massacre of Croatian civilians at Vukovar. The focus on Serb wrongdoing intensified six days later when the tribunal handed down indictments against Bosnian Serb President Radovan Karadžić and Bosnian Serb General Ratko Mladić. Even as the tribunal began to shift attention to Croat suspects, the international media remained focused primarily on Serbian atrocities.

Nevertheless, when the prosecution began to target Croat suspects, it did so strategically. Although remaining heavily dependent on Croatia and on international willingness to press Croatia to cooperate, the chief prosecutor still had the power to utilize strategies that could increase the prospect of state compliance. The strategic timing of indictments is an important tool at the disposal of the chief prosecutor, as demonstrated by Goldstone's decision to indict Bosnian Croat suspects *during* the Dayton peace talks and close in time to his indictment of Serb suspects.[70] By indicting the six Bosnian Croat suspects during Dayton, Goldstone made it difficult for Tuđman as well as U.S. negotiators to ignore the cooperation issue. In turn, Goldstone increased the likelihood that a provision binding the Balkan leaders to cooperate with the tribunal would become part of a peace agreement. And by indicting the Bosnian Croats close in time to his indictment of the Vukovar Three suspects, Goldstone signaled his intent to pursue Croat suspects with much the same vigor as he pursued Serb suspects. Although the timing of Goldstone's indictments did not lead to a firm agreement on state cooperation at Dayton, it did put the issue of Croatian cooperation squarely on the U.S. agenda. Within days of the indictment, U.S.

[70] The chief prosecutor does not have full control as to the exact timing of the official release of an indictment since a trial judge determines whether and when to confirm an indictment. However, the chief prosecutor can usually expect an indictment to be confirmed (provided that sufficient supporting evidence is submitted) soon after it is sent to the judiciary for review. In the situation discussed here, Goldstone filed the indictment against the six Bosnian Croats on November 2 and a trial judge confirmed the indictment on November 10. See "The Vice-President of Herceg-Bosna and Five Other Prominent Bosnian Croats Indicted for the 'Ethnic Cleansing' of the Lasva Valley," ICTY press release, November 13, 1995.

officials publicly called on Tuđman to transfer Blaškić, the top indicted Bosnian Croat suspect, to The Hague.[71]

The need for the tribunal to proceed strategically vis-à-vis the Croatian government was underscored by Tuđman's defiant response to the indictment of the Bosnian Croat suspects. A day after Blaškić's indictment, Tuđman appointed the Bosnian Croat general to a senior post in the Croatian army. Several days after the Blaškić promotion, the United States ambassador to Croatia, Peter Galbraith, warned Tuđman that American patience was already growing thin. "The only appointment General Blaškić can legally have now is with the international war crimes tribunal," Galbraith said.[72] Importantly, tribunal officials did not let Tuđman's defiance go unanswered, which in turn may have made it more difficult for the United States to remain silent. Goldstone and ICTY President Cassese sought and received international media attention to shame Tuđman for failing to arrest Blaškić and other Bosnian Croat suspects. At the same time, the tribunal pursued a conciliatory strategy, through visits with Croatian leaders in Zagreb, to try to persuade the government to cooperate. The tribunal's diplomatic meetings appeared to focus on two priorities: transferring Blaškić to The Hague and having the Croatian parliament adopt a domestic law on cooperation with the tribunal. Perhaps in a small concession to Tuđman, tribunal officials did not publicly press Zagreb as hard for the transfer of the five other suspects.[73]

In the wake of the early failures to implement the Dayton Accords, the United States put pressure on both Croatia and Serbia to honor their commitments on a range of issues, including cooperation with the tribunal. However, Washington exerted considerably more pressure on Croatia in the hope that its Balkan ally would be more vulnerable and that Zagreb's compliance would trigger a domino effect throughout the former Yugoslavia. The Clinton administration continued to press Croatia to hand over Blaškić through appeals by U.S. Secretary of State Warren Christopher[74] and Defense Secretary William J. Perry.[75] Under intense pressure from Tuđman, Blaškić "voluntarily" surrendered to Croatian authorities and was transferred to the tribunal on April 1, 1996.[76]

Despite his iron grip on power, Tuđman could ill afford to ignore how his handling of the cooperation issue might damage his domestic image. Indeed, aiding the tribunal's prosecution of Croatian suspects was controversial enough

---

[71] Dubravko Grakalić and Davor Ivanković, "Galbraith: The Croatian authorities are obligated to arrest and hand over suspects," *Globus*, No. 258, November 17, 1995.

[72] "U.S. tells Croatia: Hand over war crimes suspects," *Reuter's Information Service*, November 15, 1995; Wayne Corey, "Croatia/War Crimes Update," *Voice of America*, November 15, 1995.

[73] "President Cassese Takes Stock of Current Cooperation Between Croatia, the F.R.Y. and the Tribunal," ICTY press release, February 6, 1996.

[74] "Blaškić ready to give himself in to The Hague: lawyer," *Agence France-Presse*, March 1, 1996.

[75] Chris Hedges, "Croatia Arrests a Bosnian Croat Accused of War Crimes," *New York Times*, June 10, 1996, A8.

[76] "How Tuđman and Šušak sacrificed Blaškić," *Nacional*, July 2000, http://www.balkanpeace.org/hed/archive/july00/hed390.shtml.

to drive a wedge in the Zagreb government. At the same time, Tuđman's power and nationalist credentials underscored the fact that state cooperation may actually be considerably easier for an authoritarian and nationalist regime that can effectively contain protest than for a democratic government that cannot as easily do so. When he so desired, Tuđman could deliver war crimes suspects to The Hague – albeit Bosnian Croat suspects – without sparking a major political crisis on the home front.

Tuđman, however, had no plans to cooperate with Blaškić's defense, given his concerns that the Bosnian Croat general would use the evidence controlled by the government to shift blame to Zagreb.[77] Before leaving for The Hague, Blaškić expressed fear that he was being set up by Tuđman to take the fall for the massacres at Ahmići.[78] Blaškić soon realized that his fears were well-founded when Tuđman blocked his defense from obtaining evidence and access to key witnesses that might exonerate him. In many respects, Blaškić's attorneys, and other defense teams at the ICTY and ICTR, faced greater obstacles than the prosecution in their quest for state cooperation. At both tribunals, the Office of the Prosecutor had the institutional strength, diplomatic resources, and the personage of the chief prosecutor with which to battle states. But the small defense teams, which were often overburdened with their investigative and courtroom tasks, had little means to lobby states effectively.[79] In the Blaškić case, Tuđman managed to fend off efforts by both the defense and prosecution for access to valuable evidence.

Nevertheless, Blaškić's transfer to The Hague was an important victory for the fledgling tribunal, which until that point did not have such a high-ranking suspect in custody, and in fact only had two other suspects in custody. The tribunal's early decision to broaden its investigations beyond Serb war crimes was beginning to pay dividends. But the tribunal's growing success in filling its empty cells with Bosnian Croat suspects would, in Croatian eyes, produce an imbalance in the ethnic distribution of war crimes suspects awaiting trial in The Hague.

Although Tuđman could be as openly insolent as Milošević – as demonstrated by the Blaškić promotion – he also came to realize the importance of presenting a moderate and law-abiding image to the international community. Toward that end, Tuđman resisted the prosecution's request to provide investigators with access to state archives by lodging a formal appeal with the tribunal that contested its right to issue subpoenas demanding sensitive evidence.[80] At

---

[77] Marlise Simons, "Hague War Crimes Tribunal Frees a Convicted General," *New York Times*, July 30, 2004, A4.

[78] Ibid.

[79] Fieldwork interviews with ICTY and ICTR defense attorneys, The Hague, October-November 2001 and in Arusha, May-June 2000 and February-July 2002.

[80] Deputy Prime Minister Ljerka Mintas-Hodak characterized the government's approach in the following words: "We shall make use of all legal means at our disposal." "Deputy premier says Croatia will not release papers to The Hague," *BBC Monitoring International Reports, Original Source: Croatian TV satellite service*, Zagreb, July 21, 1997.

the heart of Croatia's appeal lay an attempt to win a national security exemption that would prevent tribunal investigators from gaining access to states
archives now and in the future.[81] This appeal and the prosecution's response
sparked a drawn-out "trial of cooperation" that actually took place inside one
of the tribunal's courtrooms. The battle over whether the Croatian government
would have to hand over evidence in the Blaškić case was fought in a series
of procedural hearings pitting the prosecution against Croatian government
lawyers.

Croatia's appeal sought to test the limits of the tribunal's seemingly unre-
strained authority to trump state sovereignty. The ICTY Appeals Chamber's
ruling benefited both the tribunal and the Croatian government. The Chamber ruled that the prosecution had the legal right to issue binding orders on
states, although it had to submit such orders to the state and not to particular government officials. The Chamber addressed Croatia's bid for a national
security exemption by ruling that states may invoke national security when
refusing to hand over documents. However, the tribunal also had the authority to take measures to ensure that the state's national security claim was
legitimate.[82]

Tribunal officials hailed the ruling as a pivotal moment in the tribunal's fight
for state cooperation insofar as it confirmed the prosecution's legal primacy
over states. "Everybody stopped whining, saying there's no political will, no
one helps us," recalled Chief Prosecutor Arbour. "All of a sudden we started to
have a self-perception which was accurate. We have a huge amount of power."[83]
The tribunal's growing sense of its own authority appeared to give it more confidence when engaging Croatia and other Balkan states for cooperation. However, it has been overlooked by some tribunal observers that in the Blaškić case,
state power actually trumped the legal authority of the international tribunal.
Tuđman simply ignored the Appeals Chamber's ruling to hand over evidence
badly needed by the prosecution. In this and other cases, the tribunal found
that, in contrast to obtaining custody of fugitives, it was often much more difficult to engage international attention with the more mundane, but hardly less
important challenge of gaining access to evidence.

Blaškić's defense was dealt a major blow by the Croatian government's
refusal to hand over archival evidence that might have mitigated his culpability by demonstrating Tuđman's direct role in the Ahmići massacres. In early
2000, the tribunal convicted Blaškić for his actions at Ahmići and sentenced
him to a forty-five-year prison term, which at that point was the longest sentence handed down by ICTY judges. In July 2004, however, Blaškić won a
major victory when the Appeals Chamber granted him a partial acquittal and
drastically reduced his sentence after his defense attorneys finally gained access
to exculpatory evidence withheld by Tuđman during the 1990s.

[81] "Croatia will not release classified information to Hague war crimes tribunal," *BBC Monitoring
    International Reports, Original Source: HINA News Agency*, Zagreb, July 29, 1997.
[82] Josipović, *The Hague Implementing Criminal Law*, pp. 221–228.
[83] Ignatieff, *Virtual War*, p. 127.

4.6 The Cooperation Law Debate

President Tudman initially resisted tribunal calls to adopt a domestic law[84] on cooperation since it would further oblige Croatia to aid tribunal investigations and prosecutions and provide the legal mechanisms to facilitate such cooperation. As with the Blaškić transfer, Tudman acquiesced in the face of intense international pressure. And as with the Blaškić case, Tudman quickly turned an apparent defeat into a victory of sorts. In time, the Croatian leader came to realize that passage of the cooperation law might actually serve his interests insofar it could enable Croatia to win praise internationally as a law-abiding state. That, in turn, gave the Croatian government a respite from renewed international pressure to send more suspects to the tribunal. After adoption of the cooperation law in April 1996, a year passed before the international community exerted serious pressure on Tudman to hand over more Bosnian Croat war crimes suspects. Tudman used Croatia's relatively early adoption of the law (in contrast to Milošević's refusal to consider doing the same) as a constant reminder of his commitment to the tribunal, even as he placed obstacles in the court's path.

The law, and the issue of cooperation more generally, was a source of conflict within the HDZ (Croation Democratic Union) leadership, with Foreign Minister Mate Granić favoring greater cooperation and Defense Minister Šušak taking a hard-line stance against the tribunal.[85] Anti-tribunal voices, both within and outside Tudman's governing HDZ party,[86] opposed the law even though Croatia had already consented to cooperate with the tribunal at Dayton. The parliamentary debates preceding passage of the law provide a rare window into the divisive nature of the cooperation issue during the Tudman era and foreshadowed the more severe divisions that would rent Croatian politics in the aftermath of authoritarian rule.

During the debates, opponents focused on the flaws of the tribunal and on the unwelcome prospect of the tribunal's trumping state sovereignty.[87] HDZ officials aligned with Tudman found themselves in the uncomfortable position of articulating the importance of cooperation, something that they had rarely done with domestic audiences. Granić tacitly criticized opponents in parliament for hypocrisy by reminding them that Croatia was the country that originally proposed the creation of a tribunal in the aftermath of the destruction of Vukovar.[88] Still, some members of parliament, particularly from Tudman's HDZ party, accused the government of selling out nationalist ideals.[89]

---

[84] Between 1994 and 1995, ICTY President Cassese issued four requests to Croatia to adopt a domestic law on cooperation. See "President Cassese Takes Stock of Current Co-Operation Between Croatia, The F.R.Y. and the Tribunal," ICTY press release, February 6, 1996.

[85] "Newspaper says party split over Hague tribunal," *BBC Monitoring Original Source: Globus*, Zagreb, February 23, 1996.

[86] Ibid.

[87] Josipović, *The Hague Implementing Criminal Law*, p. 207.

[88] Ibid., p. 211.

[89] Ibid., p. 209.

Following adoption of the cooperation law, Tuđman took an increasingly defiant stance toward the tribunal. In 1997, he warned that those Croatians who cooperated with the ICTY would face punishment at home. A short time later, he accused Stjepan Mesić, then a leading opposition figure, of being a traitor for giving the tribunal documents related to a war crimes investigation.[90]

The new law bought Tuđman time to delay actual progress on cooperation, but not as much time as he had hoped. What Tuđman presented as sufficient cooperation was deemed inadequate by the tribunal. In this respect, the tribunal's scrutiny of Croatia's cooperation record and its ability to garner international press attention underscored its growing "soft power" and its emerging role as an influential actor in the trials of cooperation. During the second half of 1996 and the first half of 1997, Goldstone and Cassese took steps to shame Croatia. In June, Cassese called on Western nations to expel both Croatia and Serbia from the upcoming Summer Olympics in Atlanta.[91] In September, Cassese lodged the tribunal's first formal report of non-compliance against Croatia at the Security Council.

Croatian and Serbian athletes went on to compete at the Atlanta games, and the tribunal's call for sanctions did not translate into UN sanctions. Yet the ICTY's actions were not in vain, since they served to undermine Croatia's claims that it was cooperating with the tribunal. While the Security Council failed to take action, Europe appeared to take the matter more seriously. In May, the Council of Europe voted to delay Croatia's entry into the organization, sending a clear message that Zagreb's quest to gain a foothold in Europe was in jeopardy without significant progress on cooperation. As international pressure mounted, Tuđman told domestic audiences that he would not bow to the "humiliating conditions" set forth by the Council of Europe.[92] However, he made certain to present a more palatable message to international audiences.

4.7 The 1997 Transfers of Bosnian Croat Suspects

The Blaškić transfer and the adoption of the cooperation law revealed that concerted international pressure could force Tuđman's hand. Croatia's decision to turn over eleven Bosnian Croat suspects in 1997 demonstrated above all the decisive role of Western pressure and Croatia's abiding desire to gain entrance into European institutions.

The Council of Europe's rejection of Croatia's bid for entry in early June 1996 quickly forced Tuđman to improve his worsening international image. The Croatian government took the rare step of actually arresting a Bosnian Croat suspect, rather than arranging for his "voluntary" surrender, when it

90 Human Rights Watch World Report, 1998.
91 "The President of the International Criminal Tribunal for the Former Yugoslavia calls for a sports boycott," ICTY press release, June 13, 1996.
92 "Tuđman lashes out at 'humiliating' Council of Europe conditions," *Agence France-Presse*, May 25, 1996.

apprehended Zlatko Aleksovski, a relatively minor suspect, on June 9. But Tudman made no moves to arrest several other higher-level Bosnian Croat suspects living freely in Croatia.[93] While Zagreb initially won some international points with the Aleksovski arrest, it soon lost them because of its efforts to block Aleksovski's transfer to the ICTY by making the dubious claim of the suspect's ill health. That would mark the first of Zagreb's repeated attempts to use illness as a pretext to block the tribunal from gaining custody of suspects.

International pressure soon mounted in an effort to force Croatia to send Aleksovski, and particularly Dario Kordić and Ivica Rajić, to The Hague.[94] In a warning to Croatia, the United States applied financial pressure, first to force Tudman to transfer Aleksovski to the ICTY in April 1997, and then to hand over ten more Bosnian Croat suspects in October. In July, Washington used its influence in the World Bank to postpone indefinitely the approval of a badly needed $30 million loan to Croatia.[95] Then, in September, the United States called on the Council of Europe to suspend Croatia's membership (which had been invited to join the organization after the arrest of Aleksovski) because of its failure to make progress on cooperation and to do more to resettle Serb refugees. Tudman denounced such pressure as "immoral"[96] and insisted that Croatia had no plans to sell out the Bosnian Croat suspects. "We don't want to trade people for loans," said Prime Minister Zlatko Mateša.[97] But in the end, Tudman capitulated. Just a year earlier, Dario Kordić enjoyed the protection of the Croatian government, and on one occasion had reportedly sat behind Tudman at a concert.[98] In early October 1997, Tudman arranged for the "voluntary" surrenders of Kordić and nine other Bosnian Croat suspects.[99]

The handover of the Bosnian Croat suspects softened tribunal and international criticism of Croatia. However, their transfer did not lead to a similar increase in cooperation in other vital areas, such as granting tribunal investigators access to archival evidence needed in the prosecution of these suspects.

4.8 Croatia's Counter-Shaming Offensive

At various points during its trials of cooperation with the Croatian government, the tribunal exhibited the capacity to utilize power of its own to influence the outcome of its struggle with Zagreb. The tribunal did so in large part, as

---

[93] Chris Hedges, "Croatia Arrests a Bosnian Croat Accused of War Crimes," *New York Times*, June 10, 1996, A8.

[94] "US envoy demands Yugoslavia hand over five men accused of war crimes," *BBC Monitoring International Reports, Original Source: HINA News Agency*, Zagreb, September 18, 1997.

[95] Ibid.

[96] "Croatian premier says conditions set for receiving foreign aid 'immoral,'" *BBC Monitoring International Reports, Original Source: HINA News Agency*, Zagreb, September 19, 1997.

[97] Ibid.

[98] Samantha Power, "Croatia's Threat to Peace," *New York Times*, July 18, 1996, A23.

[99] Rajić remained at large and was not transferred to the tribunal until 2003.

Goldstone acknowledged, "simply by going public"[100] and keeping the cooperation issue in the global spotlight. But the ICTY's task was not a simple
one. Just as the tribunal tried to shame the Croatian government for failing to
cooperate, the government tried to counter-shame the tribunal for its supposed
shortcomings. The tribunal's response to government attacks mattered insofar as an ineffective retort could expose the tribunal's failures and diminish its
international standing and legitimacy. That, in turn, could erode the incentive
of powerful international actors to intervene on the tribunal's behalf against a
defiant state such as Croatia.

A major component of Croatia's counter-shaming campaign was to expose
the supposed inequities of the tribunal process. Tudman attacked the court for
being biased against Croat suspects since there was now, after the handover of
the ten Bosnian Croat suspects in 1999, a disproportionate number of ethnic
Croat suspects in custody at the tribunal's detention center. Meanwhile, Serbs
insisted that the tribunal was biased against them, since when measured by the
number of indictments issued, the tribunal remained largely focused on ethnic
Serb suspects.[101]

Croatia's claims of bias did not appear to slow the tribunal's determination
to press Zagreb to cooperate. Nor did it suddenly persuade the international
community to stop pressuring Croatia. But Croatia's counter-shaming strategy
did at times put the ICTY on the defensive by raising legitimate questions about
the fairness of the tribunal process. That forced tribunal officials to fend off
criticism through frequent interviews with and statements to the international
and Croatian media. Not surprisingly, the tribunal made little headway in its
efforts to change minds in Croatia. The tribunal proved much more successful
when it came to persuading the international community about the integrity
and efficacy of its legal process. In the aftermath of Dayton, the tribunal's
international reputation steadily grew, even as it struggled to obtain adequate
financial and political support from the UN and the West. Increasingly, the
tribunal was seen, despite its flaws, as instrumental to post-war stability and
reconciliation in the Balkans.[102] In this context, Croatia and Serbia's attempts
to discredit the court were often dismissed by international diplomats as self-
interested attempts to avoid prosecution.[103]

None of this stopped Croatia from persistently attacking the tribunal on a
range of fronts. Croatian officials launched a sophisticated rhetorical assault
that detailed the skewed percentages of tribunal incarceration rates for suspects from different ethnic groups. The government assiduously tracked the

[100] Fieldwork interview with Richard J. Goldstone, Pasadena, April 2003.
[101] "Belgrade group places Croatian president on list of war crime suspects," *BBC Monitoring of World Broadcasts, Original Source: Vecernje Novosti*, Belgrade, April 8, 1996.
[102] "US envoy: Croatia must comply with Dayton on pain of economic sanctions," *BBC Monitoring International Reports, Original Source: HINA News Agency*, Zagreb, September 18, 1997.
[103] Fieldwork interviews with Western diplomats, The Hague, Croatia, and Serbia, October 2001–December 2003.

percentage of ethnic Croats in custody in The Hague. In May 1997, Croatian diplomats at the UN issued a press release claiming that ethnic Croats comprised 50 percent of the inmates. In October, following the handover of the ten Bosnian Croat suspects, it issued another press release reporting that the percentage of ethnic Croats had jumped to 70 percent. Loathe to miss a chance at statistical accuracy, the government issued another statement in December noting that the recent arrest of two more Bosnian Croats by NATO forces raised the percentage of ethnic Croats in custody at the ICTY to 73 percent.

Beyond attempting to deflect international pressure to increase cooperation, Zagreb tried to counter the predominant view of the Muslims as the main victims of the Bosnian conflict.[104] The government also claimed that the tribunal had not done enough to prosecute crimes against Croat civilians inasmuch as the alleged perpetrators of violence against Croats in Bosnia and in Croatia had not yet been brought to trial. That this situation was due to Serbian non-compliance and not to the ICTY's insensitivity to Croatian suffering did little to appease Croatian nationalists and government officials eager to shift the international focus from Zagreb's non-compliance to the tribunal's shortcomings.[105]

Tribunal officials tried to brush aside the criticisms, arguing that there were no ethnic quotas for investigations and indictments and that its prosecutions were based solely on individual wrongdoing. The tribunal countered the government's disproportionality argument by shifting the blame for its failure to prosecute more Serbs to the Serbian authorities, who refused to hand over suspects for trial. ICTY officials also frequently tried to lower expectations for prompt justice, while pledging their allegiance to impartiality. "There are great expectations from the tribunal, and they cannot be fulfilled all at the same time," said Deputy Prosecutor Graham Blewitt. "I am convinced that we will demonstrate we are not working politically, but that we are basing our work on proof."[106]

Croatia's counter-shaming offensive also included attacks on the ICTY for its "sluggishness and inefficiency,"[107] which at times made it look as inept as its counterpart in Arusha. Specifically, Zagreb condemned the lengthy period of pre-trial detention for Croat suspects. Croatian officials, for instance, repeatedly criticized the court for holding Blaškić for sixteen months prior to the start of his trial,[108] even though the delay was due in part to the government's refusal to provide vital evidence to the prosecution and defense. A more blatant charge of tribunal ineptness came in May 1997 when the government publicly assailed the prosecution for indicting a Bosnian Croat suspect, Stipo Alilović, who had

---

[104] Croatian Mission to the United Nations, Communiqué, October 8, 1997.
[105] Josipović, *The Hague Implementing Criminal Law*, pp. 238 and 244.
[106] "Bosnia War Crime Trial Opens with Leaders Still Free," *Inter Press Service*, May 7, 1996.
[107] "Croatia: No agreement on surrender of Bosnian Croat war crimes suspects," *BBC Monitoring International Reports, Original Source: Croatian TV satellite service*, Zagreb, September 11, 1997.
[108] "Croatian foreign minister says Croat war crimes suspects ready to stand trial," *BBC Monitoring International Reports, Original Source: HINA News Agency*, Zagreb, August 16, 1997.

actually died before his indictment. In a sign of the disarray in the prosecutor's office, Arbour took more than seven months to dismiss the case against Alilović.

Despite these and other mistakes, the ICTY was, as noted earlier, steadily earning a reputation among its international sponsors as a credible and effective institution. In contrast to international perceptions of the ICTR, the ICTY's mistakes tended to be regarded by Western diplomats and the international media as growing pains rather than congenital defects. In this respect, the ICTY actually benefited from the frequent comparisons the international community made with the ICTR, which, especially during the mid and late 1990s, found itself trapped in a bureaucratic quagmire.

4.9 The Battle over the Homeland War

The transfer of the ten Bosnian Croat suspects in October 1997 bought Tudman a reprieve from international pressure. That, in turn, enabled him to forestall cooperation with tribunal investigations inside Croatia aimed at collecting evidence to indict high-level officials for their role in Homeland War atrocities. In anticipation of possible indictments, Tudman took the offensive by threatening to suspend cooperation with the tribunal.[109] The government also won parliamentary backing for a resolution condemning the ICTY's numerous failures as well as its probe of the Homeland War.[110] Given the tribunal's long-held reticence to push Zagreb for cooperation with Homeland War investigations, Tudman hoped that the tribunal would acquiesce under pressure.

Croatia's strategy backfired. The threat to suspend cooperation appeared to galvanize the ICTY to pursue an adversarial approach toward Croatia, such had the tribunal's sense of its own strength grown. This strategy culminated in the tribunal's decision to formally report Croatia's non-compliance to the Security Council in late August 1999. The tribunal's protest resonated with Western leaders, who had grown exasperated with Tudman's non-compliance as well as his increasing authoritarianism and worsening human rights record.

The tribunal also blamed government officials for publicly contesting the court's right to full cooperation.[111] In its 1999 annual report, the ICTY attempted to expose the government for its relentless counter-shaming offensive against the court.[112] This annual report is noteworthy because it characterized the government's attacks on the tribunal's credibility as a form of non-cooperation since these attacks were used to justify the government's non-compliance. Thus the tribunal turned Croatia's attacks against it into a form of non-compliance. The ICTY took aim at Foreign Minister Granić's misleading report to parliament that castigated the tribunal for not prosecuting Serb crimes against Croatians and claimed that the tribunal's failure was leading to

---

[109] The government issued its first such threat in late 1997. See "Croatia's Cooperation with the UN War Crimes Tribunal: A Timeline of Developments," *Agence France-Presse*, July 16, 2001.

[110] Josipović, *The Hague Implementing Criminal Law*, pp. 244–245.

[111] Sixth Annual Report of the ICTY, August 25, 1999.

[112] Ibid., p. 28.

"an atmosphere of insecurity" in Croatia.[113] "It is also worth reiterating that all victims of crimes that fall within the jurisdiction of the Tribunal have a right to, and deserve, justice," the ICTY report said. "It is disingenuous and unacceptable, therefore, for any Government to call for investigation and prosecution of crimes allegedly committed against its citizens while simultaneously refusing to assist the Prosecutor in developing cases involving other victims."[114]

The tribunal's August 1999 complaint did not prompt the Security Council to punish Croatia. Nevertheless, the complaint and the significant press coverage it received put the Tudman regime under a harsh international spotlight. Bilateral pressure, especially U.S. threats to freeze economic assistance and cut off diplomatic relations,[115] eventually forced Croatia to promise to make some concessions. Initially, Tudman decided not to take the American threat seriously.[116] But the specter of U.S. action triggered "panic at the highest levels" of government.[117] The Croatian government soon signaled its willingness to cooperate. However, Zagreb continued to stymie the court's call for assistance with Homeland War investigations. Again, the government used its promise to transfer a Bosnian Croat war crimes suspect as a way to demonstrate compliance while staving off pressure to cooperate with the probe of Homeland War atrocities. Tudman pledged to hand over Mladen "Tuta" Naletilić, one of two Bosnian Croats indicted by the tribunal in December 1998. The Croatian leader had transferred the lower-ranking suspect, Vinko "Stela" Martinović, to The Hague in early August 1999.

The United States did not establish a firm deadline by which Croatia had to make progress on cooperation with Homeland War investigations before facing economic consequences. The United States, as well as its European allies, seemed reticent to punish Tudman because of the increasing likelihood of regime change in upcoming elections and the fear of causing a nationalist backlash that could lead to a victory for Tudman's HDZ party.[118] The terminally ill Tudman was not expected to live long and the popularity of his HDZ party was on the decline. Despite the tribunal's follow-up protests to the Security Council, the government continued to block tribunal investigators in Croatia and refused to recognize the court's jurisdiction over Operations Flash and Storm. (Tudman even backed away from his promise to deliver Naletilić, insisting that the suspect's ill health prevented him from facing trial in The Hague.)

4.10 Conclusion

It is uncertain whether sustained tribunal and international pressure might have eventually forced Tudman to cooperate with tribunal investigations of Croatian

---

[113] Ibid., p. 28.

[114] Ibid., p. 28.

[115] "Croatia: Constitutional Watch," *East European Constitutional Review*, Volume 8, Number 4, Fall 1999.

[116] Ibid.

[117] Ibid.

[118] Fieldwork interview with Western diplomat, Zagreb, November 2001.

atrocities committed during the Homeland War. The absence of such pressure, however, enabled Tuđman to go to his grave without ever doing so. To a large extent, the ICTY could decide – because of its growing international credibility and celebrity, the interest and support it garnered in the Western media, and the power of shaming – when to go on the offensive in its trials of cooperation and bring the opprobrium of the international community upon a non-compliant government. That is what the tribunal proved capable of doing when it re-ported Croatia's non-compliance to the Security Council in 1999. Although Croatia escaped economic sanctions, the tribunal's high-profile "prosecution" of Croatia at the UN sorely undermined the government's credibility and placed new obstacles in its path to European integration.

The tribunal's decision to wait so long to turn its quiet struggle with Croatia over Homeland War investigations into an openly adversarial one appeared based in part on a strategic calculation of not wanting to jeopardize Zagreb's assistance on the Bosnian Croat front. The tribunal seemed most concerned with gaining custody of the fifteen Bosnian Croat suspects under Zagreb's con-trol who were indicted between August 1995 and December 1998. Obtaining these suspects provided a crucial boost for the tribunal, given that its jail cells and courtrooms had been almost empty. Despite his obstinacy in other areas, Tuđman's cooperation was a boon to the tribunal, since it led to the handing over of thirteen of the fifteen Bosnian Croat suspects.

The tribunal paid a heavy cost for keeping its grievances concerning Home-land War investigations silent for so long. First, delay enabled Tuđman and his defense minister, Gojko Šušak, who also died in the late 1990s, to escape indict-ment and prosecution. Second, by not challenging Tuđman's defiance more aggressively, the tribunal in effect allowed Tuđman's refusal to recognize the tribunal's jurisdiction over the Homeland War to stand. However, it is unclear whether an adversarial approach would have forced Croatia's hand, because of the West's reticence to empower the tribunal to indict high-level officials, particularly Tuđman himself. Third, the tribunal's conciliatory strategy also appeared to hurt its efforts to build an international consensus to press Croatia to facilitate investigations of Homeland War atrocities. The tribunal might have received stronger backing from the Security Council in 1999 had it done more in the mid-1990s to spark international concern, although doing so presupposed a stronger voice than the tribunal has since come to develop.

Although belated, the tribunal's complaint to the Security Council signaled that it had no intention of acquiescing in Croatia's defiance nor to interna-tional ambivalence. In a few short years, the tribunal had moved from being only a weak arm of a recalcitrant international community to an institution increasingly capable of acting autonomously and forcefully.

5

The Politics of State Cooperation in Croatia's Democratic Era

5.1 Introduction

The death of President Franjo Tuđman in December 1999 and the decisive electoral defeat of his Croatian Democratic Union (HDZ) party several weeks later marked a new era in Croatian politics. After a decade of authoritarian rule, Croatian citizens voted to take the country on a democratic course. The victory of a new center-left governing coalition also marked a turning point in the tumultuous relationship between Zagreb and the International Criminal Tribunal for the Former Yugoslavia (ICTY). After years of resistance, the government pledged to aid the tribunal in its probe of Croatian atrocities committed not only in Bosnia but in the so-called Homeland War, the nation's celebrated war of independence fought against Serbs on Croatian soil. Zagreb's pledge to cooperate with the Homeland War investigations was a major step forward for the tribunal, coming as it did after years of the state's refusal to countenance tribunal investigations of Croatian atrocities in this war. At the tribunal, officials were hopeful that Zagreb's promises would lead to the first indictments and trials of high-level Croatian generals suspected of ordering atrocities during the Homeland War. Now perhaps, the "trials of cooperation" between state and tribunal would become a thing of the past.

The democratic opening, optimists in The Hague and elsewhere hoped, could start a process of national introspection in partnership with the tribunal to confront the country's recent past. In this sanguine view, state cooperation would no longer be a euphemism for compliance, but a true description of the reciprocal relationship between international justice and domestic politics. But state cooperation did not follow a smooth trajectory in the aftermath of authoritarian rule in Croatia. To be sure, cooperation generally increased compared to the Tuđman era; the state–tribunal relationship was often cordial where it was once hostile. But this relative improvement did not mean that the ICTY received the level of cooperation it required to complete investigations and prepare cases for trial in a timely manner. In fact, when it came to arrests and transfers, officials in Croatia's democratic coalition government were at times more resistant than their authoritarian predecessors.

Croatia's resistance was not a simple extension of the defiance of the Tuđman years. The new government, led by the reformed communist Ivica Račan and his Social Democratic Party (SDP), had a stronger incentive than Tuđman to cooperate. Following the demise of authoritarian rule, increased compliance with the ICTY was the key to winning the much sought after invitation to join the European Union and achieve Croatia's fervent quest to shun its Balkan heritage. Moreover, facilitating the tribunal's work did not appear to pose a direct threat to the Račan government. In contrast to the Tuđman regime, Prime Minister Račan and others in the new ruling coalition played no role in planning the war and had no reason to personally fear the outcome of tribunal investigations. Yet this did not suddenly mean that the government wished to empower the tribunal to probe Croatia's role in wartime atrocities.

The Račan government was deeply conflicted over how far to go in assisting the investigations of Croatian wartime atrocities. While the government sought the international rewards that cooperation promised, it feared the domestic repercussions of doing so. For many Croatians, the tribunal remained a detested institution that undermined state sovereignty and challenged the national narrative of Croatia as a victim country that had, against great odds, won a clean and glorious war of independence. Democratization did not bring an end to anti-tribunal sentiment or nationalism. Indeed, nationalism remained very much alive in the political and cultural fabric of the newly independent Croatia. In this context, nationalists retained great influence over the emotional issues of war, national memory, and justice. From their perch in the opposition, right-wing voices lambasted the tribunal as a biased institution that did too much to prosecute Croatians and too little to prosecute Serbs. Denouncing the tribunal soon became an effective way for nationalists to mobilize supporters and attack Račan's fledgling coalition government. Nationalist anger was directed not only at ICTY officials in The Hague, but at the tribunal's would-be collaborators in Zagreb. If Chief Prosecutor Carla Del Ponte was vilified as a foreign enemy, Račan was maligned as an enemy from within.

During the democratic era, domestic political battles over whether and how much to cooperate with the ICTY have been intense, frequently testing the viability of Croatia's governing coalition, often dominating the media, and at times inciting street demonstrations. Indeed, no issue has polarized the post-authoritarian Croatian political scene as much as the issue of cooperation with the tribunal. The new experiment in international law in The Hague at times seems to have endangered the new experiment in democratic politics in Croatia, or so its embattled leaders have frequently asserted.

Lest he be seen as a true supporter of the tribunal, Račan let it be known that Croatia needed to cooperate purely for instrumental reasons. He frequently attacked the tribunal for its supposed shortcomings by echoing the nationalist argument that indictments of individual Croatians were thinly veiled attempts to undermine the dignity and legitimacy of the Homeland War. Not surprisingly,

Račan's stance did little to build a national consensus for cooperation. The importance of creating such a consensus was underscored by the absence of a strong civil society-based campaign to support government efforts to support the tribunal. Apart from the lone voices of several small human rights organizations and a few bold politicians, such as President Stjepan Mesić, there has been no vocal domestic constituency in Croatia supporting the ICTY.

The tribunal's scrutiny of the government's cooperation record was a critical aspect of the trials of cooperation. Favorable tribunal appraisal could give Croatia's drive for EU membership momentum, while significant criticism could place new obstacles in its path to Europe. Importantly, Western diplomats closely followed the ICTY's assessments of Croatia's cooperation record. Still, the Račan government learned that it had considerable room to delay or even refuse compliance while avoiding concrete punishment. Here, the new government could exploit the international community's concern with safeguarding Croatia's delicate democratic transition. Whenever possible, the government preferred to delay a tribunal request for assistance in order to better gauge the fallout of cooperation or resistance. At other times, the government declared its intention to cooperate – which often won the West's praise and a temporary letup of pressure – and then delayed meeting its commitment. At other times, government officials tried to deflect tribunal pressure by attempting to counter-shame the tribunal for its perceived shortcomings.

For its own part, the ICTY – and Chief Prosecutor Del Ponte in particular – frequently fought back, waging its own counterattack by shaming the government before the international community when Croatia failed to comply. To a great extent, the tribunal's power lay in its ability to employ an adversarial approach to embarrass Croatia for its violation of its legal obligation to cooperate. Without tribunal vigilance and pressure, Croatia would have had considerably more opportunity to evade international scrutiny. Nevertheless, ICTY officials were cautious about overusing an adversarial approach. As much as tribunal officials bemoaned Croatia's unfilled promises, they realized that Račan represented a general improvement over the nationalists waiting in the wings. In this sense, it was also in the tribunal's interest to moderate its criticism of the Račan government in order to bolster the domestic standing of the governing coalition against the chances of a nationalist backlash. Here the tribunal favored a conciliatory approach aimed at negotiating with and offering concessions to the Račan government for its cooperation. The suggestion that the tribunal was in fact sensitive to domestic concerns and actually took measures to strengthen the democratic coalition is disputed by many Croatians, who regard tribunal indictments of Croatian war heroes as the main source of domestic turmoil.

The tribunal's conciliation did not ultimately insulate Račan from domestic discontent with his government, fueled also by Croatia's worsening economic situation. Unseating Račan's SDP party, a reformed HDZ took control of the government after its electoral victory in November 2003. The specter of the HDZ's return to power troubled tribunal officials, who feared that the window of cooperation that opened after Tuđman's death would close again. However, the HDZ victory marked a surprising turning point when it came to Croatia's policy toward the tribunal. Since the HDZ victory, state cooperation has significantly increased in the critical area of arrests and transfers of indicted war crimes suspects. Interestingly, this marked increase in cooperation has not sparked the type of nationalist protest that frequently dogged Račan's government. Zagreb's increased cooperation was driven by the pressing need to demonstrate compliance prior to the European Union's selection of candidate countries for potential membership.

In the next section, I will examine the tribunal–government relationship in the year following Račan's electoral victory in early 2000. This discussion will begin with an explanation of the factors that led to his victory and to the defeat of the HDZ party. The trials of cooperation between the Croatian government and the tribunal are best illustrated through an analysis of the political crises sparked by the handing down of indictments against high-level Croatian generals. Thus, in the following three sections, I will focus on the crises that occurred in the aftermath of tribunal indictments of these generals. This will be followed by a discussion of the improvements in cooperation that occurred toward the end of Račan's tenure. In the remainder of the chapter, I will examine how the state–tribunal relationship has changed since the reemergence of the HDZ in late 2003.

5.2 The Defeat of the HDZ and the Rise of Croatian Democracy

In the late 1990s, Tuđman's HDZ party faced rising discontent over Croatia's growing international isolation and its failure to reform the economy and curb corruption. Tuđman's success on the battlefield was not enough to ensure continued support at home. Many Croatians had expected that independence would bring about improvements in their everyday lives and, at the very least, a return to the relatively high living standards enjoyed in Tito's Yugoslavia. But the late 1990s brought a worsening in the economy for a country already reeling from the deprivation of the war years. As Croatia's domestic problems grew, so too did the prospects of the democratic opposition.

The political landscape changed dramatically within a few weeks after Tuđman's death from cancer in mid-December 1999. On January 3, 2000, the HDZ was dealt a resounding defeat in parliamentary elections, though it was still able to win 46 out of 151 seats in the parliament. A new center-left coalition of six parties, led by Ivica Račan, and his communist successor SDP (Social Democratic Party) took over and promised to reverse the anti-democratic and anti-Western policies of its predecessor. A month later, pro-democratic forces prevailed in the presidential elections with the victory of Stjepan Mesić, a former high-ranking communist and an early defector from the HDZ's ranks. The new government's rapprochement with the West entailed changing state policy in a number of areas, including speeding the return of Serbian refugees expelled from Croatia during the war, ending its meddling in Bosnia, and promising full cooperation with the ICTY. Key European countries made clear to the new government that Croatia's integration into Europe would depend on improved cooperation with the ICTY. Importantly, however, the EU's and international community's definition of sufficient cooperation would not be clearly spelled out from the start. This ambiguity would be relentlessly exploited by the Croatian government and at times by international actors, who in certain situations preferred not to hold Zagreb accountable for its non-compliance.

Several concrete actions taken by the new government fueled the tribunal's optimism that Croatia's resistance to the tribunal had been buried along with Tuđman. Within several months of taking power, the coalition government permitted the ICTY to establish a liaison office in Zagreb and transferred Bosnian Croat war crimes suspect, Mladen Naletilić, to The Hague. In an abrupt reversal of Tuđman's intransigence, the government approved a declaration that recognized the ICTY's jurisdiction over Operations Flash and Storm.

In the wake of the reformists' electoral victory, public opinion initially seemed to back the government's pro-cooperation stance. However, there were early indications that the government would face stiff resistance at home when it came to facilitating the tribunal's prosecutions of Croatians. In March 2000, the conviction and the forty-five-year sentence handed down to Bosnian Croat general Tihomir Blaškić at The Hague (at the time this was the heaviest sentence handed down by ICTY judges) sparked widespread anger and some protests in Croatia.

Despite incentives from the international community to increase cooperation, the new government proceeded cautiously. Račan, for instance, initially balked at handing over Naletilić, even though Tuđman had already cleared the way for his transfer in 1999. Even amid the government's rhetorical support of the tribunal, some observers detected fear within its ranks about a possible domestic backlash instigated by the HDZ and other nationalists in Croatia's powerful veterans' organizations. But for the first eight months of 2000, the specter of a nationalist backlash did not emerge as a serious threat.

Croatia's commitment to cooperate would not be truly tested until the tribunal handed down indictments of Croatian citizens in connection with the Homeland War. That did not happen until mid-2001, when Del Ponte indicted two high-ranking generals. But media speculation about possible indictments and the rumored progress of tribunal investigations made the cooperation issue increasingly volatile in the first year of the Račan government.[1] In August 2000, there were widespread media reports in Croatia that Del Ponte would indict General Petar Stipetić, the chief of the General Staff of the Croatian Army.[2] Nationalists seized on the rumors and railed against the prospect of Stipetić being sent to The Hague.

---

[1] Ozan Erözden, "Croatia and the ICTY: A Difficult Year of Co-operation," www.ceu.hu/cps/bluebird/pap/erozden1.pdf, 2002, pp. 13–15.

[2] *Jutarnji List*, August 12, 2000, and "Croatia's Army Chief to Testify as War Crimes Suspect," *Agence France-Presse*, March 24, 2001.

The tribunal eventually decided to call Stipetić as a witness and not indict him. But media reports that he might be indicted caused a serious rift between the coalition's two main partners, Prime Minister Račan and Dražen Budiša, leader of the HSLS (Croatian Social Liberal Party), and foreshadowed the divisiveness of the cooperation issue. The case also suggested that each indictment or credible rumor of an indictment could create a rift within the coalition.

By the end of 2000, the tribunal's trust in Račan's promise of unfettered cooperation had been tempered by government obstruction on a number of fronts. "I would like to be able to say that all problems have been completely removed, but I cannot," Del Ponte said in her annual address to the Security Council in November 2000. "Where Croatia perceives co-operation to be against its political or narrow security interests, a real difficulty still exists."[3] Del Ponte singled out problems in a number of areas, including the government's failure to fulfill its pledge to cooperate fully in investigations of the Homeland War.[4] She further criticized Zagreb for underhanded measures – such as government leaks of tribunal cooperation requests – that sabotaged the tribunal–government relationship and fostered "a negative media campaign against the Tribunal."[5] By so doing, Del Ponte, at an early date, sought to combat the government's counter-shaming attacks. In my interviews, tribunal officials acknowledged that in comparison to the past, the relationship with the Croatian government had markedly improved. Yet these officials remained frustrated that Račan did not take decisive steps to persuade the Croatian public about the moral imperative to abide by international law. "I could never understand why there was not an attempt to influence the public opinion by gradually putting out messages as to what the right thing to do should be," Deputy Prosecutor Graham Blewitt told me in an interview.[6]

5.3 The Norac Indictment[7]

The first major war crimes indictment crisis for the Račan government occurred not over an indictment issued by ICTY prosecutors but by one issued by a Croatian court. In early February 2001, a court in the seaside city of Rijeka issued an arrest warrant for Mirko Norac, a retired army general involved in the defense of the strategic town of Gospić in the Krajina region in October 1991. Norac, who later fought in Operation Storm, was a celebrated hero among Croatian nationalists. Although this crisis revolved around a domestic

---

[3] Address to the Security Council by Carla Del Ponte, November 21, 2000.
[4] Ibid.
[5] Ibid.
[6] Fieldwork interview with Graham Blewitt, The Hague, December 2003.
[7] This chapter's discussion of the Norac, Ademi, Gotovina, and Bobetko indictments, as well as parts of the introductory sections of this chapter, are largely drawn from Victor Peskin & Mieczysław P. Boduszyński, "International Justice and Domestic Politics: Post-Tuđman Croatia and the International Criminal Tribunal for the Former Yugoslavia," *Europe-Asia Studies*, Vol. 55, No. 7, 2003, 1117–1142.

war crimes case, it was a major event in the post-Tudman era that influenced the government's approach to cooperation with the ICTY.

Norac faced charges of crimes against humanity for his alleged role in the killing of approximately forty Serb civilians in October 1991. Witness testimony alleges that soldiers under Norac's command took residents, among them elderly Serbs, dragged them out of their homes and executed them. The general himself was accused of killing one woman.[8]

Croatian nationalists quickly mobilized opposition to the February 7 arrest warrant by blocking roads and organizing street demonstrations in Dalmatia. On February 11, approximately 150,000 people attended an anti-government demonstration in Split. Meanwhile, government officials warned that road closures were blocking commerce and hurting the nation's economy.[9] Norac went into hiding after the court issued the arrest warrant.

The investigation into the 1991 Gospić killings was proving to be difficult and dangerous well before the Rijeka court issued a warrant for Norac's arrest. A key witness in the Gospić investigation, Milan Levar, who had incriminating evidence against Norac and his alleged co-conspirators and who had been interviewed by both ICTY investigators and Croatian authorities, was killed in late August 2000 when a bomb exploded as he repaired a car in Gospić. Levar's murder raised the stakes of the domestic judiciary's investigation of the Gospić case.

To the protestors, the government's pursuit of Norac was tantamount to a betrayal of the Homeland War. The effort to portray the Norac investigation in this light is seen in the slogans and signs at the Split demonstration: "We are all Mirko Norac," read one placard popular among protestors. Other placards underscored the symbolic importance of the Homeland War: "Hands off our Holy War," "Amnesty for all Defenders." The government's pursuit of Norac was not the only target of the protests. The demonstrators also sought to protest the government's new policy of increased cooperation with the ICTY and the rumored tribunal indictment of Norac. To the protestors, the Norac arrest warrant and the trial of his co-conspirators in the Gospić killings were blamed on the government's readiness to give in to international pressure.

Buoyed by the electoral mandate for change, government officials moved quickly to stem the rising tide of nationalist protest. They countered the accusations of selling out the Homeland War by clearly defending the state's prerogative to prosecute war crimes and by accusing the opposition of intentionally destabilizing the government.[10] Although clearly startled by the size of the

---

[8] "Veterans Jeopardize Croatia's Fledgling Democracy," *Deutsche Presse-Agentur*, February 13, 2001.

[9] "Croatian Veterans Protest War Crimes Warrant Issued by the Croatian Authorities," *Agence France-Presse*, February 10, 2001.

[10] Opinion polls during the crisis reflected the public's opposition to handing over Norac to the ICTY. According to *Slobodna Dalmacija*, 66 percent polled were opposed to Norac's transfer to The Hague. However, 46 percent said that Norac should be tried by a Croatian court if there were evidence of his involvement in war crimes. Thirty-one percent said that Norac should

protests, government leaders articulated what was at stake. On February 9, 2001, two days after the warrant was issued, Račan told parliament that the government would not give in to pressure from those forces that wanted to undermine the legal order. To Račan, the crisis was a defining moment and "a test for a democratic and law-abiding Croatia."[11] The opposition to the Rijeka court's investigation of Norac, Račan said, constituted "a serious attack on the democratic legal order of the country." Pressure, he added, would not force the government to interfere with the independence of the judiciary and risk isolating Croatia internationally. President Mesić accused the nationalists of manipulating the Norac crisis in order to regain power.[12] In the Norac crisis, government officials presented justice for war crimes as an integral part of the process of establishing the rule of law and democratization more generally.

Interestingly, Dražen Budiša, the coalition leader most wary of cooperation with the ICTY, was particularly outspoken about the nature of the alleged crimes Norac committed. In an interview with the Croatian weekly news-magazine, *Nacional*, Budiša said his party could not defend Norac, given the severity of the indictment. "We can't defend this," he said. "Only a coward kills women and children."[13]

The momentum began to slowly shift to the government's side several days after the Split protest. Attempts by war veterans' associations to organize another large demonstration failed. The momentum continued to shift as Norac met with Mesić and Račan, apparently to discuss the possibility of surrendering. As long as Norac remained at large, the protests might continue to grow. But if Norac decided to turn himself in, the wind would likely be taken out of the nationalists' sails. Statements issued by the international community urging the government not to give in to the nationalists may have strengthened the government's resolve.[14]

It soon became apparent that the rumored ICTY indictment of the general was the central obstacle blocking his surrender. Norac told a Croatian news-paper that he would surrender only if there were guarantees that he would not subsequently be sent to The Hague.[15] It remains uncertain how close the ICTY was to actually indicting Norac, either before or after the Rijeka court issued the warrant for the general's arrest. Nevertheless, Del Ponte's decision to defer to the Croatian judiciary on February 21 clearly bolstered Račan's position

be immune from prosecution in light of his role in protecting Croatia during the war. See www.cdsp.nue.edu/info/students/marko/slodal/sldal43.html.

[11] "Premier Says He Has No Information on General Norac's Whereabouts," *BBC Summary of World Broadcasts*, February 10, 2001.

[12] Interview with TV Bosnia-Herzegovina on February 11, 2001. Text of report carried by *BBC Summary of World Broadcasts*, February 13, 2001.

[13] Peter Finn, "In Croatia, Law vs. Patriotism: Thousands Rally for Ex-General Accused of War Crimes," *Washington Post*, February 16, 2001.

[14] *Central European Review*, February 19, 2001.

[15] "Croatian War Crimes Suspect Not Sought by UN Court," *Agence France-Presse*, February 21, 2001.

vis-à-vis the nationalists and helped defuse the crisis.[16] Del Ponte's move is an important instance of tribunal conciliation and an attempt to bolster a democratic leader against domestic opponents of state cooperation. Shortly after Del Ponte's announcement, Norac turned himself in to the Croatian police. He insisted that he never intended to defy the Croatian legal system. "Fighting for this country, I also fought for its legal institutions," Norac said.[17]

The Norac trial was seen by many as a test of the Croatian courts' ability to hold trials in which ethnic Croats faced war crimes charges. Despite repeated adjournments and initial misgivings, international observers regarded it as a fair trial. In March 2003, Norac and two co-defendants were convicted on war crimes charges while another co-defendant was acquitted.[18] Norac received a twelve-year sentence, while Tihomir Orešković received fifteen years and Stjepan Grandić ten years.

In some respects, the challenge presented by the right wing in the Norac case was stronger than it would be in subsequent crises. Indeed, the massive February protest in Split would not be repeated when the tribunal issued indictments against Croatian generals. However, the domestic court's indictment of General Norac, although controversial, was not seen to be as threatening to Croatia's sovereignty as the subsequent indictments of Croatian generals handed down by the international tribunal. The Norac crisis is noteworthy because of the government's strong stand against the nationalists, the support Račan received from key coalition leaders skeptical of war crimes prosecutions, and the ICTY's conciliatory decision to defer to the Croatian judiciary. The coalition's decision to support war crimes prosecutions would turn to discord when the ICTY issued its first indictment of Croatian generals for atrocities committed during the Homeland War.

5.4 The Gotovina and Ademi Indictments

Throughout Croatia, news of the Serbian government's handover of former President Slobodan Milošević to the ICTY in late June 2001 was greeted enthusiastically. Croatians had long blamed Milošević for the destruction of Vukovar and for the loss of approximately one-third of the country's territory in 1991. Milošević's arrival in The Hague, however, would soon prompt Chief Prosecutor Del Ponte to turn her attention to Croatian generals suspected of bearing command responsibility for atrocities against Serb civilians. Del Ponte's success on the Serbian front would, she hoped, increase the chances of success on the Croatian front. With Milošević in custody, Croatian politicians now had less leverage to claim tribunal bias when protesting against indictments of their

[16] Statement by the Prosecutor Concerning the Croatian Judiciary's Investigation of General Mirko Norac, ICTY press release, February 21, 2001.

[17] Eugene Crcic, "Former Croatian General Surrenders," *Associated Press*, February 22, 2001.

[18] A fifth defendant was acquitted earlier in the trial. See "Former General, Aides Convicted in Croatian War Crimes Trial," *HINA News Agency*, March 24, 2003.

own citizens. Moreover, the timing made it easier for Prime Minister Račan to withstand the accusations of betrayal leveled by anti-tribunal nationalists if and when he moved to send the newly indicted generals to The Hague. In this respect, the timing of Del Ponte's forthcoming indictments reflected an adept understanding of the interrelatedness of Balkan politics.

On July 6, 2001, Del Ponte met government officials in Zagreb and reportedly asked them to arrest two generals named in sealed indictments and transfer them to the tribunal. The content of the indictments, which had been given to the Croatian authorities on a confidential basis in mid-June, quickly leaked to the Croatian media. One indictment charged Rahim Ademi, a Croatian general of Albanian ethnicity, with crimes against humanity for atrocities committed by his forces in the Medak Pocket area of the Krajina in 1993. The other indictment charged retired general Ante Gotovina with crimes against humanity for his role while commanding forces during Operation Storm in 1995.

The question of arresting the two generals quickly split the leaders of the two main parties in the coalition, Račan of the SDP and Budiša of the HSLS. Within days of Del Ponte's visit, four HSLS party members who were cabinet ministers in the governing coalition resigned in protest against Račan's decision to arrest the generals. Nationalists threatened to hold mass rallies. Račan publicly stated his fear of unrest.

Despite growing turmoil within the coalition, Račan initially moved swiftly on Del Ponte's request to arrest the generals. The day following Del Ponte's visit, the cabinet met in a six-hour emergency session to debate its response to the ICTY indictments. Following the meeting, Račan announced that the government would immediately hand over the generals. He issued a strong defense of the government's decision, arguing that Croatia had a legal obligation to cooperate with the ICTY and that the country's bid for entry into European institutions would be harmed by a failure to hand over the generals. "To turn down the request from the ICTY would be to plunge Croatia into the abysses of the Balkans conflict," Račan said. The Prime Minister initially appeared to forcefully articulate what was at stake for Croatia.

The government's promise to cooperate played very well internationally. For Račan, merely signaling an intention to hand over indicted suspects reaped international praise. Lawrence Rossin, the U.S. ambassador to Croatia, noted that Račan's pledge to hand over the generals would significantly strengthen support for Croatia from the United States and the international community.[19] Javier Solana, the European Union's foreign policy chief, hailed the government's "courageous" decision, adding that it "represents a very constructive step towards Europe and the respect of European values."[20] As this narrative underscores, Račan quickly realized that it often served his interests, as it did Tuđman's, to make promises even if he did not intend to keep them.

[19] *HINA News Agency*, July 9, 2001.
[20] *HINA News Agency*, July 13, 2001.

During the crisis, Račan walked a tightrope, trying to stay in the good graces of both the tribunal and nationalist groups. The resignations of the four ministers clearly posed a threat to the government. At the same time, the resignations provided Račan an opportunity to strengthen his hand by turning the crisis into a referendum on his government. In the wake of the resignations Račan called a vote of confidence. He won the July 15 vote decisively and emerged from the crisis with a stronger hand to follow through on his promise of full cooperation. Yet, ever cautious, Račan remained wary of capitalizing on his new mandate. He did not move quickly to arrest the generals.

As in the Norac crisis, various right-wing groups mounted rhetorical attacks that portrayed the ICTY indictments as an attempt to criminalize the Homeland War and cast blame on all Croatians. To bolster their arguments, these groups invoked powerful symbols of the war, such as the siege and destruction of Vukovar at the hands of the Serbs and the heroism of Homeland War generals. A coalition of veterans' associations proclaimed that the Ademi and Gotovina indictments threatened the Croatian state's survival – the decision to cooperate could have only come from "a government which does not protect national values but the policy of bargaining and betraying all values achieved in the Homeland War."[21] The Association for the Promotion of Croatian Identity and Prosperity, led by the son of the late President Tuđman, urged the government not to give in to pressure from the ICTY to hand over Croatian generals on the basis of "bizarre indictments" and stated that such a handover would call into question the "national pride, dignity and legal safety of Croatian citizens."[22] The indictments also spurred condemnation from prominent Croatian celebrities: "Croatia was the victim and its generals and soldiers were heroes. That is the only truth," said a statement issued by a group of the country's most famous athletes.[23]

In the face of such mounting opposition, Račan's announcement that he planned to arrest the generals continued to signal a new and more decisive approach to the ICTY. But he did not actually follow this pro-cooperation stance with concerted action to arrest Gotovina. Despite the lack of large anti-government protests, Račan still feared that the nationalists' vocal criticism of the government's pro-cooperation stance would resonate throughout Croatia. In an apparent bid to placate the right wing, Račan and other government officials repeated the argument that the tribunal's indictments criminalized the Homeland War. In a letter to Del Ponte, Račan claimed that the Gotovina indictment's portrayal of Operation Storm aimed at the "criminalisation and indirect denial of the Storm operation's legitimacy."[24] Specifically, Račan took

[21] *HINA News Agency*, July 7, 2001.

[22] Ibid.

[23] Jamie Wilson and Ian Black, "Goran Calls Indicted Men War Heroes," *The Guardian*, July 13, 2001.

[24] "Croatian Party Slams UN War Crimes Tribunal over Indictments," *Agence France-Presse*, July 27, 2001.

issue with the indictment's assertion that 150,000 to 200,000 Serbs were forced out of Croatia during Operation Storm. Račan, like many Croatian politicians, maintained that the Serbs left Croatia on their own accord. The government's increasing willingness to use nationalist rhetoric against the tribunal – albeit in more diplomatic tones – helped to ensure that the nationalists would continue to have a major role in framing the cooperation debate. For some tribunal officials, Račan's high-profile criticism of the wording of the indictments was exasperating since it added fuel to the nationalists' fire that the tribunal was casting collective guilt on the Croatian people. The government was trying to have it both ways, a senior tribunal official told me in a 2001 interview: On the one hand, the "government recognized . . . our mandate to investigate crimes committed by the Croatian forces during the Homeland War," but on the other, "they are objecting to our language of our indictment."[25]

The promised arrests of Ademi and Gotovina took a back seat to domestic politics as Račan and other coalition members prepared for the July 15 vote of confidence in parliament. The failure to act immediately following the July 7 cabinet meeting gave Gotovina plenty of time to elude the authorities. The government had reason to believe that delay would facilitate Gotovina's escape, given that the identity of the indicted generals had been leaked to the media and that Gotovina had, as early as July 11, indicated his intention not to face trial in The Hague.[26] By the end of July, it was apparent that Gotovina was on the run. Questions about the general's whereabouts plagued Račan throughout the Summer of 2001. But Račan tried his best to deflect responsibility for Gotovina's fugitive status. "Don't ask me every day where Gotovina is; I told you I don't know," he told journalists.[27]

In late July 2001, Ademi turned himself in to tribunal authorities in Amsterdam. In Croatia, the Ademi indictment was considerably less controversial than the Gotovina indictment, in part because Ademi was an ethnic Albanian and in part because Gotovina was held in higher esteem as commander of the Croatian armed forces in Operation Storm.

While the international community praised Račan's initial decision to arrest the generals, it did not at first strongly criticize the government for allowing Gotovina to flee, perhaps believing that arresting the general was actually beyond the government's control. A telling indication of the West's soft approach was seen in a May 2002 visit to Zagreb in which a top British diplomat issued a call for Gotovina to surrender, but then announced a 5 million pound donation aimed at helping Croatia meet European Union standards on economic, legal and educational issues.[28] Clearly, the international community

[25] Fieldwork interview with tribunal official, The Hague, October 2001.

[26] "Croatian General Rejects Trial by UN War Crimes Tribunal," *Agence France-Presse*, July 12, 2001.

[27] "Thousands Gather in Support of War Crimes Suspect," *Deutsche Presse-Agentur*, July 26, 2001.

[28] "British Minister Calls on Croat General to Surrender," *Deutsche Presse-Agentur*, May 29, 2002.

was of two minds when it came to the question of how hard to push Račan. Progress on cooperation remained, at least rhetorically, a pre-condition of European integration. But this did not mean that it would punish or even threaten to punish Croatia for failing to cooperate in a particular instance.

The fight over Gotovina between the government and tribunal soon became a fight over whether the government was at fault for his fugitive status. Tribunal officials took a hard line, blaming Gotovina's escape on the government and maintaining that it still remained in its power to arrest the general. Del Ponte said that she had provided the Croatian authorities with the sealed indictments in June 2001 in order to give the government a chance to arrest the two generals before domestic opposition mounted. The use of sealed indictments was a conciliatory strategy insofar as it could enable the government to forestall domestic opposition by secretly arranging arrests. "My trust was misplaced," Del Ponte said in her annual address to the Security Council in October 2002. "He [Gotovina] was allowed to evade arrest and according to various reliable sources he is now enjoying a safe haven in the territory of Croatia."[29] Račan protested his innocence and maintained that Croatian authorities did not know where Gotovina might be hiding. Račan's claims were bolstered by Croatian media speculation that variously located the retired general in France, Canada, or Australia.

For the government, the July 2001 crisis initially appeared to have had a beneficial, if unintended, resolution since Ademi's surrender seemed to have assuaged the West, while Gotovina's escape temporarily mollified the right wing. The lack of strong international criticism of Gotovina's escape may also have emboldened the government to use delay as a means to avoid making an arrest the next time an ICTY indictment was handed down. Nevertheless, Gotovina's escape encouraged nationalist forces by undermining the government's authority and by showing that nationalists could defy the government's policy of arresting war crimes suspects indicted by the ICTY. For several years afterward, few politicians dared to speak out about the importance of arresting Gotovina. For Croatian nationalists, Gotovina's case became a cause célèbre. Although Croatia escaped immediate punishment, Gotovina's capture would in time be used as a litmus test for Croatia's bid to join the European Union.

5.5 The Bobetko Crisis

Late September 2002 marked the beginning of a long-awaited event for many Croatians – the prosecution's case against Slobodan Milošević detailing Croatia's suffering a decade earlier at the hands of the Serbs.[30] Yet, throughout Croatia, the end of September would be remembered more for the start of the government's most serious crisis to date with the tribunal. Just days before

---

[29] Address to the Security Council by Carla Del Ponte, October 29, 2002.
[30] In February 2002, ICTY prosecutors began the trial by focusing on Milošević's alleged crimes in the Kosovo war.

the resumption of the Milošević trial, prosecutors unsealed their most explosive indictment to date against a Croatian citizen, charging Janko Bobetko, the eighty-three-year-old former army chief of staff and national hero of the Homeland War, with crimes against humanity for atrocities committed against Serbs in 1993. With the exception of Tuđman, no one in Croatia was as associated with the nation's independence struggle as Bobetko. From the prosecution's point of view, the Bobetko indictment was strategically timed and intended to have the least negative impact on the domestic standing of Račan's coalition. But when it came to such a high-ranking suspect, there appeared to be no right moment to hand down an indictment.

The Bobetko crisis underlined the increasing volatility of the cooperation issue in Croatian politics and the government's growing fear of a nationalist backlash and electoral defeat at the hands of the HDZ. Despite its continued pledges of full cooperation, the government quickly opposed the tribunal's request to arrest Bobetko and transfer him to The Hague. The government, while portraying itself as cooperative, resorted to its policy of delay. In light of the general's failing health, government officials hoped that continued delay could win him immunity from prosecution. In the end, this was an effective strategy for the Croatian government. In November, Bobetko went into the hospital with diabetes and other health problems. In early 2003, tribunal officials announced that he was medically unfit to stand trial. In late April, the general died.

An analysis of the government's initial reaction to the indictment suggests important shifts in its approach to cooperation with the tribunal. What is particularly noteworthy is that Prime Minister Račan took the lead in criticizing the Bobetko indictment rather than doing so only after nationalist forces mobilized opposition to cooperation. His criticisms of the Bobetko indictment were substantially harsher than his criticisms of the Ademi and Gotovina indictments.

With the exception of President Mesić, politicians across Croatia's political spectrum lined up behind Račan's opposition to the tribunal indictment. In late September 2002, the Croatian parliament voted unanimously to oppose the indictment. The government's response to the crisis attests to the nationalists' growing influence over the cooperation debate. At the same time, however, Račan's swift condemnation of the tribunal enabled the governing coalition to co-opt the right wing's monopoly on issues of national sovereignty.

The government's defiance was paralleled by Bobetko's own intransigence. The general, who before entering the hospital remained in his Zagreb home guarded around the clock by a group of Homeland War veterans, said he would rather die than be sent to The Hague. To Bobetko, trying suspects from the winning side of the war violated the rules of victor's justice. "There is no court on earth to have tried an army which defended and liberated its country, nor will there ever be," he said.[31] Bobetko's comments emphasize the challenge

---

[31] "General Bobetko Says He Will Not Surrender to Hague Tribunal," *HINA News Agency*, September 20, 2002.

confronting the ad hoc tribunals as well as the International Criminal Court: how to institutionalize a system of international justice in which neither winners nor losers are immune from standing trial for atrocities committed during battle.

The government portrayed itself to the international community as fully supporting cooperation while engaged in a legal conflict with the tribunal over the Bobetko indictment. Toward that end, the government filed two legal briefs with the tribunal's Appeals Chamber challenging the legality of the indictments. This strategy appeared to be designed to buy time for the government since the ICTY prosecutor enjoys clear statutory authority to indict suspected war criminals. But as long as the government was engaged in a legal struggle, it was able to deflect international criticism that it was in open defiance of its obligation to comply with tribunal requests. Del Ponte accused Račan of obstructing justice, noting that there were no justifications for challenging the indictment. In late November, the Appeals Chamber rejected the government's objection to the Bobetko indictment. Račan then broke his pledge to abide by the Chamber's ruling.

Several factors may explain the government's decision not to arrest Bobetko. First, by the autumn of 2002, Račan's coalition government had been seriously weakened since the last ICTY indictments of Croatian generals in July 2001. Rising unemployment, discontent about the speed of economic reforms, and impatience with the slow pace of integration into Europe had undermined the government's popularity. The drop in public support for the government was a boon to the opposition HDZ party, which saw its popularity grow from 5 percent in 2000 to 16 percent in May 2001 to 23 percent in June 2002 and to more than 30 percent in February 2003. The approval rating for the ruling coalition fell sharply during this period. The government's falling popularity and the prospect of early elections made Račan reluctant to act on the Bobetko indictment. Bobetko's prominence as the highest-ranking army official during the Homeland War also made his arrest and transfer to The Hague particularly difficult for the government. If the Ademi and Gotovina indictments were controversial, the charges against the elderly and popular Bobetko were explosive. Polls conducted by the Croatian Puls agency in late September 2002 indicated that 84 percent of Croatian citizens opposed sending Bobetko to The Hague; 71 percent retained the same attitude even under threat of political and economic sanctions.

The government's likely calculations of international reluctance to apply substantial pressure or impose sanctions on Croatia may have also encouraged it to postpone action on the Bobetko indictment. It is likely that Račan hoped that further delay would, on the one hand, weaken the resolve of the tribunal and the international community and, on the other hand, increase the chance that the ailing Bobetko would be declared unfit to stand trial in The Hague. Moreover, Croatian politicians surely were closely watching the tribunal and the international community's response to the non-cooperation of its neighbors in Serbia and in Republika Srpska. Despite Serbia's increased cooperation since Milošević's fall from power in October 2000, numerous indicted ethnic Serb war crimes suspects remained at large. The West's reluctance to apply sanctions against Serbia and Republika Srpska may, in the eyes of the Croatian government, have lowered the risk of not immediately acting on the Bobetko indictment.

The Croatian government's expectation of weak Western resolve was partly correct: the international community issued a number of calls for the government to arrest Bobetko, but for the most part its public statements were measured. With the exception of Britain and The Netherlands, the international community initially took no concrete actions against Croatia. In late September 2002, Denis MacShane, the British Foreign Office Minister for Europe, insisted that Croatia provide immediate and unconditional cooperation in the Bobetko case.[32] Subsequently, Britain and The Netherlands held up ratification of the stabilization and association agreement, signed between the EU and Croatia in October 2001.[33] Other EU states were reluctant to pressure the Račan government, as seen in a statement of EU foreign ministers in late October 2002, which reiterated an earlier call for cooperation but stopped short of issuing any ultimatums.[34] In November, however, EU officials suggested that Croatia's continued defiance of the tribunal risked damaging closer ties with the West.

During this period, Croatia was preparing to apply for EU membership, in the hope of entering in 2007. In early November 2002, EU official Jacques Wunenburger said he did not expect any positive statements on Croatia's application for membership of the EU until the Bobetko problem was solved.[35] Croatian officials, of course, hoped that by the time the EU considered its application, the government's inconsistent cooperation record would be a distant memory. The fact that Bobetko's ill health eventually resolved the latest conflict with the court appeared to bode well for the Croatian government's bid to join the EU. In an apparent indication that the Croatian government's handling of the Bobetko indictment might not be a deal breaker, Austria and Sweden indicated their support for Croatia's entry into the EU.[36]

The West's measured response during the Bobetko crisis reflected a view prevalent in diplomatic circles that the international community should be sensitive to the realities of Croatian politics and the weakness of Račan's coalition. The decision not to raise the level of pressure on Croatia may, unsurprisingly, have emboldened Račan to continue to delay cooperation while warning the West that increased pressure might destabilize the government. The U.S. role

[32] "Croatia: UK Urges Handover of Croatian Wartime General Bobetko," *HINA News Agency*, September 27, 2002; "Dutch Government Refuses to Sign EU Pact with Croatia over Bobetko," *Agence France-Presse*, December 20, 2002.

[33] *HINA News Agency*, October 16, 2002.

[34] "EU Ministers More Lenient with Croatia Than Had Been Announced," *HINA News Agency*, October 21, 2002.

[35] "EU tells Croatia to Hold Off Its Membership Application," *AFX News Limited*, November 5, 2002.

[36] "Austria Promises Support for Croatia's EU bid," *BBC Monitoring Europe*, February 16, 2003; "Sweden Backs Croatia's EU bid," *Agence France-Presse*, March 10, 2003.

in the Balkan conflict may also have moderated the level of pressure it exerted on the Croatian government. Washington's support of the Tuđman regime in its bid to regain territory lost to the Serbs during Operation Storm in 1995 may have dampened America's resolve to see Bobetko stand trial in The Hague. U.S. influence on Croatia (and Serbia) during the Bush administration has, in the eyes of some, also been compromised by its own human rights abuses in Iraq, Afghanistan, and Guantánamo Bay as well as by its own efforts to seek immunity from international prosecution. Its vehement opposition to the International Criminal Court (ICC) has led America to persuade many countries to sign bilateral agreements to ensure that American soldiers who might face indictment would not be handed over to the ICC. America's initiative to obtain immunity for its own forces while pressing Balkan states to hand over war crimes suspects has appeared to undermine the persuasiveness of its calls for Zagreb and Belgrade to aid in the process of international justice.

Ultimately, Zagreb's claim that Bobetko was too ill to stand trial provided it with a way out of handing the general over to the tribunal while dodging international blame. Yet again, Račan survived an indictment crisis by strategically defying the ICTY.

5.6 Rapprochement between The Hague and Zagreb

Bobetko's death ended the tribunal's efforts to bring yet another high-level Croatian suspect to trial. As with former President Tuđman, former Defense Minister Šušak, and the former head of the Bosnian Croat state, Mate Boban, a top Croat suspect had also gone to his grave without having to account. However, the tribunal scored a partial victory insofar as it had indicted Bobetko and thus made official its accusations against the general, something that it failed to do with Tuđman, Šušak, or Boban. Despite being deeply frustrated with the Croatian government, Del Ponte did not let her characteristic impatience get the better of her. Although disparaged in Zagreb and among some Western diplomats[37] for being too adversarial with Croatia, Del Ponte once again showed an ability to be conciliatory in the hopes of encouraging future state cooperation. In an April 2003 visit to Zagreb, Del Ponte cited recent progress in obtaining assistance from the Račan government and sounded a hopeful note about its commitment to finally arrest Gotovina, the only indicted Croatian war crimes suspect who remained at large. "I am confident about the commitment of [the] prime minister to locate and arrest Gotovina," she said, in a statement sharply at odds with her earlier skepticism about Zagreb's pledge to arrest a national war hero.[38] Added Del Ponte: "Perhaps the next visit will be just to thank them for full cooperation."[39]

---

[37] Fieldwork interviews with Western diplomats, The Hague, December 2003.
[38] "UN War Crimes Prosecutor Hails Croatia's Increased Cooperation," *Agence France-Presse*, April 16, 2003.
[39] "Del Ponte Praises Croatia's Co-operation with UN Tribunal," *HINA News Agency*, April 16, 2003.

Although Del Ponte remained discouraged by Račan's handling of the Bobetko and Gotovina cases, she had ample reason to reach out to him, given the growing HDZ electoral challenge to the prime minister's coalition. In the second half of 2003, Del Ponte took a number of steps apparently meant to ease the pressure on Račan and dampen the domestic volatility of the cooperation issue. First, she held off issuing new indictments against two Croatian generals until after the national elections in November 2003. Having to deal with an indictment and the likely crisis it would spark would hardly bolster Račan's electoral prospects. It is difficult to prove that the Office of the Prosecutor deliberately delayed handing down new indictments in order to boost Račan's electoral chances. Yet, among diplomats and other observers, it was well known that new indictments were nearing completion and could have been handed down prior to the election.[40]

Second, at the same time as Del Ponte relieved pressure on Račan by holding off on new indictments, she pressed the prime minister on the critical question of obtaining unimpeded access to documents held in Croatia's national archives. But along with pressure came incentives. Del Ponte, in Summer 2003, offered to give Croatia a favorable assessment in her upcoming annual report to the Security Council if the government cleared the backlog of documents that it had not yet provided to the tribunal.[41] By establishing a benchmark for what constituted sufficient cooperation, Del Ponte clearly spelled out what the government had to do, as well as the tangible benefits it could expect from the tribunal. A positive report from Del Ponte could give vital momentum to Croatia's bid for European integration, just as a negative report could lay obstacles in its path. A positive statement from the tribunal could also bolster Račan's electoral prospects by demonstrating his progress in bringing Croatia closer to Europe's door.

The government responded positively to Del Ponte's offer. From August 2003 through the end of the year, the Croatian government made very good progress on providing documents to tribunal investigators, according to diplomats I interviewed.[42] Subsequently, the government won praise from Del Ponte where it counted most – in her much noticed annual report and speech to the Security Council.[43] Her public praise was a clear demonstration of the tribunal's softening position. However, her conciliatory statements did not signal acquiescence with the Croatian government, but rather a move to obtain more cooperation. Del Ponte's public assessment of Zagreb's efforts at the Security Council was reflected in her comments in my December 2003 interview with her. In that interview, Del Ponte expressed satisfaction with Račan's recent efforts to provide documents and facilitate access to witnesses. "Since a few months ago, suddenly it was no more a battle," Del Ponte told me. "The only open issue

[40] Fieldwork interview with Western diplomat, Berkeley, March 2004.
[41] Ibid.
[42] Ibid.
[43] Address to the Security Council by Carla Del Ponte, October 10, 2003.

is Gotovina."[44] The turnaround in cooperation came, Del Ponte said, because "Croatia is on the door to enter to the European Union. It was politically extremely important that the European Union [insisted on] full cooperation [from Croatia]."[45]

Del Ponte's strategy of conciliation had mixed results. On the one hand, her bid to prod Račan on the question of outstanding documents proved quite successful. On the other hand, her bid to bolster the Račan government did not yield her preferred outcome. In late November, the HDZ, led by Ivo Sanader, defeated Račan at the polls, winning 66 of 152 seats in parliament. It is unclear whether or the extent to which the cooperation issue and Del Ponte's efforts to bolster Račan shaped the electorate's decision. While the tribunal and the chief prosecutor in particular have had a strong influence on domestic politics, they are by no means the main factor shaping electoral outcomes. It appears that the more pressing issue during this election campaign was the deteriorating health of the economy.[46]

After the election, Del Ponte and other ICTY officials I interviewed spoke apprehensively about the future of Croatian cooperation under the new HDZ government.[47] "We will see what will happen because of course now we have some worries," Del Ponte told me.[48] In Croatia and Serbia, the window of cooperation that had opened in 2000 with the rise of center-left parties appeared to be closing with the return of center-right parties. Yet, for all their similarities, the Croatian and Serbian cases were different, particularly when it came to their respective willingness to cooperate with the tribunal.

5.7 The Reemergence of the HDZ and the Quest for Europe

Fortunately for the ICTY, the new center-right governments in Serbia and Croatia approached the tribunal differently. While the new Serbian government initially curtailed cooperation, the new Croatian government signaled its intent to cooperate with the tribunal. The HDZ party that came to power in late 2003 had undergone substantial changes since Tuđman's death four years earlier, including a shift to a more conciliatory policy toward the tribunal. Like Račan's, Sanader's tribunal policy was based on instrumental calculation and not on philosophical transformation. With the European Union's decision only six months away on whether to designate Croatia an official applicant to join the EU in 2007, the utility of cooperation became increasingly apparent for the HDZ.

The EU's imminent decision greatly strengthened the tribunal's hand in early 2004. With Europe closely scrutinizing Croatia's cooperation record, Del Ponte

---

[44] Fieldwork interview with Carla Del Ponte, The Hague, December 2003.
[45] Ibid.
[46] Country Profile: Croatia, *BBC News*, July 20, 2004.
[47] Fieldwork interviews with Western diplomats, The Hague, December 2003.
[48] Fieldwork interview with Carla Del Ponte, The Hague, December 2003.

found herself in a particularly strong position to issue new indictments and press the government to quickly hand over suspects for trial. Already having failed to arrest Gotovina, the government was under increasing pressure to act decisively when Del Ponte delivered her next indictments. Failure to act quickly on the new indictments would likely derail Croatia's bid to enter the EU, according to a number of analysts.[49] In the past, both Tuđman and Račan put off handing over Croatian suspects in order to gauge international reaction. A tepid international response often encouraged further delay, as underscored by Zagreb's handling of the Gotovina and Bobetko indictments. But now with a potential invitation to Europe on the line, the negative consequences of inaction became clear both in Zagreb and in The Hague. Croatian officials feared that their dream of EU membership would be delayed by years if their country did not receive a positive assessment from European officials in Spring 2004. "You have to understand Sanader now," remarked an associate close to the prime minister. "The priority in his foreign policy is getting the European Union's positive assessment of Croatia's candidacy for membership in 2007. Without full cooperation with the Hague tribunal, this assessment ... definitely won't be positive. And the EU's negative stance would be a disaster for the country."[50]

Within a few months of the Sanader government's taking office, Del Ponte issued a series of long-anticipated indictments. In early March 2004, Del Ponte charged two high-ranking Croatian generals, Mladen Markač and Ivan Čermak, with committing atrocities against Serb civilians during and after Operation Storm in 1995. A month later, Del Ponte issued indictments against six Bosnian Croats for their role in atrocities committed against Bosnian Muslims in 1993. And in late May, the chief prosecutor indicted Mirko Norac, the retired general who had recently been convicted by a Croatian court on other charges stemming from wartime atrocities.

In sharp contrast to Račan's waffling, Sanader moved quickly to facilitate the surrender of all nine suspects. The Croatian public had been accustomed to tribunal indictments triggering domestic turmoil. But this time, tribunal indictments were followed by relatively little drama or delay. The absence of crisis sheds new light on the debate concerning the effect of international war crimes tribunals on domestic stability and democratization. To be sure, some nationalists resurrected the well-worn arguments that the tribunal sought to criminalize the Homeland War and cast collective blame on all Croatians. The leaders of two nationalist parties to the right of the HDZ condemned as treason the government's plans to facilitate the transfer of the two generals.[51] But other nationalist voices supported the transfers. Importantly, many of the veterans

---

[49] See the analysis of Barbara Peranic in "Dealing with the Hague Challenge," *Transitions Online*, March 18, 2004.

[50] Drago Hedl, "Croatia: Rewriting History," *Institute for War & Peace Reporting*, April 16, 2004, No. 353.

[51] "Croatian nationalist bodies accuse government of treason over indictments," March 10, 2004, *BBC Monitoring/HINA News Agency*, Zagreb.

who had mobilized against Prime Minister Račan in the aftermath of the Ademi, Gotovina, and Bobetko indictments remained relatively silent.

Within days of the public announcement of their indictments, Generals Markač and Čermak surrendered to tribunal authorities.[52] The government succeeded in shaping the public debate over the generals' fate by forcefully articulating what was at stake for Croatia. A key element in the government's success lay in its decisiveness. Soon after receiving the sealed indictments from the tribunal, Sanader worked quickly and quietly to build a consensus among top officials concerning the need to send the generals to The Hague. When the indictments became public, Sanader defined the imminent transfers as serving Croatia's national interest even as he continued to challenge the indictments as unfair attacks on Croatia's conduct during the war.[53] On the one hand, Sanader emphasized his commitment to the tribunal by facilitating the transfer of the two generals. On the other hand, he conveyed his commitment to the generals by condemning the tribunal indictments[54] and pledging a range of government support for their upcoming courtroom battle.[55]

Several factors help to explain why Sanader moved expeditiously to facilitate the transfer of Croatian war crimes suspects. First, Sanader's nationalist credentials insulated him from the withering attacks that Račan would likely have faced had he facilitated the handovers. Second, the political consequences of Sanader failing to move quickly to arrange the surrenders would have been particularly costly, given the EU's imminent decision on Croatia's candidacy. Third, the political repercussions of sending suspects to the ICTY were less serious for Sanader in 2004 than they were for Račan just a year earlier because the tribunal now had more ways to sweeten the bitter pill of cooperation. As discussed in Chapter 3, the prosecution's increasing focus on encouraging plea bargains increased the chances of a defendant's receiving a relatively light sentence if he pled guilty. The prospect of a light sentence may in turn have diminished the domestic political costs of the government's decision to push for Markač's and Čermak's transfer to the tribunal. In addition, the Security Council's mandated completion strategy for the tribunal increased the chances that some Croatian suspects awaiting trial in The Hague would have their cases deferred to courts back home. Suddenly the prospect of sending suspects to the ICTY did not necessarily mean they would face trial there or actually stay there for long. The prospect of having some suspects return home would doubtlessly become an important way for Sanader's government to save face with domestic adversaries of the tribunal. In Spring 2004, Del Ponte indicated that such deferrals might

---

[52] During the war, Markač served as commander of special police in the Ministry of the Interior and Čermak served as commander of the Knin garrison.

[53] "Croatian premier says some counts of Hague indictments 'unacceptable,'" March 9, 2004, *BBC Monitoring/HRT1 TV*, Zagreb.

[54] Drago Hedl, "Croatia: Rewriting History," *Institute for War & Peace Reporting*, April 16, 1004, No. 353.

[55] "Croatian justice minister confirms arrival of fresh indictments," March 8, 2004, *BBC Monitoring/HINA News Agency*, Zagreb.

include high-level suspects, such as Rahim Ademi and Mirko Norac.[56] In Fall 2005, the ICTY deferred the Ademi and Norac cases for trial in Croatia. The Ademi and Norac trial opened in Zagreb in June 2007.

Despite Croatian efforts to demonize the tribunal as a modern-day inquisition, the ICTY was a kinder, gentler court that paid close attention to a defendant's due process rights and rarely handed down long sentences, at least compared with the frequent life sentences handed down by its counterpart tribunal in Arusha, Tanzania. Moreover, the ICTY had demonstrated a capacity to correct its legal mistakes insofar as its Appeals Chamber did not simply rubber stamp first-instance convictions, but did at times overturn them and vacate sentences. The Appeals Chamber's October 2001 acquittal of the three Bosnian Croat Kupreškić brothers stands out, as does its July 2004 acquittal of Bosnian Croat suspect Tihomir Blaškić on a number of the charges he had faced and the reduction of his sentence from forty-five years to nine years.

Sanader was also dealt an easier political hand given that Markač and Čermak and the six Bosnian Croat suspects indicted in April did not enjoy the same exalted status in Croatia as either Gotovina or Bobetko. It is an open question as to whether Sanader and the HDZ could have withstood the domestic outcry that would come from sending Bobetko to trial in The Hague.

Sanader's most important allies were the generals themselves. Like good soldiers, Markač and Čermak agreed to go to The Hague without a fight. Beyond that, they were outspoken defenders of Sanader's pro-cooperation stance. Markač and Čermak publicly voiced their support for the tribunal process while insisting on their innocence. This was a far cry from Gotovina's and Bobetko's defiance of the tribunal and the cult of nationalist resistance that embraced these two generals. In an interview with Croatian television, Čermak argued that his imminent surrender was part of his duty to uphold Croatia's legal obligations and to defend the purity of Croatia's wartime conduct before the international community. "No matter how this appears to be shocking for the nation, we must understand that ... [Croatia's] constitutional law places a duty on all of us to cooperate with the tribunal," he said.[57] Čermak also argued that it was imperative to confront the accusations of Croatian ethnic cleansing in Operation Storm instead of evading them. Phrased in this way, state cooperation and standing trial before the international court was now portrayed as an act of resistance by providing a way to defend the memory of the Homeland War.

5.8 The April 2004 Indictments

In the tribunal's early years, prosecutors focused their attention on Bosnian Croat suspects. But the Office of the Prosecutor had not issued an indictment

---

[56] Ana Uzelac, "Croatian Case Heading for Local Trial?" *Institute for War & Peace Reporting*, May 28, 2004, No. 360.

[57] "Indicted Croatian general says war crimes suspects should go to Hague," March 8, 2004, report by Croatian TV.

against a Bosnian Croat suspect in six years. In early April 2004, the tribunal announced the indictments of six Bosnian Croats, including Jadranko Prlić, the former president of the breakaway Bosnian Croat republic, and Valentin Ćorić, the former commander of the Bosnian Croat military police. The others – Bruno Stojić, Slobodan Praljak, Milivoj Petković, and Berislav Pušić – were lower-level suspects. The low status of the indictees sparked criticism from tribunal backers, who wanted Del Ponte to focus on those higher up in Croatia's chain of command. Nevertheless, in the indictments of the six Bosnian Croats the prosecution cast a wider net of guilt by implicating Franjo Tuđman and Gojko Šušak in a "joint criminal enterprise" aimed at creating a Greater Croatia through ethnic cleansing of Bosnian Muslims.[58]

As with the Čermak and Markač surrenders a month earlier, the Croatian government again acted quickly to facilitate the transfer of these suspects. Some right-wing parties protested the government's latest act of cooperation, contending that the trials of the accused would unjustly cast Croatia as an aggressor.[59] But with the EU's decision on Croatia's future hanging in the balance, cooperation had become a political reality for the HDZ government. Ivica Račan, who as prime minister became a master of outmaneuvering the tribunal, declared, "Croatia has no alternative to cooperation." The six Bosnian Croat suspects surrendered to the tribunal a few days after the tribunal's indictments were sent to officials in Zagreb.

Sanader once again objected to the indictments and accused the tribunal of historical revisionism and casting collective responsibility on Croatia.[60] But with European integration at stake, Sanader came as close to providing full cooperation as the tribunal could hope for – with the exception of cooperating in the arrest of Gotovina. Within the span of a month, the tribunal had indicted eight ethnic Croats, and now had all eight in custody.

Del Ponte followed these indictments with a final one in late May, charging retired general Mirko Norac in connection with atrocities committed against Serb civilians in the Medak Pocket in 1993. In early July 2004, Norac arrived in The Hague for his arraignment. Back in 2001, the very idea of a tribunal indictment of Norac triggered one of the biggest political protests in modern Croatian history. In a strategic act of conciliation, Del Ponte helped defuse the crisis the Račan government faced by deferring the case against Norac – which concerned allegations of his role in 1991 atrocities – to the Croatian courts. Yet, when it came to Norac, there were plenty of alleged crimes to go around for prosecutors at home and abroad. While Norac faced domestic trial for his alleged 1991 crimes, Del Ponte's investigators quietly worked on building a

---

[58] Drago Hedl, "Croatia: Rewriting History," *Institute for War & Peace Reporting*, April 16, 2004, No. 353.

[59] "Tuđman's son says Hague trying to transform Croatia into 'aggressor,'" April 3, 2004, *BBC Monitoring/HINA News Agency*, Zagreb.

[60] "Premier says Croatia willing to cooperate with Hague tribunal," April 1, 2004, *BBC Monitoring/HINA News Agency*, Zagreb.

case against him for his alleged 1993 crimes. Del Ponte's concession to the Croatian government in 2001 foreshadowed her conciliation in 2004. Shortly after indicting Norac, the chief prosecutor indicated her intention of asking tribunal judges to send the case to the Croatian judiciary.

5.9 The Gotovina Challenge

With respect to Croatia, the string of surrenders in Spring 2004 underscored the rising power of the ICTY and its chief prosecutor. But Del Ponte's biggest prize from Croatia – Ante Gotovina – remained elusive. Although Prime Minister Sanader showed little sign of trying to locate Gotovina – whether he was in Croatia or elsewhere – Del Ponte appeared to be in a strong position to press Sanader. Her strength derived from the EU's pending decision on whether to designate Croatia an official candidate for membership and from the importance the EU afforded to Del Ponte's assessments of Zagreb's cooperation. But as influential as Del Ponte's assessments had become, she was mindful that possible shifts in Brussels' enlargement policy toward the states of the former Yugoslavia might speed Croatia's entry into the EU and diminish the tribunal's leverage. Indeed, even as the EU publicly declared full cooperation as a prerequisite for membership, it usually left itself the option to decide on a case-by-case basis whether to punish a state for non-compliance or to temper such a response in order to advance other policy goals. In this regard, as an EU official explained in an interview, Del Ponte's assessments on cooperation "are important, but are not everything."[61] In the aftermath of the handover of suspects in early 2004 and the international praise it received, there was a real possibility that Croatia's allies in the EU would prevail and that the Union would not vigorously press Zagreb to act on the Gotovina case.[62] Despite a reputation for boldly criticizing non-compliance, Del Ponte proceeded with strategic conciliation when it came to delivering an evaluation of Croatia's lackluster efforts to locate and apprehend Gotovina.

Meanwhile, in an apparent bid to increase the chances of Gotovina's arrest or surrender, Del Ponte made a number of concessions to Gotovina and Zagreb. First, she issued an amended and more favorable indictment against Gotovina that was made public in early March 2004. The international media barely noticed the amended indictment, but in Croatia it was closely scrutinized. In the new indictment, Del Ponte dismissed one of the five counts of crimes against humanity that had been lodged against Gotovina in the original 2001 indictment. This decision may have been warranted on legal grounds because of the

---

[61] Fieldwork interview with EU official, Brussels, December 2006.
[62] As the EU question loomed, Europe's influence over Croatia relative to the United States increased. This rising influence was highlighted by Croatia's decision not to succumb to U.S. pressure to sign a bilateral agreement to ensure that American soldiers could not be extradited for prosecution at the International Criminal Court. See "Foreign minister says Croatia won't sign non-extradition deal with US," March 21, 2004, *BBC monitoring/HINA News Agency*, Zagreb.

perceived difficulty of securing a conviction on this count. But the timing of the amended indictment may also have been designed to encourage Gotovina to surrender by demonstrating the tribunal's evenhandedness. In this sense, the decision to drop the charge seemed like a form of plea bargaining, albeit plea bargaining that occurred prior to rather than after a suspect's apprehension.

The second change to the Gotovina indictment appeared aimed at offering an olive branch to the Croatian government by reducing the initial indictment's assessment of Serb suffering during the Homeland War. The earlier indictment's estimate of the number of Serbs driven out of Croatia had been a source of bitter contention in Zagreb ever since Prime Minister Račan demanded changes to the document in July 2001. In Croatia, as throughout the Balkans, the numerical dimensions of suffering mattered greatly since they were considered indelible markers of guilt and victimization. In the 2001 Gotovina indictment, Del Ponte estimated that Croatian forces caused "the large-scale displacement of an estimated 150,000 to 200,000 Krajina Serbs" out of Croatia.[63] But in the amended indictment, Del Ponte downplayed the mass exodus of Serb civilians in the August 1995 exodus, which at the time represented the largest instance of ethnic cleansing during the Balkan wars. In the new indictment, Del Ponte dropped the term "large-scale displacement" and then lowered the number of displaced Serb civilians to "tens of thousands."[64] It is difficult to prove whether Del Ponte altered the numbers because she felt the initial ones were inaccurate or because it could serve as a relatively low-cost concession to the government. Nevertheless, in the context of Zagreb's long-standing argument with the tribunal over the size of the 1995 displacement of Serbs, the removal of the 150,000 to 200,000 estimate was a victory for the Croatian government.

Del Ponte's efforts to bring Gotovina to trial also prompted her to find other ways to entice the retired general out of hiding. For instance, she suggested that upon Gotovina's surrender to the tribunal, he might not have to remain in pre-trial detention. That was less than Gotovina had demanded but more than some other fugitives received. Del Ponte was openly signaling her willingness to negotiate the terms of Gotovina's surrender. But Gotovina remained defiant.

Despite his impressive record on facilitating the "voluntary" surrender of nine suspects and his nationalist credentials, Sanader feared that arresting Gotovina would split the HDZ and alienate key allies within the party. Britain and The Netherlands, Europe's two most vocal critics of Zagreb's cooperation record, continued to insist that they would not support Croatia's bid for EU candidate status without Gotovina's arrest. Several days after the surrender of the six Bosnian Croat suspects in April 2004, Britain stood by its long-held refusal to ratify a stabilization and association agreement with Croatia, a necessary step to joining the EU. "We consider it impossible that people in Croatia

---

[63] For the text of the initial Gotovina indictment, see http://www.un.org/icty/indictment/englishgotii010608e.htm.

[64] For the text of the amended Gotovina indictment, see http://www.un.org/icty/indictment/english/got-ai040224e.htm.

cannot locate Gotovina," said Britain's Minister for Europe, Denis MacShane. "We told Croatia's prime minister and foreign minister on several occasions that the case of Ante Gotovina is of utmost importance for Croatia's accession."[65] However, Britain, which itself faced internal EU pressure to ease its stance, indicated that it might be more forgiving toward Croatia. Short of quickly sending Gotovina to the tribunal, MacShane indicated that a government pledge to do so could ease Britain's objection's to Croatia's EU bid.[66]

As indicated earlier, Del Ponte faced a dilemma when it came to crafting her much-anticipated assessment of Zagreb's cooperation in advance of the EU's Spring 2004 decision as to whether to designate Croatia a candidate country. Censuring Croatia might have been a strategic necessity since the prospect of bringing Gotovina to trial could diminish once Croatia came one step closer to joining Europe. Yet Del Ponte likely understood that if the EU went ahead and gave the green light to Croatia's candidacy, then a sharp critique of Sanader's non-compliance might weaken her authority by demonstrating her eroding influence in Brussels. Maintaining her international standing remained essential because of the support the chief prosecutor still needed in her trials of cooperation with Croatia and Serbia as well as in her battles with the Security Council over the terms of the tribunal's "completion strategy." In April and June 2004, Del Ponte gave Zagreb high marks for its cooperation – despite its actual mediocre record in the Gotovina case – apparently in the hopes that conciliation would be favorably received in the EU and prompt an appreciative Sanader to fulfill his pledge to cooperate in tracking down Croatia's last remaining fugitive. Del Ponte's positive assessments, which a European Commission source characterized as giving Croatia "a big benefit of the doubt," were "crucial for its candidacy to go forward."[67] Following Del Ponte's April assessment, the European Commission, the EU's executive body, recommended that the EU open negotiations with Croatia on its candidacy bid. After Del Ponte's June assessment, the EU made Croatia an official candidate, and set March 2005 as the start for membership negotiations.

Apparently convinced that Croatia was on track to begin final membership talks and then soon receive a date for EU membership, the Sanader government provided little cooperation in the tribunal's quest for Gotovina. However, Sanader's lack of cooperation and his underestimation of EU resolve proved to be a serious miscalculation as far as Croatia's efforts to win an early invitation to join the Union were concerned.

By late 2004, Del Ponte went on the offensive, criticizing Zagreb's inaction and holding up its non-compliance to public scrutiny.[68] Soon after, European

[65] "Britain says its support for Croatia's EU bid conditional on arrest of fugitive general," _AFP_, April 10, 2004.

[66] "Croatia must resolve Gotovina case before getting EU support – British minister," April 9, 2004, _BBC Monitoring/HINA News Agency_, Zagreb.

[67] Fieldwork interview with European Commission official, Brussels, December 2006.

[68] Graham Bowley, "EU Postpones Talks With Croatia," _International Herald Tribune_, March 17, 2005.

support for moving forward on membership negotiations with Croatia began to wane. In mid-March 2005, a day before the scheduled start of membership talks with Croatia, the EU called off the negotiations because of insufficient cooperation from Croatia. Despite Zagreb's increased compliance a year earlier, European leaders made the Gotovina case a litmus test for the privilege of entering the EU, reaffirming its policy that an invitation would be extended only if Croatia provided *full* cooperation to the tribunal. Europe's strong stance was directed as much to Serbia as to Croatia. Officials in Brussels feared that allowing Croatia to join the EU without insisting on significant cooperation in the handover of such a high-ranking suspect as Gotovina would send a signal to Serbia that it too could continue to defy the tribunal without serious consequence when it came to the most wanted Serb fugitives – Radovan Karadžić and Ratko Mladić.[69]

The stalled EU membership talks were a major setback for the Sanader government, amounting to what one veteran Balkan analyst called "a catastrophic blow."[70] But European officials made it clear that the talks could resume as soon as Zagreb provided significant cooperation in the Gotovina case. This meant either arresting Gotovina or, if he was outside Croatia, mounting a serious effort to locate him and expeditiously passing this information on to the tribunal and relevant authorities. Croatian officials had long maintained that they should not be held responsible for arresting Gotovina, who they claimed was out of the country. But under heavy pressure from Del Ponte, the EU, in March 2005, was ultimately resolute. The message from Brussels was clear – regardless of Gotovina's whereabouts, Zagreb had a responsibility and a critical role to play in facilitating the general's arrest. Holding the Croatian government accountable for Gotovina's capture also stemmed from its evasion of its responsibility, back in June 2001, to arrest him after Del Ponte handed government officials a sealed indictment detailing the general's alleged crimes.

The EU's decision to block Croatia's entry into Europe galvanized the political leadership in Zagreb. After years of denying knowledge of where he was and doing little to find out, the government increased its efforts to track Gotovina down. Shortly after the EU's decision to delay the membership talks, Del Ponte's office and a team of trusted Croatian officials working under the direction of the Croatian State Prosecutor began to work closely on a plan to locate Gotovina.[71] Del Ponte downplayed her criticism of Croatia and sought to develop a working relationship that would allow Croatian authorities to pass on valuable information concerning Gotovina's whereabouts. This switch to a conciliatory strategy soon began to deliver results. "A solid relation of trust, based on full transparency, was established with my Office," Del Ponte later reported to the Security Council.[72]

[69] Ibid.
[70] Misha Glenny, "Backsliding in the Balkans," *The Nation*, April 11, 2005, p. 27.
[71] Address to the Security Council by Carla Del Ponte, December 15, 2005.
[72] Ibid.

Even before Gotovina's arrest, the EU, on October 3, 2005, rewarded Croatia by restarting the membership negotiations that had been stalled earlier in the year. Again, Del Ponte's appraisal would play a crucial role in Croatia's fate. Her positive assessment of Croatian cooperation, despite the fact that Gotovina was still on the run, surprised some observers who questioned whether Zagreb actually warranted such an important concession. The timing of Del Ponte's positive evaluation raised suspicion among some at the EU that she had been party to unsavory political deal-making that involved Turkey's bid for EU candidacy status. In the run-up to the October EU meeting, the question of Turkey's candidate status remained uncertain because of Austria's threat to wield its veto. Austria's veto was likely unless Britain, a strong advocate of Turkish membership, allowed EU talks to begin with Austria's close historical ally, Croatia. Moving forward on the question of Croatia's and Turkey's membership appeared to hinge on whether Del Ponte would issue a favorable assessment of Croatia's cooperation. A negative assessment could prompt Britain, a consistent tribunal supporter, to hold up Croatia's membership talks and thereby trigger Austria's veto of Turkey's membership bid.

It is not difficult to imagine that Del Ponte might well have come under intense pressure to render a favorable evaluation of Zagreb's search for Gotovina in order not to take responsibility for upsetting a political deal with far-reaching consequences for the future of Europe. Thus, suspicion arose that Del Ponte had delivered a positive report on Croatia to placate London and ease British efforts to bring Turkey into the EU. Yet, as an EU official suggested in an interview, Del Ponte may also have been concerned that a negative assessment "ran the risk of being overridden" by British officials and that Croatia would still be rewarded with membership talks. To avoid a costly split with a close ally, Del Ponte might have had an incentive to accentuate the positive.

Gotovina's imminent arrest and the increased cooperation provided by the Croatian authorities just before and after the October 2005 EU meeting would largely vindicate Del Ponte's appraisal of Croatian cooperation. In late September, Croatian officials had important information to share with Del Ponte. By monitoring Gotovina's telephone calls to his family – something that diplomats had long urged Zagreb to do – Croatian officials learned that he was abroad in Spain's Canary Islands. That information was quickly and quietly passed on to Del Ponte.[73] "This was the breakthrough for her to start to be disposed toward... giving a positive assessment," an EU official recalled.[74] However, Gotovina was one step ahead of the tribunal, leaving the Canary Islands before Spanish authorities could arrest him. Gotovina traveled to the nearby African mainland, but returned to the Canary Islands a few months later. The vigilant Croatian authorities were again able to track him down, even when he

[73] This account of the events that led to Gotovina's arrest is drawn from my interviews with EU officials in Brussels in December 2006 and from Marlise Simons, "War Crimes Case Revives Passions in a Divided Croatia," *New York Times*, December 12, 2005, A3.
[74] Fieldwork interview with EU official, Brussels, December 2006.

checked into a luxury hotel under a false name and with a false passport. That set the stage for his arrest. On the evening of December 7, just after Gotovina had ordered dinner and wine at his hotel, Spanish special forces arrested him. Within a few days, Gotovina, who had traveled the world as a fugitive, visited one destination he had hoped to avoid – The Hague.

Gotovina's arrest sparked nationalist protests back in Croatia, but did not spur instability as the government feared. In Split, some 40,000 rallied to protest the capture and impending trial of the popular war hero. But this protest, and a much smaller one in Zagreb, were dwarfed by the much larger protests held against the tribunal in 2001. The backlash against the government would likely have been much stronger had Gotovina been arrested by Croatian authorities. In this regard, the fact that Gotovina was beyond the reach of the government was a critical factor in diminishing nationalist mobilization. Still, the government played an instrumental, if behind the scenes, role in Gotovina's capture. As with the series of voluntary surrenders in 2004, the Sanader government had found a way to provide what the tribunal needed without seriously jeopardizing its domestic standing. Regardless of how long Gotovina had actually been outside Croatia after he went into hiding in 2001, the EU's insistence that Croatia was responsible for his arrest – and Del Ponte's ability to persuade the EU to take this position – established the important precedent that a targeted state could be found to be in non-compliance even if a fugitive had fled the country.[75]

5.10 Conclusion

The Sanader government's decisions to send newly indicted Bosnian Croat and Croatian suspects to The Hague in 2004 and to provide cooperation in Gotovina's arrest in the Canary Islands underscore the tribunal's growing success in achieving its mandate to bring war crimes suspects from all sides of the Balkan wars to justice. During the post-Tuđman era, the handover of five Croatian generals demonstrates that the ICTY has overcome Zagreb's entrenched resistance to cooperation. With these victories, the tribunal has also shown

---

[75] By the end of September 2007, the combined ICTY trial of Gotovina, Markać, and Čermak had not yet begun. Meanwhile, another high-profile ICTY trial concerning Croatia came to an end in late September 2007. The verdict in the trial of the Serbian Vukovar Three – for the murder of the wounded Croatian soldiers in 1991 – proved bitterly disappointing for Croatia. One of the three suspects – Miroslav Radić – was acquitted, while the other two – Veselin Šljivančanin and Mile Mrkšić – received relatively light sentences of five and twenty years, respectively. Back in 1991, the Vukovar massacre and the destruction of the Croatian town at the hands of Milosevic's JNA forces prompted the Zagreb government to request a UN tribunal in a bid for international recognition of Croatian suffering. Even as the ICTY later came to threaten the Croatian government by uncovering its complicity in war crimes, Zagreb retained an interest in having Croatia's victimization at Vukovar and elsewhere affirmed by an international court. However, the long-awaited verdict in the Vukovar case led to harsh condemnation of the tribunal from a broad spectrum of Croatian politicians, including the pro-tribunal president, Stjepan Mesić, who said that his "confidence in the court has now been seriously shaken." See "Croats Angry at War Crimes Sentences," *Associated Press*, September 28, 2007.

that when it comes to its relationship with Zagreb, its authority and autonomy have increased significantly. In important respects, the court's authority has also increased significantly vis-à-vis its powerful international patrons, the United States and the European Union. Particularly during the 1990s, the West had little intention of pressing the Croatian government to cooperate with tribunal investigations of the Homeland War. The United States, in particular, had little interest in seeing top-level suspects brought to trial, which could bring unwelcome attention to America's tacit role in encouraging Croatia's ethnic cleansing campaign against Croatian Serbs in 1995. But the tribunal's persistent lobbying and its increasing criticism of the West's passivity gradually compelled the United States and Europe to place the issue of Croatia's cooperation with investigations and prosecutions of Homeland War atrocities higher on their foreign policy agendas. Over time, the West applied strong pressure on the post-Tuđman governments of Ivica Račan and Ivo Sanader. Zagreb's susceptibility to pressure lay primarily in its abiding desire to gain entry into the European Union and to the EU's decision to link Croatia's designation as a candidate country to full cooperation with the tribunal.

As this chapter shows, the ICTY and its chief prosecutor play a crucial if often overlooked role in the battles over state cooperation. The tribunal's use of shaming and other adversarial strategies vis-à-vis targeted states have become valuable instruments for compliance. But as this chapter also shows, the ICTY's leverage vis-à-vis states is often greatly enhanced by using conciliatory strategies that are designed to lower the domestic costs of cooperation and to increase the domestic and international benefits of doing so for the state in question. The main goal of these conciliatory strategies – such as delaying indictments and deferring cases to domestic judiciaries – is to offer concessions in exchange for subsequent state cooperation. Despite her reputation as an uncompromising crusader, Chief Prosecutor Del Ponte often sought to establish a working relationship with the Zagreb government and to negotiate compromises to what she often presented publicly as firm and unbending demands. A central aim of this chapter has been to identify and highlight the ways in which the chief prosecutor uses conciliation and compromise to bring states to the bargaining table and in turn to bring fugitives into the dock.

PART III

RWANDA: VIRTUAL TRIALS, INTERNATIONAL JUSTICE, AND THE POLITICS OF SHAME

6

The Struggle to Create the International Criminal Tribunal for Rwanda

6.1 Introduction

The United Nations' first ad hoc war crimes court – the International Criminal Tribunal for the Former Yugoslavia (ICTY) – seemed, unsurprisingly, destined to be mired in conflict with the Serbian and Croatian governments that had instigated the Balkan wars in the first place. But the UN's next attempt to establish an international tribunal, in the aftermath of the Rwandan genocide, promised a much brighter future for cooperation with a state whose government leaders represented the victims. Whereas the ICTY was cast as a natural enemy of Serbs and Croats, the International Criminal Tribunal for Rwanda (ICTR) seemed poised as a likely friend of the new Tutsi-led Rwandan government that brought the 1994 genocide to a halt and took power in its aftermath. The potential for a strong alliance between the Kigali government and the ICTR could be seen in the confluence of Rwandan government and international interests in prosecuting the Hutu architects of the genocide. Despite this convergence, the tribunal–government relationship was often marked by rancor and bitterness. From the start, the threat of state non-compliance loomed. Disagreement over the blueprint for the new court prompted Rwanda, which happened to hold a temporary seat on the Security Council at the time, to cast a dissenting vote against authorizing the establishment of the tribunal. Even after the authorization, tribunal officials and diplomats feared that Rwanda might withhold vital assistance and disrupt the court's work. "It worried me a lot because there was a real danger that the Rwandan government would in fact back out," David J. Scheffer, the former United States Ambassador-at-Large for War Crimes Issues, told me in an interview. "The Rwandan government in the end had voted against [the tribunal] statute. So we always had that concern that they could" withhold cooperation.[1] At various times, the government has

---

[1] See fieldwork interview with David J. Scheffer, Washington, D.C., September 2004.

delivered on its threat, with profound consequences for the tribunal's ability to operate effectively and independently.

This chapter and the next three chapters provide a case study of the "trials of cooperation" between the ICTR and the Rwandan Patriotic Front (RPF) government. My aim is to show why the Rwandan government has enjoyed the upper hand in these "trials" and how the government has wielded non-compliance and the threat of non-compliance to control the course of justice at the Tanzanian-based international tribunal. The government has exerted direct influence over the court's prosecutorial agenda by blocking the investigations of Tutsi war crimes committed against Hutu civilians in 1994. By so doing, the Kigali government has long rendered the ICTR a de facto "victor's court" in which Tutsi RPF suspects enjoy virtual immunity from prosecution.

In contrast to the ICTY's growing capacity to prod Balkan states to cooperate and to "prosecute" them in the "trials of cooperation" for failing to do so, the ICTR has had little success in exposing Rwandan non-cooperation and generating international condemnation against the Kigali regime. The Rwandan government, not the ICTR, has enjoyed a monopoly on the mobilization of shame. Ostensibly, the government's "counter-shaming" campaign against the tribunal has been driven by the tribunal's alleged failure to deliver justice to and for the Tutsi victims and survivors of the Rwandan genocide. But beyond this purpose, the Rwandan government has used its rhetorical attacks to undermine the tribunal in the eyes of would-be international allies in the media, diplomatic corps, and human rights community. As I will demonstrate, this counter-shaming offensive intensified against the ICTR following Chief Prosecutor Carla Del Ponte's decision to investigate Tutsi RPF officers for their alleged role in atrocities against Hutu civilians. To thwart Del Ponte, the Rwandan government has cast the ICTR as yet another betrayal by the UN and the international community. Instead of providing solace to victims as the tribunal promised, the government has argued that the court's slow pace of trials, administrative scandals, and the alleged mistreatment of survivors who have testified at the tribunal have further victimized Rwanda.

Rwanda's victim status casts it in an advantageous position in its battles with the ICTR. The Tutsi-led government's assertion of victim status has resonated in an international community still shaken from the guilt of standing by passively as up to 800,000 Tutsi and moderate Hutu were massacred in the genocide. Although the Tutsi population, not the Tutsi-led government, was the victim of the genocide, the government has effectively portrayed itself as a victim deserving of international sympathy and support.

Victim status and the international community's quest for atonement for not intervening to end the genocide have not alone rendered Rwanda powerful in its trials of cooperation with the ICTR. Rwanda's leverage vis-à-vis the tribunal is also greatly strengthened by its strategic alliance with its closest Western allies, the United States and Britain. American and British diplomats have at times intervened on the tribunal's behalf in crises with the Rwandan government. Nevertheless, when it comes to Rwandan non-compliance, the United States and Britain have often been careful not to push Rwanda too strongly. Whereas the West has threatened political and economic retribution for Balkan non-cooperation with the ICTY, and has sometimes carried out such threats, it has not acted accordingly when the Rwandan government has stymied the ICTR.

At the ICTR, as at the ICTY, state cooperation is a crucial issue that ultimately shapes legal outcomes inside the courtroom. Yet in the case of Rwanda, the world has largely overlooked this issue. This oversight is symptomatic of the lack of sustained global attention paid to the ICTR. But this neglect also stems from the fact that state non-cooperation has not been the visible and chronic problem that it has been for the ICTY. The Rwandan government's overall cooperation with tribunal prosecutions of Hutu genocide suspects has actually been high, as indicated from my interviews with tribunal and government officials. The cooperation that the Rwandan government has provided derives from its interest in aiding the prosecution of its Hutu enemies, who are implicated in the genocidal massacres and, if acquitted and released, could spearhead an armed rebellion against the minority Tutsi-led government.

Yet this does not ensure that Rwanda the government will allow these genocide prosecutions if it is angered elsewhere by the tribunal's approach to justice, especially where the tribunal expects state cooperation in the investigation of Tutsi war crimes suspects. In fact, the government has impeded the prosecution of Hutu genocide defendants in order to intimidate the tribunal into forgoing its investigations of Tutsi suspects. In 2000, when the ICTR first began to investigate Tutsi war crimes, the Rwandan government refused to cooperate with the investigations despite promising that it would. In time, government anger over these investigations led it to bring the Hutu genocide trials to a temporary halt by preventing Tutsi prosecution witnesses from leaving Rwanda to testify in the trials in Arusha, Tanzania.

Long before this showdown, the ICTR and the Rwandan government were locked in battle over other aspects of the new experiment in international justice. The outcomes of these battles were crucial in shaping the power dynamic between tribunal and state in their subsequent disputes. A full rendering of the trials of cooperation in the Rwandan context involves understanding the complex history of state–tribunal relations, as well as the origins of conflict between the international court and the government. Toward that end, this chapter seeks to explain the nature of the conflict between the Tutsi-led Rwandan government and the ICTR in the aftermath of the genocide.

6.2 The Origins of the Conflict

Well before the UN allocated its first dollar to the ICTR, the Tutsi leadership, newly in power in Kigali, and the Security Council held conflicting visions of the design of the nascent tribunal. These divergent visions turned into open conflict when the question of establishing the tribunal came before the Council in the Fall of 1994.

For the Rwandan government, an international court was indispensable for delivering justice, rebuilding a broken society, and establishing an identity as a victim state. But the government's wish for international justice did not mean that it would grant unconditional consent to any court established by the UN. Tutsi leaders approached the question of post-conflict justice with the same determination and desire for control that characterized their successful military campaign – then as the RPF rebel army – to wrest power from the Hutu extremists during the genocide. The Rwandan government did not have a formal role in tribunal operations. Yet it quickly came to expect that the tribunal, on behalf of the international community, owed a debt to Tutsi victims and survivors as well as to the government itself for failing to stop the genocide. The government lobbied against several provisions of the tribunal's proposed statute that it argued would deny justice to genocide survivors. Chief among these provisions were the UN's plans to hold the trials outside Rwanda and its decision to ban capital punishment for convicted defendants.

The Rwandan government sought an ad hoc international court to spark international condemnation of the mass killings that swept the country in the Spring and early Summer of 1994. For the new Rwandan state, as for many other post-conflict states, the normative drive for justice cannot be separated from material considerations of power. For Rwanda, the pursuit of justice also became a pursuit to neutralize the former leadership of the Hutu extremist regime that, in exile, posed a military threat to Rwanda's stability. The Tutsi-led government wanted an international tribunal in part to help it defeat an enemy that had not been completely vanquished. In this respect, the tribunal, even though established after the genocide and civil war in Rwanda, still operated under conditions of war, given the ongoing hostilities in northwestern Rwanda and neighboring Zaire (renamed the Democratic Republic of Congo in 1997). Thus, as it did with the ICTY, the pale of wartime helped shape the dynamics of the ICTR. The global acknowledgment of Tutsi suffering that a tribunal could provide promised to reap political and economic benefits from the international community. Far from being unusual, this quest for victim status is common to many states engaged in or emerging from war. As a fledgling government seeks to establish its authority at home and legitimacy abroad, victim status can become a valuable form of political currency.

The next section provides a brief overview of the Rwandan genocide and the shift in power to the RPF by July 1994. I will then show how the new Rwandan government's interest in an international tribunal was directly related to bolstering the legitimacy of its hold on power. Next, I will explain where the UN's own vision of post-genocide justice clashed with the Kigali government's vision. The remaining sections of the chapter analyze the conflict between the Kigali government and the Security Council regarding the proposed blueprint of the new tribunal.

6.3 The Rwandan Genocide and the Rise of the RPF

By the beginning of July 1994, the end of the Rwandan genocide finally appeared in sight. Almost 100 days of killing left Rwanda's minority Tutsi population decimated and the country in ruins. The death toll of the Rwandan genocide – estimated at 800,000 – was approximately 265 times greater than the September 11, 2001, attacks in the United States.

Approximately 10 percent of Rwanda's population perished in one of the most organized mass murders of the twentieth century. Most victims died brutally by machetes or other blunt agricultural instruments wielded by Hutu extremists. Those fleeing for their lives had few places to hide in the densely populated country the size of Maryland. In past episodes of mass violence in Rwanda, churches had been civilian sanctuaries. But this time around, Hutu militias, often with the complicity of Hutu clergy, massacred tens of thousands of Tutsi who sought refuge in churches at Nyamata, Nyamara, Nyrabure, and other communities throughout Rwanda.[2] The genocide quickly transformed the verdant country of rolling hills into an apocalyptic landscape. Canadian Lieutenant-General Roméo Dallaire, the head of the UN peacekeeping operations in the country, vividly recalls the painful disjuncture between the beauty of the Rwandan Spring and the horror of the genocide: "It was hard to believe that in the past weeks an unimaginable evil had turned Rwanda's gentle green valleys and mist-capped hills into a stinking nightmare of rotting corpses."[3]

The UN was in a position to curtail at least some of the bloodshed, given its advance warning from Dallaire of the planned massacres and the presence in Rwanda of a peacekeeping contingent under his command. The peacekeepers were sent months earlier to safeguard a peace agreement between the Hutu government and the Tutsi-led RPF rebels. But at the start of the genocide, following the murder of ten Belgian peacekeepers, the Security Council ordered the removal of most of the UN peacekeeping force.[4] Dallaire's remaining peacekeepers saved some lives[5] but, abandoned by the UN and the international community, they were essentially helpless in the face of the Hutu extremists' lethal efficiency. The United States and other Western powers delayed characterizing the killings as genocide and chose not to intervene militarily or to take other measures such as jamming Hutu radio broadcasts used to incite the massacres. Rwanda has since become a symbol not only of unspeakable violence but of the international community's indifference to massive human suffering. Yet much less acknowledged is the responsibility that the Tutsi-led RPF rebels also bears for the events of 1994 and for forestalling international efforts that might have saved more Tutsi lives. Several weeks after the genocide began, a

---

[2] For a path-breaking study of the causes and dynamics of the genocide, see Scott Straus, *The Order of Genocide: Race, Power, and War in Rwanda* (Ithaca: Cornell University Press, 2006).

[3] Roméo Dallaire, *Shake Hands with the Devil: The Failure of Humanity in Rwanda* (Toronto: Random House Canada, 2003), p. 1.

[4] For an analysis of the UN's policy toward Rwanda leading up to and during the genocide, see Michael Barnett, *Eyewitness to a Genocide: The United Nations and Rwanda* (Ithaca: Cornell University Press, 2002); Alison Des Forges, *Leave None to Tell the Story: Genocide in Rwanda* (New York: Human Rights Watch, 1999), pp. 595–690. For an examination that focuses largely on U.S. policy toward Rwanda, see Power, *"A Problem From Hell,"* pp. 329–389.

[5] Fieldwork interview with former Rwanda-based UN peacekeeper, Kigali, July 1999.

Security Council proposal to send a larger peacekeeping contingent to Rwanda was rejected by the RPF, fearful that such a force could undermine its goal of a clear-cut military victory.[6] Moreover, there are clear indications that the RPF's emphasis on defeating the Hutu government forces delayed its efforts to rescue vulnerable Tutsi communities.[7]

While the genocide raged, the balance of power shifted to the Tutsi-led RPF rebel army. The efficient and disciplined fighting force, led by General Paul Kagame, captured key towns from the extremist Hutu government not long after the violence began with the April 6, 1994, shooting down of the Hutu president's plane. The crash of Juvénal Habyarimana's plane brought an end to the uneasy peace between the RPF and the Hutu government, in place since the signing of the Arusha Accords in August 1993. Who shot down the plane and in effect lit the match sparking the genocide would remain a mystery well after 1994. The Arusha Accords had been intended to bring an end to a civil war that had been sparked by the RPF's invasion of northern Rwanda in October 1990. The invasion had been prompted by the RPF's drive to return home to Rwanda after decades of living as second-class citizens, mainly in neighboring Uganda.[8] Many Tutsi, including a young Paul Kagame, fled Rwanda as early as 1959 to escape the repeated waves of Hutu massacres. In the mid-1980s, the Hutu government in Kigali declared that Rwanda was too over-populated to accept the repatriation of the approximately 600,000 Tutsi in exile.[9]

As the RPF solidified its control over Rwanda toward the end of the genocide, more and more Hutu extremists began to flee into the French-controlled Zone Turquoise in the southwest part of the country, and then across the border into Zaire. The UN-sanctioned French intervention in late June was supposedly intended to save Tutsi lives. However, there is great skepticism surrounding France's purported humanitarian motives given its previous support of the Hutu regime.[10] While French forces saved some Tutsi lives, they also enabled scores of the most wanted Hutu génocidaires to flee RPF capture.[11] On July 4, 1994, the RPF gained control of the capital, Kigali. On July 18, the RPF captured the last Hutu stronghold and declared victory, albeit a solemn one given the landscape of death.

6.4 A Call for Justice: Rwanda Requests an International Tribunal

As RPF officials looked to the future, the question of justice loomed as a vexing and critical issue. It was not a foregone conclusion as to the form justice would take or whether there would be a formal judicial response to the genocide.

---

[6] Des Forges, *Leave None to Tell the Story*, pp. 698–701.
[7] Ibid., pp. 698–699.
[8] Des Forges, *Leave None to Tell the Story*, p. 48.
[9] Ibid., p. 48.
[10] Barnett, *Eyewitness to a Genocide*, pp. 147–149.
[11] Ibid., p. 149.

If Rwanda's history was any guide, there would be another cycle of revenge and impunity rather than trials.[12] Since the Hutu Revolution of 1959 (when the Tutsi lost their position as the favored ethnic group under the control of Belgian colonizers), impunity had been the standard response to the aftermath of large-scale massacres of the Tutsi population. The post-genocide Tutsi-led RPF government, however, insisted on the need for trials, both at the domestic and international levels.

The irony of the genocide's aftermath was that Rwanda's prisons and communal lock-ups were overflowing with suspects, but not with those most sought by the new regime in Kigali – the government and military planners of the genocide. As a result, the fledging justice system was inundated with tens of thousands of low-level suspects, but practically devoid of any high-level ones. The most important pieces of the domestic justice puzzle – the prosecution of high-level suspects – were not in the government's control since almost all the leaders of the extremist Hutu government had fled Rwanda and sought refuge in the sprawling refugee camps of eastern Zaire, elsewhere in Africa, and in some European countries.

Rwandan courts also sorely lacked institutional capacity to carry out prosecutions. The task of prosecuting such a heavy caseload would be staggering for any country. It was infinitely more so for a country whose legal system had been destroyed. Most of Rwanda's judges and prosecutors had either been killed during the genocide, were involved in the killings, or had fled the country. The poor condition of the courts, the need to develop a domestic law on genocide, and the lack of sufficient international aid forced Rwanda to delay its own trials until the end of December 1996.[13] (The ICTR did not begin its first trial until January 1997.) Yet Rwanda's domestic trials, once they began, proceeded at a much faster rate than the international trials conducted in Arusha, the outcome of a legal system with far fewer due process protections. By early 2001, the domestic courts had tried 5,310 genocide cases, compared with just 9 completed cases in Arusha.[14] Still, the backlog of cases in Rwanda was overwhelming. In 2002, a Rwandan Ministry of Justice official estimated that it would take up to 200 years for the domestic courts to adjudicate the more than 100,000 suspects in Rwanda's prisons.[15]

When it came to the prosecution of high-ranking genocide suspects, the government quickly realized that it had to depend on the international community. For several reasons, the Kigali regime knew that it was unlikely to win extradition of these prominent suspects who had left the country. First, some Hutu suspects had fled to African countries, such as Zaire and Kenya, whose governments were sympathetic to the former Hutu regime. Second, some countries

---

[12] For a discussion of the history of the Tutsi–Hutu conflict, see Des Forges, *Leave None to Tell the Story*, pp. 31–64.

[13] Des Forges, *Leave None to Tell the Story*, p. 755.

[14] Human Rights Watch World Report, 2002.

[15] Fieldwork interview with Rwandan Ministry of Justice official, Kigali, May 2002.

would not extradite Hutu suspects for prosecution in Rwanda because of these countries' opposition to Rwanda's use of the death penalty. Third, Rwanda's lack of extradition treaties with numerous countries greatly reduced the regime's chances of apprehending fugitives.

The conventional wisdom is that the government went along with such a tribunal since it was the only way to ensure that the masterminds of the genocide were prosecuted. Yet, for the Rwandan government, international prosecution of the genocide was of fundamental importance, even though it complicated its efforts to control the course of post-genocide justice. An international court could go some way in solving the legitimacy crisis likely to arise for many Hutu from the Tutsi-led government's prosecution of high-level suspects. The absence of societal trust in Rwanda's courts had been underscored by the country's deep ethnic cleavages and the use of the legal system to favor members of the ethnic group in power. In an interview I conducted, one highly placed Rwandan government official who was pivotal in formulating the regime's justice policies explained the government's interest in an international tribunal in the following way: "It was felt that an independent, outside court, not a Rwandan court, would bring great credibility [to the justice process and] no one could turn back and say that was victor's justice."[16]

Establishing an international tribunal, Rwandan authorities thought, would also provide a way to hold the international community accountable for abandoning Rwanda during the genocide. "The tribunal also helped to remind the international community that it was its responsibility to help prevent or help stop this genocide," the same Rwandan official told me.[17] In short, it was as if the UN itself stood in the moral dock, and by running the trials would acknowledge its own guilt.

Some observers have mischaracterized or failed to recognize the complexity of the early conflict between the Rwandan government and the Security Council. A prominent example is seen in the writings of the American journalist, Philip Gourevitch. Gourevitch maintains that the government asked the UN for help in apprehending high-level genocide suspects for trial in Rwanda's own courts. Gourevitch claims the UN refused to do so and established an international tribunal instead. In this version of events, the court's establishment was an affront to the Rwandan government and was in direct conflict with its own interests. "The Rwandan government regarded the UN's decision to keep its resources to itself as an insult," Gourevitch writes in reference to the UN's establishment of the court. "The very existence of the UN court implied that the Rwandan judiciary was incapable of reaching just verdicts, and seemed to dismiss in advance any trials that Rwanda might hold as beneath international standards."[18]

---

[16] Fieldwork interview with Rwandan government official, Kigali, May 2002.
[17] Ibid.
[18] Philip Gourevitch, *We Wish to Inform You that Tomorrow We Will be Killed with Our Families: Stories from Rwanda* (New York: Farrar, Straus, and Giroux, 1998), pp. 252–253.

While Gourevitch's analysis captures the international suspicion toward Rwanda's legal system, he distorts the actual course of events behind the establishment of the tribunal – he neglects, for example, the fact that the government actually requested an international court. Indeed, even as the ICTR has been plagued by administrative problems, the government has long seen the virtues of an international court, albeit one that the government would have a substantial role in shaping. "We asked for the tribunal, but we never got what we had asked for," Joseph Mutaboba, Rwanda's deputy foreign minister and former ambassador to the UN, told me in an interview.[19] Long after the ICTR's creation, Mutaboba and other top Rwandan government officials continued to express support for the idea of an international court even as they leveled harsh criticisms against it. "We would still have asked for a tribunal, but a tribunal set up and structured as we wished," a senior government official told me in an interview, when asked whether the RPF would have wanted international prosecutions even if it had had custody of all top-level suspects.[20] Thus, despite the government's decision to vote against the establishment of the tribunal, it still won an important victory when the Security Council authorized the creation of the ICTR.

6.5 Facing the Genocide: The International Community Calls for a Tribunal

In the wake of the genocide, a consensus developed among Security Council members that the Rwandan massacres could not go unpunished by the international community.[21] For the Council and the Western powers to redeem themselves for their non-intervention required no less than their support of an international war crimes tribunal, since the UN had established a tribunal for the lesser atrocities taking place in the Balkans. Moreover, some Western diplomats, particularly in the U.S. State Department, viewed the tribunal as key to ensuring peace and stability in Rwanda and elsewhere in Central Africa. In Rwanda, as in the former Yugoslavia, international justice was presented not only as a moral imperative but also as a political necessity to prevent a new round of armed conflict and atrocity. John Shattuck, the U.S. Assistant Secretary of State for Democracy, Human Rights, and Labor, hoped that an effective tribunal and the prompt arrests of Hutu génocidaires based across the Rwandan border in the UN-run refugee camps of eastern Zaire could remove the military threat facing Rwanda.[22] Shattuck feared that without prompt arrests

---

[19] Fieldwork interview with Joseph Mutaboba, Kigali, June 2002.

[20] Fieldwork interview with Rwandan government official, Kigali, May 2002.

[21] Even as it voted to withdraw most of its peacekeeping forces from Rwanda, the Security Council condemned the violations of international humanitarian law and authorized a Commission of Experts to investigate the violence. Based on its findings, the Commission recommended in October 1994 that the Council immediately establish a tribunal.

[22] John Shattuck, *Freedom on Fire: Human Rights Wars & America's Response* (Cambridge, MA: Harvard University Press, 2003), pp. 51–76.

of high-level genocide suspects, Rwanda's de-facto leader, Paul Kagame, would follow through on his threats to send the RPF army into Zaire to crush the Hutu extremists, and even make the arrests itself.[23] As early as August 1994, Shattuck believed it was imperative that the UN take immediate steps to create a functioning tribunal. "I was convinced that unless we moved quickly to set up an international tribunal and arrest the leaders of the genocide, a new cycle of vengeance would destabilize all of central Africa," Shattuck writes in his account of his diplomatic efforts to establish the ICTR. "Rwanda was not just a tragedy we had failed to prevent; it was another crisis in the making."[24]

The ICTR's lack of enforcement powers and the unwillingness of Security Council countries to arrest Hutu fugitives in the refugee camps and stop their cross-border attacks indeed prompted Kagame to take matters into his own hands. The RPF military interventions in Congo in the mid and late 1990s dealt a blow to the Hutu extremist forces. At the same time, however, the invasion led to widespread RPF atrocities against fleeing Hutu civilians and sparked a wider regional war in Congo that, by 2003, had resulted in the deaths of more than 3 million people.[25]

The Rwandan government's shaming of the West for its inaction during the genocide also played a strong role in prodding the Security Council to take steps to create a tribunal. Still, this did not mean that the Council established the court only to appease the Rwandan government. The UN also acted to rehabilitate its own image as a moral force in the world that protected human rights and the principle of individual criminal accountability. Acting morally in the aftermath of the genocide required a legal process that reflected and expanded the evolution of international humanitarian law, especially as it pertained to due process guarantees for defendants. Such a court derived its legitimacy from being an autonomous institution mandated to protect the rights of both victims and defendants. Beyond this, the ICTR's international founders focused on the important interim role of these ad hoc tribunals for creating legal precedents for a more permanent system of global justice. As such, both the ICTY and the ICTR were not only viewed as responses to particular conflicts, but also as stepping stones for the establishment of the International Criminal Court (notwithstanding the U.S. government's subsequent opposition to this permanent tribunal).

For the Kigali regime, post-atrocity justice began and ended not with due consideration of the requisite rights for the defendant but for what the victim had suffered. The subsequent conflict between the Tutsi-led Rwandan government and the Security Council emerged in large part from these divergent orientations toward justice. The Rwandan government expected, and demanded, that the Council placate its anger at the UN's inaction during the genocide by

---

[23] Ibid., p. 63.
[24] Ibid., p. 68.
[25] "DR Congo: Africa's Worst War," *BBC News*, April 8, 2003.

revising the tribunal's proposed statute to favor the government's conception of justice for the victim.

For the UN, the tribunal was not to be a surrogate for Rwanda's devastated legal system, but created to prosecute atrocities that, as the French ambassador to the UN said, "are repugnant to the conscience of mankind."[26] That the tribunal was meant to serve the international community's conception of justice is underscored by the comments of New Zealand Ambassador Colin Keating during the November 1994 meeting in which the Council voted to authorize the establishment of the court. The tribunal, he said, "is also of great significance to Rwanda. But it is of even more fundamental importance to the international community as a whole."[27] Therefore, said Keating, the New Zealand delegation "could not support any proposals that would change the international character of the Tribunal or introduce any suggestion that the Tribunal could be subordinated to Rwandan political intervention."[28] Other Council members agreed.

6.6 From Consensus to Conflict

A. Conflict in the Chambers: Rwanda Rejects the Tribunal

Security Council members hoped that there would be unanimity on November 8, 1994, the day they planned to authorize the creation of the second-ever UN war crimes tribunal. Yet Rwanda, the state most concerned with the question of justice, had strong enough objections to cast the lone dissenting vote against the Council resolution that established the tribunal.[29]

During the November Council meeting, delegates spoke eloquently about the promise of such a court to end "the cycle of impunity," foster reconciliation, and provide a bridge to a permanent war crimes court. There was solemn talk about the barbarity of the Hutu génocidaires, but little mention of the UN's failure to intervene months earlier to stop the massacres.

The Rwandan ambassador, Manzi Bakuramutsa, began his remarks by reminding the UN of the debt owed to Rwanda for its failure to stop the genocide. "When the genocide began, the international community, which had troops in Rwanda and could have saved hundreds of thousands of human lives ... decided instead to withdraw its troops from Rwanda and to abandon the victims to their butchers," Bakuramutsa said.[30] In light of international inaction during the genocide (and generous international humanitarian assistance to Hutu refugees, including génocidaires, in the refugee camps of eastern Zaire), the Tutsi-led government felt entitled to demand international justice on its own

---

[26] Provisional verbatim record of the Security Council, forty-ninth year, 3453rd meeting, November 8, 1994.

[27] Ibid.

[28] Ibid.

[29] Citing its sympathy for Rwanda's objections to the tribunal, China abstained from voting on the resolution to authorize the establishment of the ICTR.

[30] Ibid. (Rwandan delegate's remarks).

terms. Bakuramutsa cited seven reasons for the government's decision to vote against the proposed tribunal. The regime's most serious complaints concerned the court's prohibition of capital punishment, its apparent subordinate role to the ICTY, and its likely location outside Rwanda.

Rwandan authorities also voiced concern that limiting tribunal indictments for crimes committed only during the time span of 1994 would unjustly free Hutu génocidaires from the court's prosecutorial reach. In negotiations prior to the November meeting, Council members had initially sought to authorize the tribunal only to prosecute crimes that occurred over a nearly nine-month period from the actual start of the genocide on April 6 until the end of 1994. Rwandan officials argued unsuccessfully to allow prosecution of crimes that occurred from an earlier start date to a shorter end date – between October 1, 1990 and July 17, 1994, the proclaimed end of the civil war. On the start side, the government hoped that the earlier date of October 1, 1990 would enable the tribunal to indict Hutu suspects for planning the genocide in the several years leading up to the 1994 massacres. On the end side, the government hoped that the shorter end date of July 17, 1994, would disallow tribunal prosecutions of RPF atrocities against Hutu civilians, many of which occurred after the Rwandan civil war ended in July 1994. The government won a partial victory insofar as the Council agreed to allow tribunal prosecutors to charge suspects with crimes that occurred beginning from January 1, 1994, even before the genocide began on April 6. The Council, however, held firm when it came to the December 31, 1994 end date, thus allowing more prosecutions of RPF crimes against Hutu civilians and planting the seeds for the later confrontation between the tribunal and the Rwandan government (to be discussed in Chapters 8 and 9).

Still, the Tutsi-led government scored a major yet unacknowledged victory when it came to the court's overall temporal jurisdiction of one year only. The Tutsi-led RPF army – as well as Hutu génocidaires in neighboring Zaire – would enjoy immunity from prosecution for any atrocities committed *after* 1994. The tribunal's narrow temporal mandate compromised the court's capacity to deter and prosecute post-1994 atrocities committed by both the RPF and the exiled génocidaires. And such has in fact been the case inasmuch as the Rwandan army, during its subsequent invasions of Congo, has carried out large-scale massacres against both Hutu génocidaires and Hutu civilians.

Rwandan officials also objected to the lack of clearly delineated rules concerning the setting of priorities for the crimes that the tribunal would prosecute. The government feared that the tribunal could divert its limited resources from prosecuting genocide to prosecuting lesser crimes. This appears to have been a veiled attempt by the Rwandan government to make the Council ensure that the ICTR would not have the legal authority to indict RPF officers suspected of carrying out non-genocidal massacres against Hutu civilians. The Council would obviously not prioritize such lesser crimes, but nor would it ensure that such crimes had to be forcefully pursued by the tribunal's chief prosecutor. This subtle ambiguity in the tribunal's legal mission would come to bear directly on the issue of victor's justice at the ICTR.

The Kigali regime also protested the absence of any provision preventing France from nominating judges to serve at the tribunal. As a close ally of the former Hutu regime, the Tutsi-led government bitterly accused France of aiding the génocidaires and playing a high-profile role in the civil war. The Council declined to prohibit French judges from serving at the tribunal. Interestingly, however, the UN has never appointed a French judge to serve as a trial judge at the ICTR.[31] This stands in contrast to the UN practice of appointing French judges to serve as trial judges at the ICTY. Finally, the Rwandan government objected to the provision in the tribunal statute that stipulated that convicted war criminals be imprisoned outside Rwanda. Subsequent to the November 1994 Council meeting, the UN changed the ICTR statute to allow convicted defendants to serve their sentences in Rwanda.[32]

B. The Battle over Capital Punishment

Chief among the Rwandan government's objections to the tribunal's proposed statute was the prohibition of death sentences for convicted génocidaires. To the government, the death penalty was a punishment commensurate with the gravity of the crime of genocide. The death penalty lay at the emotional core of what justice meant to many genocide survivors.[33] Moreover, a disturbing disparity existed in that while a life sentence was the harshest punishment facing high-level Hutu suspects in international custody, lower-level suspects in Rwandan courts faced the death penalty. In his remarks to the Security Council, Bakuramutsa argued that the UN's prohibition of the death penalty would create just such an unfair discrepancy in punishments. "This situation," Bakuramutsa claimed, "is not conducive to national reconciliation in Rwanda."[34] Council members took a completely opposite view: authorizing the tribunal to hand down death sentences would only inflame Hutu–Tutsi conflict and undermine reconciliation, they argued.

The Council's notion of just punishment did not emerge from a particular analysis of the Rwandan genocide but from the evolution of international humanitarian law since Nuremberg and Tokyo, when death sentences were legion. In short, the growing trend toward the international abolition of capital punishment stems from the belief that the protection of a "right to life" is a universal right. For most Council members, capital punishment had long become a barbaric relic of medieval times. Abolition of capital punishment, rising

---

[31] Claude Jorda of France served as an ICTR Appeals Chamber judge. The ICTR and ICTY share the same Appeals Chamber judges, many of whom, such as Jorda, are recruited after serving as ICTY trial judges.

[32] As of July 2007, no convicted ICTR defendant has been sent to Rwanda to serve his sentence.

[33] Victor Peskin, "Conflicts of Justice: An Analysis of the Role of the International Criminal Tribunal for Rwanda," *International Peacekeeping*, Volume 6, Nos. 4–6, July-December 2000, pp. 128–137.

[34] Provisional verbatim record of the Security Council, forty-ninth year, 3453rd meeting, November 8, 1994.

throughout the first and third worlds in the 1980s and 1990s, had become a core value for an increasing number of UN member states. Even if two of the five permanent Council members – the United States and China – used capital punishment in their domestic legal systems, there was virtually no chance that the Council would permit executions in the newly created international tribunals. Madeleine Albright, then the U.S. ambassador to the UN, expressed sympathy for Rwanda's advocacy of the death penalty. However, she conceded that "it was simply not possible to meet those concerns and still maintain broad support in the Council."[35]

The death penalty issue would continue to spark controversy in Rwanda and rankle the government for several years to come. Yet there was little the government could do in light of the Council's steadfast position. The Council would, however, offer some compromises when it came to Kigali's other objections to the tribunal's statute.

C. Pragmatic Concerns and Problems of Institutional Capacity

Some of the Rwandan government's most serious criticisms of the tribunal's proposed statute were based on perceived flaws that would undermine the international endeavor to hold genocide suspects criminally accountable. During the November 1994 Council meeting, the government leveled two pragmatic criticisms against the tribunal's design. First, the government protested the decision to authorize the construction of only two courtrooms at the tribunal. Ambassador Bakuramutsa presciently argued that with only two trial chambers, the trial process would be greatly compromised. The ICTR was in fact frequently overwhelmed with cases and sorely in need of additional courtrooms and judges. The Council allowed for the possibility that additional trial chambers could be added as needed by both tribunals. Belatedly, in the late 1990s, the Council authorized a third chamber for the ICTR and the ICTY. In March 2005, the ICTR completed construction of a fourth trial chamber.

The government's second pragmatic criticism focused on its fear that the ICTR would be treated as an extension of the ICTY rather than as a freestanding institution. Publicly, the ICTR was presented as having its own chief prosecutor and its own appeals chamber. But, in reality, both the ICTR and the ICTY shared the same chief prosecutor and the same appeals chamber. This official presentation was meant to indicate that the ICTR was not subordinate to the ICTY, notwithstanding the fact that both the chief prosecutor and the appeals chamber were based at the ICTY in The Hague. Rwanda complained that this arrangement was unsatisfactory because it subordinated the prosecution of the Rwandan genocide to the prosecution of the ethnic cleansing campaigns in the Balkans. Moreover, the government argued – correctly, as events would show – that forcing the ICTR to share a chief prosecutor and appeals chamber with the ICTY would undermine the efficiency of the ICTR's prosecutorial and judicial missions.

[35] Ibid.

Some journalists simply repeated the government assertion that the ICTR had been subordinated to the ICTY. Such is the interpretation advanced by Philip Gourevitch, who characterizes the ICTR as "essentially a subset"[36] of the ICTY. However, Gourevitch ignores how much the initial concept of the tribunal had changed since the UN Commission of Experts recommended that the ICTR be subsumed into the ICTY. The situation was more complex, with the Security Council ultimately making the ICTR by and large a separate institution, notwithstanding its common chief prosecutor and appeals chamber. Although not having its own chief prosecutor and appeals chamber hampered the ICTR's efficacy, the court remained a separate institution with its own statute, budget, trial judges, prosecutors, and administrators. Separate, of course, is not necessarily equal – in certain respects, there is merit to calling the ICTR a poor relation of the ICTY.

The Rwandan government's displeasure at the limits placed on the ICTR's institutional capacity gave it an opening to attack the UN's motives for establishing the court. Government officials charged that the Council created the tribunal out of guilt and not out of a genuine commitment to make the institution succeed. "My delegation," Bakuramutsa said, "considers that the establishment of so ineffective an international tribunal would only appease the conscience of the international community rather than respond to the expectations of the Rwandese people and of the victims of genocide in particular."[37] Noteworthy is the fact that the Rwandan government accurately predicted the administrative problems that would plague the tribunal well before its actual establishment. By pointing to these early warnings, the government would, years later, bolster its efforts to embarrass the tribunal and the UN for betraying their promise to provide speedy justice to the victims of the genocide.

D. The Politics of Location: Finding a Home for the ICTR

Of the Rwandan government's seven objections to the proposed tribunal, perhaps none was as vehemently argued as its objection to locating the court outside Rwanda. The government lobbied vigorously to have the tribunal headquartered in Kigali, where Rwandans could actually see the trials taking place. The government's objections to locating the ICTR outside Rwanda were closely connected to its reasons for wanting an international tribunal in the first place. To the government, a tribunal could serve as a pedagogic tool. "Above all," Bakuramutsa told his Security Council colleagues in November 1994, "we requested the establishment of this Tribunal to teach the Rwandese people a lesson to fight against the impunity to which it had become accustomed since 1959 and to promote national reconciliation. It therefore seems clear that the seat of the International Tribunal should be set in Rwanda; it will have to deal

---

[36] Gourevitch, *We Wish to Inform You that Tomorrow We Will be Killed with Our Families*, p. 252.
[37] Provisional verbatim record of the Security Council, forty-ninth year, 3453rd meeting, November 8, 1994.

with Rwandese suspects responsible for crimes committed in Rwanda against Rwandese."[38] Notwithstanding the potential of "palpable justice"[39] to foster stability – if not the much more elusive goal of reconciliation – locating the tribunal in Rwanda could afford the government a degree of influence over the court that it might not otherwise have.

The question of location would be contested so ardently because it also represented an important way for the government to remain a participant in international justice even though it had no formal role in the actual court proceedings. A UN decision to locate the court inside Rwanda could be used by the government as a demonstration of power over the international community and the Hutu masterminds of the genocide. But as long as the tribunal remained out of the country – even in neighboring Tanzania – it ran the risk of being seen by Rwandans as an abstract international enterprise. The remoteness of the tribunal was magnified by the poor communications links between Tanzania and Rwanda and the tribunal's anemic efforts at publicizing its work and bringing news of the trials to the people of Rwanda.[40]

During the November 1994 debate, several Council members expressed their support for locating the tribunal in Rwanda. However, they reserved final judgment until Secretary-General Boutros Boutros-Ghali completed an assessment of possible sites for the tribunal. The report, delivered to the Council in mid-February 1995, recommended against locating the tribunal in Rwanda. The Secretary-General favored the northern Tanzanian city of Arusha. Boutros-Ghali based his recommendation on two criteria: (1) fairness and independence, and (2) administrative efficiency. On both counts, the report concluded that it would be more advantageous to locate the tribunal outside war-torn Rwanda.

The UN worried that by placing the tribunal in Kigali, the Rwandan government would wield too much influence over it and thereby undermine the institution's independence. Although the international character of the tribunal would prevail even if it were located in Kigali, Boutros-Ghali's report concluded that it was necessary "to ensure not only the reality but also the appearance of complete impartiality and objectivity in the prosecution of persons responsible for crimes committed by both sides to the conflict. Justice and fairness, therefore, require that trial proceedings be held in a neutral territory."[41] Although the genocide was over, security concerns sparked by the continuing instability in northwestern Rwanda were cited by some at the UN as another reason for basing the ICTR in Tanzania.

---

[38] Ibid.
[39] John Shattuck uses this evocative phrase in his discussion of the Rwandan government's interest in having the ICTR based in Rwanda. See Shattuck, *Freedom on Fire*, p. 70.
[40] For a discussion of the tribunal's belated attempts to increase its visibility in Rwanda, see Victor Peskin, "Courting Rwanda: The Promises and Pitfalls of the ICTR Outreach Programme," *Journal of International Criminal Justice*, Vol. 3, No. 4, September, 2005, 950–961.
[41] Report of the Secretary-General Pursuant to Paragraph 5 of the Security Council Resolution 955, February 13, 1995.

The Rwandan government ended up supporting the Secretary-General's recommendation to base the court in Arusha in order, as Bakuramutsa said, to foster a spirit of cooperation. Yet the government never dropped its bid to see international trials held in Kigali and, over the years, pressed the tribunal to hold some genocide trials in Rwanda. Although the Council designated Arusha as the official seat of the ICTR, it granted a concession to the Kigali government by allowing the tribunal discretion to hold trials elsewhere, including Rwanda. The government's ongoing campaign to have trials moved to Rwanda has kept the issue of the tribunal's remoteness in the public eye.

From an early stage, the Council felt it was an important symbolic step to place the court in Africa. The UN gave serious consideration to locating the tribunal in Nairobi, which presented numerous advantages over other African sites, given its available infrastructure and its location in an urban area with a large UN presence and significant international press corps. However, the Kenyan government refused to enter into negotiations, likely because President Daniel arap Moi was a backer of the former Hutu regime. The UN then turned its sights to Arusha. Arusha's lack of infrastructure and its distance from larger East African cities made it less than satisfactory for a war crimes tribunal. The infrastructure challenges meant that it would be several years before all the necessary improvements were made to the building the tribunal occupied, a fact that slowed progress at the new court. Arusha, however, had symbolic importance because it was where Hutu and Tutsi factions signed a 1993 power-sharing agreement. But for many in Rwanda, Arusha was the wrong symbol in light of the failure of the Arusha Accords to prevent the genocide.

6.7 Conclusion

Despite its complaints to the contrary, the Rwandan government actually received significant concessions from the Security Council when it came to designing the new international court. The government's strong objections to locating the ICTR outside Rwanda prompted the UN to grant the government a major concession by locating the deputy prosecutor's office in Kigali. This concession was made, according to Richard J. Goldstone, the first ICTR (and ICTY) Chief Prosecutor, "to placate the feelings of the Rwandan government."[42] This entailed basing the entire investigative division, along with members of the prosecutor's staff, in Rwanda. By contrast, none of the countries of the former Yugoslavia had anywhere near that level of ICTY presence within its borders. Instead, ICTY investigators traveled to the Balkans on short missions and then returned to their offices in The Hague. To be sure, with the exception of the Bosnian Muslim-dominated government in Sarajevo, none of the other Balkan governments welcomed a sizeable tribunal presence.

The Council also permitted the ICTR to move trials to Rwanda if it so chose and also agreed that its decision to authorize only two trial chambers could be

---

[42] Goldstone, *For Humanity*, p. 110.

revisited if there became a need to do so. The UN made another key concession to the Kigali regime when it changed the tribunal statute to allow Rwanda to imprison convicted ICTR defendants. In addition, the UN has maintained a practice of not appointing French judges to serve at the ICTR in Arusha.

An even greater concession to the Rwandan government came from the UN parameters placed on the tribunal's temporal jurisdiction. By limiting the prosecution's jurisdiction to atrocities committed during 1994, the Council effectively, if unintentionally, ensured that the RPF's subsequent conduct in neighboring Congo would go unscrutinized by the tribunal. The UN's decision to limit the prosecution's temporal reach was no doubt welcomed by a Rwandan government that, in the wake of the genocide, anticipated armed intervention to stem future Hutu reprisal attacks being launched from refugee camps in eastern Congo. In time, the UN's action turned out to be a major concession for a government that sought to bolster its claim for victim status even as it increasingly became a perpetrator in its own right.

By an accident of history that gave it a temporary seat on the Council, Rwanda arguably had more influence over the blueprint of the ICTR than its counterparts in the Balkans when it came to designing the ICTY. But perhaps more important than its Council seat was Rwanda's growing international standing as a victim state deserving of international sympathy. However, international atonement for inaction during the genocide did not mean that the new Tutsi-led government had a free hand in shaping the future tribunal. As this chapter has demonstrated, the UN and the Rwandan government clashed repeatedly in the negotiations leading up to the November 1994 decision to create a new ad hoc war crimes tribunal. When it came to issues of vital importance to the Kigali regime, especially the use of capital punishment and the location of the tribunal, the government suffered a defeat. Prohibiting capital punishment and locating the tribunal's courtrooms outside the volatile environment of war-torn genocide Rwanda became virtually non-negotiable for the Security Council.

Rwanda's vehement and long-standing criticism of Security Council insensitivity created an inaccurate impression among many international observers that Rwanda came away empty-handed in the negotiations preceding the creation of the ICTR. By so doing, the government, from an early date, often successfully cast the UN and the tribunal itself as spoilers with little regard for Rwandan victims and survivors. Abandoned by the UN during the massacres of Spring 1994, Rwanda claimed to be abandoned again by the UN when it came to designing the international legal response to the genocide in the Fall of the same year. In this way, the government laid the foundations for its later efforts to exert influence over the tribunal by shaming the UN and the court for doing too little, too late for Rwanda. The government vote against the tribunal signaled its ongoing determination to fight for its conception of international justice, and underscored the uncertainty of its future cooperation with the tribunal. In the years to come, Rwandan officials also sought to overturn some of the Security Council's actions, specifically the decisions to hold the trials outside

Rwanda and to require that the ICTR and the ICTY share the same chief prosecutor.

For all practical purposes, the clash between the Rwandan government and the Security Council in the Fall of 1994 marked the beginning rather than the end of the political and legal skirmishes over the direction of the International Criminal Tribunal for Rwanda. A special, but unannounced sore spot for the government was the tribunal's mandate to allow prosecutions of RPF atrocities that occurred in Rwanda during 1994. In keeping the window of jurisdiction open for the entire year of 1994, the Council thwarted Kigali's wishes for immunity for the RPF in the several months after the genocide. The central issue in Chapters 8 and 9 will be the mounting crisis of cooperation over the Rwandan government's attempts to prolong RPF immunity.

7

"Trials of Cooperation" and the Battles for Karamira and Barayagwiza

7.1 Introduction

A "trial of cooperation" refers to the battles fought between a tribunal and a targeted state over the terms and timing of that state's cooperation with tribunal investigations and prosecutions. This chapter centers on the narratives of two defining "trials of cooperation" that occurred between the International Criminal Tribunal for Rwanda (ICTR) and the Rwandan government, from the tribunal's turbulent beginning in late 1994 through early 2000. These virtual trials played a crucial role in shaping the tribunal–government relationship for years to come and helped set the stage for the Tutsi-led Rwandan government's subsequent success in blocking tribunal indictments of its own military officers suspected of massacring Hutu civilians during 1994. The outcome of these early trials of cooperation created a tribunal dynamic of acquiescence vis-à-vis the Rwandan government. This, in turn, emboldened the government to strategically withhold cooperation in order to control the court at key junctures and to shame the tribunal for its missteps and shortcomings.

This chapter begins with a brief discussion of the tribunal's initial efforts to establish a diplomatic relationship with the Rwandan government following the Security Council's November 1994 resolution authorizing the creation of the court. We then examine the two major trials of cooperation. The first "trial" occurred in 1996 and centered on Froduald Karamira, a notorious genocide suspect wanted by both tribunal prosecutors and the Rwandan government. Given that the tribunal enjoys legal primacy over Rwandan courts, the tribunal had an undisputed legal right to obtain custody of Karamira and prosecute him. However, the tribunal's first chief prosecutor, Richard J. Goldstone, quickly bowed to Rwandan government pressure and handed the case over for prosecution by a domestic court in Kigali. The second "trial," that began in late 1999 and lasted through early 2000, also involved the fate of a high-level genocide suspect. In this case, the government suspended cooperation with the tribunal in a successful bid to force the tribunal's Appeals Chamber to reverse a controversial ruling that would have released the suspect, Jean-Bosco Barayagwiza, to remedy the prosecution's violation of his due process rights.

7.2 Diplomacy in Kigali: Goldstone Goes to Rwanda

The ICTR was born in crisis. It remained uncertain whether the Rwandan government, which cast the sole dissenting vote against creating the tribunal in the Security Council, would provide the tribunal the cooperation it required to function. Chief Prosecutor Goldstone – who also served as chief prosecutor of the International Criminal Tribunal for the Former Yugoslavia (ICTY) and was at the time the only employee of the ICTR – realized that his first task was to repair an already strained relationship between the UN and the Rwandan government. Before Goldstone could wear his prosecutor's robe, he had to don his diplomat's hat.

Sensing the threat of non-cooperation, Goldstone traveled to war-torn Rwanda, despite resistance from UN officials in New York, who saw no pressing need for the trip and even balked at paying for his flight. In the end, Goldstone turned to Switzerland, a non-UN member state at the time, to cover the cost of his flight to Rwanda.[1] "It was fairly obvious that getting the [Rwandan government's] cooperation was going to be crucial," Goldstone told me in a 2003 interview.[2] "If you need people to cooperate and help you, you have to meet people face to face. You can't do it by telephone calls let alone email or faxes." The timing of his December 1994 trip was also critical, Goldstone said in the same interview: "It was crucially important that I went there when I did. If I had taken the advice of the legal office in New York it...could have been a fateful error...By delaying it, [the government] would have seen it as insensitivity and not caring. And I wouldn't have blamed them."[3] With his characteristic diplomatic skills, Goldstone explained to Rwandan officials the constraints that the Security Council's decision of a month earlier imposed on the structure of the tribunal. Goldstone's early visit to Kigali appears to have played a key role in establishing trust with the government and ensuring that the tribunal could establish an office in Rwanda and begin genocide investigations in 1995.

Goldstone was adept at forging timely pieces of diplomacy that advanced the tribunal's capacity to shape events and become a political actor in its own right. However, his strategic actions also sowed a tribunal dynamic of deference toward the Rwandan government that mirrored the international community's accommodation to the new Tutsi-led Rwandan Patriotic Front (RPF) government. In the aftermath of the genocide, international guilt for not intervening to save lives often translated into an attitude of permissiveness toward the RPF government. This attitude was stoked by the government's skillful reminders of

---

[1] Goldstone, *For Humanity*, pp. 110–111.
[2] Fieldwork interview with Richard J. Goldstone, Pasadena, April 2003.
[3] Ibid.

the debt owed to it as the representative of Tutsi victims and survivors. In time, Goldstone and his successors, Louise Arbour, Carla Del Ponte, and Hassan Jallow would slide into an accommodative posture that weakened the tribunal's position vis-à-vis the Rwandan government. To be sure, the ICTR did not simply bow to Rwandan government demands on a variety of issues or cede control to the government. After all, the tribunal's statute ensured that international judges and prosecutors would have sole authority to make decisions about the direction of the legal process in Arusha. Tribunal officials, nevertheless, were constantly mindful of not further angering the Rwandan government and jeopardizing the steady flow of cooperation. So too was the Security Council which, shortly after creating the tribunal, tried to assuage Rwandan anger at having the tribunal headquartered in Tanzania by locating the tribunal's deputy prosecutor and investigations offices in Rwanda.

7.3 The Battle for Théoneste Bagosora and Froduald Karamira

In a trial of cooperation, a tribunal seeks to "prosecute" a non-cooperative state for its violation of its legal obligation to aid the tribunal. This virtual prosecution depends on publicly exposing and shaming the state. But, as discussed in Chapter 1, trials of cooperation also allow opportunities for closed-door negotiation and conciliation to replace antagonism. The battle between the tribunal and the government over the fate of the genocide suspect Froduald Karamira underscores this point. This trial of cooperation occurred almost entirely out of public view, and today is known by few people either inside or outside the tribunal's walls. Nevertheless, the outcome of this dispute helped establish a pattern of Rwandan government intimidation and tribunal accommodation.

Karamira's role in the hate campaign against the Tutsi minority both before and during the genocide earned him notoriety in Rwanda. Although ethnically Tutsi, Karamira rose to prominence in the early 1990s as a vocal proponent of the Hutu Power ideology that demonized and dehumanized the Tutsi minority. In the waning days of the genocide, Karamira and other top-level suspects fled the country to avoid capture by the advancing RPF army. Most Hutu fugitives sought refuge in Tanzania, Zaire, Kenya, Cameroon, and elsewhere in Africa. Karamira went further afield and fled to India. His role in the genocide naturally made him a potential target of tribunal prosecutors. By 1996, however, Chief Prosecutor Goldstone and his investigators had not yet identified Karamira as a suspect worthy of investigation and indictment. Nor, apparently, did they know his whereabouts.

The Rwandan government was much more familiar with Karamira and his role in stoking the genocide. Moreover, the government was determined to see him stand trial in front of a domestic court in Kigali. As discussed in Chapter 6, the Rwandan government's need for an international tribunal stemmed in no small part from its realization that it had little chance to obtain custody of top-level Hutu suspects who had fled the country. Yet Rwandan officials retained a deep interest in prosecuting some high-level genocide suspects such as Karamira. To the government's consternation, most of the more than 100,000 Hutu in the country's jails and communal lock-ups bore little or no command responsibility for the genocide.

The Rwandan government's first attempt to obtain custody of a prominent Hutu fugitive ended in failure. In early 1996, Rwandan officials learned that the alleged mastermind of the genocide, Théoneste Bagosora, and several of his close associates had been apprehended in Cameroon. The Cameroonian authorities arrested Bagosora after Belgium filed an international arrest warrant for him.[4] Belgium had an interest in prosecuting Bagosora because of his alleged involvement in the murder of ten Belgian UN peacekeepers at the start of the genocide. The Rwandan government moved to bring Bagosora and his associates to Kigali by also filing an extradition request with the Cameroon government. After this, Goldstone filed a competing claim to have Cameroon send the suspects to Arusha. The tribunal's statute empowered Goldstone with the authority to gain custody of Bagosora, even though Belgium and Rwanda, not the tribunal, were first to initiate extradition proceedings.

The prospect of losing the opportunity to prosecute Bagosora on Rwandan soil, where he would face the death penalty, was difficult for the Rwandan government to accept. In what Goldstone described to me as a "very tense" and "difficult" meeting, government officials pressed him to drop his extradition request with the Cameroon government for Bagosora.[5] In my 2003 interview, Goldstone reported that he remained resolute and defended the tribunal's right to decide what suspects it would prosecute. In the interview, Goldstone recalled his encounter with Rwandan officials over Bagosora: "I think they realized that I wasn't just threatening, that I meant it when I said that I preferred to suggest closing down the tribunal than to defer a major criminal involved in the genocide."[6] Goldstone's comment is striking because it expresses a belief that maintaining the tribunal's autonomy may in certain circumstances be in conflict with maintaining the court as an institution. Goldstone explained that gaining custody of Bagosora was crucial because he "was the Milošević of Rwanda."[7] Acquiescing in this situation, Goldstone told me, "would be like saying we will defer to the Belgrade judges and have them try Milošević."[8] In January 1997, the Cameroon government sent Bagosora and three other genocide suspects to the ICTR in Arusha. In deference to the tribunal's legal primacy, Belgium had withdrawn its extradition request for Bagosora back in July 1996.[9]

The Rwandan government remained determined to bring a high-level Hutu suspect to trial in Kigali if and when the opportunity arose. Froduald Karamira

---

[4] Paul J. Magnarella, "Judicial Responses to Genocide: The International Criminal Tribunal for Rwanda and the Rwandan Genocide Courts," *Africa Studies Quarterly* (The Online Journal for African Studies), Vol. 1, Issue 1, 1997, http//web.africa.ufl.edu/asq/v/1/1/2.htm.

[5] Fieldwork interview with Richard J. Goldstone, Pasadena, April 2003.

[6] Ibid.

[7] Ibid.

[8] Ibid.

[9] Magnarella, "Judicial Responses to Genocide," *Africa Studies Quarterly*.

represented the next opportunity. Once again, the Rwandan government proved more resourceful than the better-funded tribunal by locating Karamira in India. Government officials in Kigali were successful in getting India to send Karamira back to Rwanda.

However, en route to Rwanda in early June 1996, Karamira attempted to escape when his plane landed in Addis Ababa, Ethiopia. The incident soon came to Goldstone's attention. Goldstone quickly issued a request to the Ethiopian authorities to have him transferred to the tribunal in Arusha. Although the tribunal enjoyed the legal right to trump Rwanda's extradition request, politics, not law, would decide Karamira's fate. The Ethiopian authorities held Karamira until his legal fate could be determined.

Attorneys hired by Karamira's family tried to block his extradition to Rwanda and instead have him sent to Arusha, where he would have no chance of facing execution.[10] Karamira also applied for asylum status in Ethiopia, and his Kenyan attorney, Kennedy Ogetto, flew to Addis Ababa in early July to try to ensure that he would end up at the ICTR in Arusha.[11] In a letter to the United Nations High Commissioner for Refugees, Ogetto argued for the primacy of the ICTR: "If Mr. Karamira played any role in the 1994 mass killings in Rwanda, then, there is the International Criminal Tribunal for Rwanda at Arusha, Tanzania, which should try him. This is exactly why the said Tribunal was set up by the UN."[12]

Taking preventive action not to be trumped again by Goldstone, the Rwandan government this time took a much tougher stance toward the chief prosecutor. The government threatened to suspend all cooperation with the tribunal if Goldstone went ahead with his efforts to obtain custody of Karamira and bring him to trial in Arusha.[13] Goldstone quickly changed course and dropped his request to the Ethiopian authorities, though he did not try to wrest a guarantee from Rwandan officials that Karamira would not face execution if convicted. Karamira was soon put on a Rwanda-bound plane. After a three-day trial, Karamira was convicted of genocide in a Rwandan court in early 1997.[14] A year later he was executed publicly, along with twenty-one other Rwandans implicated in the genocide. Although the Karamira trial was relatively short, due in part to the civil law court system that places an emphasis on the submission of written evidence, the trial apparently conformed to international standards of due process.[15] William A. Schabas, a leading authority

[10] Fieldwork interview with Kennedy Ogetto, Arusha, April 2002.

[11] Ibid.

[12] Letter from Kennedy Ogetto to UNHCR Regional Representative, Addis Ababa, Ethiopia, re: Mr. Frodouald Karamira, July 12, 1996.

[13] Fieldwork interviews with Richard J. Goldstone, Pasadena, April 2003, and Filip Reyntjens, Antwerp, Belgium, December 2003.

[14] *Integrated Regional Information Network* Special Feature on Rwandan Trials, February 19, 2007.

[15] William A. Schabas, "Genocide Trials and Gacaca Courts," *Journal of International Criminal Justice*, Vol. 3, No. 4, September 2005, p. 887; Des Forges, *Leave None to Tell the Story*, p. 758.

on war crimes prosecutions observed the trial on behalf of Amnesty International. He reported that the trial "had all the appearances of fairness" and that the judge gave Karamira and his lawyer "every chance to rebut the charges."[16]

The story of how Karamira ended up in a Rwandan jail remains contested. While tribunal sources reported to me in interviews that the government threatened to suspend cooperation if Goldstone did not acquiesce, Rwandan government officials deny this assertion. "We didn't even make threats. We had a tug of war," Rwandan Attorney General Gerald Gahima told me in a 2002 interview. "Goldstone for some reason decided to defer to us...I think he did it out of the spirit of cooperation because [we] have to work with each other. Any [one] knows that cooperation takes give and take."[17] Government officials have also claimed that Goldstone, in the earlier meeting over the Bagosora issue, promised that in the future the ICTR would not seek custody of suspects that Kigali had already begun to pursue.[18] Goldstone reportedly said he never made such a promise.[19]

Few people, even those in the Office of the Prosecutor, were privy to the tribunal–government dispute. However, Filip Reyntjens, a prominent scholar of Rwanda from Belgium who had provided expert testimony on behalf of the prosecution in other cases, learned of the matter and appealed to the Office of the Prosecutor not to bend to Rwandan pressure.[20] It is unclear if Reyntjens' protest, which was issued to a prosecution official, ever reached Goldstone.

In my 2003 interview, Goldstone explained that he had issued the request for Karamira to the Ethiopian government without knowing that Rwanda had already done so and had thus unintentionally challenged Rwanda's bid to gain custody of Karamira. Before Goldstone heard back from the Ethiopian authorities, he recalls that he "got a huge protest from Kigali to say that [Karamira] had been sent from India to Ethiopia at their request. Had I known that Karamira had been sent from India to Ethiopia at their instance, I wouldn't have sent a letter to Ethiopia without consulting them," Goldstone told me. "I didn't know. It had been withheld from me. I would never have done that. Had I known, it would have almost been a fraud on them to have gone behind their back and use their sleuthing work...especially immediately after the Bagosora incident, and grab Karamira."[21]

---

[16] William A. Schabas, "Genocide Trials and Gacaca Courts," *Journal of International Criminal Justice*, Vol. 3, No. 4, September 2005, p. 887.

[17] Fieldwork interview with Gerald Gahima, Kigali, May 2002.

[18] Madeline H. Morris, "The Trials of Concurrent Jurisdiction: The Case of Rwanda," *Duke Journal of Comparative and International Law*, Vol. 7, No. 2, Spring 1997, footnote 91. Morris recounts aspects of the Karamira case in a footnote. She refers to the matter as a "brief 'tug of war,'" but does not make mention of any government threat issued to the tribunal.

[19] Ibid., footnote 91.

[20] Fieldwork interview with Filip Reyntjens, Antwerp, December 2003.

[21] Fieldwork interview with Richard J. Goldstone, Pasadena, April 2003.

To Goldstone, building trust and developing a close working relationship with the Rwandan government were crucial components of being a prosecutor and ensuring that the tribunal received the cooperation it needed from Kigali. In this regard, Goldstone's willingness to respond quickly to government pressure in the Karamira case parallels his sensitivity to its anger following the UN's establishment of the ICTR in late 1994. Back in December 1994, his swift diplomacy cost no more than the price of an airplane flight to Rwanda.

But now, diplomacy involved making a compromise that, although ensuring continued cooperation from Kigali, rendered the tribunal vulnerable to future government threats. In the Bagosora case, Goldstone showed a willingness to stand up to the government and incur its wrath. Yet, as Goldstone himself admits, the Bagosora battle frayed relations with the Rwanda government and appeared to make him cautious about sparking another confrontation. Insisting on prosecuting Karamira in Arusha would have jeopardized the tribunal's relationship with the government, Goldstone said. "Once I put down my foot on Bagosora it made it even more difficult to insist on Karamira," Goldstone told me. "It would have clearly been another souring of the relationship. It would have been seen justifiably by them as a breach of faith from somebody that they've learned to trust."[22] The execution of Karamira left Goldstone feeling "bloody awful," but it did not prompt him to regret his decision.[23] "Politically . . . I don't think I had any options," Goldstone said. "It would have been the end of our relationship and the end of cooperation."[24]

To Goldstone, the Bagosora and Karamira cases appeared to hold different lessons. In the Bagosora case, Goldstone felt it was critical to remain steadfast in light of the stature of the suspect. The Karamira case seemed to hold a contrary lesson – that it is justified to strike a compromise with a state (or at least a so-called victim state) when the accused in question is not deemed to be a major suspect. In Goldstone's estimation, Karamira "wasn't such an important person. He wasn't so important to the tribunal as Bagosora was."[25] It is certainly true that Karamira was not as important to the tribunal as Bagosora, the alleged mastermind of the genocide. However, veteran Rwanda experts such as Filip Reyntjens maintain that Karamira was a high-level suspect who deserved to be prosecuted before an international tribunal. It remains unclear if Goldstone and his troubled Office of the Prosecutor – that at the time was struggling to identify and investigate the many players who orchestrated the genocide – fully appreciated the importance of Karamira either as a suspect or a potential insider witness.

The cost of Goldstone's acquiescence in this case was two-fold. First, it appeared to embolden the Rwandan government and make it easier for it to threaten the tribunal in the future. Second, relinquishing the right to prosecute

22 Ibid.
23 Ibid.
24 Ibid.
25 Ibid.

Karamira may have hampered the tribunal's subsequent efforts to prosecute other top-level genocide suspects on trial in Arusha. In addition to being a valuable suspect, Karamira might have been a valuable insider witness in the prosecution of Bagosora and other high-level Hutu defendants. Reyntjens asserts that Karamira would have been an "absolutely crucial witness" had he agreed to cooperate with the prosecution.[26] Reyntjens recalled in my interview that he tried unsuccessfully to use this argument to persuade the Office of the Prosecutor to obtain custody of Karamira:

I told them, 'You can't do that. You can't send him to Kigali because there will probably be a summary trial and he may well be executed and you will lose a crucial witness.' I thought this was more convincing to them than saying I think it is immoral to extradite someone to somewhere where he won't have a fair trial.[27]

In 2002, when Bagosora finally went on trial in Arusha after more than five years in pre-trial detention, the beleaguered prosecution team responsible for the case found itself greatly in need of insider witnesses to link "the Milošević of Rwanda" to the massacres that swept Rwanda in 1994.[28]

7.4 The Barayagwiza Crisis

A. Setting the Stage for Acquiescence

The next major trial of cooperation between the ICTR and the Rwandan government also involved the fate of a notorious genocide suspect. But whereas the Karamira dispute occurred almost entirely behind closed doors, this dispute occurred mostly in the international public spotlight. And whereas the Rwandan government threatened to suspend cooperation during the Karamira dispute, it actually followed through on its threat this time around. The dispute arose in early November 1999 when the tribunal's Appeals Chamber ordered Jean-Bosco Barayagwiza – a top Hutu genocide suspect who had played a central role in the media campaign exhorting the Hutu population to massacre Tutsi – to be unconditionally released and not face trial. During the genocide, Barayagwiza was a high-level official in the Rwandan Ministry of Foreign Affairs and a leader of an anti-Tutsi political party called the Coalition for the Defense of the Republic. Barayagwiza had been one of three defendants in the much-anticipated Media Trial, named for their alleged role in using media outlets to hasten the spread of the genocidal killings in 1994. The tribunal's Appeals Chamber ordered Barayagwiza's release as a remedy to a number of due process

---

[26] Fieldwork interview with Filip Reyntjens, Antwerp, December 2003.

[27] Ibid.

[28] On the other hand, Karamira's death may have also been a loss for Georges Rutaganda, a Hutu genocide suspect who wanted Karamira brought to Arusha to testify on his behalf in one of the early trials at the ICTR. Rutaganda's defense lawyer, Tiphanine Dickson, appealed to the trial chamber hearing the Rutaganda case to request that the Rwandan authorities allow Karamira to travel to Arusha to testify for the defense in this case. The tribunal judges rejected Dickson's motion.

breaches, including the prosecution's failure to charge him within the legally specified time period and his delayed arraignment. The Rwandan government immediately responded by announcing that it would withhold cooperation from the ICTR until the Appeals Chamber reversed its decision. The government's move sparked panic at the tribunal and quickly reinforced a tribunal dynamic of accommodation toward the government.

As we know from the Karamira case, the Barayagwiza controversy was by no means the first time that the Rwandan government had registered its dissatisfaction with the tribunal's approach to genocide prosecutions. Moreover, the tribunal's administrative tribulations in its first five years of life and its failure to bring more suspects to trial triggered a torrent of harsh criticism from Kigali. Even as Rwandan officials called for improvements at the ICTR, they reaped significant political gains from the institution's dysfunctions and from international sympathy for the frustrating wait for tribunal justice. Shaming the tribunal for its failures enhanced Kigali's standing as an aggrieved victim government and increased the tendency of Western observers and commentators to conflate the victimization of the Tutsi during the genocide with the victimization of the Tutsi-led government. Shaming the tribunal also served the added purpose of keeping tribunal officials on the defensive and increasing the likelihood that they would acquiesce to government demands when a hotly contested issue arose. The government's ability to persuade the Appeals Chamber to reverse its decision in the Barayagwiza case must therefore be seen in the larger context of the tribunal's troubled early years.

A prominent example of government shaming of the tribunal prior to the Barayagwiza case occurred during Chief Prosecutor Louise Arbour's visit to Kigali in May 1997. A government-backed demonstration by several hundred Tutsi genocide survivors greeted the prosecutor when she arrived at the tribunal's offices in Kigali.[29] The demonstrators protested the ICTR's lack of progress in convicting Hutu suspects and called for Arbour's resignation and the appointment of a full-time chief prosecutor. The protest reportedly shook Arbour and contributed to a feeling among top officials in the Office of the Prosecutor that the tribunal was a victim of an unfair government-sponsored campaign to undermine the court.[30] "We had a feeling of a big injustice because she was there to do her job. But she was treated like a criminal," a prosecution official who accompanied Arbour on her trip to Kigali told me in a 2003 interview.[31] Both the tribunal and the government, with its closely aligned Tutsi survivor groups, felt victimized by the other. But the advantage fell to the government; following the demonstration, the government and the survivor groups came away with renewed international attention for their claim of being betrayed by a careless and incompetent institution.

---

[29] "Rwanda: Genocide survivors protest against ICTR prosecutor," *Integrated Regional Information Network Weekly Round-up*, May 26, 1997.
[30] Fieldwork interview with former tribunal official, The Hague, December 2003.
[31] Ibid.

B. Conflicting Visions of Justice

The prosecution's blunder in the Barayagwiza case did not come as a surprise either to tribunal employees or observers who had grown accustomed to a dysfunctional court. Yet the tribunal's latest misstep proved particularly costly to its reputation and to its troubled relationship with the Rwandan government.

To the Appeals Chamber judges, the tribunal's failure "to prosecute the case with due diligence" was not a problem that could be overlooked.[32] In its November 1999 decision, the five-member Appeals Chamber called the prosecution's failure "tantamount to negligence" and "egregious."[33] The ninety-day indictment deadline was, the judges wrote, a cornerstone of the tribunal's obligation to protect the due process rights of defendants and the right to limited pre-trial detention.[34] The following passage from the Appeals Chamber decision underscored the importance of the legal principles at stake:

The Tribnal – an institution whose primary purpose is to ensure that justice is done – must not place its imprimatur on such violations. To allow the Appellant to be tried on the charges for which he was belatedly indicted would be a travesty of justice. Nothing less than the integrity of the Tribunal is at stake in this case ... As difficult as this conclusion may be for some to accept, it is the proper role of an independent judiciary to halt the prosecution, so that no further injustice results.[35]

To the Appeals Chamber, the Barayagwiza case was fundamentally about deterring prosecutorial abuse of power and holding the prosecution accountable to the judiciary. But to the Rwandan government, the case was about holding the Appeals Chamber accountable to Rwanda. To the government, the judiciary's role did not include freeing a notorious genocide suspect without trial in order to remedy a prosecutorial mistake. The Barayagwiza controversy presented in sharp relief the conflicting visions of justice held by the international court, which emphasized the protection of defendant rights, and the government, which emphasized the protection of victim rights. In short order, the case also turned into a contest for control of the court and the degree to which a state that has no formal role in the court operations acquires the power to shape legal outcomes.

The Appeals Chamber decision prompted the government to announce a suspension of all cooperation with the tribunal until the Chamber reversed its decision. Without the government's cooperation, Rwandan prosecution witnesses would be prevented from traveling to Arusha and ongoing trials would be brought to a standstill. The new chief prosecutor, Carla Del Ponte, warned that the worst case scenario – in which the court would be forced to close its

---

[32] Jean-Bosco Barayagwiza v. The Prosecutor, Appeals Chamber Decision, November 3, 1999, paragraph 101.

[33] Ibid., paragraph 106.

[34] Judge Mohamed Shahababuddeen filed a dissenting opinion that disagreed with some of the majority's arguments but agreed with the Appeals Chamber's decision to release Barayagwiza and dismiss the indictment.

[35] Ibid., paragraph 112.

doors and release the suspects in its custody – was just around the corner unless the Appeals Chamber reversed its decision.

The Rwandan government made no effort to hide its non-compliance as governments often do during trials of cooperation. On the contrary, emboldened by its ardent belief that it was the victim of a grave injustice, the government argued that withdrawing its cooperation was fully justified. The government used its suspension of cooperation as a way to focus international attention on and shame the tribunal for its negligence. Following the Appeals Chamber decision, Rwanda's representative to the United Nations, Joseph Mutaboba, invoked the theme of betrayal when speaking to reporters in New York. The tribunal's action, he said "was a stab in the back" to Rwanda. "The ends of justice are not served by penalizing once again the people of Rwanda for the shortcomings of a United Nations prosecutor," he said.[36]

The government was not the only critic of the ICTR. Within the tribunal, the decision led to heated and at times bitter debate. Even some tribunal judges, not on the Appeals bench, voiced their discontent with the ruling. "If you have these kinds of allegations I don't see how you can let [Barayagwiza] walk away on a technicality," one judge told me in a 2000 interview. "You can't just let him walk away, that's not justice."[37] Leading international human rights organizations also criticized the tribunal. In early November 1999, Human Rights Watch "deplored prosecutorial incompetence" at the tribunal.[38] "This decision should jolt the prosecutor's office and the international community in general, reminding everyone of the need for prompt and exemplary justice," said Human Rights Watch's Alison Des Forges, a leading authority on the ICTR and the Rwandan genocide. "The early bumblings and delays of the poorly funded prosecutor's office have led to a decision that distresses but should not surprise us."[39] Human Rights Watch stopped short of insisting that the Appeals Chamber reverse its decision, and instead said that Barayagwiza should at least be tried in Cameroon, where he had initially been arrested. While not condoning Rwanda's move to withhold cooperation, American diplomats voiced concern that a suspect as important as Barayagwiza would simply be allowed to leave his jail cell without first facing trail.

The Barayagwiza crisis posed a complex challenge for the tribunal. In the Karamira case, Goldstone alone could defuse the crisis by quickly (and quietly) withdrawing his request to gain custody of the suspect from the Ethiopian authorities. But Del Ponte had far less power in the current situation. The key to unlocking the crisis lay primarily with a panel of five appeals judges located thousands of miles away in The Hague, and not with the chief prosecutor. Moreover, the judges had staked the very credibility of the tribunal on their

---

[36] Press conference by Permanent Representative of Rwanda, November 11, 1999.
[37] Fieldwork interview with ICTR judge, Arusha, June 2000.
[38] "Prosecutorial Incompetence Frees Rwandan Genocide Suspect," Human Rights Watch press release, November 8, 1999.
[39] Ibid.

decision and dismissed the case with prejudice,[40] thus raising the bar for any potential prosecutorial appeal that Del Ponte might file.

With the future of the court on the line, Del Ponte rushed to Africa to mend fences, just as Goldstone had done several years earlier. Del Ponte had taken up her position two months earlier as chief prosecutor of both the ICTY and ICTR and had yet to visit her offices in Arusha or in Rwanda. In a show of defiance, the Rwandan authorities refused to grant her and other senior tribunal officials visas to enter the country. Del Ponte remained in Arusha for two weeks until the Appeals Chamber announced its decision to hold a hearing to reconsider its initial ruling.[41]

Del Ponte's primary battle was with the Appeals Chamber, not the Rwandan government. At every turn, Del Ponte stressed her empathy with the government's anger and pledged to work to overturn the Chamber's decision. Besides assuaging the government and ensuring continued cooperation, Del Ponte had a strong interest in prosecuting Barayagwiza and thereby redeeming the tribunal's international image.

The government carried through on its threat to suspend cooperation by stopping tribunal investigations from taking place in Rwanda. During late 1999 and early 2000, tribunal investigators already in Rwanda reported that they consistently encountered hostility from the government and from government-backed survivor groups.[42] This hostility culminated in a large government-sponsored demonstration outside the tribunal's offices in Kigali. Interestingly, however, the government did not block Rwandan survivors selected to testify on behalf of the prosecution from traveling to Arusha. The government's actions suggest that while it wanted to punish the tribunal to obtain international sympathy and force the Appeals Chamber's hand, it did not actually want to disrupt the trials of Hutu genocide suspects. Nevertheless, the government claimed in its press statements that it had withdrawn cooperation across the board, likely in an attempt to increase international pressure on the tribunal. Some Western journalists took the Rwandan government at its word without recognizing that it had not blocked the trials in Arusha from taking place.[43] The government's partial suspension of cooperation came as a relief to tribunal prosecutors. "The witnesses were still coming," one veteran prosecutor recalled in a 2002 interview. "The day I hear there are no witnesses coming over, then I'll worry...then how do you prosecute?"[44]

The tribunal was not without allies in this crisis. In bilateral contacts with Joseph Mutaboba, Rwanda's ambassador to the UN, diplomats pressed the

[40] Jean-Bosco Barayagwiza v. The Prosecutor, Appeals Chamber Decision, November 3, 1999, paragraph 108.

[41] However, some tribunal officials were barred from traveling to Rwanda for several months. Fieldwork interviews with ICTR official, Arusha, February 2002.

[42] Fieldwork interviews with tribunal investigators, Kigali, June 2000 and April-May 2002.

[43] Bill Berkeley, *The Graves Are Not Yet Full: Race, Tribe and Power in the Heart of Africa* (New York: Basic Books, 2001), pp. 275–276.

[44] Fieldwork interview with ICTR prosecutor, Arusha, February 2002.

Rwandan government to cooperate with the tribunal.[45] Yet international pressure was muted, at least compared with the level of pressure that the Serbian and Croatian governments typically faced from Western governments. One reason for the lack of sustained international pressure was that the ICTR did not call upon the UN to intervene on its behalf with Rwanda. Yet nothing would have stopped the Security Council from taking stronger action on its own since it had an obligation to enforce international law. Despite Rwanda's open admission of blocking cooperation, the Council refrained from even issuing a statement reminding Rwanda of its legal obligation to cooperate. The limited international pressure also stemmed in part from an international consensus that the tribunal's problems were of its own makings and that it held the power to resolve this crisis by putting Barayagwiza on trial.

C. The Barayagwiza Appeal

Del Ponte turned her focus to the Appeals Chamber, first by filing a request for a review of its decision, and second, by underscoring the tribunal's dire predicament in interviews and press statements. Barayagwiza's defense attorney declared "the case closed" and dismissed Del Ponte's efforts as "the last kick of a dying horse."[46] However, in early 2000, the Appeals Chamber granted the prosecution a new hearing. The Chamber had rendered its first decision without holding a public hearing. Now, in an apparent attempt to present a more transparent process, the Appeals Chamber scheduled a hearing and decided to hold it in Arusha, rather than The Hague, where the Chamber is based. The Rwandan Attorney General, Gerald Gahima, traveled to Arusha and gave an impassioned plea to the Appeals Chambers to reverse its decision, arguing that releasing Barayagwiza would defeat the tribunal's goals to deter future Hutu massacres and foster national reconciliation.[47] The prosecution made a similar argument.[48] The hearing provided a rare instance for Rwandan authorities to literally have their day in court, and it offered an unusually public demonstration of the new alliance between the Office of the Prosecutor and the Rwandan government.

Del Ponte's plea to the Appeals Chamber to reverse its decision and her comments to the media were based on both a legal and a political logic. To the Appeals Chamber, Del Ponte argued that the discovery of "new facts" demonstrated that the prosecution was not at fault in the Barayagwiza matter and that survivors of the genocide deserved to see him brought to justice.[49] But

[45] Fieldwork interview with Joseph Mutaboba, Kigali, June 2002.

[46] "Barayagwiza's defense accuses prosecutor of political motives," *Hirondelle News Agency*, November 24, 1999.

[47] Fieldwork interview with Gerald Gahima, Kigali, June 2002. Also see amicus curiae brief of the Government of the Republic of Rwanda, filed February 15, 2000.

[48] Jean-Bosco Barayagwiza v. The Prosecutor, Decision: Prosecutor's Request for Review or Reconsideration, March 31, 2000.

[49] "Prosecutor v. Jean-Bosco Barayagwiza," ICTR press briefing, February 22, 2000.

especially in her press statements and interviews, Del Ponte also issued a plea based on the exigencies of the moment, as seen in the following quote:

If I don't get cooperation from Rwanda, I can't do my work. If I don't get it, I can first open the door at the detention center and set them all free and then second I can close the door to my office because without them I cannot do anything [at] all. That means that I'll have to go to the Secretary-General and say, we're closed, we can't do anything.[50]

Implicit in Del Ponte's remarks was an acknowledgment that concession and compromise were integral parts of guaranteeing state cooperation and safeguarding the tribunal's future. The Appeals Chamber initially argued that releasing Barayagwiza was essential to upholding the integrity of the court. Now Del Ponte argued that putting Barayagwiza on trial was essential for the survival of the court.

Del Ponte, of course, was only stating the obvious. But some Western diplomats cringed when they heard her characteristically blunt language since they believed it would render the tribunal even more vulnerable to the criticism that it had succumbed to political pressure if the Appeals Chamber ended up reversing its initial decision.[51] Del Ponte's language aside, accusations of a politically motivated decision were sure to haunt the tribunal. Citing "new facts" presented by the prosecution, the Appeals Chamber ultimately reversed its decision and ordered Barayagwiza to stand trial. But in a nod to its earlier ruling, the Chamber stipulated that if Barayagwiza were found guilty, his sentence would be reduced as a remedy of the violation of his rights, and that if found not guilty, he would receive monetary compensation.[52] In the wake of this decision, the government quickly restored its cooperation with the tribunal.

In the eyes of the government and some tribunal officials, Rwanda walked away from the crisis the clear winner. "This was a no-win situation for the tribunal. There was no way to come off looking good," a veteran tribunal official told me in an interview.[53] The government had forced the tribunal's hand while escaping international condemnation for doing so. In the process, the government had learned that it could withhold cooperation to great effect with little adverse consequence, particularly in situations in which it could portray the tribunal as an irresponsible institution impeding justice for genocide survivors. In an interview, Rwandan Attorney General Gahima told me that the government had "no regrets" about the government's decision to suspend cooperation in light of the Appeals Chamber's "unacceptable" ruling.[54] Tribunal officials publicly defended the Chamber's decision and maintained that it had been made on

[50] J. Coll Metcalfe, "An Interview with United Nations' Chief War Crimes Prosecutor, Carla Del Ponte," *Internews*, February 15, 2000.
[51] Fieldwork interview with Western diplomats, Kigali, May 2002.
[52] The Prosecutor v. Fredinand Nahimana, Jean-Bosco Barayagwiza, Hassan Ngeze, Summary, December 3, 2003.
[53] Fieldwork interview with tribunal official, Arusha, June, 2002.
[54] Fieldwork interview with Gerald Gahima, Kigali, June 2002.

the legal merits. But among many ICTR staff members, doubts emerged about the autonomy of the tribunal from Rwandan pressure.

The Barayagwiza crisis prompted reflection from ICTR judges and prosecutors alike as to how to strike a better balance between judicial independence and accountability to Rwanda. In interviews I conducted in May and June 2000, several tribunal judges spoke with a new awareness of the need to consider victims' interests. "A court cannot operate in a vacuum," a judge told me in an interview. "So even if a court and judges are independent . . . I think it would be wrong when deciding a case not to see how [it] would be seen in the country." It is inadvisable, the judge said, to render "a legal decision that is wrong in the reality of the world."[55] Still, a fundamental philosophical clash existed between the goals of the international tribunal and those of the Rwandan legal system.

The end of the crisis made way for the start of the trial of Barayagwiza and of his two co-defendants in the Media Trial, Ferdinand Nahimana and Hassan Ngeze. When the trial began in October 2000, Barayagwiza protested by withdrawing his cooperation in the legal process and refusing to appear in court. Barayagwiza denounced the tribunal as a tool of the Tutsi-led Rwandan government. "I refuse to associate myself with a show trial . . . the outcome of which is dictated by the government of Rwanda," he said in a statement delivered the day the trial started.[56] The trial chamber upheld Barayagwiza's right to flaunt the court. The trial took several years to complete. But the December 2003 guilty verdicts against all three defendants on incitement of genocide charges established an important legal precedent concerning the relationship between hate speech and violence. All three defendants received life sentences. However, the trial chamber, citing the prosecution's failure to issue a timely indictment against Barayagwiza years earlier, reduced his sentence to thirty-five years.[57]

7.5 Conclusion

The end of the Barayagwiza crisis ushered in a détente between the ICTR and the Rwandan government. The tribunal began to demonstrate its responsiveness to Rwandan government concerns. In its public statements, ICTR officials spoke more frequently of the need to make the tribunal's work relevant to Rwanda. After initially showing little concern about Rwandan perceptions of the tribunal, officials in Arusha began to take some remedial steps. The ICTR launched an outreach program and several public relations initiatives in an effort to rehabilitate the tribunal's image in Rwanda. Del Ponte pledged to work on a plan to hold some ICTR trials in Rwanda, which had been sought by the Kigali government since before the tribunal's creation. Judging from

---

[55] Fieldwork interview with ICTR judge, Arusha, June 2000.

[56] "Rwandan Media Suspects Boycott Start of Their Trial," *Hirondelle News Agency*, October 23, 2000.

[57] The Prosecutor v. Fredinand Nahimana, Jean-Bosco Barayagwiza, Hassan Ngeze, Summary, December 3, 2003.

tribunal and government statements, it was tempting to conclude that the combative relationship between Arusha and Kigali had been repaired. Although overdue in some respects, the tribunal's conciliatory approach toward Kigali was disquieting to many tribunal employees, who were already disturbed by the precedent of state power that had been established in the Barayagwiza case.

The Barayagwiza crisis also underscored the fact that the trials of cooperation in the Rwandan context differed, at least initially, from those in the Balkans. Balkan states withheld cooperation primarily for one purpose – to block tribunal prosecutions of members of their own national or ethnic group. But Rwanda apparently had withheld cooperation for the opposite reason – to ensure tribunal prosecutions of its enemies. Withholding cooperation risked incurring the wrath of the international community. For the most part, however, Rwanda had avoided any negative international reaction during this period. In the language of the trials of cooperation, the government had successfully defended itself against charges of non-compliance. Doing so was relatively easy, in part because Rwanda enjoyed the international legitimacy of a victim state and the sympathy of its two closest Western allies, the United States and Britain. While displeased with Rwanda's tactics, both allies shared an interest in seeing Barayagwiza stand trial. The government's success in the trials of cooperation was also due to its skill in shaming the tribunal for its failure to bring a timely indictment against Barayagwiza and to the tribunal's lackluster "prosecution" of Rwandan non-compliance. The tribunal's chief prosecutor and chief justice refrained from criticizing Rwanda's non-compliance.

In their much-watched annual reports to the Security Council, both Chief Prosecutor Carla Del Ponte and Chief Justice Navanethem Pillay made no mention of Rwanda's obstruction of justice months earlier. The ICTR's silence in this important forum stood in sharp contrast to the ICTY's strongly worded complaints against Serbian and Croatian non-compliance. Whereas confrontation was often the ICTY's preferred approach in the Balkans, conciliation was often the ICTR's preferred approach in Rwanda. By allowing Rwanda to blatantly withhold cooperation without issuing any criticism of its actions, the ICTR rendered itself more vulnerable to a repeat performance by the Kigali government and signaled its reticence to fight back in the future.

8

Investigating Rwandan Patriotic Front Atrocities and the Politics of Bearing Witness

8.1 Introduction

Despite the mutual pledges of friendship and understanding in the aftermath of the Barayagwiza crisis, the International Criminal Tribunal for Rwanda (ICTR) and the Rwandan government were soon enmeshed in a new confrontation that threatened the tribunal's independence and its hope for uninterrupted state cooperation. The government's determination to block Chief Prosecutor Del Ponte's investigation of Rwandan Patriotic Front (RPF) massacres of Hutu civilians would become the central battleground of state–tribunal conflict.

In the first part of this chapter, I examine the political context in which Del Ponte embarked on her investigations of the RPF in 2000. The idea of prosecuting atrocities committed by all sides of an armed conflict is a foundational principle of the contemporary ad hoc tribunals as well as the International Criminal Court. Yet Del Ponte's decision to probe the RPF's role in atrocities against Hutu civilians was controversial because in the aftermath of the genocide, the Tutsi-led RPF and the Tutsi population in general were widely recognized internationally as victims deserving sympathy, not scrutiny.

In the second part of the chapter, I examine the government's response to the tribunal's early attempts to prod Rwanda to cooperate with these investigations. The centerpiece of the government's response was a "counter-shaming" campaign against the tribunal aimed at undermining its reputation and diverting international attention away from the government's attempts to stop the RPF investigations. The government's counter-shaming offensive had two elements. First, it increased its attacks on the tribunal for being an ineffective and incompetent United Nations institution that had betrayed Rwanda's quest for justice. Second, the government strategically mobilized Tutsi survivor groups to carry the banner of protest and attack the tribunal for its alleged mistreatment of survivors. As I will show, the tribunal's ongoing problems provided the government and survivor groups with no shortage of ammunition with which to embarrass the tribunal. Two scandals at the ICTR in 2001 – the hiring of Hutu defense investigators implicated in the murder of Tutsi during the genocide and a courtroom incident in which a panel of judges laughed during the testimony of a Tutsi rape victim – fed the attacks of the survivor groups against the tribunal.

In the third part of the chapter, I demonstrate how the Tutsi survivor groups, with strong government backing, took center stage in the trials of cooperation with the tribunal during the first half of 2002. In early 2002, the anger of the survivor groups with the tribunal culminated in a decision to boycott the tribunal by urging Tutsi survivors not to speak to investigators or otherwise cooperate with the court. The boycott further undermined the tribunal's legitimacy and dealt a serious blow to its genocide investigations, since the cooperation of Tutsi survivors was necessary to bring indictments and prosecutions of Hutu genocide suspects.

8.2 A Short-lived Détente

Fallout from the Barayagwiza crisis, coupled with the slow pace of trials at the tribunal and its ongoing administrative travails, increasingly placed the ICTR on the defensive in its relationship with the Rwandan government. That, in turn, solidified a tribunal dynamic of conciliation toward the Kigali regime. The tribunal's conciliation was driven by its interest in lessening the chances that disgruntled leaders in Kigali would again withdraw cooperation and in fulfilling the tribunal's Security Council mandated goal to become a relevant force in the reconstruction of post-genocide Rwanda. Toward these ends, the ICTR in 2000 launched a series of "outreach" initiatives aimed at doing more to inform the Rwandan citizenry about the tribunal's work and to increase Rwandan support for the court. Although poorly funded, this effort was a first step toward making the tribunal's work more visible in Rwanda and tempering the government's long-standing grievance that the court held little relevance for Rwandan society. Outwardly, the tribunal–government relationship improved dramatically in the months following the Appeals Chamber's decision in early 2000 to reverse its initial ruling and put Barayagwiza on trial. The government not only promised to cooperate but provided timely support when it came to tribunal investigations of Hutu genocide suspects. This détente was short-lived, however. By the end of 2000, the seeds of a new conflict had been planted.

The origin of this new confrontation lay neither in the tribunal's bureaucratic dysfunction nor in the jurisdictional battles over high-level genocide suspects. Rather, the conflict was triggered by the tribunal's attempt to investigate and indict Tutsi war crimes suspects. Chief Prosecutor Del Ponte's decision in 2000 to expand the ongoing probe of Tutsi suspects placed the ICTR in direct opposition to the government and posed a challenge to its claim of sole possession of victim status in Rwanda. In effect, as a Western diplomat suggested in a 2002 interview, the tribunal had now become a "a swivel gun"[1] pointed at Tutsi suspects and the Tutsi-led government.

The opening public salvo in this new conflict occurred in December 2000 when Del Ponte announced an ongoing investigation of Tutsi RPF army officers suspected of committing atrocities against Hutu civilians during 1994.[2] Following Del Ponte's announcement, the government promised to cooperate with the so-called special investigations.[3] However, Del Ponte soon found herself in a contentious battle with the Kigali regime that would threaten not only the tribunal's autonomy but its survival. Del Ponte risked more than just failing in her bid to bring RPF suspects to justice. Her investigation of the RPF jeopardized the Rwandan government's cooperation with the tribunal even when it came to prosecutions of Hutu genocide suspects.

8.3 RPF Atrocities: To Investigate or Not to Investigate?

A. *The Approaches of Richard Goldstone and Louise Arbour*

As much as the contemporary international tribunals look to the World War II-era tribunals for legal guidance, they also have taken deliberate steps to improve on the flaws of these seminal institutions. One such flaw is the problem of "victor's justice" that has tainted the Nuremberg and Tokyo tribunals. A fundamental aim of the contemporary tribunals has been to bring more fairness to the process of deciding whom to place on trial. Today's tribunals have sought to do so by prosecuting war crimes suspects from both the winning and losing sides of armed conflicts.[4] Thus, the ICTR has a mandate not only to prosecute Hutu suspects accused of carrying out the genocide against the Tutsi minority, but also those Tutsi suspects accused of carrying out non-genocidal massacres of the Hutu majority.

At an early date, Richard Goldstone, the first chief prosecutor of the ICTY and ICTR, established the precedent of indicting war crimes suspects from opposing ethnic groups involved in the Bosnian war. His decision to do so won him praise in the West for establishing the ICTY as a balanced, fair, and legitimate legal institution. But at the ICTR, Goldstone took a markedly different approach and did not investigate atrocities committed by the Tutsi-led RPF army.

The ICTR investigators who arrived in war-torn Rwanda in 1995 were consumed with the formidable tasks of investigating the genocide and building an international tribunal from scratch. These tasks were made even more challenging by the lack of adequate international community support and a tribunal bureaucracy hobbled by incompetence and nepotism. Even if Goldstone's Office

---

[1] Fieldwork interview with Western diplomat, Kigali, July 2002.

[2] "Prosecutor Outlines Future Plans," ICTR press release, December 13, 2000.

[3] "UN to Charge Tutsis for War Crimes," *BBC News*, December 13, 2000; "UN Confirms Secret Probe of Tutsi War Crimes," *National Post*, December 15, 2000.

[4] Victor Peskin, "Beyond Victor's Justice? The Challenge of Prosecuting the Winners at the International Criminal Tribunals for the Former Yugoslavia and Rwanda," *Journal of Human Rights*, 4: 213–231, 2005.

of the Prosecutor had been a model of bureaucratic efficiency, it is likely that he would still have initially focused attention on investigating the genocide rather than on the lesser evil of crimes against humanity. In a 2003 interview, Goldstone told me that the magnitude of genocidal crimes wrought by the Hutu extremists so outweighed the RPF's massacres that the prosecutorial choice was clear. "My attitude ... was to give priority in investigations and prosecutions to the most guilty," Goldstone told me in the interview.[5] "We didn't have enough resources to investigate all the nines and the tens," he said, referring to a hypothetical ten-point scale of atrocity. "And the RPF, who acted in revenge, were at ones and twos and maybe even fours and fives."[6]

Issuing indictments against RPF officers without sufficient evidence of atrocities was for Goldstone unsound prosecutorial policy. "I certainly didn't have evidence of massive crimes committed by the RPF," he said. "I wouldn't have issued an indictment against [Bosnian Muslims] for the sake of ... saying what an even-handed chap I am. I think crimes have to be of the magnitude that justify doing it."[7] Goldstone's short tenure at the ICTR (November 1994 to September 1996), coupled with the pressing task of establishing the Office of the Prosecutor and launching genocide investigations, may have justified his decision not to embark on RPF investigations. Yet significant evidence of RPF atrocities did exist as far back as 1994. The United Nations Commission of Experts, an investigative body created by the Security Council prior to the establishment of the ICTR, found evidence of significant RPF abuses, and recommended in its December 1994 report that in addition to prosecuting Hutu genocide suspects, a tribunal should also prosecute these RPF crimes.[8]

The issue of RPF atrocities was reportedly brought to Goldstone's attention by Filip Reyntjens, the prominent Belgian scholar and Rwanda specialist, in 1995.[9] In a telephone conversation that took place when Goldstone was in Brussels for a conference, Reyntjens, as he told me in a 2003 interview, asked what Goldstone planned to do about reports of RPF atrocities. Goldstone reportedly said he did not know that such evidence existed. Reyntjens said Goldstone's response puzzled him in light of Reyntjens' knowledge that significant documented evidence of RPF atrocities existed. "Goldstone told me, 'I find this absolutely shocking because as far as I can see there is not the slightest prima facie evidence of the RPF having committed any such crimes.' Well that was the end of the conversation."[10] To Reyntjens, even in 1995, such a statement was "absolutely ridiculous ... because there was much more than prima facie evidence."[11] Still, Reyntjens said that he is "willing to accept

---

[5] Fieldwork interview with Richard J. Goldstone, Pasadena, April 2003.
[6] Ibid.
[7] Ibid.
[8] Final Report of the Commission of Experts, Established Pursuant to Security Council Resolution 935, December 9, 1994, paragraph 95.
[9] Fieldwork interview with Filip Reyntjens, Antwerp, December 2003.
[10] Ibid.
[11] Ibid.

that [Goldstone] didn't know" about RPF atrocities, given the prosecution's general lack of detailed knowledge about Rwanda.[12] "I can imagine that Goldstone didn't know that much about Rwanda. I mean who knew about Rwanda before 1994 anyway?"[13]

In my 2003 interview, Goldstone did not mention the threat of Rwandan retribution against the tribunal as a factor in his decision not to investigate the RPF.[14] Nevertheless, he was likely aware of Rwanda's possible reaction, given the government's turbulent relationship with the ICTR and its earlier threat to suspend cooperation in its bid to put Froduald Karamira on trial in Kigali. From a strategic point of view, Goldstone had little to gain and much to lose from investigating RPF atrocities, an endeavor that could target the inner circle of the RPF military and political establishment and even implicate Paul Kagame, Rwanda's de-facto leader. Targeting the RPF could stir resistance from the Tutsi-run government and military without increasing the prospect of cooperation from the Hutu forces that had fled into exile at the end of the genocide and were now stateless.

After Goldstone's departure from the ICTR and ICTY, the question of RPF investigations became a growing concern for the Office of the Prosecutor. With the tribunal's increasing awareness of the crimes committed by the RPF also came an awareness of the political dangers of investigating these abuses. Louise Arbour, Goldstone's successor, spelled out the risks in an interview with the Canadian journalist Carol Off. "How could we investigate and prosecute the RPF while we were based in that country? It was never going to happen. They would shut us down," Arbour said.[15] Government spying presented another obstacle for investigators. "The Rwandan government was reading my mail," recalled Arbour. "We were infiltrated. They knew what I was doing. So if I sent someone off to do an investigation of the RPF, they might be killed. I wouldn't do it."[16] Some former senior ICTR officials who worked in Rwanda during this period expressed skepticism in my interviews that the Kigali government would have actually taken the extreme step of harming investigators.[17] However, Arbour's statement underscores the palpable sense of fear among some at the ICTR that the government was determined to intimidate the tribunal in order to keep it focused exclusively on prosecuting Hutu suspects.

Nevertheless, Arbour – who held the chief prosecutor post at the ICTR and ICTY from September 1996 until September 1999 – decided, toward the end of her tenure, to open a preliminary probe into RPF atrocities. The probe, carried out quietly and cautiously, laid the groundwork for Del Ponte's subsequent investigation of specific RPF war crimes suspects.

---

[12] Ibid.
[13] Ibid.
[14] Fieldwork interview with Richard J. Goldstone, Pasadena, April 2003.
[15] Off, *The Lion, the Fox,& the General*, p. 331.
[16] Ibid, p. 331.
[17] Fieldwork interview with Cess Hendricks, Harlaam, The Netherlands, December 2003.

B. Del Ponte's "Special Investigations"

For Del Ponte, the political imperative of not upsetting the tribunal's delicate relationship with Kigali was not the only factor she had to consider when deciding whether to initiate a full-fledged investigation of RPF atrocities. Issuing some RPF indictments – if only several token indictments of low-level military officers – was fundamental to realizing the tribunal's mission of fairness and safeguarding its legitimacy. Continuing to ignore RPF crimes threatened to undermine the tribunal's efforts to win acceptance among Rwanda's majority Hutu population. That, in turn, would likely have thwarted the tribunal's mandate to contribute to national reconciliation between Hutu and Tutsi. How, critics increasingly asked, could the tribunal foster reconciliation in Rwanda if it did not acknowledge the extent of Hutu suffering and bring Tutsi suspects to account? With the end of the tribunal's mandate approaching, Del Ponte decided that she could not delay a full-fledged investigation of RPF suspects. By 2000, it became increasingly apparent that both the ICTR and ICTY would be pressed by the Security Council to close their doors by the end of the decade and complete all investigations by the end of 2004.

Del Ponte faced an uphill battle when it came to investigating, indicting, and ultimately prosecuting RPF officers. The main obstacle, of course, was the Rwandan government's determination to keep Tutsi RPF officers out of the dock in Arusha. Influential international actors also posed a formidable obstacle to Del Ponte's efforts to obtain the cooperation she needed to indict and prosecute RPF officers. The ICTR relied on the international community to act as a surrogate enforcer by pressuring Rwanda to abide by its legal obligation to cooperate with the tribunal. In contrast to Rwanda, in the Balkans, particularly during the post-authoritarian era, the Western powers often assumed a surrogate enforcer role by using their economic and political leverage – and the incentive of European Union membership – to prod Serbia and Croatia to cooperate. And in the Balkans, the West had considerably more leverage to compel the states of the former Yugoslavia to cooperate. Nevertheless, the West and the international community more generally retained significant leverage over Rwanda insofar as they could make much-needed economic aid to the government conditional on cooperation with the ICTR.

Del Ponte had some maneuvering room to pressure and persuade powerful international actors to prod Rwanda to cooperate with the RPF investigations. Her best hope for success depended on convincing these actors that RPF investigations were a vital part of the tribunal's mission and that Rwanda's non-compliance was an unacceptable violation of international law. However, as we will see, Del Ponte failed to shame Rwanda effectively in the eyes of the international diplomatic community and the international media.

In the Balkans, Del Ponte's shaming campaign against non-compliant states was bolstered by the ICTY's growing international stature and international outrage at Serbia (and Croatia to a lesser extent) over its role in wartime atrocities. Serbia and Croatia's efforts to counter-shame the ICTY usually failed, at least in the eyes of the international community, for the same reasons. But when it came to playing the shame card in the Rwandan context, it was the Kigali government, not the ICTR that enjoyed the upper hand. The government had long used shame effectively to attack the ICTR for its shortcomings, both perceived and real. The tribunal's failure to shame Rwanda and Rwanda's success at counter-shaming the tribunal was a function of the court's tattered international reputation and the Kigali government's standing as a victim state. The ICTR's disappointing performance[18] – as measured by the pace of completed genocide trials – undermined the leverage it might have had to lobby international actors to pressure the Rwandan government to cooperate in the RPF investigations. At the time Del Ponte announced her investigations of RPF atrocities in December 2000, the tribunal had completed only eight genocide cases, three of which were the results of pre-trial plea bargains.

International attention to RPF war crimes had indeed increased since the Goldstone and Arbour eras. Still, during Del Ponte's tenure, these crimes remained a marginal issue for the international community. To a significant extent, the lack of international interest in prosecuting RPF officers was an outgrowth of the lopsided distribution of violence that ravaged Rwanda in 1994 and the fact that the genocide against the Tutsi minority constituted one of the most horrific mass murders of the twentieth century. The number of RPF killings of Hutu civilians indeed pale by comparison with the toll of the genocide. Human Rights Watch's minimum estimate is that the Tutsi-led RPF killed approximately 25,000 to 30,000 Hutu during 1994.[19] Amnesty International estimates that 60,000 Hutu civilians were killed between April and July 1994.[20] The lack of thorough investigations and the challenges posed to documenting the killings have raised questions about the accuracy of these estimates.[21] In contrast to the killings carried out by Hutu extremists, the RPF massacres committed in 1994 were not part of a genocidal plan to eliminate the Hutu ethnic group. Thus the crimes committed by the two sides were fundamentally different, although the anguish of individual and familial loss among Hutu and Tutsi was often difficult to distinguish. In my interviews, top Rwandan government officials did not deny that some Hutu were killed during 1994. However, these officials minimized the numbers of Hutu killed and attributed their deaths to isolated acts of revenge. Evidence suggests that the pattern of massacres was too extensive and systematic to be solely attributed to individual actions.[22]

---

[18] It should be noted, however, that by the late 1990s, the ICTR had significantly outpaced the ICTY in bringing high-level suspects into custody. This success was due to the cooperation of states in Africa and Europe that arrested numerous Hutu fugitives and transferred them to the ICTR. By the end of July 2007, eighteen genocide suspects indicted by the tribunal – including its most wanted fugitive, Felicien Kabuga – remained at large.

[19] For a detailed discussion of RPF atrocities, see Des Forges, *Leave None to Tell the Story*, pp. 692–735.

[20] See "Appeal to the UN Security Council to ensure that the mandate of the International Criminal Tribunal for Rwanda is fulfilled," Amnesty International press release, December 12, 2006.

[21] Des Forges, *Leave None to Tell the Story*, p. 734.

[22] Ibid., pp. 692–735.

Given the RPF's cohesive command structure and its well-disciplined soldiers, it is possible that a sizeable number of killings were in fact carried out with the knowledge of or ordered by the higher echelons of the RPF. Human Rights Watch cites the decrease of atrocities in late Summer 1994, under U.S. pressure, as proof that the Rwandan government had control of its forces.[23]

It is important to emphasize that estimates of Hutu deaths refer only to RPF killings that occurred during 1994, the temporal scope of the tribunal's prosecutorial mandate. As discussed in Chapter 6, the tribunal has no legal authority to investigate atrocities – whether committed by Tutsi or Hutu forces – that occurred after December 31, 1994. Excluded from the tribunal's scrutiny are the RPF killings of tens of thousands of Hutu that occurred when RPF forces invaded neighboring Zaire in 1996[24] and then again later in the decade.

In the aftermath of the genocide, international attention, not surprisingly, focused on Tutsi suffering and the negligence of the international community to save Tutsi lives. In the wake of such evil, knowing when and how to acknowledge and prosecute the crimes committed by the victims is not clear. Many scholars and journalists writing on Rwanda made little, if any room, for discussing RPF atrocities. Nor was there a rigorous examination of the ways in which the RPF's invasion of Rwanda, launched from neighboring Uganda in October 1990, helped trigger the series of events that led to the genocide. Not infrequently did Western writers, such as the American journalist Philip Gourevitch, portray the Tutsi-led RPF government as a heroic victim that brought the genocide to an end. Gourevitch viewed the Rwandan tragedy through the lens of the Holocaust, identifying one side as victim and the other side as perpetrator. But the reality was a good deal more complicated given that the RPF, the purported victim of the genocide, was also a perpetrator of atrocities, albeit not nearly of the same magnitude as that of the Hutu génocidaires.[25]

The benevolent portrayal of the new Kigali regime – popularized by Gourevitch in his National Book Critics Circle Award winning account of the genocide[26] – helped bolster American and British policy goals in the African Great Lakes region. In the aftermath of the genocide, Western governments, particularly the United States and Great Britain, provided an outpouring of political and economic support to the fledgling Tutsi-led government. Sympathy for Rwanda's suffering and guilt for the West's complacency during the genocide strengthened the Kigali government. In light of their strategic goals in Rwanda, Washington and London had little interest in pressing the Kigali regime to cooperate with tribunal investigations of RPF atrocities. Nor did the United States

---

[23] Ibid., p. 735.
[24] Human Rights Watch, "Democratic Republic of Congo: What Kabila Is Hiding: Civilian Killings and Impunity in Congo," October 1997.
[25] Howard W. French, *A Continent for the Taking: The Tragedy and Hope of Africa* (New York: Alfred A. Knopf, 2004), p. 143 and pp. 231–232.
[26] Gourevitch, *We Wish to Inform You that Tomorrow We Will Be Killed With Our Families*.

and Britain have an interest in shining a spotlight on the wave of post-1994 RPF atrocities against Hutu génocidaires and innocent civilians who had fled to Congo.[27]

8.4 The Battle for Cooperation: Opening Salvos

The trials of cooperation between the ICTR and the Rwandan government would not surface publicly for a year and a half after Del Ponte's December 2000 announcement of the start of her investigations of RPF atrocities. By then, her quiet attempts to prod the Rwandan authorities to assist her probe came to an end. In April 2002, Del Ponte issued her first public criticism of Rwanda's refusal to aid her investigations of RPF atrocities.

During the period from December 2000 to April 2002, Del Ponte chose not to pursue the confrontational, media-centered stance that characterized her approach to the Serbian and Croatian governments. When it came to her job in The Hague, Del Ponte quickly earned a reputation for her dogged pursuit of war crimes suspects harbored by the governments of the former Yugoslavia. But without firm international backing for her pursuit of RPF officers in Rwanda, such an aggressive approach could alienate potential international supporters. When it came to dealing with the Rwandan government, Western diplomats often counseled the tribunal to tread carefully. Del Ponte appeared to realize, at least initially, that public silence was the prudent approach.

For its own part, the Rwandan government also had an interest in maintaining public silence on the question of its cooperation with the tribunal's "special investigations" of RPF crimes. Clearly the government preferred not to open a public discussion that might raise questions about its narrative of the genocide and the actual role played by the RPF. Several years after the genocide, RPF atrocities remained a taboo topic, rarely discussed publicly by Rwandans or Westerners in Rwanda.

As Del Ponte worked behind the scenes to secure government assurances to cooperate, Rwandan officials took the offensive. The government launched a counter-shaming campaign against the tribunal long before Del Ponte sought to publicly "prosecute" the government for its failure to cooperate. Despite their silence over the RPF investigations, Rwandan leaders sought indirectly to undermine Del Ponte's international diplomatic support for these investigations by attacking the tribunal for the slow pace of the genocide trials and its administrative tribulations.

The Rwandan government also expanded its offensive against the tribunal by encouraging and aiding closely aligned Tutsi survivor organizations to wage a counter-shaming campaign against the court. The injection of "civil society" actors into the trials of cooperation with the tribunal was a strategic gambit that strengthened the government's bid for the political and moral high ground. The attacks of the survivor groups on the tribunal – and their stinging accusations

[27] French, *A Continent for the Taking*, pp. 141–142.

of victim and witness mistreatment – further eroded the ICTR's international standing by magnifying the government's long-running complaint that the tribunal had betrayed Tutsi survivors. As with the government's counter-shaming campaigns, the survivor groups made some important critiques of the tribunal process and called attention to issues of witness treatment and protection that had not been adequately addressed by the tribunal. Nevertheless, the critiques also doubled as political attacks with the larger aim of boosting the government's attempts to delegitimize the tribunal and block the prosecution of Tutsi suspects. In the remainder of the chapter, I will examine how the mobilization of the Tutsi survivor organizations shaped the battle between the tribunal and government over the unresolved issue of state cooperation with RPF investigations.

8.5 Counter-Shame and the ICTR's Self-Inflicted Wounds

A. Overview
An explanation of how the Rwandan government and Tutsi survivor organizations counter-shamed the tribunal must take into account the way in which they exploited the tribunal's missteps. When it came to Rwanda's counter-shaming offensive, the ICTR was its own worst enemy. Two embarrassing incidents at the tribunal in 2001 were used by the government and then by Tutsi survivor groups to highlight their claim of tribunal mistreatment of victims and witnesses. In the first incident, the tribunal arrested a veteran Hutu defense investigator after discovering his alleged role in massacres of Tutsi during the genocide. In the second incident, the Rwandan government and Tutsi survivor groups accused a panel of ICTR judges of demeaning and unprofessional conduct after the judges laughed during the cross-examination of a Tutsi rape victim. The tribunal tried unsuccessfully to limit the public relations damage by arguing that the arrest of the Hutu defense investigator – and the subsequent arrest of another ICTR defense investigator – were isolated incidents and that the judges' courtroom behavior had been misinterpreted. These incidents remain landmark events in the tribunal's troubled relationship with the Rwandan government and Tutsi survivor organizations.

B. The Enemy Within: Genocide Suspects as Defense Investigators
That the tribunal had long and unknowingly employed a Hutu defense investigator who was actually a high-level genocide suspect wanted by the ICTR was a stunning revelation. News of the tribunal's arrest of the suspect, Siméon Nshamihigo, followed by the discovery of other genocide suspects on the tribunal's payroll, sparked harsh condemnation from Kigali.[28] Additional revelations over the next year of more genocide suspects employed by the tribunal fueled these charges and further eroded Rwandan and international trust in the tribunal.

---

[28] Victor Peskin, "Rwandan Ghosts," *Legal Affairs*, September/October 2002, pp. 21–25.

For almost three years, Sammy Bahati Weza led a typical life of a defense investigator at the ICTR. By all accounts, Bahati Weza, who held a Congolese passport, was well liked by those who knew him. He was reportedly a diligent investigator who spent long hours following the genocide trials from the public gallery, as a number of other defense investigators commonly do.

Bahati Weza's life began to unravel one day in early May 2001 when a Rwandan recognized him in the halls of the tribunal as someone he once knew in Rwanda. Some time afterward, this person notified tribunal authorities and told them two things that were extremely unsettling. First, Bahati Weza was not a Congolese national, but actually Siméon Nshamihigo, a Rwandan who had served as a deputy prosecutor in Cyangugu Prefecture in southwestern Rwanda. And second, Nshamihigo was allegedly involved in planning the massacres that took place in Cyangugu shortly after the genocide against the Tutsi minority began in early April 1994. Within several weeks, the tribunal arrested Nshamihigo and charged him with genocide and crimes against humanity. "I was very surprised," one senior tribunal official told me in a 2002 interview. "Sammy was such a nice guy. But he was just playing a game, and he was playing the game good. Nobody knew."[29]

The dilemma facing the tribunal in the aftermath of Nshamihigo's arrest was that there was no guaranteed way to ensure that other Hutu defense investigators were not playing a similar game of deception. About 90 percent of the approximately fifty defense investigators working at the tribunal were Hutu. The Registry, the tribunal division in charge of recruitment and hiring, did not conduct rigorous security screening of prospective defense investigators. The revelation that genocide suspects were on the staff exasperated diplomats who had grown impatient with the tribunal's administrative problems. "Imagine Klaus Barbie working for the defense at Nuremberg," a European diplomat in Kigali told me in an interview.[30] The tribunal's public relations unit, which was also run by the Registry, tried its best to downplay the tribunal's responsibility for having employed a possible mass murderer by maintaining that defense investigators were not actually tribunal employees, but "independent contractors recruited by defense counsel."[31] Moreover, inured to stories of scandal and administrative incompetence, the news that a genocide suspect had worked at the court did not seem to shock many at the tribunal.

In Rwanda, this latest travail of the tribunal became the lead story in the country's pro-government newspaper, *The New Times*. In fact, *The New Times* ran front-page stories about the defense investigator issue well before Nshamihigo's arrest. The newspaper reported government allegations, first made in March 2001, that the ICTR was employing several genocide suspects as defense investigators. The government's warning, however, was met with a passive tribunal response. The Registry's failure to investigate these charges redoubled the

[29] Fieldwork interview with tribunal official, Arusha, April 2002.
[30] Fieldwork interview with European diplomat, Kigali, May 2002.
[31] "Defense Investigator Arrested," ICTR press release, May 21, 2001.

government's anger and the potency of its criticism of the tribunal following Nshamihigo's arrest.

Nshamihigo's arrest was more than just a disconcerting story about a bold mass-murder suspect who eluded capture by hiding in the very institution created to prosecute him while making a small fortune in Rwandan terms.[32] Fallout from this incident would have far-reaching implications for the relationship of the government and survivor groups with the tribunal as well as for the future of cooperation with the international court. In Rwanda, rumors spread quickly that many, if not most, of the Hutu defense investigators working at the tribunal were wanted for genocide.

Rwandan resentment of the tribunal was exacerbated by the operation of its legal aid program established to provide genocide defendants in Arusha a right to a fair trial. The privileged role of the defendant at the tribunal and the marginal role of victims had long been a sore point for the government. But anger from the government and survivor organizations also can be attributed to abuses of the legal process by Hutu defendants and their defense teams. Defendants had little difficulty exploiting the system, as illustrated by many untruthful claims of indigence to obtain free legal aid and illegal fee-splitting arrangements with their defense attorneys. The tribunal also came under attack for not doing more to stop the defendants hiring friends and relatives to work as defense investigators on their cases. "It's a mafia," one senior tribunal official lamented in a 2002 interview, in reference to the abuses of the court's legal aid system.[33]

In fairness, it is important to note that such abuses of the legal aid system were not limited to the ICTR. Two investigations by the UN Office of Internal Oversight Services found support for allegations of fee-splitting arrangements at both the ICTR and the ICTY.[34] However, the issue of fee splitting did not become a major bone of contention between the ICTY and the states of the former Yugoslavia. By contrast, the Rwandan government featured the fee-splitting scandal as a major component of its counter-shaming campaign against the ICTR.

In the aftermath of the Nshamihigo arrest, the Rwandan government pressured the tribunal to address the flaws in its screening procedures of prospective employees. Interviews I conducted at the tribunal during the first half of 2002 suggest that the tribunal's Registry remained ill-equipped to address the formidable task of screening current and prospective Rwandan employees. Developing a rigorous screening procedure was a difficult challenge, especially when it came to verifying the government's allegations that certain defense

---

[32] In 2002, ICTR defense investigators earned up to $2,500 a month, a huge sum in Rwanda, where civil servants typically make about $200 a month. The salary offered to defense investigators may have been especially attractive to Hutu refugees, thousands of whom struggle to earn a living in exile.

[33] Victor Peskin, "Rwandan Ghosts," *Legal Affairs*, September/October 2002, pp. 21–25.

[34] "Statement by the Registrar Concerning Change of Counsel under the Tribunal's Legal Aid Programme," ICTR press release, November 5, 2002.

investigators had participated in the genocide. In fact, it was relatively easy for the Rwandan government to cast blame on defense investigators without probable cause simply by adding that person's name to the country's wanted list of genocide suspects. In this way, Hutu defense investigators confronted the very real possibility of being unjustly added to the Rwandan government's list of suspects as a means to further attack the tribunal. This placed Hutu defense investigators in serious danger of being falsely accused and becoming pawns in a larger game of blame and retribution.

Following Nshamihigo's arrest in May 2001, the ICTR's Registrar, Adama Dieng of Senegal, took action to stem the rising tide of anger in Rwanda. In July 2001, Dieng held a press conference to announce that the contracts of four defense investigators would not be renewed because of evidence that they had participated in the genocide.[35] These four investigators were among those added to Rwanda's most-wanted list and were the ones the Rwandan government had identified as genocide suspects back in March. Dieng's attempt to assuage the government did little to quell the controversy. The government strongly criticized Dieng for allowing the dismissed genocide suspects to walk free instead of arresting them or handing them over to Rwanda for prosecution.[36]

In December 2001, another ICTR defense investigator, Joseph Nzabirinda, was arrested in Belgium and charged by the tribunal with genocide. Once again, the arrest of a defense investigator occurred because of a chance event and not because of any improvements in the Registry security measures.[37] The arrest fueled a new round of charges from the Rwandan government and survivor groups that the tribunal had become a haven for Hutu génocidaires.[38] Astonishingly, several years later in 2006, the question of how many genocide suspects may be on the ICTR payroll had not been resolved. In June 2006, the tribunal announced an investigation of twelve Hutu employees suspected by the Kigali government of participating in the genocide.[39]

Outrage over the defense investigator issue bolstered the capacity of the government and the survivor groups to counter-shame the tribunal, and leant

---

[35] "Statement by the Registrar, Mr. Adama Dieng, on the Non-Renewal of the Employment Contracts of Certain Defense Investigators," ICTR press release, July 16, 2001.

[36] The Registrar's attempt to resolve the defense investigator issue also sparked condemnation from another corner – the tribunal's defense attorneys. Soon after Dieng's July press conference, the defense team that had hired one of the dismissed investigators charged that the Registrar had falsely accused the investigator and unfairly tarnished his reputation. The investigator in question, Aloys Ngendahimana, shared the same name as the man wanted by Rwanda, but he was actually thirteen years older and came from a different part of Rwanda. The incident raised questions about how thoroughly the Registry had reviewed the list of genocide suspects on the ICTR payroll provided by the Rwandan government.

[37] Fieldwork interview with tribunal official, Arusha, March 2002.

[38] Nshamihigo's trial did not start until September 2006, more than four years after his arrest. By the end of July 2007, the trial had not yet concluded. In a plea agreement, Nzabirinda, who had originally been charged with genocide and crimes and against humanity, was convicted of one count of murder as a crime against humanity and sentenced in February 2007 to seven years' imprisonment.

[39] "Rwanda: UN tribunal investigating 12 on its payroll," *Integrated Regional Information Network*, June 29, 2006.

renewed credence to their claims of tribunal indifference to victims and witnesses. The presence of Hutu genocide suspects at the tribunal posed a serious
threat to the safety of Tutsi prosecution witnesses who traveled to Arusha to
testify. While the identity of most of these Rwandan witnesses was shielded
from the public and from most tribunal employees, the defense investigators
had easy access to their identities. With this information in the hands of genocide suspects, it was feared that the safety of prosecution witnesses could be
imperiled. In the months to come, the government and survivor groups gave
voice to these fears and to what they claimed was the tribunal's insufficient
response.

C. The "Witness TA" Affair: Laughter in the Courtroom, Outrage in Kigali

The Witness TA affair draws its name from the pseudonym given to shield the
identity of a Tutsi rape victim who testified as a prosecution witness at the
tribunal. On October 31, 2001, a three-judge panel presiding over the Butare
trial at the ICTR laughed as a Kenyan defense attorney posed sexually explicit
questions to Witness TA concerning her claims of being repeatedly raped by
the former governor of the Butare province, Shalom Ntahobali. Ntahobali was
one of six Hutu defendants on trial in the Butare case.

The defense attorney's effort to undermine the veracity of Witness TA's testimony by asking detailed questions about the rape appeared to unsettle the
judges. The presiding judge, William Sekule of Tanzania, unsuccessfully prodded the defense attorney to speed up his questioning of the witness. But the
defense attorney remained dogged in pursuing his line of inquiry. After repeatedly trying to limit the attorney's questions, the judges laughed when the attorney again questioned the witness.

The political fallout from the judges' laughter did more to damage the institution's image and undermine its morale than perhaps any other single incident
in the tribunal's history. Leaders of Ibuka and Avega,[40] the two principal Tutsi
survivor organizations, sought to turn Witness TA into a symbol of the plight
of every Tutsi witness who had testified in Arusha. Regardless of the judges'
actual intent, the perception in Rwanda and neighboring countries was that
their laughter constituted harassment of Witness TA, as seen in the headline
of a Ugandan newspaper: "UN Judges Laugh at Rape Victim!"[41] In the highly
politicized climate, the episode became a central exhibit in the government and
survivor groups' "prosecution" of the tribunal.

The tribunal responded to the crisis defensively. The ICTR's chief justice
(and president), Navanethem Pillay, issued a press release that defended the
judges and refuted the accusations that they were actually laughing at Witness
TA.[42] With two lengthy footnotes, Pillay's press release resembled a legal brief

---

[40] Ibuka is the largest Tutsi survivor association in Rwanda. Avega is an association of Tutsi
widows.
[41] "UN Judges Laugh at Rape Victim!" AFP, *The Monitor*, December 3, 2001, p. 13.
[42] "Statement of Judge Pillay, President of the Tribunal," ICTR press release, December 14, 2001.

more than a convincing attempt to impart compassion for Rwandan genocide survivors who had testified before the tribunal. Moreover, Pillay seemed more intent on laying blame on others – by criticizing Chief Prosecutor Del Ponte for her "highly unfortunate" critical remarks of the Butare trial judges – than in accepting responsibility for the judges' actions.[43] Tribunal staff members were stung by the harsh attacks on the court that many considered to be inaccurate and politically motivated. Yet many staff members I interviewed acknowledged that the incident highlighted long-standing problems with the ICTR judiciary, especially its frequent failure to control and hasten courtroom proceedings.

Rwandan anger over the Witness TA incident opened up a new line of attack against the tribunal's courtroom treatment of witnesses. Fundamental aspects of the adversarial courtroom process, such as cross-examination, now became fair game for Rwandan critics. The tribunal's mistreatment of witnesses, the survivor organizations alleged, forced survivors to relive their trauma rather than move beyond it. "Witnesses are tortured when they go to Arusha," a survivor association official told me in a 2002 interview in Kigali.[44] Regardless of the political motives of the survivor associations, such allegations posed a direct challenge to the claim advanced by tribunal officials that the experience of testifying in international trials helps victims come to terms with their loss.

8.6 Boycotting the ICTR: Tutsi Survivor Groups Suspend Cooperation

In late January 2002, Ibuka and Avega, with pivotal backing from the Rwandan government, raised their counter-shaming campaign against the ICTR to a new level by announcing their refusal to cooperate with the tribunal and calling on all Tutsi survivors to do the same. By doing so, the survivor groups reinforced the government's efforts to delegitimize the tribunal and divert international attention away from the government's continuing refusal to abide by its obligation to cooperate with Del Ponte's investigations of RPF atrocities.

With the launching of the boycott, the tribunal now faced an unprecedented crisis of cooperation. The ICTR found itself in a battle with non-state actors who held the key to the continuation of the courtroom trials. In contrast to government officials, non-state actors such as survivor organizations do not have a legal obligation to cooperate with the tribunal. Moreover, these non-state actors possess the moral standing of actual victims, which made it particularly challenging for the tribunal to pressure them to alter their position.

In justifying their boycott, Ibuka and Avega took aim at the alleged humiliating treatment meted out to Rwandan witnesses at the ICTR and to the threat posed to witnesses by the alleged presence of yet more Hutu genocide suspects employed by the court. The survivor associations claimed that they had tried to raise their concerns with the tribunal but were rebuffed.[45] Ibuka and Avega

---

[43] Ibid.
[44] Fieldwork interview with Ibuka official, Kigali, April 2002.
[45] Ibid.

also issued a call for immediate and comprehensive reform to bolster the rights of witnesses and victims – an unrealistic request given the existing constraints on the tribunal. Still, the survivor groups were determined to use the boycott to bring international opprobrium on the tribunal. Ibuka announced in a statement that the boycott would continue "until [the tribunal] has corrected all its mistakes and accorded sufficient importance to victims"[46] and "that as long as all the above mistakes are not corrected, the court's decisions will only constitute stop-gap measures and a mockery of the genocide victims in the place of equitable justice."[47]

Many tribunal officials, including some who were sympathetic to Ibuka's complaints, felt there was little they could quickly do to meet Ibuka's long list of demands and thereby persuade the organization to halt its boycott.[48] In their meetings with Ibuka, tribunal officials promised better treatment of witnesses and additional steps to safeguard witnesses and shield their identities.[49] But according to tribunal officials I interviewed, Ibuka leaders expressed little interest in the reforms pledged by the tribunal. Increasingly, tribunal officials who dealt with witness-protection issues came to view the Ibuka boycott as an effort to exploit its victim status in order to exert control over the tribunal and significantly alter the balance between the rights of defendants and victims.

As the survivor groups took on the tribunal, the government, in early 2002, uncharacteristically took a back seat in the counter-shaming offensive. Juxtaposed against the bold defiance of the survivor associations, the government appeared to be a moderate force, a view it sought to reinforce by offering to mediate the dispute between the associations and the tribunal. By so doing, the authoritarian government tried to create the appearance that the boycott was a genuine act of Rwandan civil society and, in turn, a demonstration of a burgeoning democracy.

Western diplomats based in Kigali and other veteran tribunal observers I interviewed during this period doubted the claim that the boycott was the work of independent civil society organizations since few of them could exist in such an authoritarian state as Rwanda. According to well-placed Rwandans, the government played an active role in supporting the boycott and providing damaging information about the tribunal for the survivor groups to use in their attacks against the court.[50] Still, the close government–survivor group collaboration did not necessarily mean that the government initiated the survivor group boycott or exerted full control over it.

Despite the heavy hand of the Rwandan state, there was room at certain periods for some independent political expression by non-state actors, particularly

[46] "UN Tribunal Registrar Leaves Kigali Amid New Standoff," *Hirondelle News Agency*, January 27, 2002.

[47] Mary Kimani, "Genocide Survivor Groups Suspend Co-Operation with ICTR," *Internews*, January 28, 2002.

[48] Fieldwork interviews with tribunal officials, Arusha, February-March 2002.

[49] Fieldwork interviews with tribunal officials, Kigali, June, 2002.

[50] Fieldwork interviews with Rwandan government officials, Kigali, April-May 2002.

Tutsi survivor groups. Indeed, the relationship between the government and the survivor groups was not always a smooth one.[51] Tensions between the two entities stemmed from their different experiences during 1994 and their different post-genocide status in Rwandan society. While the RPF sought to portray itself internationally as a government of survivors, its most powerful leaders were Tutsi who only returned to Rwanda following the genocide after spending many years in exile, particularly in Uganda and other Anglophone African countries. Whereas many of the Anglophone Tutsi returnees enjoyed access to economic and political opportunity, most of the Francophone Tutsi survivors had little access to either. In the mid and late 1990s, this political and economic disparity and a number of disagreements led to friction between the government and Ibuka. In 2000, the Rwandan government took steps to purge Ibuka's leadership and forced some of its leaders into exile. The government was then instrumental in installing a new, more compliant Ibuka leadership.[52] From that point on, Ibuka grew much closer to the Kagame government and rarely took action that went against the government's political interests.

Most officials and staff members at the ICTR headquarters in Arusha regarded the boycott as more of a headache than a crisis. This feeling was reinforced by the fact that the boycott had little visible effect on the trials in Arusha.[53] Throughout the Winter and Spring of 2002, Tutsi witnesses selected to testify on behalf of the prosecution continued to travel to testify in a number of genocide trials. However, the boycott inflicted heavy damage on the tribunal's pre-trial investigations in Rwanda, reducing by as much as half the number of survivors willing to give testimony to field investigators.[54] This significantly compromised the tribunal's ability to build cases against Hutu genocide suspects.

It was not for want of trying that the survivor groups were unable to dissuade more survivors from testifying in Arusha. The tribunal's success was due in large part to the efforts of its Witness and Victims Support Section to persuade survivors to bear witness in the genocide trials.[55] In my interviews, witness unit staff members in Kigali reported that many prospective witnesses agreed to testify in Arusha only after having long discussions with the staff. The witness unit benefited greatly from its inclusion of Rwandan employees – some of whom were survivors themselves – who could empathize with the

---

[51] Human Rights Watch World Report, Rwanda, 2001.
[52] Fieldwork interviews with representatives from Rwanda-based international non-governmental organizations, Kigali, June-July 2002.
[53] The sense of complacency at the ICTR was somewhat shaken in early April when two genocide survivors, citing the Ibuka and Avega boycott, refused to go to Arusha to testify on behalf of the prosecution in the Juvénal Kajelijeli trial. The prosecution was forced to rest its case without the benefit of testimony from its final two witnesses.
[54] Fieldwork interviews with tribunal officials, Kigali, April-May 2002.
[55] Fieldwork interviews with Witness and Victims Support Section officials, Kigali, June-July 2002; Arusha, July 2002.

prospective witnesses, prepare them for the trial experience, and persuade them of the importance of aiding the prosecution's efforts to convict genocide suspects. The efforts of this small, under-funded unit charged with transferring witnesses from Rwanda to Arusha and protecting them during their journey remain an untold story.

What the Tutsi survivor groups were unable to do during the first part of 2002 – namely, stop a significant number of witnesses from traveling in Arusha – the Rwandan government was later able to do by virtue of its control over the country's borders. In June 2002, the government again took center stage in the trials of cooperation by blocking Tutsi witnesses from traveling to Arusha to testify against Hutu genocide suspects. By so doing, the government raised the stakes in its battle with Carla Del Ponte over her investigations of RPF atrocities.

8.7 The Ibuka Boycott and ICTR Diplomacy

A. *Adama Dieng Responds*

For much of its duration, the boycott crisis was left to the Registry, the tribunal division officially charged with handling external relations and witness protection. Leaving the problem to the Registry appeared to suit Del Ponte who, according to tribunal sources, felt it was not her responsibility to deal with the survivor groups.[56] Del Ponte's willingness to cede the issue to the Registrar, Adama Dieng, was part and parcel of her lack of consistent diplomatic engagement in Rwanda.

Dieng happened to be in Kigali when Ibuka and Avega announced the boycott of the tribunal. Although the announcement caught Dieng off guard, he recognized the potential danger of the boycott. If Dieng was quick to appreciate the nature of the threat, he was less adept at imparting a diplomatic response. "It is important that they reverse that decision, otherwise they will be responsible for what I could call an injustice to victims," Dieng said, referring to the survivor groups.[57] "If I were a victim I would prefer to be harassed than see the person who had raped me swaggering down the streets of Europe and the world." Dieng paid another visit to Kigali a month later to try to launch an initiative in which a number of UN agencies based in Rwanda would devise a plan to help address a range of concerns raised by the survivor groups, including the question of economic assistance to survivors. The move was intended to address some of the groups' grievances while delegating responsibility to other UN organizations.

In a sign of their growing radicalization, the survivor associations rejected Dieng's invitation to attend the Kigali conference to discuss his new initiative. Association representatives refused to meet with Dieng until the tribunal met

---

[56] Fieldwork interviews with tribunal officials, Arusha, February-March 2002.
[57] "UN Tribunal Registrar Leaves Kigali Amid New Standoff," *Hirondelle News Agency*, January 27, 2002.

their demands to arrest genocide suspects on the court's payroll and provide added security for witnesses. A frustrated Dieng reiterated his call for the groups to cooperate with the ICTR, and said they would only have themselves to blame if the boycott brought an end to the genocide prosecutions and the release of Hutu defendants.[58] The war of words between Ibuka and Dieng became the lead story in *The New Times*: "Ibuka, ICTR lock horns," read the large front-page headline. In the narrative advanced by the pro-government newspaper, the genocide survivors were engaged in a David and Goliath struggle with the international court.

Following Ibuka's refusal to meet with him, Dieng changed his approach by engaging the government instead of the survivor groups. The change in strategy enabled Dieng to regain the diplomatic initiative. By appealing to the government to intervene, Dieng was implicitly arguing that the government, its denials notwithstanding, had the power to resolve this crisis if it so wished.

B. The Tribunal–Government Commission Proposal

Conciliation was the centerpiece of Dieng's diplomatic initiative. In early March 2002, he proposed a joint ICTR–Rwandan government commission to investigate the claims of the Rwandan government and survivor groups of witness mistreatment.[59] The proposal to invite the government to play a role in investigating long-standing accusations of witness mistreatment was unprecedented. Neither the Rwandan or Balkan governments had any legal claim to play an official role in the legal or administrative functions of the ICTR and the ICTY. Rwandan leaders had long complained of being excluded from the operation and oversight of the international court. In my interviews, Rwandan officials spoke enviously of the new hybrid war crimes tribunal in Sierra Leone that provided the Freetown government with the power to appoint the deputy prosecutor, one judge to each of the two three-judge panels, and two of the five appellate judges. But now, at least in a small way, Dieng's proposal for a joint commission promised to change the status quo at the ICTR.

To Dieng, the seriousness of the allegations of witness mistreatment aired by the survivor groups and the government made it "absolutely vital to work together to verify the validity of the allegations openly and fairly."[60] A joint ICTR–Rwandan government report detailing allegations of witness mistreatment and recommendations could signal the tribunal's sensitivity to the problems outlined by the survivor associations.

Dieng's commission, scheduled to begin on April 1, sparked a bitter tug-of-war with the Rwandan government over the ground rules of the joint body. The government took issue with what it considered the commission's narrow mandate. Government officials argued that the commission should also have

---

[58] Ibid.
[59] "Tribunal Proposes Joint Committee with Government of Rwanda to Verify Allegations of Mistreatment of Witnesses from Rwanda," ICTR press release, March 13, 2002.
[60] Ibid.

the authority to examine the tribunal's recruitment of Rwandan employees to ensure that no genocide suspects remained on the court's payroll. The government also charged that Dieng had promised that the commission would have such powers. The Registrar strongly denied making such a promise and pointed to a March 4 letter in which he said that the commission would be charged only with investigating allegations of witness mistreatment. While the Rwandan government criticized the proposal for not going far enough, defense attorneys, as well as some judges, feared that the commission's investigation would have a chilling effect on their courtroom conduct and the right of the defense to vigorously cross-examine prosecution witnesses.

An opportunity for cooperation soon descended into conflict and mutual suspicion. The disagreement over the terms of the commission was played out first in an exchange of angry letters between Dieng and the Rwandan Minister of Justice Jean de Dieu Mucyo and then in the Rwandan media. Mucyo's accusation that Dieng had gone back on his promise was countered with Dieng's accusation that the government was attempting to usurp the tribunal's independence by trying to control recruitment and hiring practices. The stalemate between the tribunal and the government persisted for several weeks, with no signs of a breakthrough. In mid-April, Dieng withdrew the proposal for a joint commission.[61] The source of the conflict aside, Dieng's proposal for a joint commission may have been more trouble than it was worth for the tribunal. The clash between Dieng and Mucyo underscored how quickly such a commission could be engulfed by contention and attempts at political manipulation. This conflict provides a cautionary tale about the difficulty some tribunals might confront when sharing authority with domestic governments.

8.8 Conclusion

Dieng's withdrawal of the commission proposal was, not surprisingly, condemned in Rwanda and cited as further evidence of the tribunal's insensitivity to survivors. Soon the counter-shaming offensive of the government and survivor groups went a step further. Later in the Spring of 2002, the survivor groups called for Dieng's resignation. The story of the stillborn commission underscores the growing climate of contention between the tribunal and the Rwandan government. In past crises, such as the Karamira and Barayagwiza incidents, the tribunal used conciliation, even acquiescence, to try to secure Rwandan cooperation. But the dispute over Dieng's proposal for a joint tribunal–government commission demonstrated the limits the tribunal now faced when trying to be conciliatory toward the Rwandan government. Despite Dieng's inclination to assuage government officials, there was a limit to how far he was willing or able to go with the commission proposal because of the need to protect the tribunal's autonomy and to temper the objections of the court's increasingly vocal defense

---

[61] "The Registrar Decides to Withdraw his Proposal to Establish a Joint Commission to Investigate Allegations of Mistreatment of Witnesses from Rwanda," ICTR press release, April 17, 2002.

attorneys. The Rwandan government may have had principled objections to the mandate of the proposed commission, regardless of the unprecedented level of participation in the tribunal it was offered. Nevertheless, the government's reluctance to reach a compromise stemmed from its uncompromising position on a more fundamental objection to the tribunal – Chief Prosecutor Del Ponte's continuing efforts to hold RPF suspects accountable for their role in atrocities against Hutu civilians.

9

Victor's Justice Revisited

The Prosecutor v. Kagame

9.1 Introduction

The contentious relationship between the International Criminal Tribunal for Rwanda (ICTR) and the Tutsi-led Rwandan government came to a head when Rwanda blocked Chief Prosecutor Carla Del Ponte's imminent indictments of Rwandan Patriotic Front (RPF) military officers. The ability of the government to avoid significant international censure as it thwarted Del Ponte undermined a foundational principle upon which the contemporary international war crimes tribunals was founded: that individuals from all sides of an armed conflict suspected of committing serious violations of international humanitarian law should not enjoy immunity from prosecution. This chapter focuses on the period beginning in April 2002 and ending in August 2003 – from Del Ponte's first public criticism of Rwandan non-cooperation with her probe of RPF atrocities, to the government's successful move to have the Security Council dismiss her as chief prosecutor of the ICTR. The chapter concludes with an analysis of the way Del Ponte's replacement, Hassan Jallow, has approached the question of RPF atrocities and why, after nearly four years, he has refrained from indicting RPF suspects.

The tacit backing of Rwanda's closest Western allies – the United States and Great Britain – played a crucial role in enabling the Kigali government to outmaneuver Del Ponte's efforts to prosecute RPF officers for war crimes against Hutu civilians. The role of the West during this period underscores a recurring theme in this study: without strong and consistent international political support, tribunals will rarely succeed in prodding recalcitrant states to cooperate in the prosecution of members of their own national or ethnic groups. However, Del Ponte and other senior tribunal officials could have done much more to work for state cooperation, both through diplomacy with Rwandan authorities and key international players. Still, it is arguable that a more determined tribunal diplomacy could have triggered the world support needed to force the Tutsi-led Rwandan government to cooperate in the prosecution of Tutsi military officers. To be sure, the raw power of the Rwandan state to block cooperation was no match for the lack of enforcement powers of the ICTR. Moreover, the Rwandan government had long ago staked out the political and moral high ground when it came to its dealings with the ICTR, which helped thwart tribunal attempts to obtain cooperation. Nevertheless, this chapter demonstrates that the tribunal relinquished important opportunities to increase its leverage vis-à-vis the Rwandan government.

The ICTR failed on two counts: first, to effectively "prosecute" the Rwandan government for violating its legal obligation to provide full and immediate cooperation, and second, to articulate to the international community – particularly Western diplomats and the media corps – the legal and political imperative of bringing Tutsi RPF war crimes suspects to justice. The tribunal's attempts to shame Rwandan officials for obstructing the course of international justice hardly resonated internationally. In the "trials of cooperation," it was the Rwandan government, not the ICTR, that launched an effective "prosecution" through its instrumental use of shame. A key to the government's success lay in its reframing the debate away from non-compliance and toward the tribunal's lackluster performance in prosecuting Hutu genocide suspects. To achieve this end, government officials also targeted Chief Prosecutor Del Ponte and the alleged failures of the Office of the Prosecutor. This strategy made it considerably easier than it might otherwise have been for international actors, such as the United States and Britain, to withhold the political backing that the tribunal needed to prevail.

9.2 In Pursuit of the Rwandan Patriotic Front

At the outset of her RPF probe, Del Ponte pursued a strategy of quiet negotiation with the Kigali regime, apparently in the hope that this would increase her chances of gathering sufficient evidence to bring indictments against RPF officers. But after nearly a year and a half without tangible results, Del Ponte realized the futility of this approach. In time, the trials of cooperation moved out of the shadows of closed-door meetings between Del Ponte and Rwandan President Paul Kagame and into the public arena of heated rhetorical battles pitting the tribunal against the state. Del Ponte's first criticism of Rwandan non-compliance, in April 2002, marked the beginning of an escalating confrontation with the Kigali government.

From the start, Del Ponte faced an uphill battle. A tribunal's efficacy in "prosecuting" a state's non-compliance depends in large part on its ability to shame the state for its failure to abide by its legal obligation to cooperate. However, states rarely remain passive when confronted by a tribunal. The Rwandan government demonstrated a keen ability to counter the tribunal's offensive in several ways. First, the government disputed the tribunal's contention that it was not providing cooperation. Second, government officials insisted that RPF crimes – which they downplayed as isolated acts of revenge by aggrieved Tutsi soldiers – should be handled exclusively by Rwandan courts. Third, the government sought to establish a moral basis for Tutsi exceptionalism, and thereby win international assent for its bid for immunity from tribunal prosecution. Government leaders argued that the United Nations had relinquished any moral right to prosecute RPF military officers when the world organization stood by passively during the genocide. According to this logic, it was the Tutsi-led RPF government, which had actually brought the genocide to a halt, that retained the exclusive right to pass judgment on its own crimes. Fourth, Rwandan officials answered the tribunal's efforts to "prosecute" the government by launching an effective counter-shaming offensive that deflected international attention away from its violation of international law and focused it on the tribunal's shortcomings.

Del Ponte's first public criticism of Rwandan non-compliance was accompanied by a warning that she would hand down indictments of RPF officers by the end of 2002. The chief prosecutor's warning was "a shot across the bow," one Western diplomat told me in an April 2002 interview in Kigali.[1] Western diplomats whom I interviewed in Rwanda interpreted Del Ponte's warning as an indication that she actually had the capacity to issue indictments against RPF officers. Del Ponte's trump card was the incriminating evidence she could obtain both from Hutu refugees who had fled Rwanda at the end of the genocide and from those Tutsi who had left Rwanda more recently after falling out with the repressive Kagame regime. Still, Del Ponte relied heavily on Rwandan government cooperation when it came to prosecuting RPF atrocities. First, she most certainly needed access to state and military archives to bolster any indictments she might issue and to build a strong case if and when indicted Tutsi suspects ever stood trial in Arusha. Second, she needed Kigali's cooperation to gain custody of any indicted Tutsi officers living inside Rwanda.

Some Western diplomats have blamed Del Ponte's shift to an adversarial approach for worsening her chances of persuading President Kagame to cooperate with her "special investigations" of the RPF. Moreover, according to these sources, going on the offensive against the Kigali regime likely increased the prospect that Kagame would retaliate by blocking cooperation altogether and would thereby bring the trials of Hutu genocide suspects to a halt. "Some of [Del Ponte's] public statements were a little too blunt on this issue [and said] in such a way that she antagonized the Rwandan government," recalled one senior United States official.[2] A similar criticism has been privately voiced by some ICTR officials. "When you're doing this type of operation you keep your mouth shut...and then when it is time to go into action you do it," a veteran tribunal investigator told me in a 2005 interview. "You don't advertise it in the newspapers [and you don't say] 'I'm investigating you and I will have charges against you in six months or by such a date.'"[3] These critiques reveal a larger truth about the power of the post-genocide Rwandan state in international affairs (and consequently, the weakness of the ICTR). For all intents

---

[1] Fieldwork interview with Western diplomat, Kigali, April 2002.
[2] Fieldwork interview with U.S. government official, Washington, D.C., September 2004.
[3] Fieldwork interview with tribunal investigator, Freetown, Sierra Leone, March 2005.

and purposes, the Tutsi-led government had established itself as an authoritative victim that could demand sympathy and deference from the international
community. This reality, diplomats explained, required all international actors
to tread carefully when dealing with the Rwandan government.

9.3 The RPF and the Role of the International Community

International reluctance to press the Kagame government to cooperate in the
tribunal's investigations of RPF atrocities stems in large part from two related
factors: atonement for the West's failure to stop the genocide and a deeply
held view of the RPF Tutsi-led government as a benevolent force that rescued
the country from genocide and that has worked diligently to create a new
society based on the reconciliation of Hutu and Tutsi. Viewing the Rwandan
government in this light has been an article of faith for many Western policy
makers, journalists, and scholars during the post-genocide period.

This narrative has contributed to Western inattention to the RPF government's human rights record of atrocities committed during 1994 – the length of
the ICTR's temporal mandate – and afterward. For many commentators, the
enormity of the genocide against the Tutsi leaves little or no room to mention
the much lesser atrocities committed by the Tutsi-led RPF. Nevertheless, such
atrocities, far short of genocide as they may be, fall unmistakably under the
tribunal mandate of crimes against humanity and warrant prosecution. Some
of the most authoritative Western accounts of the genocide – such as Samantha
Power's Pulitzer Prize-winning book, *"A Problem From Hell:" America and the
Age of Genocide* – do not discuss the RPF atrocities.[4] As Howard French, the
former *New York Times* Africa correspondent, argues in the following passage,
the media's perpetuation of the pro-RPF narrative has obscured the RPF's role
in post-genocide atrocities, particularly in Rwanda's invasion of Zaire:

There were no good guys in Rwanda's catastrophic modern history, and the same was
true for Zaire's civil war. We in the press were far too slow in seizing upon the recklessness
of Rwanda's invasion, and by the time the true dimensions of the tragedy it had unleashed
could be discerned, almost no one cared.[5]

Over time, some observers have come to question the dominant narrative
about the Rwanda government, in light of its repressive practices at home and
its military intervention in Congo.[6] In interviews I conducted in Kigali during
the Spring and Summer of 2002, some Western diplomats expressed growing
doubt about the story line that has trumpeted the authoritarian, minority-led
Rwandan government as an agent of reconciliation deserving unquestioned
international political support. Yet the shift in the international conversation

---

[4] Power, *"A Problem From Hell,"* pp. 329–389.
[5] French, *A Continent For The Taking*, p. 143.
[6] See, for instance, Johan Pottier, *Re-Imagining Rwanda: Conflict, Survival and Disinformation
in the Late Twentieth Century* (Cambridge: Cambridge University Press, 2002); Eltringham,
Accounting for Horror, 2004.

about Rwanda remains minor and has not prompted a fundamental rethinking of Western policy toward Rwanda. The Rwandan government still benefits from the widely held perception in the West that it is a victim state with a strong political and moral claim to continued international backing.

Western reluctance to pressure the Rwandan government to cooperate with the tribunal's investigations of RPF officers has also been driven by a number of strategic considerations. One concern was that exerting pressure on Rwanda to aid Del Ponte's RPF investigations might jeopardize international efforts to prod Rwanda to withdraw its troops from Congo and thus complicate efforts to bring the war to an end. Just as Del Ponte began to turn up the heat on Rwanda in the Spring and Summer of 2002, international diplomats were trying to reach a negotiated peace settlement to the devastating Congo conflict that, since Rwanda's invasion in 1998, had triggered a regional war involving six African nations. Here we see again the conflict of interests between peace and justice that complicated the judicial process of the ICTY.

Some Western diplomats also expressed concern that Del Ponte's "special investigations" – and the possible indictment and apprehension of RPF suspects – could destabilize Rwanda by causing a serious rift between President Kagame and his own Tutsi-run military that he relies on to remain in power. Diplomatic caution, particularly among the Americans and the British, may also have been colored by an interest in bolstering the Kagame regime and, in turn, advancing Anglo-American political and economic influence in mineral-rich Congo. Some international human rights activists doubted that tribunal indictments of RPF officers could actually trigger instability. In this view, Del Ponte was not accorded the same power to cause domestic backlash in Rwanda as she was in Serbia and Croatia. Such an argument had merit, given that the authoritarian Tutsi-led RPF regime enjoyed a far higher degree of political control over Rwandan politics and society than did the much weaker and internally divided democratic coalitions newly in power in Belgrade and Zagreb. Still, assessing the domestic consequences that might arise from potential RPF indictments was a difficult task that could not be verified in the absence of indictments.

Despite a lack of international backing, Del Ponte's bid to issue indictments against RPF officers was not destined to fail. From the start of her RPF probe, she failed to build support among Western diplomats in Rwanda or to keep them adequately apprised of important developments in her battle for cooperation with the Rwandan authorities.[7] Del Ponte's vigorous lobbying of Western nations to back the ICTY in its efforts to prod Balkan states to cooperate was much less evident when it came to the ICTR. This failure of diplomacy was part and parcel of a larger institutional problem that had long disadvantaged the ICTR – the chief prosecutor traditionally gave priority to the ICTY. This problem was accentuated by Del Ponte and the UN's twenty-month delay – between May 2001 and January 2003 – to hire a permanent deputy prosecutor to run the Office of the Prosecutor (OTP) on a day-to-day basis. A key function

---

[7] Fieldwork interviews with Western diplomats, Kigali, April-May and June-July 2002.

of the deputy prosecutor is to act as a consistent diplomatic presence in Kigali with Rwandan officials and Western diplomats as well as to set and articulate prosecutorial strategy. "There is no one interlocutor for the OTP here to engage in dialogue with Rwandan officials," a source close to the prosecution told me in a 2002 interview in Kigali. "In order to maintain cooperation [it is] something you do on a sustained basis."[8] The delay in hiring a deputy prosecutor also hampered genocide prosecutions in Arusha by leaving the OTP without strong leadership. "It takes someone running the office on a regular basis to solve our problems," the same source said, lamenting that the UN is "investing $100 million a year in the tribunal, but no one is watching the store."

Waging an effective campaign for state cooperation also required developing political and diplomatic expertise within the tribunal itself. This lesson appeared to have been learned a few years earlier at the ICTY. In the late 1990s, Chief Prosecutor Arbour hired two specialists to act as her political advisors when it came to dealing with international actors and the governments of the former Yugoslavia. Del Ponte had continued this practice at the ICTY. These advisors played a critical, if unacknowledged, role by providing the chief prosecutor with insight about her interlocutors in the Balkan governments and advice on crafting the tribunal's diplomatic strategy.[9] Although Del Ponte had experienced aides whose duties included advising her on ICTR diplomacy, she did not hire specialists with extensive knowledge of Rwandan politics and history, as she did in the case of the ICTY. In the battle for cooperation with the Rwandan government, there was much that was not in the tribunal's control. Yet, as this discussion underscores, the tribunal could still have taken significant action in its virtual "trials" with the Kigali regime.

9.4 "Trials of Cooperation" and the Witness Crisis of 2002

ICTR officials heralded June 2002 as the beginning of a new era for the tribunal because it would mark the first time that trials would occur simultaneously in all three of its courtrooms. But the tribunal's plans did not come to pass. On the morning of Friday, June 7, the Rwandan authorities at the airport in Kigali blocked a group of Tutsi genocide survivors scheduled to testify on behalf of the prosecution from boarding the UN plane that regularly ferries witnesses to and from the courtrooms in Arusha. In the following weeks, the government continued to prevent Tutsi genocide survivors from leaving the country for Arusha. The government's measures forced tribunal judges to repeatedly postpone two trials and sowed uncertainty about when, or indeed whether, another genocide case would be heard at the ICTR.[10]

---

[8] Fieldwork interview with source close to the prosecution, Kigali, July 2002.

[9] Fieldwork interviews with ICTY officials, The Hague, October-November 2001 and December 2003.

[10] The third ICTR trial took place because it was then in the defense phase and therefore was hearing testimony from defense witnesses, most of whom resided outside Rwanda. These witnesses could thus travel to Arusha unimpeded by the Rwandan government.

The Rwandan government did not portray its decision to stop the witnesses from traveling as deliberate non-compliance or as an attempt to intimidate Del Ponte into dropping her imminent RPF indictments. Of course, announcing such an obstructionist intent ran the risk of provoking international censure. Instead, Rwandan officials maintained that their move was a necessary and temporary bureaucratic measure to ensure the safety of Rwandan witnesses, who were allegedly endangered by the tribunal's lax witness protection procedures. The witnesses would be able to travel to Arusha, government officials said, as soon as the tribunal's Witness and Victims Support Section complied with new government document regulations. In this way, government officials amplified the complaints of witness mistreatment that Tutsi survivor groups had cited months earlier as the reason for their continuing boycott of the tribunal. As in the Barayagwiza crisis, the Rwandan government appeared to be using the withdrawal of cooperation as a means to force the tribunal to right a perceived injustice. In that crisis, the injustice targeted by the government was the Appeals Chamber's decision to release a notorious Hutu genocide suspect prior to trial to remedy the prosecution's violation of his due process rights. Now the injustice the government targeted was the supposed poor treatment and endangerment of tribunal witnesses. But whereas the government's motivation in suspending cooperation was straightforward in the Barayagwiza crisis, it was much less clear in the witness crisis.

The government's actual motivation cannot be known with full certainty. However, interviews I conducted with a range of tribunal officials and Western diplomats in Rwanda during this period suggest that the government blocked witnesses from traveling to Arusha to warn the tribunal of what could happen if and when Del Ponte fulfilled her promise to indict RPF officers.

The grounding of the UN plane in June 2002 caught many ICTR officials off guard despite the ongoing survivor group boycott and the tribunal's increasingly strained relationship with the Kigali government. Initially, tribunal officials hoped that the government would resume witness travel as soon as the Witness and Victims Support Section obtained the necessary documents the government now required in order to allow every genocide survivor to leave the country. The government's demand for tribunal compliance with the new immigration regulations turned the tables on the tribunal. Cooperation had long been a one-way street: The tribunal regularly told the state what it expected, and the state was bound by international law to deliver without exception. But now it was the state that was telling the tribunal to comply. Throughout June, tribunal witness protection officers in Rwanda endured a Kafkaesque search for the required documents. After traveling the country to track down and cajole regional government officials to provide the necessary papers for witness travel, the witness protection officers would be informed that they had still other documents to obtain.

Only after several adjournments did the judges presiding over the two interrupted trials in Arusha issue an order for the Rwandan government to allow witness travel. Yet, in an apparent effort not to antagonize the Kigali regime, tribunal officials refrained from issuing any public criticism of Rwanda's action for several weeks or from making any official announcement of the crisis in press releases or on the tribunal's website.[11] Several prosecutors and defense attorneys were more outspoken in expressing their frustrations to the judges in open session. Attorneys defending the Hutu suspects in the stalled trials were particularly vocal about the culpability of the Kigali government in disrupting the trials and the need for the judges to take a tougher stand.[12] "The court should condemn publicly the illegal behavior of the Kigali government towards this Tribunal," said defense attorney Nicole Bergevin.[13]

The witness crisis provided a compelling story about the clash between the new system of international justice and the prerogative of state sovereignty. But the international media all but ignored the story, in no small part because tribunal officials sought to downplay the crisis. As a consequence, the shutting down of the trials, one of the most serious cooperation crises to occur in the history of either the ICTR or the ICTY, went virtually unreported in the international media.

The tribunal's virtual silence during the witness crisis enabled the government to go unchallenged when it announced that the newly implemented witness restrictions were needed to safeguard vulnerable witnesses, fostering the impression that Rwanda had a legitimate right to temporarily block witness travel. Some Western journalists reported an interruption in trials, but attributed it to the ongoing survivor group boycott that had begun in January. However, these reports typically offered no substantiation for this claim.[14] In early July, *The New York Times* made its first mention of the crisis with a one-line statement, in a news brief on another tribunal matter, that some trials had been postponed "because witnesses have feared facing suspects."[15] The *Times* did not mention that the genocide survivors had been blocked from traveling by their own government. Some international journalists initially reported the interruption of trials in Arusha not as a fact, but merely as a tribunal accusation against the government.[16] Yet, even if one accepted the government's justification for stopping witnesses, it remained abundantly clear that the trials had in fact come to a standstill. In the eyes of the media, the burden of proof fell on the tribunal to show that the government's actions not only constituted a willful act of non-compliance but that they actually brought

[11] See ICTR Archive of 2002 press releases, http://www.ictr.org/ENGLISH/PRESSREL/2002/index.htm.

[12] "Rwanda Delays Travel of Genocide Witnesses, Says Tribunal Official," *Hirondelle News Agency*, June 10, 2002.

[13] "Butare Trial Adjourned to October as Protests Bar Witnesses," *Hirondelle News Agency*, June 28, 2002.

[14] Chris McGreal, "Witness boycott brings Rwandan genocide trials to a halt," *The Guardian*, July 29, 2002.

[15] Marc Lacey, "World Briefing Africa: Rwanda: Tribunal Tries to Cut Backlog," *New York Times*, July 9, 2002, A12.

[16] "Rwanda pressed over genocide trials," *BBC News*, June 28, 2002.

the genocide trials to a halt. The tribunal initially remained largely silent on the matter.

The ICTR's lackluster response to the witness crisis stemmed not only from a belief that patience was the most prudent course of action, but also from a preference on the part of some tribunal officials to shift responsibility to others at the tribunal. Initially, Del Ponte preferred to keep a low profile, reportedly citing the issue of witness travel as the sole responsibility of the Registry.[17] As the official responsible for handling external relations as well as witness protection, Registrar Adama Dieng could certainly have been more engaged in the witness crisis. Instead, he too conveniently took a low-profile stance. He did so, according to tribunal insiders, because he claimed that the stopping of prosecution witnesses was an issue best handled by the chief prosecutor. In short, the tribunal's internal struggles further delayed a prompt and effective response to the growing crisis.

A prime example of the tribunal's conciliation occurred when judges in the two interrupted trials opted in late June 2002 to adjourn the proceedings until August and October. After issuing several short adjournments during June in the hope that the trials would soon resume, the judges grew increasingly frustrated with the witness crisis. Still, the judges could have continued to reschedule the resumption of trials, as opposed to adjourning the trial until the Fall, in order to send a message to the government that the judges were intent on seeing the trials resume as quickly as possible. This could also have served to alert the international community that the government remained in violation of its legal obligation to allow unimpeded witness travel. By adjourning the trials until the Fall, the judges relinquished a critical opportunity to expose Rwandan non-compliance.

Gathering such evidence of non-compliance is a crucial component of a tribunal's effort to "prosecute" a state and persuade the international community to intervene on the tribunal's behalf. In short, the tribunal needed all the evidence it could muster to substantiate its claims of Rwandan non-cooperation, particularly in light of the government's insistence that its new requirements for witness travel were not intended to stop the trials in Arusha. The need for such evidence was heightened by the inadequate media coverage that failed to report the full extent of the witness crisis.

9.5 Protest at the Gates

In a bid for a diplomatic resolution of the witness crisis, top tribunal officials traveled to Kigali at the end of June to meet with high-level government officials. But the prospects for a productive summit with Rwandan leaders appeared slim given the increasingly tense political climate in Kigali. With government backing,[18] Ibuka and Avega, the two largest Tutsi survivor organizations, planned a

---

[17] Fieldwork interviews with ICTR officials, Kigali, June-July 2002.
[18] Fieldwork interviews with Western diplomats, Kigali, June-July 2002.

major march and demonstration at the gates of the ICTR compound in Kigali. The demonstration was timed to coincide with Chief Prosecutor Del Ponte and Registrar Dieng's visit to Kigali. The ostensible goal of the protest was to call attention to Ibuka and Avega's ongoing boycott of the tribunal and to their long-standing complaints of tribunal mistreatment of survivors who had testified at the ICTR. Although the government-supported protest was presented by the survivor groups as an independent civil society action, it appeared to be a thinly veiled effort to further damage the court's hope for international backing during the witness crisis.

The image of thousands of genocide survivors protesting at the gates of the tribunal compound in Rwanda did nothing to improve the tribunal's reputation. Nor did the survivors' vocal call for the resignations of Del Ponte and Dieng. "Go home, you are nothing worse than Interahamwe," an Ibuka speaker shouted, equating Del Ponte and Dieng with the infamous Hutu militia responsible for many of the genocidal killings.[19] The survivors focused their grievances on two points – the alleged harassment of prosecution witnesses in Arusha and the revelations from a year earlier that the tribunal had hired Hutu genocide suspects as defense investigators. "The tribunal is there to only create employment opportunities and enrich the relatives of genocide suspects; the only solution is to dissolve it, because as long as it continues... justice will remain a myth in Rwanda," said one protestor.[20]

News of the protest did not make the front-page of Western newspapers, as the government would no doubt have wanted. Still, the coverage of the protest appeared to work in the government's favor by eliciting some negative coverage of the tribunal without a critical examination of the government's role in the protest or its possible motives for blocking trials in Arusha. Once again the government and its "civil society" proxies had managed to put the tribunal on the defensive. By doing so, they further undermined Del Ponte's bid for international support to prosecute RPF atrocities.

Del Ponte and Dieng left Kigali with no assurances of a quick resumption in witness travel to Arusha. Nor, unsurprisingly, did Del Ponte make any headway in her latest effort to prod Rwandan officials to cooperate in her investigations of RPF military officers. A month later, Del Ponte went to the UN Security Council in New York to lodge a formal complaint against the Rwandan government.

9.6 The ICTR Goes to New York

Filing a formal complaint at the Security Council is the strongest action a tribunal can take to counter the defiance of a non-cooperative state since in theory it is supposed to trigger decisive Council action. Yet lodging a complaint with the Council also entails risks. A delayed or lackluster UN response can further

[19] Victor Peskin, "Rwandan Ghosts," *Legal Affairs*, September/October 2002, p. 22.
[20] "Rwanda: Genocide victims demonstrate against UN tribunal officials," *BBC Monitoring Original Source: RNA News Agency*, June 27, 2002.

weaken the tribunal's leverage vis-à-vis the targeted state and thus embolden the state to continue to defy the tribunal with impunity. That appears to have happened when the ICTR lodged a formal complaint against the Rwandan government with the Council in late July 2002.

The ICTR's complaint seemed to have little effect on its efforts to secure cooperation from the government when it came to the issue of Del Ponte's RPF investigations. The Council waited close to six months to take action on the tribunal's complaint.[21] When it finally acted, the Council went no further than to remind Rwanda of its obligation to fully cooperate with the tribunal.[22,23] Nevertheless, in the aftermath of the tribunal's complaint, the United States exerted pressure on the Rwandan government to allow the Tutsi survivors to travel to Arusha and testify in the genocide trials.[24] It is unclear whether Kigali had actually acquiesced because of international pressure or if it chose to resume witness travel out of its own desire to see the genocide trials continue. From the start of the crisis on June 7, the government had left ambiguous the question of how long it would block witness travel.

In any case, the ICTR's formal complaint marked an intensification of its "prosecution" of the Rwandan government. In the following months, Del Ponte launched a wider campaign to shame the Kigali regime and obtain much needed international support for her RPF investigations. Still, her shift to an adversarial approach did not appear to strengthen her hand vis-à-vis the Rwandan government. Soon the government launched a sophisticated counter-shaming campaign aimed at putting the ICTR and Del Ponte herself on trial in the court of world opinion.

In their previous counter-shaming attacks, Rwandan authorities sought to deflect attention away from the RPF issue by attacking the tribunal for its failure to deliver more justice for the victims of the 1994 genocide. Now, with the issue of RPF atrocities out in the open, the government intensified this line of attack. At the UN, a few days following Del Ponte's complaint to the Security Council, Rwandan Attorney General Gerald Gahima sought to turn the focus away from the issue of Kigali's compliance with international law and to the failures of the "pathetic" and "mismanaged" tribunal.[25] Echoing earlier attacks by the government and survivor groups, Gahima hammered away at the ICTR for the defense investigator and fee-splitting scandals. Gahima also intensified his personal attack on Del Ponte and on the negative consequences of the Security Council's decision, back in November 1994, to appoint a single prosecutor

---

[21] "Statement by the President of the Security Council," Colombia, December 18, 2002.

[22] Ibid.

[23] In subsequent resolutions, the Security Council called on the Rwandan government to cooperate with tribunal investigations of RPF atrocities. For example, see Security Council Resolution 1503, relating to the split of the chief prosecutor's duties for the Rwanda and Yugoslavia tribunals, August 29, 2003.

[24] Human Rights Watch Rwanda Annual Report, 2002.

[25] Jim Wurst, "Rwanda: Gov't, U.N. Prosecutor Trade Barbs over Lack of Cooperation," *UN Wire*, July 25, 2002.

for both the ICTR and the ICTY. "How can a genocide that claimed a million people be a person's part-time job?" Gahima asked.[26]

Now the Rwandan government not only targeted the tribunal's shortcomings, but also took aim at the chief prosecutor herself. Laying blame for the tribunal's problems at Del Ponte's feet would soon come to underpin its demand to have the Council remove her from her role as chief prosecutor of the ICTR. While Del Ponte was responsible for the mismanaged and poorly supervised Office of the Prosecutor, many of the ICTR's problems lay outside of her purview. In fact, responsibility for many of the tribunal's most embarrassing scandals – including the defense investigator and fee-splitting incidents – did not belong to Del Ponte at all. Nevertheless, Rwandan officials increasingly used Del Ponte and her neglect of the ICTR as a central component of their counter-shaming offensive against the tribunal.

Gahima's press conference at the end of July succeeded in shifting attention away from the tribunal's accusations of Rwandan non-cooperation. International press accounts, including the UN's own news service,[27] paid considerably more attention to Gahima's accusations of tribunal mismanagement than to the government's success in bringing the ICTR's trials to a halt.

The government opened yet another front in its efforts to block Del Ponte's indictments by attacking one of her key justifications for pursuing RPF indictments. Del Ponte argued that indicting RPF officers was critical because it would right an imbalance in the tribunal's treatment of the Rwandan conflict. But the government alleged that this quest for balance would only bolster the Hutu extremists' revisionist history and fuel denial of the genocide. In so doing, the Rwandan government sought to tar Del Ponte with the brush of ethnic divisionism, a frequent criticism the government leveled against perceived enemies of the state. Del Ponte "is deeply immersed in the ethnic arithmetics and negationist theories of 'equal guilt.' This remains unacceptable," charged Martin Ngoga, the Rwandan government representative to the tribunal.[28]

9.7 A War of Words

A heated altercation ensued in the months following Del Ponte's complaint to the Security Council at the end of July. Del Ponte appeared to ease her criticism of the Kigali regime when it began to allow prosecution witnesses to travel again to Arusha in August. But she went on the offensive again in late October during her annual address to the Council, reporting that the government remained defiant when it came to its refusal to cooperate with her probe of RPF atrocities.[29] In an effort to thwart Rwanda's counter-shaming campaign against

---

[26] Ibid.
[27] Ibid.
[28] "UN Prosecutor Rallies UK Support to Investigate Rwandan Army," *Hirondelle News Agency,* November 29, 2002.
[29] Address to the Security Council by Carla Del Ponte, October 30, 2002.

the tribunal, Del Ponte urged the Council to focus on Rwanda's violations of international law:

I would urge the Council not to become distracted from the only issue at stake here: the obligation of Rwanda to co-operate with all lawful requests from the Tribunal, irrespective of the subject matter. No State can place itself above its international obligations, and co-operation, even on sensitive issues, must be unconditional.[30]

In the following weeks, the government found new ways to put Del Ponte on the defensive by making her conduct at the ICTR *the* story covered by the international media. In November, Del Ponte met in The Hague with Hutu refugees – including members of a Hutu rebel group – apparently to bolster her investigations of Tutsi war crimes suspects. The Rwandan government garnered new headlines by portraying Del Ponte as "consorting with génocidaires" and arguing that she "has lost her moral authority to prosecute" genocide cases.[31] With this criticism came the government's first formal call for her resignation. The government had once again placed the prosecutor on the defensive.

Del Ponte regained the upper hand in early December in a speech to British parliamentarians in which she defended her November meeting with the Hutu refugees and called for punitive action to enforce Rwanda's obligation to cooperate with her probe of Tutsi atrocities.[32] Del Ponte vigorously dismissed the government's charge, insisting that it was her prerogative to meet with any individual or group that might have relevant information for her investigations.

The end of 2002 came and went without Del Ponte handing down her promised indictments against RPF officers. In fact, her "special investigations" appeared to have been put on hold not long after the Rwandan government permitted the resumption of witness travel to Arusha. The witness crisis and the lack of concerted international pressure on Kigali appeared to contribute to Del Ponte's decision to suspend the investigations. Del Ponte insisted that the suspension was temporary and that the RPF investigations would be resumed in November 2002.[33] However, a well-placed tribunal source told me in an interview that the investigations had effectively come to a halt not long after the witness crisis ended.

In the trials of cooperation, the Rwandan government appeared to have the clear advantage. Yet the government was not content with the impasse, still fearing the real possibility that Del Ponte had the capacity to indict RPF officers based on evidence her investigators had collected from Rwandan refugees living in exile. The Office of the Prosecutor had sufficient evidence to support indictments of RPF officers prior to the suspension of the "special investigations," according to several sources I interviewed. Moreover, the incriminating

[30] Ibid.
[31] "UN Prosecutor Rallies UK Support to Investigate Rwandan Army," *Hirondelle News Agency*, November 29, 2002.
[32] Ibid.
[33] Arnaud Grellier and Frederic Legrand, "There has been a two and a half week break in investigations into RPA," Interview with Carla del Ponte, *Judicial Diplomacy*, December 4, 2002.

evidence implicated senior RPF army commanders who were in a position to give orders on the battlefield. The evidence, one tribunal source told me in an interview, went "all the way to the top."

9.8 Chief Prosecutor Del Ponte on "Trial"

In late 2002, the battle over RPF indictments entered a new phase when government officials began to call for Del Ponte's ouster. Again, powerful international actors would tip the balance of power in Kigali's favor. Fortunately for the Rwandan government, the approaching end of Del Ponte's four-year term (in mid-September 2003) created an opportunity for it to mount a campaign at the UN against her. By July 2003, after extensive lobbying of UN delegations, the Rwandan government appeared to have secured the support of the United States and Britain to dismiss Del Ponte from her position as chief prosecutor of the ICTR, while retaining her as chief prosecutor of the ICTY.[34]

Del Ponte's bid to retain her job was dealt a further blow when UN Secretary-General Kofi Annan supported just such a reorganization, recommending that the Security Council appoint a chief prosecutor for each tribunal, dismiss Del Ponte from her ICTR responsibilities, and retain her at the ICTY.[35] Del Ponte initially fought back, accusing the Rwandan government of trying to block RPF indictments and indicating that she might resign her post at the ICTY in protest. She traveled twice to New York in the Summer of 2003 in an effort to save her job. But during these trips – as she told me in a December 2003 interview – she felt her chances of holding on to her position in Arusha slipping away. In the end, Del Ponte did not put up a vigorous fight to keep her post at the ICTR, nor did she resign from her role as chief prosecutor of the ICTY, as some American officials feared she would. Del Ponte explained in the December 2003 interview that the Swiss government and others persuaded her to remain as prosecutor in The Hague to complete the prosecution of Slobodan Milošević.[36]

UN Secretary-General Annan maintained that the plan to separate the prosecutor's positions was motivated solely by administrative concerns, most notably the need to speed the closure of the tribunal by the end of the decade. The message here was that the tribunal's long-documented managerial failures required new leadership. Yet the belated push for two separate chief prosecutors is suspect on several counts. First, the UN's bid for a management shake-up only centered on removing Del Ponte and did not extend to other problem-plagued divisions at the tribunal, particularly the Registry, whose own inaction regarding witness treatment helped the Rwandan government conceal its own resistance to RPF indictments. Second, the UN, as well as an independent audit it

[34] Marlise Simons, "Rwanda is Said to Seek New Prosecutor for War Crimes Court," *New York Times,* July 28, 2003, A2.
[35] Felicity Barringer, "Annan Seeks Separate War Prosecutors," *New York Times,* July 30, 2003.
[36] Ibid.

had commissioned three years earlier, had previously maintained the importance of having a single prosecutor to oversee both tribunals. In the face of intense Rwandan pressure, the timing of the plan to split the chief prosecutor's portfolio leaves the Security Council open to the charge that it sacrificed Del Ponte to appease Rwanda's anger and stop the tribunal from issuing RPF indictments.

The reasons for Del Ponte's dismissal are complex. Suspicion of the Security Council's motives was not quelled by American and British diplomats who denied RPF influence in Del Ponte's dismissal[37] despite the wording – in the Council resolution authorizing the split of the chief prosecutor's position – that Rwanda cooperate with the tribunal's probe of RPF atrocities.[38] Yet, at the same time, the single-prosecutor arrangement had long been an impediment to the ICTR. Not surprisingly, therefore, the Security Council's impending decision to appoint separate chief prosecutors at the ICTY and ICTR did not elicit condemnations from the international human rights community. However, in early August 2003, Human Rights Watch, along with three other human rights groups, called on the Security Council to ensure that Annan's proposal would not undermine the tribunal's RPF investigations. Importantly, these influential organizations stopped short of opposing Del Ponte's departure.[39]

Del Ponte's dismissal, she told me in December 2003, was meant to prevent her from gathering enough evidence to issue Tutsi indictments. "It's a political decision," she said. "What I know is that the United States [and Britain] didn't want...RPF indictments."[40] To Del Ponte, her dismissal followed naturally from previous American and British pressure to drop the RPF investigations and allow Rwandan courts to handle the matter. In my interview, Del Ponte sharply criticized the combined U.S. and British insistence that she negotiate with Kigali in order to allow Rwandan courts to handle RPF prosecutions. "It was absolutely unacceptable because they are doing nothing for seven years and so they will not start now to do it," Del Ponte told me, in reference to the Rwandan government's poor record in prosecuting RPF officers.[41] Del Ponte identified Claire Short, Britain's minister of international development and a close ally of President Kagame's, as being "very aggressive" in her attempts to persuade Del Ponte to drop her investigations. "'You have enough to do with the genocide trials. It is politically not acceptable because President Kagame is a very good president; he's trying to install real democracy in Rwanda, so what are you doing?'" Short said, according to Del Ponte.[42]

---

[37] Fieldwork interviews with Western diplomats, The Hague, December 2003.

[38] Security Council Resolution 1503, relating to the split of the chief prosecutor's duties for the Rwanda and Yugoslavia tribunals, August 29, 2003.

[39] "Joint Letter to Security Council Members on ICTR," Human Rights Watch, Lawyers Committee for Human Rights, Fédération Internationale des Ligues des Droits de l'Homme, and Rencontre Africaine pour la Défense des Droits de l'Homme, August 6, 2003.

[40] Fieldwork interview with Carla Del Ponte, The Hague, December 2003.

[41] Ibid.

[42] Ibid.

According to Del Ponte, other Western officials were less aggressive toward her, but apparently no less trusting of the Rwandan regime's willingness to prosecute RPF atrocities. Del Ponte reported that Western officials used the prospect of instability in the wake of RPF indictments as a way to try to convince her to drop the investigations. Yet Del Ponte believed that other concerns were at play, particularly the Bush administration's campaign to win Rwanda's signature on a bilateral agreement that would ensure the Kigali government would not extradite any indicted U.S. soldiers to the International Criminal Court.[43]

Even without Del Ponte's dismissal, the United States and Britain, the two states with the most potential to influence Rwanda, did not exert the magnitude of pressure that might have swayed Rwanda to cooperate with her probe of the RPF. For Del Ponte, the lack of international pressure was the crucial variable in explaining her failure to elicit cooperation. "You are independent theoretically, but in reality you depend a lot on the international community," Del Ponte said.[44] Yet the Rwandan government's success in shaming her and the tribunal for their shortcomings and missteps played an important role in her demise. In this regard, Del Ponte shares a fair portion of blame for her own fall because there is much that she could have done to improve the tribunal's performance and its international reputation.

9.9 Assessing Del Ponte's Approach

Del Ponte's decision to open a full-fledged investigation of RPF atrocities marked a significant break with the tribunal dynamic of conciliation toward the Rwandan government. Despite the likelihood of government retaliation, particularly in light of the punitive steps it took in the Barayagwiza crisis, Del Ponte opened these investigations to bring a semblance of balance to the tribunal's prosecutorial agenda and to withstand Kagame's campaign to turn the ICTR into a victor's court. How should we understand the outcome of Del Ponte's investigations? Did the fact that in the final analysis she did not issue any RPF indictments signal a political accommodation to the realities of pursuing such a controversial endeavor?

In Del Ponte's narrative, Rwandan obstruction and the political agendas of the United States and Britain were solely responsible for the tribunal's inability to issue any RPF indictments. However, interviews I conducted with current and former prosecution officials as well as with sources close to the tribunal indicate that Del Ponte had actually collected enough evidence from investigations conducted outside Rwanda to issue indictments of some RPF officers.[45] These sources suspect that Del Ponte likely chose not to issue the indictments either because of intense American and British pressure or in order to safeguard her reappointment at the ICTY in the run-up to the Security Council's

---

Ibid.
Ibid.
Fieldwork interviews with current and former tribunal officials, The Hague, December 2003.

decision on her fate in the Summer of 2003. Del Ponte maintains that she did not issue indictments because the Rwandan government blocked her investigators from gathering sufficient evidence, a stance that denied complicity with international opposition to RPF indictments.[46] As early as December 2002, Del Ponte acknowledged that she had "drafts of indictments" of RPF suspects, but still lacked sufficient evidence to render the indictments final.[47] When pressed on the necessary evidentiary requirements, Del Ponte told me that simply having a "prima facie" case is not sufficient. Her litmus test for indictments had grown stricter in recent years, she said, and now depended on whether prosecutors were ready to bring the case to trial. "It must be trial ready."[48]

Knowledgeable sources close to the ICTR Office of the Prosecutor told me that Del Ponte had gathered a significant amount of evidence and could have issued indictments against RPF officers. "They had massive information, I thought... they could indict if they wanted," said Filip Reyntjens, the Belgian Rwanda scholar.[49] Issuing RPF indictments could certainly have prompted the Rwandan government to block witness travel once again. However, handing down these indictments might have given Del Ponte the upper hand by bringing global attention to the RPF's role in atrocities and its efforts to obstruct justice. Del Ponte's indictments could also have helped guard against Rwandan efforts to remove her from office, if only because the government's motives for her dismissal would have become more transparent.

Rwandan resistance and American and British opposition to RPF indictments did not leave Del Ponte much room to maneuver. Yet she was not powerless. The way Del Ponte approached the Rwandan government and the international community, at times, decreased her political leverage. In this regard, a number of observers believe that Del Ponte unnecessarily undermined her chances of obtaining Rwandan cooperation. One former senior U.S. government official described Del Ponte's general posture in the following way:

She simply did not approach the job as a diplomat [who] understands the significance of what one might say to the media, to the press. She approached it as a good, hard-nosed prosecutor... There is an advantage to that. But there is also an enormous risk that you say things which in fact have the effect of derailing cooperation... You need a sixth sense... Carla didn't simply have it in her gene pool and that's not a criticism of her. I would love to have Carla in any prosecution.[50]

The critique of Del Ponte as an overly adversarial prosecutor does at times have merit, as even some of her own prosecutors and investigators acknowledged in my interviews. Yet a chief prosecutor is no different from a diplomat when confrontation is necessary, as Del Ponte believed in light of the Security

---

46 Fieldwork interview with Carla Del Ponte, The Hague, December 2003.

47 Arnaud Grellier and Frederic Legrand, "Interview with Carla Del Ponte," *Judicial Diplomacy*, December 4, 2002.

48 Fieldwork interview with Carla Del Ponte, The Hague, December 2003.

49 Fieldwork interview with Filip Reyntjens, Antwerp, December 2003.

50 Fieldwork interview with former U.S. government official, Washington, D.C., September 2004.

Council's increasing pressure to bring an end to all tribunal investigations by the close of 2004. What has gone largely unacknowledged is that Del Ponte, prior to going public with her complaints of Rwandan non-cooperation in April 2002, had indeed pursued quiet diplomacy with Kigali for almost a year and a half. Perhaps a more apt criticism is that she kept the issue of RPF investigations and Rwanda's defiance out of the public eye for too long. Del Ponte's failure to expose Rwanda's non-cooperation during the course of 2001 may then have contributed to her subsequent difficulties in building international attention and support for RPF investigations.

It is difficult, in any case, to imagine that the Rwandan government would have reacted favorably to RPF indictments if Del Ponte had simply waited another year or two or if she had spoken in more diplomatic tones. It is unclear what if anything Del Ponte might have been able to offer Kagame by way of a suitable compromise short of agreeing to the Rwandan leader's insistence on trying RPF cases domestically. During this period, Del Ponte had begun to offer concessions to the Balkan governments – such as the prospect of provisional release and plea-bargaining – as incentives to arrest and transfer war crimes suspects to The Hague. But in the Rwandan context, such concessions were not attractive to Kagame because of his staunch opposition to tribunal indictments of RPF officers and the lack of international pressure to make him reconsider. Offering assurances that her investigations would stay focused on low-level suspects would likely have done little to assuage Kagame's fears, given the possibility that these suspects would have based their courtroom defense on shifting culpability to senior commanders, including Kagame, the former head of the Tutsi-led RPF rebel army. There was speculation that Del Ponte and Kagame would agree on the indictments of several RPF officers who had fallen out of favor with the government. But such a prosecution might still have been unacceptable to Kagame since the disgruntled RPF officers in question might have had a greater incentive to implicate high-level RPF commanders.

That Del Ponte found herself between a rock and a hard place does not relieve her of responsibility for how she handled the RPF issue. Del Ponte's greatest mistake was in not doing more to build international support for her investigations or to insulate the prosecutor's office from Rwanda's predictable counter-shaming offensive. In terms of building more international support for RPF investigations, Del Ponte could have done more to persuade Western diplomats about the importance of supporting this endeavor. Toward that end, it was essential for Del Ponte to have consistently engaged Western diplomats in Kigali in order to keep them appraised of progress at the tribunal and to quickly counter the frequent attacks by government and survivor groups on the tribunal. Del Ponte's infrequent visits to Rwanda, coupled with her failure to appoint a permanent deputy prosecutor for nearly two years, further eroded the tribunal's image among diplomats in Rwanda during the critical Spring and Summer months of 2002. This meant that diplomats in Kigali often found themselves left with the task of trying to find authoritative tribunal contacts to evaluate the veracity of the latest Rwandan charge of tribunal malfeasance.[51]

9.10 After Del Ponte: Chief Prosecutor Jallow and the RPF Question

The witness crisis of 2002 followed by Del Ponte's departure from the ICTR in 2003 cast a long shadow over the tribunal and its already fragile relationship with the Kagame government. These two events were defining moments in the tribunal's history that reinforced its acquiescence toward Kigali. Nearly a decade after its establishment, the tribunal never seemed more dependent on Rwanda for cooperation, more vulnerable to its counter-shaming attacks, or more susceptible to Rwandan pressure. Yet this did not mean that the tribunal's tradition of acquiescence was set in stone – particularly when it came to whether Del Ponte's replacement would hand down indictments of RPF suspects. On the RPF matter, to be sure, Chief Prosecutor Hassan Jallow of Gambia confronted many of the constraints and risks that had dogged Del Ponte. Her travails provided a cautionary tale of how a supposedly independent prosecutor could fall victim to political forces and actors beyond the courtroom. But Jallow, even in the face of his inherited political weakness and the court's diminished soft power, has possessed the same amount of legal authority held by other UN tribunal chief prosecutors. With the ample evidence left by Del Ponte's investigators, Jallow could, if he chose, indict RPF suspects and thereby bring a semblance of proportionality to the tribunal's treatment of atrocity in Rwanda in 1994.

However, in almost four years as chief prosecutor, Jallow has not made RPF atrocities against Hutu civilians a priority. By the end of July 2007, he had not issued any public indictments of RPF suspects. The issue of RPF indictments, the flash point in tribunal–government relations during the Del Ponte era, is rarely mentioned by the new chief prosecutor. With the tribunal's scheduled closing just a few years away in 2010 – and with its indictment deadline already passed – it appears unlikely that any RPF suspects will ever be brought to trial at the ICTR. Still, the possibility that such indictments could yet be issued has fueled the Rwandan government's intimidating posture and occasional threats of non-cooperation, and, in turn, the tribunal's compliant approach to Kigali.

Jallow's lack of concerted action on the RPF file has gone hand in hand with retaining the Kigali government's cooperation in genocide prosecutions before the court's impending closure. Jallow's efforts to make up for time lost to the bureaucratic quagmire of the tribunal's early years and to the previous chief prosecutors' neglect of the court have yielded impressive results. Under his on-site direction, the number of completed trials has notably increased, a result also attributable to a range of tribunal reforms. The contrast with Del Ponte's tenure and her hands-off managerial style is striking, according to a long-time ICTR

---

[51] Fieldwork interviews with Western diplomats, Kigali, April-May and June-July 2002.

trial attorney: "Jallow's a big improvement...he's there for all the meetings, he's personally involved, and he's managing it much better."[52] In this regard, the Council's appointment of a single chief prosecutor based in Arusha has been productive for the ICTR, despite the political circumstances and implications of this decision. With Jallow and Chief Justice Erik Møse at the helm, the tribunal demonstrated significant improvement in the efficiency of trials. By July 2007, thirteen years after the end of the genocide, the ICTR had completed the cases of thirty-four defendants, resulting in twenty-nine convictions and five acquittals. Since its establishment, the tribunal had obtained custody of seventy-two of its ninety indicted suspects. Still, by the end of July 2007 the ICTR had yet to hand down judgments in two of its most important cases – the landmark Bagosora trial that began in 2002 and the Butare trial that began in 2001.

The progressive success of the prosecution of Hutu genocide suspects in Arusha underscores the tribunal's dependence on the Kagame regime, and thus bears directly on Jallow's cautious approach to the question of RPF atrocities. Rwanda's power to once again block witnesses from traveling to the ICTR remains a specter over the court. With so much on the line, Jallow is hardly eager to move forward on RPF indictments.

From a strategic point of view, Jallow is not as weak as it might appear from his delay. He could use Rwandan retaliation against hypothetical RPF indictments to his advantage by publicly holding up Kigali's obstruction as the key obstacle to the realization of the Security Council-mandated "completion strategy." The Council's insistence on closing the ICTR's doors by 2010 to relieve the UN of the costly burden of funding the tribunal could actually bolster Jallow's leverage. If the Kagame government blocked witness travel, the Council would likely have a strong interest in pressing Rwanda to allow the genocide trials to resume and reach completion. In this regard, the government's prospective non-compliance might be much less acceptable internationally than it was during the witness crisis of 2002. A strategic chief prosecutor could also make Rwanda's ardent bid to win referrals of ICTR genocide suspects for domestic prosecution contingent on a government agreement not to retaliate in the event of RPF indictments and to promise to hand over indicted RPF suspects to the tribunal. However, Jallow's leverage in this regard is somewhat limited because of pressure he faces from the Security Council to refer genocide cases to Rwandan courts and to other countries in order to clear the tribunal's docket before its scheduled closing date. The preparedness of Rwandan courts to undertake these high-level genocide cases and to assure fair trials remains a matter of contention.[53] Even as he prepared to seek judicial approval to send some ICTR cases to Rwanda, Jallow acknowledged in his December 2006 address to the Security Council that the Rwandan courts were not yet ready to prosecute. In

---

[52] Telephone interview with ICTR trial attorney, July 2006.

[53] See Amnesty International's December 12, 2006, press release, "Appeal to the UN Security Council to ensure that the mandate of the International Criminal Tribunal for Rwanda is fulfilled."

June 2007, Jallow asked tribunal judges to refer one genocide case back to Rwanda and indicated that he had plans to ask that sixteen more cases be sent to the Rwandan courts. The move was prompted by the Kigali government's recent decision to abolish the death penalty, which had long been a precondition for the referrals. With the abolition of capital punishment, the government – long at odds with the ICTR over the tribunal's refusal to apply the death penalty – dropped a fundamental element of its own judicial approach to genocide.[54] In return, the government may finally prevail in its attempts to try some high-level genocide suspects at home.

Jallow's approach to the RPF issue has been marked by ambiguity. On the one hand, he has defended his right to pursue the RPF. In a June 2005 speech to the Security Council, Jallow asserted his prerogative to issue RPF indictments beyond the deadline set by the Council. But on the other hand, he has claimed that he is restrained by the Council from doing so. Jallow's statements on the RPF issue often appear directed at justifying inaction, such as claiming that he needs more time to conduct further investigations,[55] without yet asking the Council for more time to extend the tribunal's mandate. For example, in his December 2006 speech to the Council, Jallow said that in 2007 he expected to complete his RPF investigations and then decide how to proceed. However, in his June 2007 address to the Council, Jallow again said he needed more time to continue his probe "until we are in a position to finish that aspect of our mandate."[56] He has also implied that his prosecutorial discretion to pursue RPF suspects has been curtailed by the UN-mandated completion strategy.[57] In a November 2004 speech, Jallow said the Council "dictated" a prosecutorial strategy that focuses "on those bearing the greatest responsibility for the genocide, the leaders of the genocide."[58] Missing from this speech was an acknowledgment that, first, the Council had not stripped him of his authority to hold RPF suspects accountable for massacres of Hutu civilians and, second, that such accountability is central to the tribunal's mission of combating impunity and advancing reconciliation between Hutu and Tutsi insofar as it would demonstrate that no side of the conflict is above the law. Jallow has stated elsewhere, "that the Council expects the Prosecutor to investigate [RPF] allegations and to decide whether or not to indict."[59] Here, Jallow appears to

---

[54] It is important to note that there have been no legally sanctioned executions of convicted génocidaires in Rwanda since April 1998.

[55] Addresses to the Security Council by Hassan Jallow, December 15, 2005, and December 15, 2006.

[56] Address to the Security Council by Hassan Jallow, June 18, 2007.

[57] My analysis here is informed by Luc Reydams' insightful article, "The ICTR Ten Years On: Back to the Nuremberg Paradigm?" *Journal of International Criminal Justice*, Vol. 3, No. 4, September 2005.

[58] Hassan Jallow, "The OTP-ICTR: Ongoing Challenges of Completion," speech to the International Criminal Court, November 1, 2004.

[59] Hassan Jallow, "Prosecutorial Discretion and International Criminal Justice," *Journal of International Criminal Justice*, Vol. 3, No. 1, March 2005.

dilute the intent of the tribunal's mandate to prosecute both sides of the Rwandan conflict by suggesting that he would fulfill his obligations as long as he investigates the RPF, even if he decides not to issue indictments.

That Jallow has not yet issued any public RPF indictments does not preclude his doing so or the possibility that he has already issued secret indictments. In fact, some observers believe he is waiting to hand down indictments toward the end of the tribunal's tenure when Rwandan obstruction can no longer hold Tutsi witnesses and the trial process hostage. In anticipation and apparent approval of this scenario, Human Rights Watch and the International Federation of Human Rights called on the Security Council in June 2006 to promise Jallow that in the event he issues RPF indictments late in the ICTR's tenure, the tribunal will be given the time it needs to conduct trials of RPF suspects. In this respect, Jallow's current sidestepping of the RPF issue may be a strategic gambit designed to forestall conflict with the Rwandan government and secure its ongoing cooperation. Some tribunal insiders believe that Jallow has a strong interest in issuing indictments if for no other reason than to counter charges that he is a handmaiden of the Kagame regime. Indicting RPF suspects would in fact be a "big feather in his cap," suggested a veteran ICTR trial attorney.[60] Thus, for Jallow as for Del Ponte, RPF indictments may be something to aspire to as well as fear.

Indictments, even if belated, would establish an important precedent that even atrocities committed by a victim group deserve to be criminalized rather than forgotten to history. At the same time, it is uncertain whether indictments issued at the eleventh hour of the ICTR's life could be anything more than a face-saving move to salvage the tribunal's reputation. Even if the Security Council gave the tribunal an extension to allow for RPF trials, the question of government cooperation in the arrest and transfer of indicted suspects would pose a vexing obstacle to actually conducting prosecutions in Arusha. As in the Balkans, the handing down of indictments marks the beginning of a long battle between tribunal and state over whether the state will actually fulfill its obligation to hand over suspects. Given that such trials of cooperation can take years for a tribunal to win, there is reason enough for Jallow to issue public indictments earlier rather than later in order to cultivate international allies and build pressure against the Rwandan government. And there is all the more reason for him to lobby the Security Council now for more time to prosecute RPF suspects later. In this regard, Jallow's inaction and his silence on the matter in a December 2006 Council meeting stands in sharp contrast to Del Ponte's forceful call at the same meeting for extending the ICTY's mandate to prosecute Radovan Karadžić and Ratko Mladić.

In the event that Jallow does indict RPF suspects, a possible outcome could be a negotiated settlement in which the Rwandan courts prosecute RPF cases. In fact, in speeches to the Security Council in June 2004 and December 2005, Jallow acknowledged that such negotiations were taking place with the

---

[60] Telephone interview with ICTR trial attorney, July 2006.

Rwandan government, an admission of the tribunal's willingness to diminish its own authority. If he handed RPF cases to Rwanda, Jallow would hope for a sympathetic international response based on the growing norm, embodied in the International Criminal Court statute, to allow states to prosecute their own war crimes suspects when these states are deemed willing and able to do so. The failure of the Rwandan courts over the last decade to undertake serious prosecutions of RPF crimes underscores the problematic nature of the tribunal's handing over of RPF cases to Rwanda even under ICC rules. Since the Kigali government also removed applicable provisions of the Geneva Conventions from domestic law in 2004, it is unlikely at present that the Rwandan courts would have jurisdiction to prosecute RPF atrocities.[61]

For the tribunal, the costs and benefits of pursuing criminal accountability for RPF atrocities have been starkly illuminated by the events of late November 2006, when a French investigative judge in Paris issued arrest warrants for nine of President Kagame's close associates following a long-running investigation into the 1994 plane crash that killed Rwandan President Juvénal Habyarimana. The case was initiated at the behest of the families of the French crew killed in the crash. Lacking the authority to indict Kagame under French law because of his immunity as a head of state, Judge Jean-Louis Bruguière instead called on the tribunal to prosecute the Rwandan president for war crimes.

The plane crash sparked the onset of the genocide and, in turn, the RPF's successful military campaign to control Rwanda. Bruguière's allegations directly link the RPF and Kagame to the downing of the airplane. This finding challenges the received wisdom that Hutu extremists killed the moderate Habyarimana in order to carry out a coup and provide a pretext for the genocide, and that Kagame's army resorted to combat to bring the genocide to an end. Bruguière's report alleges that "Kagame had deliberately opted for a modus operandi that, in the particularly tense context . . . could only lead to bloody acts of retribution against the Tutsi community, which provided him with the legitimate motive to restart hostilities and take power with the support of the international opinion."[62] If proven, the allegations could severely undermine the veracity and legitimacy of the RPF's narrative as defender of the nation and render it culpable for contributing to the circumstances that led to the genocide.

Bruguière's bombshell put both the Rwandan government and the tribunal on the defensive. In Kigali, the French arrest warrants and the call for Kagame's prosecution at the ICTR created a political furor, leading Rwanda to break off diplomatic relations with France and expel the French ambassador. Days later, the government organized a 25,000 strong anti-French protest in Kigali that recalled the government-sponsored protest at the tribunal's Kigali compound

---

[61] "Appeal to the UN Security Council to ensure that the mandate of the International Criminal Tribunal for Rwanda is fulfilled," Amnesty International press release, December 12, 2006.

[62] Katrin Bennhold, "French Judge Seeking to Bring Rwandan President before UN Tribunal," *International Herald Tribune*, November 21, 2006.

during the witness crisis. Kagame denounced the French investigation and sought to delegitimize its findings by invoking Rwanda's victim status and flaunting France's shameful role as a supporter of the genocidal regime. "They should first try themselves because they killed our people," Kagame said.[63]

Kagame's harsh response and the atmosphere of crisis sparked by Bruguière's arrest warrants raise the political stakes for Jallow if he decides to indict RPF suspects, either in connection with the plane crash or with the atrocities of Hutu civilians. Jallow, like his predecessors, maintains it is not in the tribunal's mandate to investigate the crash. (During Chief Prosecutor Arbour's tenure, a confidential memo that still remains under seal was authored by an ICTR investigator and implicated Kagame in the crash.) Bruguière's call for the tribunal to indict Kagame for the plane crash raises the specter that any RPF indictments by Jallow for atrocities against Hutu civilians would be effectively delegitimized by Kagame as mere acquiescence to French pressure. Jallow could have insulated the tribunal from such a charge by handing down indictments before Bruguière completed his long-anticipated case. Ironically, Bruguière's call for Kagame's prosecution at the ICTR may provide Jallow political cover to forego indicting RPF officials both in connection with the plane crash and RPF atrocities by casting his refusal to indict the RPF as a legitimate act of autonomy in the face of unwarranted pressure on the tribunal. Tribunal spokesman Everard O'Donnell almost said as much following Bruguière's public call for ICTR action against Kagame: "The prosecutor takes instructions from nobody in the world."[64]

Still, in the aftermath of Bruguière's warrants, tribunal indictments of the RPF – particularly on the question of atrocities against Hutu civilians – may come at a relatively advantageous time because further inaction would solidify both the perception and reality of the tribunal's accommodation to the Kagame regime. Indeed, regardless of the political legitimacy of the Bruguière investigation and the truth of his charges, the French judge's action (issuing warrants for the arrest of President Kagame's associates) underscores the extent of the tribunal's prosecutorial passivity when it comes to holding the victims and victors of the Rwandan conflict accountable. In time, Bruguière's action on the plane crash investigation may pierce Rwanda's victim status, making it easier for Chief Prosecutor Jallow to indict RPF suspects for atrocities against Hutu civilians. Yet time is running short for the tribunal.

The last chapter in the tribunal–RPF story has not yet been written. The current ICTR chief prosecutor may yet issue RPF indictments and pursue prosecutions. Whether or not he does, whether trials will be held at the tribunal, and whether he indicts foot soldiers or reaches higher up the RPF hierarchy will have a lasting influence on the tribunal's legacy. Failure to indict and prosecute RPF suspects will spell failure for the tribunal, according to some ICTR

---

[63] "Kagame Slams French Judge over Prosecution Call," *Agence France-Presse*, November 22, 2006.

[64] "France Issues Rwanda Warrants," *BBC News*, November 23, 2006.

officials. "If we close the door at the ICTR, if we lock it, and we turn the lights off ... without doing anything about the RPF then we haven't done our job," a veteran tribunal investigator told me in a 2005 interview.[65] "We have only investigated ... the loser, the Hutu, the génocidaire. And the winner gets away with murder ... There is no justice there."

---

[65] Fieldwork interview with tribunal investigator, Freetown, March 2005.

PART IV

CONCLUSION

10

The Present and Future of International Criminal Justice

10.1 Overview

The international war crimes tribunals that emerged in the early 1990s sought to distance themselves from the first generation of tribunals established by the victorious Allied powers at Nuremberg and Tokyo nearly half a century earlier. This new model of justice would be truly independent and fully international in origin and operation. Such autonomy and neutrality would ensure the new tribunals' legitimacy, and thereby help fulfill their ultimate mission of rehumanizing nations, communities, and individuals rent by atrocity and trauma. Whereas the Nuremberg and Tokyo military tribunals prosecuted only the crimes of the losers, the United Nations International Criminal Tribunals for the Former Yugoslavia and Rwanda would prosecute war crimes suspects from all sides of an armed conflict. And whereas the Nuremberg and Tokyo courts were arms of the Allied occupation forces, the ICTY and ICTR were intended to be free from control by any state or group of states. But being created without a standing army was not meant to leave today's tribunals powerless. The UN Security Council endowed the tribunals with the legal authority to carry out their mandate to prosecute war crimes, crimes against humanity, and genocide without state interference. When called upon by these courts, all UN member states would be legally bound to cooperate without delay. This requirement of state compliance would particularly oblige those nations complicit in atrocities to hand over the suspects, witnesses, and evidence essential for the trial process and the survival of the tribunals.

In reality, the ICTY and the ICTR have found themselves dependent on these targeted states to follow through on this obligation to provide cooperation. Despite their legal primacy over states, the ad hoc tribunals have been confronted by persistent state obstruction. However, the dynamics of state resistance vary across the cases under study in this book. Unlike Serbia, Rwanda and Croatia each claim the entitlement of a victor's court to mete out victim's justice at The Hague and Arusha, respectively, to its defeated oppressors. Unlike

Croatia, Rwanda's claim has so far succeeded in the ICTR insofar as no RPF suspects have yet been prosecuted for atrocities against Hutu civilians. By contrast, the ICTY has thwarted the Croatian government's attempts to have its army generals win immunity for their alleged involvement in atrocities against ethnic Serbs. But like Serbia and Croatia, Rwanda's claim for victim's justice has increasingly become a way to subvert prosecution of its own suspected war criminals. As much as this book acknowledges the differences, it has been yet more emphatic about the similarities between and among Rwanda, Croatia, and Serbia in the politics of state cooperation. Given the Western or Eurocentric bias that treats Africa as a continent apart from all others, it is all too easy to overlook the commonality of obstacles that all three states put in the way of the tribunals' prosecutions of war crimes.

Understanding the political forces that move targeted states to relinquish or maintain their resistance to tribunal authority has been the broad subject of this book. The first major conclusion is that *without decisive international community intervention on behalf of war crimes tribunals – whether in the form of persuasion, incentives, or coercion – cooperation from targeted states will rarely be forthcoming.* Given the tribunals' lack of enforcement powers, the international community – and particularly the Western powers – is often in the position to act as a surrogate enforcer of the targeted state's obligation to cooperate. When international actors choose not to intervene on the tribunals' behalf – which is in itself a violation of their commitment to support these institutions – state authorities will continue to shield fugitives, withhold witnesses, and hide evidence.

International pressure is of course, not the only force at work when it comes to a state determining whether it will cooperate. One cannot understand the politics of state cooperation without recognizing that domestic politics is critical in shaping a state's decision. This leads to the second major conclusion of the book: *notwithstanding international pressure and incentives, a targeted state will often withhold cooperation when domestic anti-tribunal actors threaten state authority and stability.* The question of whether a targeted state will empower a tribunal to uncover the criminal actions of suspected nationals can be extremely volatile domestically. This volatility is fanned by nationalists playing on fear at home that tribunal prosecutions of individual suspects will brand the state an aggressor and humiliate the nation on the world stage. The prospect of the government's arresting fugitives and sending them to a tribunal for trial can dominate a country's political life and sow instability by sparking anti-government protests and causing deep fissures in governing coalitions. Beset by domestic opposition that may erode a leader's standing and derail his political agenda, leaders tread carefully when deciding whether to submit to international pressure to cooperate with the tribunal. State resistance can play out as much in transitional democracies as in authoritarian regimes, as underscored in the Balkan case-study chapters. Established democracies may also be antagonistic to tribunals that can prosecute their own nationals, as seen by the United States' rejection of the International Criminal Court.

Despite their dependence on external actors, the tribunals do not necessarily sit passively in the shadows of international and state power. This brings us to the third main conclusion of the book, and a central focus of this chapter: *at critical junctures, the tribunals, and particularly their chief prosecutors, have garnered state cooperation by the use of adversarial and conciliatory strategies – from shaming to negotiation.*

However slowly and imperfectly, the tribunals have delivered a significant measure of justice by skillfully mobilizing their "soft power" to bring recalcitrant states into compliance. In the face of once seemingly insurmountable odds of state defiance and international indifference, the tribunals have succeeded in ways that skeptics once thought impossible. Indeed, the tribunals have registered and wrested cumulative successes in the area of state cooperation. Most notably, numerous suspects – long hidden and protected by state authorities – have in fact been brought to account for wartime atrocities. Despite formidable resistance, the ICTY and ICTR have each developed their own capacity to act strategically in the "trials of cooperation" to bring war crimes suspects to trial. In the process, these tribunals have established important precedents for newer international tribunals.

The "trials of cooperation" framework, introduced in Chapter 1, helps us to conceptualize the three-way interaction between tribunal, targeted state, and international community. The battle over cooperation is formulated as a virtual trial in which the tribunal seeks enforcement by resorting to (1) shaming the recalcitrant state in order to generate international pressure against the state, and (2) to conciliation where concessions and compromises are traded for state cooperation.

The tribunals' soft power derives from their perceived legitimacy as guardians of justice and accountability in much of the international community. But legitimacy is not an entitlement. It depends on the extent to which tribunals make significant progress toward meeting their goals while avoiding flagrant missteps that erase the awareness of and credit for real achievement. Targeted states are eager to politicize the tribunals' shortcomings by magnifying the inequities of international justice, both real and perceived. In this way, states attempt to knock the tribunals off their moral pedestals, shaming as they have been shamed.

The comparative nature of this book – which undertakes an examination of two tribunals' approaches to the problem of state cooperation – underscores the fact that there is nothing assured about the extent or efficacy of a tribunal's soft power. The ICTR has been stymied and stigmatized by its own missteps – shortcomings that the Rwandan government has ably exploited. By comparison, the ICTY has generally proved more effective both in the reality and international perception of its performance and in neutralizing the counterattacks of the Serbian and Croatian governments.

10.2 The Chief Prosecutor as Strategic Actor

We now take a closer look into the tribunals' use of soft power, which in essential ways lies in the hands of the chief prosecutor. The prosecutor occupies two positions at once: first, as the trial lawyer who marshals evidence to convict war crimes suspects and, second, as the political strategist who maneuvers through the relatively unchartered shoals of the trials of cooperation to obtain state compliance for his or her courtroom mission to convict. In the courtroom, the prosecutor must heed the Rules of Procedure and Evidence. But in the virtual trials for cooperation, there are no rules to guide or govern the chief prosecutor's quest for state compliance. The next section of this chapter records and interprets the chief prosecutor's political terms of engagement that have been pivotal in moving states to cooperate. For all the precedents that Nuremberg and Tokyo established for today's international tribunals, none exist for the chief prosecutor's political mission. The victor's justice that drove the Nuremberg and Tokyo tribunals obviated any need for their chief prosecutors to politically engage Germany and Japan. Unconditional surrender made state cooperation unconditional.

A. Shaming and its Limits

State recalcitrance spurs tribunal officials to employ adversarial strategies, notably shaming, to activate international pressure against the state and to raise the political costs of violating its legal obligation to cooperate. But shaming cannot by itself produce increased cooperation. Overemphasis on condemning a state's actions to the exclusion of other less confrontational strategies can seriously undermine the tribunal's bid for cooperation. Excessive shaming can undermine the prospects of cooperation by backing the government into a corner, leaving it little room to reverse course without being seen by domestic constituencies as losing face and sacrificing national sovereignty to an unpopular international institution. Even if the government does cooperate, the tribunal pressure that may have preceded its decision to do so may increase domestic hostility toward the tribunal and exacerbate a perception in the targeted government or society as a whole that the tribunal is at war with the state. Excessive shaming can be particularly counter-productive for a tribunal when the government is undergoing a democratic transition and represents a significant improvement over the nationalist opposition waiting in the wings.

Although tribunal officials often feel they have no other option but to repeatedly condemn state recalcitrance and call for international punishment of the state, doing so can undermine the tribunal's long-term bid for cooperation by sparking a debilitating political crisis at home. Transitional democracies, as in Croatia and Serbia, find themselves in the politically difficult position of balancing tribunal pressure to cooperate with domestic pressure to resist. Persisting with an adversarial strategy bent on exacting full cooperation from the state can intensify the crisis and risk bringing down the government. This danger is particularly great when the tribunal seeks the arrest and transfer of high-level suspects lauded at home as national heroes.

A chief prosecutor does well to cultivate the empowering image of a human rights crusader who tirelessly pursues prosecutions and state cooperation without regard to reputation or personal security. Still, a prosecutor who emphasizes shaming to the exclusion of conciliatory measures runs the risk of alienating international allies. To these allies as well as to targeted states, Carla Del Ponte, more than Louise Arbour and Richard Goldstone before her, has appeared to be relentlessly prosecutorial. Yet, while Del Ponte's actions may appeal to the human rights image of hot pursuit, she has also been mindful of mitigating nationalist resistance. For her part, Del Ponte speaks thus of the chief prosecutor's work: "You must stay in contact, you must persuade, you must argue about the necessity to conduct investigations and trials. It is extremely important. You cannot isolate yourself by staying in [the] office."[1]

Excessive shaming can magnify a tribunal's powerlessness. The tribunal's cautious approach to lodging official complaints of state non-cooperation with the Security Council is a case in point. Using the Council complaint process represents the most high-profile way by which a tribunal has tried to shame a resistant state. But the danger lies in the Council's predictable failure to take decisive action. Frequent complaints followed by Council inaction may send a message that a state can withhold cooperation without serious consequences. Not to be taken seriously by one's sponsors may be the most undermining of all a tribunal's travails. Unsurprisingly, the ICTY and ICTR have used the Council complaint process sparingly.

The challenge facing the chief prosecutor is to employ shaming to create rather than foreclose opportunities for diplomatic interaction and negotiation with these states. Indeed, shaming is not an end in itself, but a means to negotiate agreements for the handover of evidence, suspects, and witnesses. For a tribunal, realizing this aim relies on balancing pressure, ostracism, conciliation, and persuasion. While there is no formula for tribunal officials to achieve this difficult task, learning the language of diplomacy and the art of cultivating allies from among adversaries are indispensable components of soft power.

B. Negotiation and its Limits

Unlike diplomats who speak the language of negotiation and compromise, chief prosecutors rarely acknowledge that they take part in negotiations lest they undermine a tribunal's legitimacy by being seen to contravene their pledge to act free of political considerations. The negotiating function of the chief prosecutors is largely absent in most practitioner and scholarly accounts. David J. Scheffer, the former United States Ambassador-at-Large for War Crimes Issues, acknowledges, however, that a tribunal prosecutor "has to be as much of a diplomat as a criminal prosecutor . . . The only way the court efficiently operates is if the prosecutor in particular successfully negotiates their way to cooperation

---

[1] Fieldwork interview with Carla Del Ponte, The Hague, December 2003.

state by state. What is unrealistic for these courts is for the prosecutor to deign to assume that he or she can order the states to do anything."[2]

By necessity, a tribunal's position of weakness often compels its chief prosecutors to bargain with states and offer concessions in order to secure promises of cooperation or to forestall threats to disrupt cooperation altogether. At other times, however, a tribunal is driven to negotiate with states not from its weakness, but because of the actual or anticipated weakness of the targeted state. The prosecutor may offer concessions to a targeted state to offset the domestic instability that an uncompromising pursuit of state cooperation may cause. Negotiation toward this end is especially evident when a tribunal is dealing with a transitional democracy, such as Serbia or Croatia, or an otherwise weak democratic government that faces rebellion at home from nationalists if it moves too readily to provide cooperation. Less evident but no less important is the possibility that tribunal indictments and an uncompromising tribunal campaign for the handover of indictees may also imperil stability in authoritarian states. At the ICTR, for example, indictments of Tutsi RPF officers would likely cause deep fissures between President Kagame and the military he relies on to remain in power. This, Kagame might fear, would also weaken the minority Tutsi government's hold on power and lead to a destabilizing power struggle between Tutsi and Hutu forces. The ultimate fear is that instability in Rwanda could spark a return to mass violence, dwarfing the political turmoil witnessed in post-war Serbia and Croatia.

Whether in a democracy or a dictatorship, the prospects of instability may pose a serious threat to a tribunal since the further weakening of the government may reduce the prospects of future cooperation, while the government's collapse may dash hopes for cooperation entirely. Even as prosecutors have an interest in steadfastly maintaining that international justice aids the cause of stability – which, after all, is a foundational objective of the contemporary war crimes tribunals – they must be mindful of the ways in which the pursuit of state cooperation can trigger domestic turmoil.

In sum, the power of chief prosecutors is paradoxical. On the one hand, they are fundamentally weak insofar as they must rely on targeted states for many aspects of investigating and prosecuting war crimes cases. But, on the other hand, they can become powerful by virtue of the damage they might inflict on domestic governments through issuing war crimes indictments and triggering a domestic backlash against the government. The power of the chief prosecutors is not necessarily consistent but changes over time, particularly with shifts in domestic governance and the structure of state–society relations. Thus, this power over states often has more to do with the internal dynamics of a state than with any change within the tribunal.

Negotiation and the chief prosecutor's offer of limited concessions should ideally strengthen a tribunal's leverage over the state and bolster its effort to obtain cooperation. But the line is thin between making concessions that bolster

---

[2] Fieldwork interview with David J. Scheffer, Washington, D.C., September 2004.

and making concessions that undermine. Not surprisingly, the best assessments of where this line lies are made in hindsight. The Rwanda case study demonstrates how concessions can devolve into acquiescence and undermine a tribunal's influence vis-à-vis a targeted state.

Closed-door meetings are not the only way a chief prosecutor carries out negotiations with government officials. A key element of the negotiation process also occurs through actions taken and signals sent outside the context of a particular meeting. As the case-study chapters reveal, a chief prosecutor has a range of conciliatory measures at his or her disposal to encourage cooperation from the state. These include:

1. Tempering or foregoing criticism of a state's cooperation record and highlighting areas of improved cooperation.
2. Granting a new government a honeymoon period in which the prosecutor abstains from pressuring the state to cooperate.
3. Creating benchmarks that the state must meet in order to receive favorable evaluations in tribunal reports to the Security Council and to regional bodies such as the European Union.
4. Allowing suspects who surrender to the tribunal for arraignment to be provisionally released during the long pre-trial period.[3]
5. Deferring war crimes cases to domestic courts to stem domestic opposition to the transfer of a war crimes suspect to the tribunal.
6. Altering aspects of an indictment in order to downplay the alleged culpability of the suspect or the state in question.
7. Strategically timing indictments to mitigate domestic opposition to the arrest and transfer of indictees.
8. Delaying indictments until after pivotal events such as upcoming national elections and the signing of peace treaties in order to bolster the government's domestic political prospects.
9. Indicting suspects from a state's own ethnic, national, or political group whom government leaders wish to see removed from the country and prosecuted for political reasons.
10. Spearheading initiatives to make the tribunal more legitimate to domestic audiences, such as holding some tribunal trials in the country and honoring the state's wartime suffering by the prosecutor's paying visits to important gravesites.

Government leaders determined to maintain a tactical advantage over the tribunal have little interest in acknowledging instances in which the prosecutor offered concessions and sought compromise. Doing so can undermine the state's rhetorical attacks against the tribunal as an uncaring institution incapable of demonstrating sensitivity to domestic concerns. Indeed, particularly in

---

[3] Tribunal judges decide whether a defendant will be provisionally released prior to trial. However, the chief prosecutor plays an important role in this decision by either lending or withholding support to a defendant's request for provisional release.

Serbia and Croatia, and even during the democratic era, the image of an inflexible chief prosecutor who threatens state sovereignty is an enduring one in the public mind, burnished by government officials and the national media. Not surprisingly, the prosecutor's visits to the Balkans are anticipated in the government and the media with dread, as if the prosecutor were a headmaster sure to deliver a scolding. Such dread is not far from the truth, given the stinging criticism that the chief prosecutors (particularly Del Ponte) have leveled against governments in the region.

The tribunals' own need to avoid projecting a public image of negotiation aggravates a state's suspicions of tribunal intransigence. Publicly acknowledging that negotiations do take place can jeopardize the tribunals' leverage at the bargaining table in a number of ways. Such an admission may undercut the strongest card that the ICTY and the ICTR have to play in their struggle for cooperation – namely, the tribunals' legal primacy over the states. Thus it remains important for a chief prosecutor to publicly insist on full state cooperation, and only through more subtle channels indicate willingness to reach compromises with the state.

Negotiation itself, rather than only the public acknowledgment of negotiation, is also fraught with danger. Overemphasis on negotiating the tribunal's way through impasses with a targeted state can send a message to that state that the tribunal's demands can be bargained away. Influential international actors can play a key role in reinforcing this message if they either publicly or privately call for a negotiated settlement to a state–tribunal conflict over an outstanding request for cooperation. An international call for a negotiated resolution to such a conflict usually deals a blow to the tribunal's negotiating leverage because it undercuts the tribunal's public insistence that state cooperation is a matter of binding international law.

Such a scenario was played out during and after the witness crisis in Rwanda in the Summer of 2002 when Western diplomats privately stressed the need for the tribunal and the government to resolve the crisis through dialogue.[4] The Security Council went a step further, several months later, when it passed a resolution explicitly calling on the ICTR and the Rwandan government (as well as the ICTY and the states of the former Yugoslavia) to resolve their differences through "constructive dialogue."[5] The Council's endorsement of this approach – despite its insistence that "dialogue or lack of dialogue must not be used by States as an excuse"[6] not to cooperate – demonstrated that Rwanda's legal obligation was less than absolute. Too much emphasis placed on negotiation may also encourage a defiant state to use the cover of ongoing negotiations to portray itself as cooperative and to delay actual cooperation. In time, the state may initiate new rounds of negotiations with the tribunal for this very purpose of delay.

---

[4] Fieldwork interviews with Western diplomats, Kigali, June-July 2002.
[5] Statement by the President of the Security Council, ICTY/ICTR, December 18, 2002.
[6] Ibid.

The negotiated concessions that a prosecutor provides to one state may also undermine the tribunal's efforts to press for cooperation from other states without also offering comparable concessions. This scenario applies to the chief prosecutor at tribunals such as the ICTY or the International Criminal Court that have political relationships with various targeted states. The failure to offer the second state a concession of similar magnitude offered to the first state may decrease the prospects of cooperation from the second state. An assessment of whether to negotiate with a state should therefore be evaluated with an eye not only toward how it may alter the tribunal's short and long-term leverage with this state, but how it may alter that leverage with other states as well. This, of course, adds greatly to the complexity of the chief prosecutor's diplomatic task.

In sum, continuous negotiation is a critical aspect of what is needed to prod recalcitrant states to cooperate. At the same time, the culture of deal-making that can arise may undercut a tribunal's larger goal of obtaining legitimacy from targeted states and winning domestic support for the norm of international justice. The prevalence of bargaining – even when it leads to beneficial concessions for targeted states – may increase skepticism at home and abroad toward the tribunal by imparting the lesson that the tribunal and the state are involved in an exercise that has more to do with politics than with law.

10.3 Beyond Shame

Those involved in the tribunal drama often blur the distinction between compliance and cooperation – that is, between a state's submitting to a tribunal's orders and a state's working with a tribunal in a spirit of embracing the norms of international justice to address and redress crimes against humanity. While the tribunal's short-term goal is to obtain the state's compliance, its long-term goal is to affect a deep change in state and societal attitudes toward international justice. This deeper intent is codified in the tribunals' founding documents. Accordingly, the tribunal strives for a level of cooperation in which the state provides assistance not because of material incentives or out of fear of international retribution but from an evolving conviction of responsibility to confront its atrocities. Such deep cooperation is perhaps the only way for the tribunal someday to achieve its other objectives of deterring new rounds of violence, fostering peace and reconciliation, and strengthening the rule of law in post-conflict societies.

For the ICTY and ICTR, legitimacy and this deeper form of cooperation were based not on the victor's justice of the Nuremberg and Tokyo tribunals but on the impartiality of the rule of law. At best, garnering deep cooperation is a work in progress due in large part to crises of legitimacy that the ICTY and ICTR face in Serbia, Croatia, and Rwanda. Aside from missteps of their own, the tribunals' crises owe much to the targeted states' denial of their wartime culpability and their contempt for any institution that would pierce the state's self-proclaimed victimhood. Even as the idea of international justice gains global credibility, the tribunals have confronted intense opposition from states that fear prosecutions.

National leaders do not measure today's tribunals against the improvements that these courts have instituted since the days of Nuremberg and Tokyo. Rather, these leaders assert their preferred vision of justice in which tribunals ignore the state's wartime conduct, while prosecuting the conduct of the state's enemies. Still, the full scope of legitimacy must come to include these very intransigent opponents of the tribunals.

Even as the ICTY and ICTR have done much to modernize and humanize international law, the basic adversarial nature of international criminal justice has not been changed. For targeted states, the tribunals are still institutions of judgment and punishment. Considering the still open wounds of the Balkan and Rwandan conflicts and the persistence of denial, hate, and anti-tribunal propaganda in these regions, it comes as no surprise that the ICTY and ICTR have yet to establish their legitimacy in the states for which they were created. As David J. Scheffer writes, the tribunals were created "to pursue justice and, over the long term, influence the attitudes of perpetrators and victims. No one ever assumed that they would have a significant short-term impact on warring parties."[7] In fact, a number of tribunal observers do operate under this assumption, judging the tribunals against the test of short-term progress in obtaining societal legitimacy, deterring atrocities, and contributing to peace and reconciliation.[8] For some of these observers, war crimes tribunals can only be deemed successful and the resources devoted to them justifiable if they have shown an immediate effect on repairing and rehabilitating broken societies. But favoring a short-term appraisal of success betrays a misunderstanding of the complex relationship of law to political and social change. Even under ideal conditions – in advanced industrial societies that enjoy a robust tradition of rule of law – courts often do not rapidly alter behavior and attitudes. It is only in the long run – not simply while the tribunals are still operating, but long after their doors have closed – that we will be able to determine whether international courts have upset carefully constructed and historically entrenched belief-systems of national suffering that delegitimize and dehumanize the suffering of other societies. In this respect, the tribunals' legacies are not necessarily fixed, but may change over time as the domestic perceptions of the past and the domestic politics of the present change. It is useful to envisage a future retrospective study that establishes the long-term effects of the tribunal process.

The problem for the contemporary war crimes tribunals is how to foster deep cooperation and encourage the internalization of the norms of justice while winning the battle for compliance with defiant states at the same time. A central predicament is that the adversarial strategies the tribunals use with some success to induce compliance can quickly undermine their prospects of receiving deeper cooperation from targeted states. In this regard, a tribunal's use of shaming is a double-edged sword: wielding it to exact compliance might inflict a new

---

[7] David Scheffer, "Jostling Over Justice," *Foreign Policy*, May/June 2006, Letters, p. 4.

[8] For example, see Helena Cobban, "International Courts," *Foreign Policy*, March/April 2006, pp. 22–28.

wound on the state of being considered an outcast among nations. Self-interested politicians in these states can turn this wound of humiliation to domestic political advantage by demonizing a tribunal in the same unflattering light.

In one sense, it would seem a luxury for a tribunal – hampered by a lack of enforcement powers, confronted with persistent and ingenious state defiance, and facing pressure from international corners to deliver justice promptly – to heed and temper the potentially negative domestic repercussions of pursuing state compliance for an unassured deeper cooperation. This is particularly true when ad hoc tribunals like the ICTY and ICTR confront imminent deadlines for the completion of their mandates. Locked in battle with a state determined to obstruct justice, a chief prosecutor may share Cicero's remorseless principle: "Let them hate us, so long as they fear us." Still, by failing to move significantly beyond the politics of shame, a chief prosecutor and a tribunal more generally may leave a diminished legacy to regions devastated by mass atrocity. Even generations later, that tribunal may then be remembered not for its actual success in moving beyond victor's justice in its courtroom trials, but for imposing a new kind of victor's justice in the virtual trials over state cooperation.

The risks inherent in shaming should give us pause and lead us to consider the possible benefits for a tribunal if it abandoned an adversarial approach altogether. An alternative approach would be to allow a society to take responsibility for prosecutions itself or to forego prosecutions altogether and pursue alternative mechanisms of accountability, such as truth commissions, reparations, and lustrations. Indeed, the matter of accountability should ideally emanate from within because domestic processes – at least in democratic societies – are more likely to affect domestic populations and receive legitimacy from them.

The recognition of the vital role of national justice and state sovereignty is a central pillar of the International Criminal Court. In contrast to the ICTY and ICTR, which enjoy legal primacy, the ICC is based on the principle of complementarity, which only grants the Court the right to proceed with prosecutions when a state is either unwilling or unable to carry out genuine prosecutions itself.

There are significant disadvantages in non-adversarial paths to cooperation. International forbearance can give a state license to delay accountability indefinitely and legitimize the state's denial of its role in war crimes. That a state will hand over suspects to a tribunal of its own accord overlooks the real likelihood that compliance may come, if it comes at all, too late either to exact justice (because key suspects and witnesses may already be dead or incapacitated) or to serve as an agent of deterrence. The state's denial protects and implicitly valorizes suspected war criminals, emboldening and empowering them and their followers to again plunge the state and region into instability, crisis, and violence. In many post-conflict societies, denial has a long half-life, prolonged by the myth of victimization that makes it difficult for people to accept the suffering their state has inflicted on others.

Insisting that a state complicit in atrocities abide by its legal obligation to comply with tribunal orders will almost certainly lead to conflict between tribunal and state as well as within state and society. Such conflict will often bring varying degrees of political instability with it. It is incumbent on the chief prosecutor to try – through the aid of political advisors and in consultation with experts outside the tribunal – to anticipate and contain the destabilizing effects that indictments may create. By the same token, it is incumbent on those domestic leaders who value state cooperation to also take preventive action to contain rather than passively watch crises at home worsen, thereby handing nationalists another reason for blaming the tribunal.

Handing over high-level suspects to a tribunal for prosecution can be essential for a state's efforts to remove threats to the government and move beyond an era of criminality. This in turn may sow the seeds for legal reform and a new recognition of the role that both international and domestic law can play in protecting the rights of the individual and limiting the state's abuse of power. Thus, even as the battles over state cooperation with the tribunals stir domestic resistance and threaten stability, they can become, if fought to the end, a foundation for normative change as well as for a more stable and just society. But tribunals do not operate in a vacuum. Much depends on what the international community does to foster political, legal, and economic reform and integrate the country into regional and international organizations. In this regard, the promise of European Union membership for those Balkan states that demonstrate sufficient cooperation with the tribunal represents an important opportunity for these states.

The foundation for just societies depends in no small measure on whether tribunals can overcome state obstruction and prosecute all sides of a conflict equitably, thereby arriving at a comprehensive truth about what happened and who bears responsibility. It is, of course, extremely difficult for different societies to accept a common truth, because ethnic or national identity can hold a country in rigid thrall. But by uncovering and representing the truth about a conflict, the tribunals hope not only to establish a credible record of human rights violations, but also to hold norms of truth and justice in trust, so to speak, for countries such as Serbia, Croatia, and Rwanda that are currently unable or unwilling to fully hold these norms for themselves. Perhaps if and when domestic circumstances change in these countries, this international record can be reclaimed by all citizens of the former Yugoslavia and Rwanda.

10.4 The Next Generation: The Special Court for Sierra Leone and the International Criminal Court

The following analysis of the next generation of international war crimes tribunals, which focuses on the Special Court for Sierra Leone and the International Criminal Court, shows that the growing proliferation of new tribunals by no means assures that the problem of state cooperation has been overcome. These courts represent the next step on the historical trajectory of international war crimes tribunals in regard to the changing balance of tribunal authority and state sovereignty.

As arms of the conquering Allied forces, the Nuremberg and Tokyo tribunals had near absolute power over the targeted state. At both the ICTY and ICTR, the tribunal's authority continued to trump state sovereignty insofar as targeted states and all other UN members were legally bound to comply. But, in fact, states – even small and relatively weak states riven by years of war and economic decline – could often trump the tribunal and violate their obligation to cooperate. At the Special Court for Sierra Leone – and the East Timor and Cambodia tribunals – the concept of state–tribunal collaboration is built into the very fabric of these courts insofar as they are hybrid international–domestic institutions that include judges and prosecutors from both jurisdictions. This presents a different model that envisions state–tribunal comity in the pursuit of accountability. The hybrid concept makes more credible the claim of the international tribunals that a state is not in the judicial dock, only indicted individuals. However, depending on the ratio of domestic to international players, power at these hybrid tribunals either tilts toward more authority for the international judges and prosecutors, as in the Sierra Leone tribunal, or toward more authority for the domestic judges and prosecutors, as in the Cambodia tribunal. At the Sierra Leone tribunal, the international–state alliance is also reflected in the requirement to negotiate to resolve disputes that may arise if the Freetown government withholds cooperation.

Finally, the International Criminal Court empowers state sovereignty more than ever before by giving states that have ratified the Court's statute the first right to try their own nationals for serious violations of international humanitarian law. In this regard, the ICC waits in the wings as a court of last resort to prosecute cases only when states are unwilling or unable to prosecute their own nationals. The ICC statute takes state sovereignty yet further by exempting states that have not ratified the statute from the requirement to cooperate with the Court.

Even as the ICC is hailed as a permanent and global court, its legal authority has thus been significantly curtailed compared with the Nuremberg and Tokyo tribunals, on the one hand, and the Yugoslavia and Rwanda tribunals, on the other. It remains to be seen if such clear deference to state sovereignty mitigates the Court's adversarial quest for cooperation as well as alleviates the need to hide the politics of negotiation behind closed doors.

A. *The Special Court for Sierra Leone*
The Special Court for Sierra Leone was created in 2002 to prosecute atrocities committed during the civil war that ravaged that West African nation. Notably, the Special Court's legal authority to move defiant states and indifferent international community actors is very limited. Not only does it lack enforcement powers like its predecessors, the ICTY and ICTR, but it has not been invested with the Chapter VII powers of the UN Charter requiring compliance from all UN member states. Although there are serious limitations to the utility of these Chapter VII powers, as described in the case-study chapters, these powers have served as the ICTY and ICTR's foundation for their campaign for state

compliance. Their legal authority to turn to the Security Council for enforcement has enabled the ICTY and ICTR to effectively mount pressure and mobilize shame against a state's violation of its obligation to cooperate. The tribunals' Chapter VII powers are "a very useful battering ram with other governments," observes David J. Scheffer, the former United States Ambassador-at-Large for War Crimes Issues.[9] For the Special Court for Sierra Leone, its relative lack of legal authority has, if anything, created an imperative to forge new strategies in its quest for state cooperation.

In contrast to the ICTY and ICTR, the Special Court for Sierra Leone is not directly operated by the UN or regularly overseen or monitored by the Security Council. Whereas those ad hoc tribunals were created by Council resolutions, the Sierra Leone tribunal was established by a treaty agreement between the UN and the Sierra Leone government. When it comes to Sierra Leone's obligation to cooperate, the treaty establishing the Special Court is quite clear. Pursuant to Article 17 of the treaty, the Sierra Leone government is obliged to "cooperate with all organs of the Special Court at all stages of the proceedings ... [and] comply without delay with any request for assistance by the Special Court."[10] In spelling out the government's obligation to cooperate, the Special Court agreement stipulates that any conflict that may occur between the government and the Court "concerning the interpretation or application of this Agreement shall be settled by negotiation, or by any other mutually agreed-upon mode of settlement."[11] Making negotiation a requirement is a radical departure from the ICTY and ICTR tribunals' insistence that negotiation is not an option.

The lack of an official UN complaint mechanism has not adversely affected the Special Court's efforts to obtain cooperation from the Sierra Leone government. Indeed, several senior Court officials reported in interviews during March 2005 that the government's cooperation had been exemplary. The Court's relationship with the Freetown government has been smooth and devoid of acrimony, due in part to the fact that the government both requested the establishment of the Court and played a role in its creation.[12] However, the Sierra Leone-based court faced a prolonged struggle unlike any encountered by the ICTY or ICTR: the refusal of a non-targeted state to hand over a war crimes suspect it had been harboring. The struggle over obtaining custody of its most wanted suspect, the former Liberian President Charles Taylor, was waged between the Court and Nigeria, the country where Taylor had been granted exile in August 2003. As the Special Court agreement does not stipulate a legal obligation for governments other than Sierra Leone to comply with court orders, persuading Nigeria to revoke Taylor's safe haven status posed a formidable

---

[9] Fieldwork interview with David J. Scheffer, Washington, D.C., September 2004.

[10] Article 17 of the "Agreement between the United Nations and the Government of Sierra Leone on the Establishment of a Special Court for Sierra Leone."

[11] Article 20 of the "Agreement between the United Nations and the Government of Sierra Leone on the Establishment of a Special Court for Sierra Leone."

[12] Fieldwork interviews with Special Court officials and Sierra Leone cabinet ministers, Freetown, March 2005.

challenge to the Office of the Prosecutor. The former warlord Taylor, who is charged with war crimes and crimes against humanity in connection with atrocities committed in Sierra Leone, had been allowed to leave Liberia for exile in a plush seaside villa in Nigeria. The United States and Britain played a leading role in brokering this arrangement to prod Taylor to relinquish power and prevent further bloodshed in Liberia's civil war.

From the start of Taylor's exile until his dramatic arrest at a remote Nigerian border crossing and his immediate transfer to Freetown in March 2006, the Court was engaged in its most difficult and high-stakes cooperation battle. In the end, it was international pressure, particularly from the United States, that forced Nigeria to end Taylor's asylum. Especially during 2005, the Special Court played an instrumental role in building international pressure for Taylor's arrest, a venture whose success is as impressive as any use of soft power by the ICTY to enlist the cooperation of the international community. Court officials waged a campaign – at the European Union, the United Nations, and in Washington – to obtain resolutions calling on Nigeria to transfer Taylor to the Special Court.[13] In February 2005, the Court won an important victory when it persuaded the European Parliament to approve a resolution calling on the EU "to build international pressure in order to bring about Charles Taylor's extradition."[14] For the ICTY and ICTR, such resolutions, while certainly welcome, do not have the same urgency because of the tribunals' explicit statutory obligation on all UN member states to cooperate. But for the Special Court, creating such an explicit legal basis for Taylor's transfer was a critical step in its diplomatic efforts to apprehend the former Liberian leader. "Now we have a resolution to take to governments," a Special Court official told me in a 2005 interview in Freetown, in reference to the European Parliament resolution. "It gives us something to work with [and to] parlay one thing to the next."[15]

The European Parliament's action gave the Special Court momentum to prosecute Taylor. In early May 2005, the U.S. House of Representatives passed a resolution calling on Nigerian President Olusegun Obasanjo to send Taylor to Freetown for trial. The U.S. Senate followed a week later with the same resolution. As with the transfer of Slobodan Milošević to the ICTY in 2001, the arrest and transfer of Taylor to the Special Court would come to depend in large part on U.S. pressure, both from Congress and the White House. The House of Representatives' resolution was timed to coincide with Obasanjo's May 2005 visit to Washington. During that visit, President Bush and Secretary of State Condoleezza Rice discussed the Taylor issue with Obasanjo. Although Obasanjo did not publicly commit himself to revoking Taylor's safe haven status, there were indications that the Nigerian leader would soon be inclined to

---

[13] Fieldwork interview with Special Court Prosecutor David Crane, Freetown, March 2005.

[14] See "EU: Press Nigeria to Hand Over Charles Taylor," Human Rights Watch, February 24, 2005.

[15] Fieldwork interview with Special Court official, Freetown, March 2005.

send Taylor to the Special Court.[16] Meanwhile, Court officials hoped that the Congressional resolutions would bolster their efforts to win a Security Council Chapter VII resolution that would legally require Nigeria to transfer Taylor to Freetown for trial. The Council rebuffed the Court, but did pass a much weaker resolution that noted "the importance of ensuring that all those indicted by the Court appear before it."[17]

The diplomatic offensive by the Special Court – and by like-minded international human rights organizations such as the Coalition for International Justice – played an important role in prodding the Bush administration to lobby Nigeria to end Taylor's asylum. Court officials and human rights groups effectively argued that Taylor had violated the conditions of his exile by communicating with his associates in Liberia and by planning to sow instability in advance of the Fall 2005 Liberian presidential elections.[18]

Even as Nigeria refused to hand Taylor over to the Special Court, it indicated that it would eventually do so if a democratically elected Liberian president made the request. Democratic change in Liberia came in January 2006, when Ellen Johnson-Sirleaf, who won the presidential election, took office. Even so, intense pressure from Washington was required before Obasanjo terminated Taylor's asylum following Johnson-Sirleaf's formal request in mid-March 2006. In any case, it would soon become apparent that Taylor's capture was anything but assured.

Obasanjo balked at actually arresting Taylor, telling Johnson-Sirleaf that since she was the one who had requested his handover, it was up to her to send Liberian authorities to make the arrest. Nor did the Nigerian leader take measures to tighten the lax security around Taylor's seaside compound to ensure that he did not flee. In another indication that Obasanjo was reluctant to make the arrest or prevent his escape, his spokeswoman announced that Taylor was "not a prisoner."[19] Within a few days of Obasanjo's announcement that Taylor's asylum would come to an end, Taylor disappeared. Taylor's escape, which had been anticipated given Obasanjo's failure to arrest him, prompted a *New York Times* editorial entitled, "The Least Surprising Jailbreak Ever."[20] The escape sparked fear of a coup attempt in Liberia and the possibility that the warlord might find his way back into the country and imperil the new-found peace there.[21]

Back in Nigeria, Taylor sought to flee into neighboring Cameroon at an isolated border crossing some 600 miles away from his seaside villa. Just as the four-wheel drive vehicle he was in was about to cross into Cameroon,

[16] Bryan Bender, "US, Nigeria Step Up Bid to Bring Taylor to Trial," *Boston Globe*, May 6, 2005.
[17] Security Council Resolution 1610, June 30, 2005.
[18] Fieldwork interviews with Special Court officials, Freetown, March 2005.
[19] Lydia Polgreen, "Liberian Seized to Stand Trial on War Crimes," *New York Times*, March 30, 2006, A1.
[20] "The Least Surprising Jailbreak Ever," *New York Times*, March 29, 2006, A26.
[21] Lydia Polgreen, "Nigeria Says Ex-President of Liberia has Disappeared," *New York Times*, March 29, 2006, A3.

Nigerian security officers spotted Taylor and arrested him. On the same day, March 29, he was flown to the Liberian capital, Monrovia, before landing by helicopter in the Special Court's heavily guarded compound in Freetown. It was a defining moment for the Court, as a prosecution official underscored in an email to colleagues: Taylor "arrived last night and looked very forlorn and broken. It was truly a historic moment and the cheers that were heard from all the people of Sierra Leone as they stood on roof tops and in roads at the noise of the in-coming helicopters was just incredible."

For the Special Court and for many Sierra Leonians, Charles Taylor's arrival was no less significant of an event than the arrival of Milošević in The Hague five years earlier.[22] Taylor's arrest marks the first African head of state to face charges of war crimes and crimes against humanity at an international tribunal. The very lack of a statutory obligation of a non-targeted state's compliance spurred the Special Court to take its own direct action to solicit the help of the European Union and the United States, in an effort that riveted the world's attention.

B. State Cooperation and the Future of the International Criminal Court

In contrast to the ICTY and ICTR, which were created by the Security Council, the International Criminal Court owes its establishment to the Rome Statute approved by 120 states (in July 1998) and to the ratification of this treaty by 105 states (as of the end of July 2007). The representative manner in which the ICC was established enhances its legitimacy and gives it significant moral and political leverage in its trials of cooperation. However, the ICC's wide international backing and the detailed rules governing state cooperation in the Rome Statute[23] do not eliminate significant obstacles. The ICC lacks the support of some of the world's most powerful and populous nations, specifically the United States, China, Russia, and India. The states that have chosen not to ratify the ICC statute are, with limited exceptions, neither subject to the Court's jurisdiction nor obliged to provide cooperation. Whereas the ICTY and ICTR impose a strict legal obligation on all UN member states to cooperate, the ICC renders this obligation voluntary for states that have not ratified the Rome Statute.[24] Herein lies an essential root of the cooperation problem for the ICC.

---

[22] Following Taylor's arrest, the Special Court sought to conduct his trial in The Hague (using a courtroom in the International Criminal Court) because of concern that a trial in Freetown could cause regional instability. In June 2006, the Security Council approved the new venue for the trial, which began in June 2007. In August 2007, the trial was postponed until January 2008 to give Taylor's new attorney ample preparation time.

[23] Part 9, International Cooperation and Judicial Assistance, Articles 86–102, "Rome Statute of the International Criminal Court."

[24] States that are party to the Rome Statute are under an obligation to fully cooperate with the ICC. If a State party fails to cooperate, the matter can be referred to the Assembly of States Parties. The Assembly of States Parties is the body – comprised of states that have ratified the Rome Statute – that oversees the ICC. However, the Assembly of States Parties, in contrast to the Security Council, has no recourse to sanction non-compliant states. The matter of state non-cooperation can also be referred to the Security Council in those instances in which the Council originally asked the ICC to investigate and prosecute certain crimes. See Article 87, "Requests

Without the backing of major world powers – most importantly, the United States, which has vehemently opposed the Court – the ICC's cooperation problem is, in key respects, likely to be greater than that faced by the UN ad hoc tribunals. The U.S. decision not to become a State party to the Rome Statute renders prospective American war crimes – including those that may have been committed in Iraq and Afghanistan since the Court's statute went into force on July 1, 2002 – immune to ICC prosecution. The lack of U.S. support will also have lasting implications for the ability of the ICC to bring war crimes suspects to trial from other countries. In sharp contrast to the ICTY, ICTR, and the Special Court for Sierra Leone, the ICC has not been able to turn to Washington for much needed support in providing evidence of atrocities that have occurred in targeted states and in pressuring these states and rebel groups therein to cooperate with Court investigations.

For the Bush administration and its Republican allies in Congress, the ICC has been perceived as a threat to American exceptionalism, despite the procedural safeguards that place strong limits on the chief prosecutor's authority and indictment powers. Washington's opposition to the ICC culminated in the American Service Members' Protection Act of 2002 barring the U.S. government from lending support to the ICC. The law includes what has been dubbed the "Hague invasion clause," which authorizes the President to "use all means necessary and appropriate" to free American personnel held in custody by the ICC and provides for the withholding of U.S. military aid for governments ratifying the Rome Statute.[25] Still, it is important to note that the law provides an exemption that permits the U.S. government to provide direct cooperation to the ICC.

Even as Washington maintains that it will not join the Court, there are signs that its staunchly anti-ICC position is softening – in part as a corrective to the backlash against the administration's unilateralism and a realization that the United States may benefit from providing selective cooperation to the Court. When the Security Council considered where suspected perpetrators of the Darfur atrocities in western Sudan should be prosecuted, the United States backed away from its categorical opposition and showed a new pragmatism. In early 2005, Washington had opposed a Security Council resolution to refer the Darfur case for ICC investigation. Under the Rome Statute, a Security Council referral was the only way for the ICC to obtain jurisdiction because Sudan is not a State party to the Statute. (A Security Council resolution is one of three triggering mechanisms for the ICC chief prosecutor to initiate an investigation. Pending judicial approval, an ICC investigation can also be initiated by the prosecutor himself or when he receives a referral from a State party.) In an effort to derail Europe's support for ICC prosecutions of the Darfur conflict, the Bush

for cooperation: general provisions," paragraphs 5b and 7, "Rome Statute of the International Criminal Court."

[25] "The United States and the International Criminal Court," Human Rights Watch, http://www.hrw.org/campaigns/icc/us.htm.

administration had proposed the creation of an ad hoc tribunal based in Arusha and jointly operated by the African Union and the United Nations. "We don't want to be party to legitimizing the ICC," explained Pierre-Richard Prosper, the then U.S Ambassador-at-Large for War Crimes Issues.[26] A U.S. victory for its ad hoc proposal would have dealt a blow to the ICC's relevance as an institution capable of responding to ongoing atrocities. However, in the face of strong European pressure, the rising death toll in Darfur, and the lack of international military intervention to stop the killing, the United States withdrew its counter-proposal for an ad hoc tribunal. On March 31, 2005, the Security Council voted to refer the Darfur conflict to the ICC. In an important victory for the Court and its backers, the United States, not long after its initial opposition, abstained rather than vote against the Council resolution.

The U.S. abstention was not an embrace of the Court but, even more significantly, neither was it a rejection. By allowing the ICC jurisdiction in the high-profile Darfur case, the U.S. also signaled that its stance toward the Court could be open to further change, particularly in Darfur. In June 2007, John B. Bellinger III, the State Department legal advisor, articulated further change in the U.S. approach to the ICC, underscoring Washington's need to be perceived as a supporter of international justice. "The very seriousness with which we approach international law is sometimes mischaracterized as obstructionism or worse," Bellinger said in a speech in The Hague.[27] While reiterating the administration's concerns about the Court, Bellinger indicated that the United States would consider assisting the ICC's investigations in Darfur if requested. The apparent easing in U.S. policy has come as a welcome surprise to the ICC. Still, the United States is far from offering itself as a surrogate enforcer that would vigorously press Sudan and other non-compliant states to cooperate with the ICC.

The United States is not the only major impediment to the Court's quest to overcome the resistance of targeted states. Although many of the 105 States parties to the Rome Statute are avid sponsors of the Court, providing funding and logistical support, they have put little diplomatic pressure on targeted states to cooperate in investigations and hand over indicted suspects.[28] This lack of political support poses a serious threat to the Court's efforts to bring suspects into custody and thus demonstrate that it can actually hold a significant number of trials. Although championing the Court and defending it against Washington's attacks, European leaders have been reluctant to press targeted states, such as Sudan, that are refusing to cooperate with ICC investigations. Such reluctance raises serious questions as to whether the European Union will follow through on its commitment to the ICC and play the role of international enforcer on the

---

[26] Warren Hoge, "U.S. Lobbies U.N. on Darfur and International Court," *New York Times*, January 29, 2005.

[27] Nora Boustany, "Official Floats Possibility of Assistance to Hague Court," *Washington Post*, June 12, 2007, A20.

[28] Fieldwork interviews with ICC officials, The Hague, June 2007.

Court's behalf. That is part of the larger question concerning whether the EU can take a more prominent role in global politics. The answer to both questions depends in large part on the extent to which the EU will remain distracted by its recent enlargement to twenty-seven members. For ICC advocates, there are some optimistic signs that "the Hour of Europe"[29] in the realm of international justice may soon be upon us. For example, the EU, as this book has demonstrated, has become an increasingly vital source of political support for the ICTY's cooperation battles, even turning to the ICTY to help appraise whether a state's cooperation is sufficient enough to warrant advancement toward EU membership.

Europe's capacity to exert influence is significantly greater with the Balkan states on its doorstep than with states in Africa where the ICC is at present (2007) carrying out investigations. To be sure, Europe's leverage over those African states where ICC investigations are taking place will be diminished without the inducement of EU membership. Yet the EU does have at its disposal other instruments of pressure, especially the threat of sanctions, to prod defiant states into compliance. Since the ICC has so far limited its investigations to atrocities committed in four African countries – Sudan, Uganda, Congo, and the Central African Republic – the African Union (and the Arab League to a limited extent) also has an important role by pressuring African states to cooperate with the ICC. However, it is doubtful whether the fifty-three-nation African organization will form a consensus to act decisively to move non-compliant states to hand over war crimes suspects.

The ICC's long-term survival will depend in no small part on a chief prosecutor who can, first, obtain jurisdiction to investigate major atrocities in Africa and elsewhere and, second, cultivate the Court's soft power to overcome entrenched state resistance to cooperation. For the ICC, rigorous indictments, prompt arrests, and efficient prosecutions of high-level suspects in the conflicts in Darfur, Uganda, Congo, and the Central African Republic will go a long way toward establishing the Court's credibility and prominence. That, in turn, may give the ICC the political leverage to bring other suspects in other conflicts to trial. In time, such momentum may bolster the ICC's lobbying efforts and increase the pressure on holdouts such as the United States as well as pro-ICC states in Europe and beyond to tangibly support the Court's pursuit for cooperation from targeted states. If the ICC grows effective in prosecuting the world's worst atrocities – and if it does so without the scandals and institutional turmoil that have undermined the ICTR – it may become increasingly costly for Washington, Moscow, and Beijing to stand on the sidelines.

The ICC's stature, internationally and in targeted states, may also depend on the extent to which it is seen to be a neutral actor. Maintaining the reality and the perception of neutrality may be particularly complicated in situations such

---

[29] "The Hour of Europe" was the erroneous prediction of Luxembourg's foreign minister, Jacques Poos, when referring in mid-1991 to the ability of European diplomats to bring the Croatian war to an end.

as Uganda, where the state has invited the ICC into the country to prosecute atrocities perpetrated by rebel groups. By not indicting suspects tied to state-sponsored atrocities or in long delaying doing so, the ICC's neutrality may be undermined to stay in the good graces of the government upon which the Court relies for cooperation. Being perceived as a neutral actor, then, will depend on whether the ICC Chief Prosecutor, Luis Moreno-Ocampo of Argentina, follows the ICTY's precedent of prosecuting war crimes suspects from all sides of an armed conflict or instead follows the ICTR's precedent of prosecuting suspects from only one side of a conflict.[30] Judging by the ICC's publicly issued arrest warrants for Ugandan and Sudanese suspects (as of the end of October 2007), the chief prosecutor so far appears to be following the ICTY precedent. In Uganda, he has charged Lord's Resistance Army leader Joseph Kony and four commanders of his rebel group with crimes against humanity and war crimes.[31] However, Moreno-Ocampo has not charged any suspects in connection with Ugandan army atrocities against civilians. Again, in the Darfur conflict, the chief prosecutor has charged two suspects tied to the Sudanese government with crimes against humanity and war crimes, but has not sought prosecutions of war crimes suspects from the anti-government rebels. In May 2007, the ICC issued arrest warrants for these two suspects – Ahmad Muhammad Harun, a Sudanese government minister, and Ali Kushayb, a leader of the government-backed Janjaweed militia.

It is too early to make firm assessments of prosecutorial trends in this regard, especially given that the ICC is building its investigative capacity. A case in point comes from the Ituri region of eastern Congo, where Moreno-Ocampo has indicted two militia leaders from opposing ethnic-based militias – Thomas Lubanga, on charges of conscripting and abusing children, and Germain Katanga, on charges that include sexual slavery. Suspects from other Congolese factions in Ituri – and Ugandan army officers suspected of atrocities in Ituri – have not yet been charged by the ICC. To date, the Court has obtained custody only of Lubanga and Katanga, who were transferred to the ICC from Congo in March 2006 and October 2007, respectively.

It should be noted that the ICC, given its potential global reach, will issue far fewer indictments for a particular armed conflict than either the ICTY or the ICTR. According to ICC officials, this restriction on indictments will go hand in hand with a higher threshold for the type and magnitude of atrocities that are grave enough to warrant prosecution. This could lead to a situation in which the atrocities of one side of a conflict could be legitimately excluded from prosecution if the gravity threshold is not reached. But, the higher gravity threshold must be closely scrutinized because it can give carte blanche to

---

[30] It is important to note that the Special Court for Sierra Leone has followed the ICTY's prosecutorial precedent. Under the direction of its first chief prosecutor, David Crane, the Special Court indicted and prosecuted suspects from all sides of the conflict in Sierra Leone.

[31] Raska Lukwiya, one of the LRA commanders charged by the ICC, was killed by the Ugandan army in combat in August 2006.

the ICC prosecutor to avoid undertaking prosecutions that may be politically controversial.

The normative argument for justice is necessary but not sufficient for the ICC to win over the international community. To cultivate support for investigations and arrests, Chief Prosecutor Moreno-Ocampo and other Court officials will have to persuade both the states that have and have not ratified the Rome Statute to become surrogate enforcers on behalf of the Court. Therein lies the importance of the campaign by the ICC and the international human rights movement to demonstrate to these states the political benefits of international justice. The ICC, as well as the Yugoslavia, Rwanda, and Sierra Leone tribunals, have staked their legitimacy on the promised capacity of international law to transform deeply divided communities and create a culture of human rights. International war crimes prosecutions, we are told, will succeed in this endeavor by reconciling enemies, deterring revenge killings, and bringing an end to a culture of impunity. If ICC officials can demonstrate the beneficial outcomes of indictments and prosecutions for peace and stability, they may be able, perhaps only slowly at first, to garner support from powerful actors such as the United States that hold cooperation and justice in the balance. But persuading skeptics in this endeavor will depend on whether ICC prosecutions actually help deter new cycles of violence or instead exacerbate armed conflict and sow regional and domestic instability. This question is on the minds of many Ugandans, diplomats, and human rights activists who are debating whether the ICC arrest warrants of leaders of the Lord's Resistance Army have jeopardized or fostered efforts to reach a lasting peace settlement to the long-running conflict in northern Uganda. There is also an emerging debate as to whether the ICC's arrest warrants related to the Darfur conflict will help or hinder international efforts to end the violence there.

Here we see the reemergence of a central theme of this book – the peace and justice controversy. It is my hope that this book has not become part of the familiar polarization of this controversy, but has recognized the complex interaction between peace and justice. For many tribunal advocates, the power of international justice to end impunity has become an article of faith. For tribunal skeptics, international justice is a force that interferes with the diplomat's search for peace and undermines a nation's quest to recover from war on its own terms. The examination of the Serbia, Croatia, and Rwanda cases lends credence, at various times, to both points of view. To be sure, tribunal indictments can run the risk of backing an indicted head of state or rebel leader into a corner and thereby jeopardizing the prospects for ceasefires and peace agreements. That, in turn, can actually lead to an intensification of armed conflict. A tribunal's bid to press a recalcitrant state to cooperate by subjecting that state to shame and condemnation can also activate domestic instability by mobilizing nationalists against the tribunal and the government in power. But tribunal indictments can also galvanize international resolve to hasten a war's end and erode an indicted leader's domestic and international support. Once a state leader is indicted, he may find himself castigated and shunned as an international pariah by powerful nations that once tolerated his crimes and kept him in power. A tribunal's shaming of a non-compliant state, along with international pressure, might thus set in motion political and moral forces that prod that state to move against nationalist challengers who threaten domestic and regional stability.

These scenarios underscore the complex interplay between peace and justice and suggest some of the ways in which efforts to prosecute war crimes suspects may both enhance and complicate efforts to achieve and maintain peace. It is in this context that the ICC will interject itself in today's armed conflicts. And it is also in this context that the ICC and its advocates will have to convince doubters of the practical value of a standing international war crimes court. It is the abiding hope of this new experiment in international law that skeptics will become adherents, seeing the ICC not only as serving their political interests, but as a moral good in and of itself. It is only then that the International Criminal Court will inaugurate a permanent place for global justice.

Bibliography

This bibliography consists of books and journal articles cited in the footnotes. Newspaper articles, speeches, press releases, and tribunal, UN, and human rights reports are listed in the footnotes only.

Albright, Madeleine K. (2003) *Madame Secretary*. New York: Miramax Books.

Askin, Kelly Dawn (1997) *War Crimes Against Women: Prosecution in International War Crimes Tribunals*. The Hague: Martinus Nijhoff Publishers.

Baker III, James A., and Thomas M. DeFrank (1995) *The Politics of Diplomacy*. New York: G. P. Putnam's Sons.

Barnett, Michael (2002) *Eyewitness to a Genocide: The United Nations and Rwanda*. Ithaca: Cornell University Press.

Bass, Gary Jonathan (2000; 2002) *Stay the Hand of Vengeance: The Politics of War Crimes Tribunals*. Princeton: Princeton University Press.

Berkeley, Bill (2001) *The Graves Are Not Yet Full: Race, Tribe and Power in the Heart of Africa*. New York: Basic Books.

Bob, Clifford (2005) *The Marketing of Rebellion: Insurgents, Media, and International Activism*. Cambridge: Cambridge University Press.

Cigar, Norman (2001) *Vojislav Koštunica and Serbia's Future*. London: Saqi Books in association with The Bosnian Institute.

Cigar, Norman, and Paul Williams (2002) *Indictment at The Hague: The Milošević Regime and Crimes of The Balkan Wars*. New York: New York University Press.

Clark, Wesley K. (2002) *Waging Modern War: Bosnia, Kosovo, and the Future of Combat*. New York: Public Affairs.

Cohen, Lenard J. (2001; 2002) *Serpent In The Bosom: The Rise and Fall of Slobodan Milošević*. Boulder: Westview Press.

Cohen, Roger (1998) *Hearts Grown Brutal: Sagas of Sarajevo*. New York: Random House.

Côté, Luc (2005) "Reflections on the Exercise of Prosecutorial Discretion in International Criminal Law," *Journal of International Criminal Justice*, Vol. 3, No. 1, March.

Dallaire, Roméo (2003) *Shake Hands with the Devil: The Failure of Humanity in Rwanda*. Toronto: Random House Canada.

Des Forges, Alison (1999) *Leave None to Tell the Story: Genocide in Rwanda*. New York: Human Rights Watch.

Elster, Jon (2004) *Closing the Books: Transitional Justice in Historical Perspective*. Cambridge: Cambridge University Press.

Eltringham, Nigel (2004) *Accounting for Horror: Post-Genocide Debates in Rwanda*. London: Pluto Press.

Erözden, Ozan (2002) "Croatia and the ICTY: A Difficult Year of Co-operation," www.ceu.hu/cps/bluebird/pap/erozden1.pdf.

French, Howard W. (2004) *A Continent for the Taking: The Tragedy and Hope of Africa*. New York: Alfred A. Knopf.

Glenny, Misha (2003) "The Death Of Đinđić," *The New York Review of Books*, July 17.

Glenny, Misha (1992) *The Fall of Yugoslavia: The Third Balkan War*. New York: Penguin Books.

Goldstein, Ivo (1999) *Croatia: A History*. London: Hurst & Company.

Goldstone, Richard J. (2000) *For Humanity: Reflections of a War Crimes Investigator*. New Haven: Yale University Press.

Gourevitch, Philip (1999) *We Wish to Inform You that Tomorrow We Will be Killed with Our Families: Stories from Rwanda*. New York: Farrar, Straus, and Giroux.

Gow, James (2003) *The Serbian Project and its Adversaries: A Strategy of War Crimes*. Montreal: McGill-Queen's University Press.

Hagan, John (2003) *Justice in the Balkans: Prosecuting War Crimes in The Hague Tribunal*. Chicago: The University of Chicago Press.

Hazan, Pierre (2004) *Justice in a Time of War: The True Story Behind the International Criminal Tribunal for the Former Yugoslavia*. College Station: Texas A & M University Press.

Holbrooke, Richard (1998) *To End a War*. New York: Random House.

Ignatieff, Michael (2000) *Virtual War: Kosovo and Beyond*. New York: Metropolitan Books.

Jallow, Hassan B. (2005) "Prosecutorial Discretion and International Criminal Justice," *Journal of International Criminal Justice*, Vol. 3, No. 1, March.

Josipović, Ivo (2000) *The Hague Implementing Criminal Law: The Comparative and Croatian Implementing Legislation and the Constitutional Act on the Cooperation of the Republic of Croatia with the International Criminal Tribunal and the Commentary*. Zagreb: Informator, Hrvatski Pravni Center.

Judah, Tim (2000) *The Serbs: History, Myth & the Destruction of Yugoslavia*. New Haven: Yale University Press.

Kerr, Rachel (2004) *The International Criminal Tribunal for the Former Yugoslavia: An Exercise in Law, Politics, and Diplomacy*. Oxford: Oxford University Press.

Kritz, Neil (editor) (1995) *Transitional Justice: How Emerging Democracies Reckon with Former Regimes*, Vol. I, General Considerations; Vol. II, Country Studies; Vol. III, Laws, Ruling, and Reports. Washington, D.C.: United States Institute of Peace Press.

Kurspahić, Kemal (2003) *Prime Time Crime: Balkan Media in War and Peace*. Washington, D.C.: United States Institute of Peace Press.

Lakatos, Alex C. (1995) "Evaluating the Rules of Evidence for the International Tribunal in the Former Yugoslavia: Balancing Witnesses' Needs Against Defendants' Rights," *Hastings Law Journal*, March.

MacDonald, David Bruce (2002) *Balkan Holocausts? Serbian and Croatian Victim-Centered Propaganda and the War in Yugoslavia*. Manchester: Manchester University Press.

Magnarella, Paul J. (1997) "Judicial Responses to Genocide: The International Criminal Tribunal for Rwanda and the Rwandan Genocide Courts," *Africa Studies Quarterly* (The Online Journal for African Studies), Vol. 1, Issue 1, 1997, http//web.africa.ufl.edu/asq/v/1/1/2.htm.

May, Richard, and Marieke Wierda (1999) "Trends in International Criminal Evidence: Nuremberg, Tokyo, The Hague, and Arusha," *Columbia Journal of Transnational Law*.

Moghalu, Kingsley (2005) *Rwanda's Genocide: The Politics of Global Justice*. New York: Palgrave.

Morris, Madeline H. (1997) "The Trials of Concurrent Jurisdiction: The Case of Rwanda," *Duke Journal of Comparative and International Law*, Vol. 7, No. 2, Spring.

Mundis, Daryl A. (2001) "Reporting Non-Compliance: Rule 7*bis*," In Richard May, et al. (editors), *Essays on ICTY Procedure and Evidence in Honour of Gabrielle Kirk McDonald*. Great Britain: Kluwer Law International.

Neier, Aryeh (2003) *Taking Liberties: Four Decades In The Struggle For Rights*. New York: Public Affairs.

Neier, Aryeh (1998) *War Crimes Brutality, Genocide, Terror, and the Struggle for Justice*. New York: Times Books.

Neuffer, Elizabeth (2001) *The Key to My Neighbor's House: Seeking Justice in Bosnia and Rwanda*. New York: Picador.

Nye, Jr., Joseph S. (2004) *Soft Power: The Means to Success in World Politics*. New York: Public Affairs.

Off, Carol (2000) *The Lion, The Fox & The Eagle: A Story of Generals and Justice in Rwanda and Yugoslavia*. Toronto: Random House Canada.

Owen, David (1995) *Balkan Odyssey*. New York: Harcourt Brace & Company.

Paris, Erna (2000) *Long Shadows: Truth, Lies and History*. Toronto: Alfred A. Knopf Canada.

Peskin, Victor (2005) "Beyond Victor's Justice: The Challenge of Prosecuting the Winners at the International Criminal Tribunals for the Former Yugoslavia and Rwanda," *Journal of Human Rights*, Vol. 4, No. 2.

Peskin, Victor (2000) "Conflicts of Justice: An Analysis of the Role of the International Criminal Tribunal for Rwanda," *International Peacekeeping*, Vol. 6, Nos. 4–6, July-December.

Peskin, Victor (2005) "Courting Rwanda: The Promises and Pitfalls of the Arusha Tribunal Outreach Program," *Journal of International Criminal Justice*, Vol. 3, No. 4, September.

Peskin, Victor (2002) "Rwandan Ghosts." *Legal Affairs* September/October.

Peskin, Victor, and Mieczysław P. Boduszyński (2003) "International Justice and Domestic Politics: Post-Tudman Croatia and the International Criminal Tribunal for the Former Yugoslavia," *Europe-Asia Studies*, Vol. 55, No. 7.

Pottier, Johan (2002) *Re-Imagining Rwanda: Conflict, Survival and Disinformation in the Late Twentieth Century*. Cambridge: Cambridge University Press.

Power, Samantha (2002) *A Problem From Hell: America and the Age of Genocide*. New York: Basic Books.

Reisman, Michael, W., and Chris T. Antoniou (1994) *The Laws of War: A Comprehensive Collection of Primary Documents on International Laws Governing Armed Conflict*. New York: Vintage Books.

Reydams, Luc (2005) "The ICTR Ten Years On: Back to the Nuremberg Paradigm?" *Journal of International Criminal Justice*. Vol. 3, No. 4, September.

Risse, Thomas, Stephen C. Ropp, and Kathryn Sikkink (1999) *The Power of Human Rights: International Norms and Domestic Change.* Cambridge: Cambridge University Press.

Robertson, Geoffrey (1999) *Crimes Against Humanity: The Struggle for Global Justice.* New York: The New Press.

Roht-Arriaza, Naomi, and Javier Mariezcurrena (editors) (2006) *Transitional Justice in the Twenty-First Century: Beyond Truth versus Justice.* Cambridge: Cambridge University Press.

Schabas, William A. (2005) "Genocide Trials and Gacaca Courts," *Journal of International Criminal Justice*, Vol. 3, No. 4, September.

Scharf, Michael (1997) *Balkan Justice: The Story Behind the First International War Crimes Trial Since Nuremberg.* Durham: Carolina Academic Press.

Sell, Louis (2002) *Slobodan Milošević and the Destruction of Yugoslavia.* Durham: Duke University Press.

Shattuck, John (2003) *Freedom on Fire: Human Rights Wars & America's Response.* Cambridge: Harvard University Press.

Sikkink, Kathryn, and Carrie Booth Walling (2006) "Argentina's Contribution to Global Trends in Transitional Justice," in Naomi Roht-Arriaza and Javier Mariezcurrena (editors), *Transitional Justice in the Twenty-First Century: Beyond Truth versus Justice.* Cambridge: Cambridge University Press.

Silber, Laura, and Allan Little (1997) *Yugoslavia: Death of a Nation.* New York: Penguin Books.

Slaughter, Anne-Marie (1992) "Law and the Liberal Paradigm in International Relations Theory," International Law and International Relations Theory: Building Bridges – Elements of a Joint Discipline, 86 *American Society of International Law Proceedings*.

Stover, Eric (2005) *The Witnesses: War Crimes and the Promise of Justice in The Hague.* Philadelphia: University of Pennsylvania Press.

Stover, Eric, and Gilles Peres (1998) *The Graves: Srebrenica and Vukovar.* Zurich: Scalo.

Stover, Eric, and Harvey Weinstein (editors) (2004) *My Neighbor, My Enemy: Justice and Community in the Aftermath of Mass Atrocity.* Cambridge: Cambridge University Press.

Straus, Scott (2006) *The Order of Genocide: Race, Power, and War in Rwanda.* Ithaca: Cornell University Press.

Tanner, Marcus (2001) *Croatia: A Nation Forged in War.* New Haven: Yale University Press.

Teitel, Ruti G. (2000) *Transitional Justice.* Oxford: Oxford University Press.

Trueheart, Charles (2000) "A New Kind of Justice," *The Atlantic Monthly*, April.

Williams, Paul R., and Michael P. Scharf (2002) *Peace with Justice? War Crimes and Accountability in the Former Yugoslavia.* Lanham: Rowman & Littlefield Publishers.

Woodward, Bob (1996) *The Choice.* New York: Simon & Schuster.

Index